Essential Clinical Social Work Series

Series Editor

Carol Tosone

For further volumes:
http://www.springer.com/series/8115

James W. Drisko · Melissa D. Grady

Evidence-Based Practice in Clinical Social Work

James W. Drisko
Smith College School for Social Work
Lily Hall 215
Northampton, MA 01063
USA

Melissa D. Grady
Catholic University of America School
  of Social Service
Shahan Hall
Washington, DC 20064
USA

ISBN 978-1-4614-3469-6   (hardcover)   ISBN 978-1-4614-3470-2   (eBook)
ISBN 978-1-4614-6484-6   (softcover)
DOI 10.1007/978-1-4614-3470-2
Springer New York Heidelberg Dordrecht London

Library of Congress Control Number: 2012934663

Printed on acid-free paper

Springer is part of Springer Science+Business Media (www.springer.com)

Preface

There are many recent books about evidence-based practice (EBP) in social work, psychiatry, and in other mental health professions. In reviewing these books, it appeared to us that the majority were written by researchers, bringing a particular point of view and skill set to the technicalities of EBP. These books are useful because EBP involves a lot of technical detail about research design, methods, and interpretation that are not always covered in other social work texts.

On the other hand, the lack of a more direct practice, client-centered, viewpoint seemed to leave out many of the day-to-day realities clinical social workers confront in learning and using EBP. We thought this was important to emphasize as the context in which clinical social workers practice EBP. Second, lengthy case examples were missing in most EBP texts. The technicalities were described very well, but real people in real situations seemed oddly omitted or only briefly illustrated. This book seeks to illustrate through several cases how important clinical knowledge and expertise are to doing EBP well. It also seeks to point out clearly how client preferences and common resource limitations shape and limit EBP. Third, most EBP books did not provide detailed examples of high quality systematic reviews. We wanted to be sure clinical social workers were 'walked through' the kinds of materials, terminology, and analyses found in Cochrane Collaboration and Campbell Collaboration systematic reviews. We understand these are not the only sources of solid research knowledge for practice, but they are very important. Systematic reviews include terminology, methods, and statistics not often found in social work research textbooks. Fourth, the books on EBP also seemed to lack much in the way of a broad, critical, perspective on EBP as a social movement shaping policy, agency practice, and views of what constitutes 'good' research. As we looked to these books as resources for our students, they seemed a bit unbalanced and lacking in breadth. Micro-, messo-, and macro- perspectives on EBP all seemed important to us and to practicing clinical social workers. Finally, the step in EBP in which the client and clinician discuss the results of outcome research too often seemed to be a 'top down' interaction. We think the best treatment decisions in mental health are shared decisions made collaboratively between client and clinician. The client's active role and participation in EBP are equally important—or more important—than knowing what the research shows is effective. In mental health services, clients are not passive recipients of treatments, but active agents of change. Having several ideas, we set off to write a text that explored EBP more fully. We seek to introduce the core ideas and practice of EBP, to critically explore them, and then illustrate them by applying the concepts and process to real-world cases. We are very appreciative of EBP but also want to examine its limitations and challenges.

We, the authors, are both clinical social workers with practice experience in a variety of settings. We are also academic researchers. We have worked in community mental health, public schools, psychiatric inpatient and outpatient services, as well as private practice. Day-to-day practice challenges are very familiar to us both. Each of us has done quantitative and qualitative research on many aspects of practice theory, practice process, and practice outcomes. Further, we are both teachers of clinical social work practice. We are committed to social work's core values and to the many merits of the person-in-environment perspective that distinguishes social work from related professions. While we think that EBP represents a very useful practice decision-making process and approach to policy making, we also think it is a complex social movement. As social workers, we take a broad view of social phenomena and believe that EBP is best understood from several perspectives.

We intend this book for clinical social workers in practice. It will also be suitable for master's and doctoral students in social work and in allied professions. Many introductory level books on EBP emphasize procedures without much perspective or much detail. We seek to offer greater perspective, depth, and detail. This includes detailed examination of systematic reviews and resources on practice research. Further, we view many of the technical chapters of the book as *reviews* of research content, not initial introductions to the content. That said, we have tried to make the technical chapters clear, but with enough detail for them to be useful to clinical social workers doing practice.

In our terminology and our examples of EBP we have focused on the identification of treatment alternatives. We understand—and address—how EBP may be more broadly applied to the study of alternative diagnostic procedures, prognoses, prevention, prevalence, and economic analyses. We chose to focus our examples more narrowly to fit the interests of our intended audience of clinical social workers and social work practitioners. We also have made an effort to locate our exploration of EBP in the context of social work professional values. We think that the person-in-environment perspective can make a major, useful, contribution to EBP conceptualization. We also believe it has implications for EBP methods.

In Chapter 1, this book will detail EBP as an important practice decision-making process, but it will also critically examine EBP in context. We provide a brief history of EBP and evidence-based medicine (EBM) from which it developed. We employ the contemporary model of EBP that includes four components: (1) the current clinical circumstances of the client, (2) the best relevant research evidence, (3) the client's values and preferences, and (4) the clinical expertise of the professional clinician. Research is just one part of the EBP practice decision-making process. Client values and clinical expertise are equally valued in this model, though in many discussions of EBP they are not emphasized. We aim for balance among the four components of EBP.

In Chapter 2, we will look at EBM and EBP as public ideas that are actively promoted by economic and political interests to shape public perceptions and social policy. We believe that clinical social workers who read this book will already be aware of how EBP is used to shape access to specific treatments and services, and often to shape or limit funding for clinical services. Chapter 2 also explores the way EBM and EBP are reshaping research funding priories and research education. EBM and EBP have established hierarchies of research knowledge based upon the use of specific research designs and methods. This was done purposefully to prioritize experimental research evidence with strong interval validity. Yet the impact of this hierarchy may be to devalue other forms of research and knowledge that have been actively promoted by social workers and others in the "science wars" of the last 20 years. We think that large-scale experimental research has great merit, but is just one of many valuable ways of knowing. Experiments are only as good as the conceptual base upon which they draw, the measures that operationalize concepts and theories, and the samples they use. Many aspects of research on clinical practice are neither simple nor fully resolved. Some of these unresolved and contentious issues relate to social work values on social justice and research. We want clinical social workers to have enough information to draw their own conclusions about the EBM and EBP research hierarchies.

In Chapter 3 we lay out the steps of EBP as a practice decision-making process. This process is what most people think of 'as' EBP. We hope to introduce clinical social workers to this useful process and to identify both its strengths and its limitations. We differ on one point: that some lists of the steps of EBP include practice evaluation (Gibbs, 2002). Our view is that case-by-case quantitative practice evaluation is an essential part of all good practice, but that it draws on a very different logic than does the rest of the EBP model. We hope to help clinical social workers better understand the differences between the EBP practice decision-making model and single case practice evaluation.

In Chapter 4 we explore assessment in EBP. As experienced clinical social workers, we find it odd that the EBP practice decision-making model does not include standards for assessment. We appreciate that the EBP practice decision-making model is intended to be generic and widely applicable, but we also believe a thorough and wide ranging assessment is the only appropriate basis for treatment and service planning. Social workers use many different models of assessment, five of which we explore in some depth. Our goal is to help social workers better identify how to selectively use each model. However, many assessment models, including the American Psychiatric Association's assessment and diagnostic model, exclude or de-emphasize issues of concern to clinical social workers. We also know that the realities of most managed care practice require very brief or single session assessment, often with a very narrow focus on symptoms and risks. Such brief assessment procedures may not provide sufficient information to guide the best use of the EBP practice decision-making process. Limited assessment procedures may also omit aspects of social diversity and attention to both the positive and limiting influences of the client's social environment. To fail to attend to these issues is inconsistent with social work's core professional values and ethical principles (National Association of Social Workers, 2008). We also are quite aware that the DSM-V will revise some diagnostic categories and add others in ways that will matter for both research and practice.

Chapters 5–10 detail the EBP practice decision-making process. Chapter 5 addresses how to locate the best available research evidence in print and online sources. It also begins the complex process of evaluating the quality of research and the fit of the available research to your client's needs and circumstances. Many useful resources for EBP are identified. Chapters 6–8 provide detailed information about how to appraise research reports. Chapter 6 reviews research designs and the terminology used to describe them in EBM and EBP. This terminology frequently differs from the terminology used in social work research textbooks. Chapter 7 examines methodological issues including sampling, tests and measures, defining treatments, and statistical analyses. Chapter 8 explores systematic reviews, the most highly regarded form of evidence in the EBM and EBP models. Chapter 8 also examines meta-analysis, the statistical technique used to compare mathematically the results of multiple studies on the same topic. Neither systematic reviews nor meta-analysis are covered in most social work research textbooks. Both are crucial to the EBM and EBP process.

Chapters 9 and 10 address how to bring EBP research knowledge back to the client. We find many EBM and EBP textbooks do not place enough attention on these crucial steps in treatment or service planning. Contemporary EBP models require clinicians to discuss available treatment or service options directly with the client before a treatment plan is finalized. We go a step further and argue that informed, shared decision making by the client is a co-equal component in EBP. The client's role is just as important as research knowledge or clinical expertise. Contemporary EBP models also empower clients to reject options that do not fit their values and preferences—even if these options are the 'best' alternatives based on research evidence. EBP is not a top-down authoritative enterprise, but a shared, cooperative one. Formally documenting that the steps of EBP have been followed and evaluation of practice are also examined.

The second part of this book, Chapters 11 through 16, centers on the application of the EBP practice decision-making process through six lengthy case vignettes. The cases include various diagnoses, various ages and needs, various ethnicities, and illustrate varying success in finding and implementing evidence-based treatments or services. We link each case directly to a detailed search for relevant high quality research, and to a critical analysis of the resulting research. We seek to illustrate the challenges of assessment and of identifying a single priority question to orient the EBP process. We also seek to illustrate how to engage clients in the EBP practice decision-making process. We examine how practice proceeds when research evidence is lacking, or if research supported services are unavailable.

The third part of this book, Chapters 17–19, examines EBP in clinical social work education and supervision. These chapters are intended to address important contextual issues. EBP has already had some impact on the content of social work education. It may also impact social work accreditation standards, though it is not yet specifically mentioned in the current Council on Social Work Education (2008) standards. Doing EBP will require new skills from clinical social workers, access to new resources such as electronic data bases, and may require new content in supervision. Chapter 17 explores issues in clinical social work education related to EBP. Chapter 18 examines issues related to clinical social work practice that are either intended or unintended consequences of the implementation of EBP. This chapter will also examine several issues of interest to clinical social workers that are not directly or adequately addressed by EBP research and procedures. Chapter 19 offers a set of conclusions and some recommendations for clinical social work practice, advocacy, and education.

We also offer an extensive glossary. Many terms in the glossary have extended descriptions in order to make them more useful to clinical social work practitioners. Finally, we offer two appendices. The first is an outline of a social work biopsychosocial assessment framework. The framework illustrates the complexity and scope of a thorough social work assessment. The second appendix is a bullet point summary of the strengths and limitations of EBP. We hope a succinct summary will be useful for review and reflection on the complexity of EBP.

Our overall purpose is to help clinical social workers understand EBP and to use it in practice. There is much to learn to do this successfully. At the same time, we hope clinical social workers will be critical consumers of EBP. EBP is a complex social movement with many dimensions and many components. We hope to keep EBP in context as we explore its merits and its limitations. Attentive engagement and critical thinking are strongly encouraged!

Northampton, MA, USA   James W. Drisko
Washington, DC, USA   Melissa D. Grady

Acknowledgments

We would like to thank Dr. Carol Tosone, the series editor, for her request that we undertake this project. Carol has been a steady source of support and many good ideas, as well as a keen editing eye. We thank you.

Jennifer Hadley of Springer helped us do our first academic book. We thank her for her guidance and help through the process. Springer's production team was very efficient and helpful as well.

We are very grateful for the comments and suggestions of our wonderful external reviewers. You all were both very affirming and pointed to some valuable ways to strengthen the book. Thank you!

I (JD) am the child of two social workers who would be very proud to see this book completed. They pointed me in the direction of intellectual excellence. I am so grateful. My wife Marilyn watched the whole project progress, and was very patient with the time it took to refine and finish. She even kindly agreed to proofread when deadlines approached. Thank you! My daughters Ann and Meghan might have wondered if I had a real job, seeing me typing when they woke up and still at it at lunchtime. (Yes, I do have a real job.)

In addition to the individuals mentioned above, I (MG) would like to thank my co-author who has been a tremendous mentor. I would also like to thank my parents who pushed me even when I resisted. Finally, I would like to thank my family, Ryan, Maggie and Elizabeth for being tolerant with their mom when I needed to work, and to my always supportive husband Mark. You have always been my biggest cheerleader and I would not have been able to accomplish this without your support.

Contents

Part I
What is Evidence-Based Practice and How It Influences Clinical Practice

Chapter 1
Introduction and Overview

Evidence-based practice (EBP) now strongly influences medical and mental health practice, research and policy. In a relatively short time, it has become a major part of clinical training in all the mental health professions. Some authors even call it a "paradigm shift" in practice (Edmonds et al. 2006, p. 377). EBP has also become quite prominent in the social work professional literature. Several new journals have been started to share knowledge about EBP, including one in social work focused exclusively on evidence-based social work practice.

Despite this growing influence and expansion of EBP, there is little consensus on what EBP is and how to best implement it (Powell et al. 2010). In fact, Rubin and Parrish (2007) found a wide range of views about the nature and practice of EBP in a national survey of social work faculty! Terminology, emphasis and application in practice vary from author to author, practitioner to practitioner and researcher to researcher. This leaves many social workers at a loss regarding how to define and ultimately practice using the principles of EBP. EBP is a complex social movement with several important dimensions. To begin this book, we will start with some definitions and some background to set the stage for a more detailed exploration of EBP in clinical social work.

What is Evidence-Based Practice?

Greenhalgh (2010) offers one definition of evidence-based medicine (EBM) as "the use of mathematical estimates of the risk of benefit and harm, derived from high quality research on population samples, to inform clinical decision making in the diagnosis, investigation and management of individual patients" (p. 1). That is, the key feature of EBM and EBP is the application of results from research on populations to service planning for individuals. It is the application of large-scale research results to decision making in everyday clinical practice. This definition

J. W. Drisko and M. D. Grady, *Evidence-Based Practice in Clinical Social Work*,
Essential Clinical Social Work Series, DOI: 10.1007/978-1-4614-3470-2_1,
© Springer Science+Business Media New York 2012

connects EBM and EBP to its origins. It also leaves quite undefined just how to make the best use of these research results in clinical practice. This book will address both what EBP is and how it influences the work and training of clinical social workers. The goal of this book is to identify the many strengths of EBM/ EBP while also identifying its limitations and unresolved issues. Further, this book will show how to apply critically EBP in clinical social work practice.

EBP has had such a profound impact on the medical and mental health professions that it is also a social movement: an effort by a group of people to make a social change. The extent of this social movement is so widespread that both the definition of EBP and its application can become confusing. As most often used in clinical social work circles, EBP refers to a practice decision-making process. The goal here is to include the use of the "best available research evidence" in everyday client services (Sackett et al. 1996, p. 71). However, EBP is also used to specify methods and processes in research. In this second instance, the goal is to set standards for the kinds of evidence considered worthy for application in the practice decision-making process. Further, EBP is applied administratively to require the use of specific treatments by clinicians based on the quality of the research evidence that supports their benefit to clients. In this third instance, the administrative goal is to reduce costs while promoting quality care. Beyond issues of just what constitutes 'good enough' evidence and how to make the best use of research evidence in clinical practice, issues of professional autonomy and professional standards are also raised in EBP discussions (Groopman 2010). Understanding EBP in its many applications can be confusing. To begin, we will explore how EBM and EBP originated. This will clarify the core features of EBP and provide definitions for further exploration.

The Foundations and History of Evidence-Based Practice

Some scholars locate the origins of evidence-based medicine (EBM) and EBP in the very early efforts of physicians to identify the specific symptoms of medical disorders. Indeed, Park (1990) argues that the work of Persian healer Avicenna (Ibn Sinā) introduced the ideas of quantification and experimentation into medicine as early as 1025. Later, in France and England in the 1700s, physicians observed and counted numbers of patients with specific symptoms. Compiling data across many patients, these physicians began to reliably link clusters of symptoms with distinct medical disorders. By using observational research, the characteristics of many medical disorders were empirically identified (Kelsey et al. 1996). These early European efforts allowed for more accurate diagnosis of disorders and began what is today the science of epidemiology. Being able to diagnose disorders accurately was a pivotal conceptual and empirical step in providing more specific and effective treatments. Indeed accurately identifying the problem to be treated is vital to today's EBP clinical practice decision-making process.

What is called EBM and EBP today is grounded in the pioneering work of Scottish physician Archibald Cochrane. His life story clearly illustrates why having some knowledge of what works to treat specific disorders is so important for practice. Dr. Cochrane volunteered to fight in the Spanish Civil War and later served as a Captain in the British army in Crete during World War II. He was captured and became a prisoner of war in 1941. Cochrane became the medical officer in charge of prisoners in Hildburghausen, Elsterhorst and Wittenberg an der Elbe prisoner of war camps in Germany. He provided services to large numbers of Allied prisoners living in very difficult and traumatic conditions. Cochrane (1972, p. 5) writes of a clinical question about tuberculosis that illustrates his interest in distinguishing treatments that help from those that may injure:

> At Elsterhost all the POWs with tuberculosis (most of whom were far advanced) of all nationalities, were herded together behind the wire. Conditions were in many ways not too bad. Through Red Cross parcels we had sufficient food; we were able to 'screen' patients and do sputum 'smears' but radiographs [X-rays] were very limited. We could give our patients bed rest, pneumothorax and pneumoperitoneum…
>
> …I had considerable freedom of clinical choice of therapy: my trouble was that I did not know which [therapy] to use and when. I would gladly have sacrificed my freedom for a little knowledge. I had never heard then of 'randomised controlled trials,' but I knew there was no real evidence that anything we had to offer had any effect on tuberculosis and I was afraid that I shortened the lives of some of my friends by unnecessary intervention…

Not knowing what treatments 'work' made selecting treatments almost an arbitrary process. All professionals seek to use their knowledge and clinical expertise to help their clients improve and grow. Including research knowledge as a routine part of clinical practice should improve results for individual clients. It also helps clinicians to be more confident in their own decision making.

While Cochrane strongly advocated for the use of the scientific knowledge in making treatment choices, he was also a practitioner with a heart. Cochrane describes a case showing how important both human caring and accurate diagnosis can be:

> Another event at Elsterhost had a marked effect on me. The Germans dumped a young Soviet prisoner in my ward late one night. The ward was full, so I put him in my room as he was moribund [near death] and screaming and I did not want to wake the ward. I examined him. He had obvious gross bilateral cavitation and a severe pleural rub. I thought the latter was the cause of the pain and the screaming. I had no morphia, just aspirin, which had no effect.
>
> I felt desperate. I knew very little Russian then and there was no one in the ward who did. I finally instinctively sat down on the bed and took him in my arms and the screaming stopped almost at once. He died peacefully in my arms a few hours later. It was not the pleurisy that caused the screaming but loneliness. It was a wonderful education about the care of the dying. I was ashamed of my misdiagnosis and kept the story secret. (Cochrane with Blythe 1989, p. 82)

Clinical expertise must always guide good clinical practice. Understanding the client fully and accurately is still the foundation on which in current models of EBM and EBP are built.

In 1972 Cochrane, who became a distinguished Professor of Tuberculosis and Chest Diseases in Wales, published the influential book that started the contemporary evidence-based approach in medicine. His book *Effectiveness and Efficiency: Random Reflections on Health Services* argued for the use of experimentally based research in both clinical practice and in policy making. Cochrane argued that because health care resources would always be limited, they should be used to provide equitably those treatments and services which had been shown to be effective through rigorously designed research. He promoted the use of research results to distinguish (1) treatments that are effective from, (2) treatments that are harmful and ineffective and from (3) treatments that are benign but ineffective. Cochrane heavily emphasized the importance of drawing evidence from experimental randomized controlled trials (called RCTs) because these provide compelling information about the effects of treatments. A central idea of the EBP process—using the best available research knowledge to help decide what treatment is likely to be the most effective—was introduced. Knowledge based on experimental research or RCTs was also clearly prioritized.

Cochrane's writing points out the significance of accurate and thorough assessment, coupled with attention to available resources as well as using the best available research knowledge. Note, too, that several different types of professional expertise are combined with the knowledge provided by quality research. Current approaches to EBP still draw on these core ideas, but add to them actively engaging clients to include their preferences and their willingness to participate in any proposed treatment plan. Current approaches to EBM/EBP also heavily emphasize clinical expertise as combining and integrating all these components of assessment and treatment.

The Overall Goals of Evidence-Based Practice

Cochrane (1972) sought (1) to increase the number of truly helpful treatments, (2) to reduce the use of harmless treatments that did not help the target disorder and (3) to eliminate harmful treatments that did not lead to improvement but caused other harm. This overall goal remains a fundamental policy-level focus of EBP and EBM today. The goal of reducing harm may seem more applicable to medical practice than to clinical social work practice. Yet there are costs (harms) in the effort, expense and time taken by ineffective and potentially harmful treatments. Further, in some circumstances, risk of death and bodily harm are real issues for mental health patients. Where clients are asked to undertake treatments that may exacerbate risk (such as risk of suicide for people who improve from severe depressions), the same concerns apply to clinical social work practice. For all health and mental health professionals reducing harmful treatments and increasing helpful treatments, remains a very appropriate and critical goal.

Cochrane thought that doing EBM/EBP should lead *both* to improved outcomes for individual clients as well as more efficient use of available monies, resources and services. That is, the EBP model allows for more efficient and effective use of health-care resources at the policy level while pointing to the most effective treatment options for individual clients. Gains in both improved client outcomes and in making optimal use of health-care resources should result.

Of course, these gains may appear only in the aggregate. Evidence-based policy decisions may not automatically improve services for any given individual (Groopman 2010). In the United States, some policy-level decisions may exclude certain patients from coverage and specific types of treatment, differentiating policy- and patient-level results. Such difficult policy choices have also been made in other Western countries. Because EBP has both micro- or client-level application and macro- or policy-level implications, it is always important to be clear about how EBP is being viewed in any given article or report.

Defining the Evidence-Based Medicine/Evidence-Based Practice Decision-Making Process

While we have emphasized the impact of Archic Cochrane in originally promoting the concepts behind EBM, many authors credit other physicians as the originators of EBM and EBP. Indeed, the so-called 'McMaster Group,' led by Dr. David Sackett, promoted the incorporation of research knowledge into practice in the 1980s. Another member of the McMaster group, Dr. Gordon Guyatt (Guyatt et al. 2008, p. xx) states that the first published use of the term evidence-based medicine was in an article of his in 1991. The McMaster Group promoted and systematized the process of EBM in a series of articles published in the 1990s. These Canadian physicians organized and advocated for the EBM practice decision-making process that gave form to Cochrane's pioneering ideas. Their work made EBM an international social movement.

An early and widely cited definition of EBM in clinical practice was offered by Sackett et al. (1996, pp. 71–72):

> Evidence-Based medicine is the conscientious, explicit and judicious use of current best evidence in making decisions about the care of individual patients. The practice of evidence-based medicine means integrating individual clinical expertise with the best available external clinical evidence from systematic research.

Following Cochrane, their initial emphasis was on actively including population-based research knowledge in the individual practice decision-making process. While including research knowledge in practice decision making is the defining feature of EBM and EBP and a great strength, its everyday application proved neither simple nor straightforward.

This early definition of EBM had some serious limitations when applied to real-world clinical practice. Haynes et al. (2002a, p. 38) note that the early definitions of EBM and EBP "de-emphasized traditional determinants of clinical decisions" and "overstated the role of research in clinical decision-making." They do not mean to imply that research knowledge is unimportant, only that it is one part of several that shape practice decision-making. To make EBP more useful in practice, current definitions are simpler and more balanced: emphasizing that "research alone is not an adequate guide to action" (Haynes et al. 2002a, p. 38).

The current definition by the same group of Canadian physicians is that EBM is "the integration of best research evidence with clinical expertise and patient values" (Sackett et al. 2000, p.x). Here research findings are one part of a multi-part process that also includes current clinical circumstances, patient preferences and views all weighed and integrated through professional clinical expertise.

This contemporary definition has also been applied in social work definitions of EBP by Rubin (2008), Gibbs and Gambrill (2002) and Mullen and Shlonsky (2004). Rubin (2008, p. 7) states that "EBP is a process for making practice decisions in which practitioners integrate the best research evidence available with their professional expertise and with client attributes, values, preferences and circumstances." This definition of the EBP practice decision-making process will be used throughout this book. Yet as we will see, EBP may be defined differently for purposes other than practice decision making. These different perspectives on EBP may not involve such balanced consideration of research knowledge with professional expertise and client preferences.

What Makes up the Evidence-Based Medicine/Evidence-Based Practice Decision-Making Model?

Haynes et al. (2002a) state that the contemporary EBP practice decision-making model actually has four parts. They are (1) the current clinical circumstances of the client, (2) the best relevant research evidence, (3) the client's values and preferences and (4) the clinical expertise of the professional clinician. They emphasize that the professional expertise of the clinician is the 'glue' that combines and integrates all the elements of the EBP process. It is the cement that holds the other parts of the model together. Note, too, that the client has active input into the clinical decision-making process. Research evidence is indeed one key ingredient, but it is not privileged over other factors. Clinical practice decision making is an active, multidimensional process. Figure 1.1 graphically illustrates the four parts of EBP and how clinical expertise is the overarching and integrating component of the model.

Gilgun (2005a) states that just what is meant by patient values has neither been well conceptualized nor well examined in current EBP models. This is an area of great interest to social workers that deserves further study. Religious and cultural values, individual beliefs and concerns, personal principles and attitudes would all appear to be aspects of client values. In addition, past experiences with health-care providers and systems as well as other people with power and authority, may shape client preferences and actions. Socially structured differences and oppression may profoundly influence comfort, use, trust and openness in health and mental health-

Fig. 1.1 The components
of the evidence-based
practice model from
Haynes et al. (2002a)

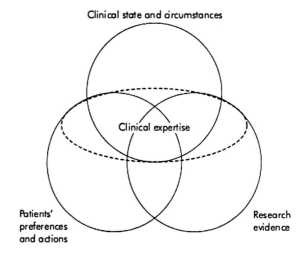

care delivery. All these factors may impact on a client's decision to seek, to stick
with and to actively participate in mental health services.

Clinical expertise "encompasses a number of competencies that promote
positive therapeutic outcomes" (American Psychological Association 2006,
p. 276). These basic professional competencies should be possessed by all grad-
uate-level clinical practitioners. These core competencies include the ability to
conduct a clinical assessment, make diagnoses, systematically formulate cases and
develop treatment plans, each with a clear rationale and justification. They also
include the ability to implement treatments, to monitor progress and to evaluate
practice outcomes. Clinical expertise has a strong interpersonal component,
requiring that clinicians can form therapeutic alliances, self-reflect and understand
the impact of individual, cultural and contextual differences on treatment. Such
contextual differences also include practical and resource limitations that influence
practice decision-making.

Despite this clear statement, Gilgun (2005a) argues that clinical expertise still
warrants better conceptualization and further study. We may know what clinical
expertise is, in general, but may lack knowledge of its important specific details.

Clinical expertise is required to assess the client's clinical state and circumstances.
It is also required in facilitating the client's sharing of their preferences and values. Both
of these processes may take place in stressful circumstances and under time pressure.
Both clinical and research expertise is needed to find, appraise and link research
evidence with the client's particular circumstances. EBP, as a practice decision-making
process, is made up of several components. It is important that clinical social workers
have a clear understanding of EBP as a practice decision-making process.

Not only are there several definitions of EBM and EBP in print, there are a
number of similar endeavors. These efforts are not quite the same as EBP, but may
share a focus on integrating research results into practice and policy. It is important
to distinguish EBP from other uses of research evidence to inform practice and/or
policy.

How the Evidence-Based Practice Decision-Making Process Differs From

'Empirically Supported Treatments' and 'Best Practices'

A related issue appears in terminology. Clinicians may read about 'empirically supported treatments' (ESTs) or 'evidence-based interventions' (EBIs) or 'best practices.' These may be similar to EBP but often reflect quite different research-informed models and applications. Unfortunately, these terms have different definitions and sometimes apply a very different logic than does EBP. For example, 'ESTs' or 'evidence based treatments' (EBTs) are *usually* based on ideas from the Division 12 (Clinical Psychology) of the American Psychological Association (APA) (Chambless and Hollon 1998). APA was attempting to better identify the research support for specific treatments. Note that this is a very different goal that the clinical practice decision-making process of EBP which focuses on the needs of specific clients. An APA task force argued that treatments can be rated on the basis of their research support. Specifically, treatments supported by two or more carefully completed experiments, or 10 or more single systems design studies, can be called 'empirically supported treatments (ESTs).' They also required use of a treatment manual and that persons other than the originator of the treatment under study complete some of the outcome research (Chambless and Hollon 1998). When this model is applied, the treatments that demonstrate statistically significant improvement using these research methods may be called ESTs.

The emphasis in ESTs is on showing that specific treatments have demonstrated effectiveness. Note, however, that this terminology and model focuses on rating specific *treatments* for specific populations or targeted issues, rather than on *how to make decisions about treating a specific client*. ESTs are helpful at the policy planning level, or possibly as a starting point in making clinical decisions, but are not based on the EBP practice decision-making model.

'Empirically supported interventions' (ESIs) usually apply a similar approach to rating programs or interventions. ESIs are more likely to address entire service programs with many components rather than just a single, specific treatment (as in an EST). This makes the ESI approach useful for some services of interest to clinical social workers, such as programs for substance abuse that might involve individual, group and residential components. Unfortunately, there is no clear, consensus definition of an ESI. Researchers and policy makers apply the terminology inconsistently since the ESI label is not based on a single, consensus, set of standards.

Best Practices

The label 'best practices' is sometimes applied to treatments or interventions using the EST approach, but the label is used inconsistently in the literature and lacks a single consensus definition. Best practices generally refers to techniques or interventions that have consistently shown superior results to those achieved by other means (Bogan and English 1994). It is a concept that originated in business administration and strategic management. Identifying best practices is a feature of some management standards, including the ISO 9000 model used in manufacturing and business. ISO 9000 is a set of self-assessment standards and guidelines relating to quality management systems. It involves ongoing, thorough, internal auditing to insure quality. ISO standards represent industry self-regulation as an alternative to mandatory or legislated standards.

The concept of best practices implicitly points to a single way of doing a task that is the superior to all others. However, there may be several 'very good practices' that work more or less effectively in different circumstances, or in response to specific consumer/client preferences rather than just one ideal practice. That is, different contexts may call for different practices or adaptation of best practices that have superior results for particular people, or in different settings, or with people from different cultures. The best practices model does not easily allow for differences among client situations or among client preferences. It is an aggregate model of considerable value, but requires adaptation to settings in which consumer preferences must be considered and valued.

Groopman and Hartzman (2011b) define best practices in medicine as involving "a group of experts who come together and designate how they think services should be provided to patients with a certain condition." As in manufacturing, these medical experts seek to define practices that achieve the best results for a specific disorder. It is important to bear in mind that these experts will often draw upon research findings, but how the experts select and interpret findings may not always be made clear to professionals or consumers.

Groopman and Hartzman (2011a, b) add that the use of best practices has two distinct aspects. In certain situations, such as a specific surgical procedure or acute treatment of heart attacks, standardized procedures can be very helpful in producing positive outcomes and reducing harms. These procedures fit best in emergency or high acuity situations. In such circumstances, best practices may be fairly well defined and routinized. Patient involvement in such medical decisions may be limited or impractical. However, in other situations that involve active patient participation and choice, or where choices among possible risks and benefits are complex and unclear, Groopman and Hartzman argue that best practices may be difficult to identify. Indeed, they argue that:

> many of these expert committees have overreached and they're trying to make it one-size-fits-all and dictate that every diabetic is treated in this way, or every woman with breast cancer should be treated this way, or mammograms are only really beneficial for women older than 50 but not less than 50. But if you step back, you see that you can have different groups of experts coming out with different best practices and what that tells you is there is no one right answer when you move into this gray zone of medicine. (2011b, para 74)

Groopman (2010) states that many decisions about best practice involve key value judgments. He notes, for example, that a government task force decided that mammograms for women in their forties should no longer be recommended routine practice. The task force estimated a high rate of false positives among these women could lead to considerable unwarranted stress and anxiety. They also noted that mammograms involved radiation exposure, though researchers cannot fully quantify the risks of such exposure. Using 2008 statistics, Groopman states that routine mammograms could possibly prevent 12,000 deaths per year among women in their forties. In comparison, for women in their fifties for whom mammograms *are* recommended, Groopman states that 15,000 deaths per year could be possibly be prevented. Why would a best practice not address the possible risk of death from breast cancer for the 12,000 women per year in their forties while recommending the very same procedure to possibly aid 15,000 women per year in their fifties? Groopman argues that policy makers do not simply base such a judgment solely on research results, but must make value judgments in the interpretation and prioritization of research findings. He states that best practices are complex social processes that should not be understood as simply based on research results. Groopman (2010) also states that political and economic interests can heavily shape views about best practices. Social workers—and our clients—must be critical consumers of best practice recommendations from several dimensions.

Some states, insurance companies and health-care agencies use lists of best practices to guide administrative and policy-level practice decision making. Groopman (2010) and Groopman and Hartzman (2011a, b) point out that there is a tension between some uses of best practices and both client participation and client autonomy in health-care decision making. Best practices may be very useful where acute care needs limit client participation in service planning and optimal outcomes are clear cut. On the other hand, in complex, non-emergency healthcare situations, client participation in health and mental health-care planning is often crucial to service planning success. Views on optimal outcomes may vary considerably among clients. Social work's professional ethics also strongly affirm client autonomy and active participation in decision-making.

At this time, only EBP and ESTs have clear definitions. Clinical social workers must be able to distinguish among EBP as a practice decision-making process and designated ESTs or ESIs that have some research support for their effectiveness. Clinical social workers must also critically evaluate claims of best practices by reviewing their evidence base and consistency with the EBP practice decision-making process. Unfortunately authors, policy makers and administrators do not always use this terminology consistently or with rigor, forcing practitioners to be careful and critical consumers of research reports and summaries.

Evidence-Based Practice in Social Work

In social work, EBP arose as the single case evaluation effort declined in prominence. In the 1980s and early 1990s, many social work researchers advocated the use of single subject or single system research designs to evaluate and document the outcome of social work practice efforts and improve accountability (Bloom and Fischer 1982; Kazi and Wilson 1996; Kratochwill 1978; Tripodi 1994). Social work researchers called this movement 'empirically based practice' (Reid 1994) although its focus and methods were quite different from today's EBP. The goal of this effort was to improve accountability. Specifically, empirically based practice sought to demonstrate that social work services were effective on a case–by–case basis. This is a sharp contrast with EBM and EBP that focus on large scale, population level, research results. Of course as stated in the National Association of Social Worker's (NASW) *Code of Ethics* (2008, 5.02a), "social workers should monitor and evaluate. . . practice interventions."

While single case evaluation is a useful approach, the limitation of the effort was that single case research designs do not conclusively show that the treatment or program *caused* any benefit or harm that occurred. Single subject evaluation can document whether or not a client improved, but a single application cannot demonstrate that the treatment, rather than other factors, caused this change. Importantly for the profession, this single case evaluation effort affirmed that evaluation is a key part of professional practice, though social workers use a number of different qualitative and quantitative evaluation methods.

As EBM gained prominence in the late 1990s, social work began to adopt the contemporary EBP model as a more data-grounded way to guide treatment decision-making before treatment starts. Note carefully that deciding what treatment or intervention to use with a specific client is a very different process than is outcome evaluation for an individual client. Practice evaluation is routinely discussed in social work practice texts (see, for example, Gambrill 2006b; Hepworth et al. 2010; Sheafor and Horejsi (2011). However, the linkage between EBP and practice evaluation is not clearly stated. Hepworth and colleagues (2010, pp. 33 ff) affirm the use of both quantitative and qualitative "measures" to evaluate practice. Single case evaluation is still a valuable method for evaluating treatment impact on a specific case.

In the twenty-first century, the empirically based practice movement with its focus on single case evaluation was replaced in prominence by EBP and its emphasis on using large-scale, population-based, research to inform the selection of assessments and/or treatments before they are started. Some social work researchers now argue for combining EBP with single case evaluation measures (Gibbs 2002). Indeed, Gibbs makes the evaluation of individual cases outcomes a step in EBP. The authors of this book instead view EBP and practice evaluation as quite different endeavors.

In 2001 the Council on Social Work Education [CSWE] accreditation standards required content on "empirically based knowledge, including evidence-based interventions" be taught in all accredited BSW and MSW programs. In the 2008 CSWE accreditation standards, "research-informed practice" and "practice-informed research" must both be taught in conjunction with critical thinking and clear attention to diverse client views (CSWE 2008, EP 2.1.6). CSWE used this language to allow social work education programs some flexibility in how they characterize and implement content on including research in treatment decision making. Unfortunately, "practice-informed research" is a standard with no further definition: "Social workers use practice experience to inform scientific inquiry" (CSWE 2008, EP 2.1.6). One approach to teaching "research-informed practice" may be to focus on EBP, but this is not the only way social work programs can meet this accreditation standard. Programs may use other types of research than those most valued in EBP to meet this standard. Since an accredited degree is crucial to obtaining licensure to practice, clinical social workers matriculating from accredited programs should be knowledgeable about the intersection of research and practice. Understanding the linkage of practice and research involves valuable knowledge, values and skills for contemporary clinical social work practice.

Today's emphasis on EBP often makes clinical social workers question if there was any research evidence that their efforts were beneficial in prior years. The answer is that there is an extensive research foundation for clinical practice in social work and in the allied mental health fields. It has been developed over more than 100 years. This research base takes many different forms and asks a wider range of questions than does the EBP model. What EBP brings is a specific focus on population-based research using experimental methods.

Was There Not Any Previous Evidence that Treatments Worked?

Clinical social work practitioners have many questions about their clients and their practice efforts. Are the assessment methods we use accurate? Do they address both psychological and social needs? How can we individualize treatments to best meet the needs, values and 'style' of each client? What are the markers of progress toward larger outcomes we can use to guide our efforts? Do clients make meaningful change? Do these changes last? Do some people get worse even with treatment? How can we better help people who drop out or never really engage? Overall, mental health practitioners are curious people who ask many questions, who can tolerate partial answers and ambiguity and who use many types of evidence to answer these complex questions in changing circumstances (Drisko 2001; Elks and Kirkhart 1993; Goldstein et al. 2009; Ventimiglia et al. 2000). Practitioners want to know a lot about several different, complex issues.

Over the past 20 years calls for greater professional accountability, concerns about healthcare costs and efforts to improve treatment outcomes have all come together to force mental health professionals to better demonstrate that what they do 'works.' In 1999 the United States Surgeon General David Satcher published a comprehensive review of mental health concerns and treatments. The report was based on a review of "more than 3,000 research articles and other materials, including first-person accounts from individuals who have experienced mental disorders" (U.S. Department of Health and Human Services, 1999). The report clearly stated that mental health is a fundamental part of overall health and that mental health disorders are real health issues. This careful review of research supported two major findings: (1) that the "efficacy of mental health treatments is well documented," and

(2) "that a range of treatments exists for most mental disorders" (Chapter 8). Based upon these key findings "the single, explicit recommendation of the report is to seek help if you have a mental health problem or think you have symptoms of a mental disorder" (Chapter 8). Expert clinicians and researchers working for the United States government after an extensive professional review, found a strong evidence base for the effectiveness of mental health treatments and encouraged their use.

That mental health services are generally effective was not a new finding in 1999. Since the 1930s many research studies have demonstrated that psycho-therapy is generally effective across theoretical orientations and intervention techniques (Bergin and Garfield 1971, 1978, 1986, 1994; Lambert 2004; Wampold 2001, 2010). Of course this does not mean that all treatments work or that there are no harmful, or unethical, or culturally insensitive interventions. Yet there is a massive body of evidence, based on multiple research methods and outcomes, that indicates many forms of psychotherapy are effective.

In the 1970s a research technique called meta-analysis was developed to aggregate and compare the experimental outcomes of different therapies for a single disorder such as depression or anxiety. (We will explore meta-analysis in depth in in Chapter 8). A growing number of meta-analyses demonstrate that, in general, the effects of therapy are as good, or better, than is found for most medical procedures (Wampold, 2001, 2010). This is especially impressive when one considers that the outcomes of therapy and mental health services address not only specific symptoms, but also intrapersonal quality of life, interpersonal functioning, engagement in community social roles and in school or job performance. Further, psychotherapy produces enduring outcomes that are likely to continue after the end of formal treatment (Lambert and Ogles 2004). Mental health services may be costly to provide, but they have also been found to reduce both medical and hospital costs in some cases.

While the Surgeon General and the United States Department of Health and Human Services was studying mental health services, evidence-based practice (EBP) emerged as a growing influence on mental health practice and policy. Since the late 1990s discussion of the delivery of mental health services has become strongly linked to EBP, with almost all public and private payers advocating for its implementation. Indeed, the rise in influence of EBP has occurred hand-in-hand with important efforts to reduce health and mental health-care costs while maintaining or improving service quality.

To look in detail at how EBP is linked to research, clinical practice and policy a recent example may be informative. The complex interplay of the quality of research methods, selected target outcomes applications to practice and policy issues are reflected in a very public discussion about how to treat depression.

An Example: Is Medication Useful for Treating Depression?

A series of articles and letters illustrate a number of issues about EBP and doing clinical practice in the era of EBP managed care. Specifically a recent meta-analytic summary of studies on depression was published in a prestigious medical journal (Fournier et al. 2010). The authors are well qualified mental health professionals from several high profile medical research centers. They aggregated the results of several large-scale, high quality, experimental studies on depression. Their work largely conformed to the standards of EBM and EBP research. Their article reported that medications are not helpful for treating depression unless one is severely depressed. For mild to moderate depression, study results show, medication is no more effective than is psychotherapy, placebo or the passage of time. This was a very controversial finding.

In heated response a newspaper column questioned the new study's methods and findings and further claimed that it included too few studies and too few medications to draw such a firm conclusion (Friedman January 11, 2010). The author of this newspaper column is a well-qualified professor of psychiatry from another high profile medical center. The column's author also stated that the real test of an effective antidepressant is not just that it relieves symptoms but that it should also keep depression from returning. Later re-occurrence of depression is known to become more likely with each depressive episode, but this was not a measure of outcome in the original summary article. This summary of evidence, the critic claims, was both poorly done and did not target some important issues.

Other letters expanded on these themes; with another psychiatrist (who was the past-president of a psychiatric organization) noting that depression responds to psychotherapy and always warrants a thorough diagnostic assessment (Freedman January 11, 2010). Another letter from a prominent psychiatrist and researcher stated that mild to moderate depressions were often not diagnosed or treated and again noted that psychotherapy was often under-utilized by general practitioners who more commonly treated all severities of depression with medications (Price January 11, 2010). Yet another letter from a psychologist (and former president of a state psychological association) noted that this exchange of views pitted "competent researchers against clinicians" (Brush January 11, 2010). He added that "the best clinicians practice flexibility in approach, depending on the needs of their patients."

This set of exchanges among professionals shows that in learning and practicing EBP many points of view exist and that simple conclusions about best practices are often lacking or must be viewed as partial and tentative. The ongoing issues include: Does useful evidence exist on the topic I need to know about? Does the research address the specific kinds of outcomes I and my client seek? Is the research comprehensive and valid? Were the study participants like my client? Does the research point to a single best treatment? Are other treatments available which were not fully studied but which may be helpful to my client? How does my client view the best treatments reported in the literature? Are there cultural or practical factors that may make this treatment a poor fit for this client in this situation? Are these practices ethical? Can I deliver this treatment or are there other nearby services that can provide it? Are there any ethical issues in working with managed care payers? EBP has many dimensions and, while a very helpful part of practice, it does not replace careful and ethical practitioner decision making.

Behind the evidence are differences in perspective about the quality and comprehensiveness of research on treatment outcomes and differences on approaches to practice (Goodheart et al. 2006; Mace et al. 2001; Petr 2009; Trinder and Reynolds 2000). Legitimate and longstanding differences exist on the quality of available research and the methods by which summary conclusions are drawn. Further, some scholars note that the 'active ingredients' of many treatments are unknown or not well specified, or that some treatments do not actually qualify as legitimate psychological interventions (Wampold 2010). It may be that simple summaries of treatments omit attention to vital factors that help make the treatments work.

Still, some authors claim that using any treatment lacking a strong evidence base is unethical; a form of malpractice (Myers and Thyer 1997). Yet it may also be unethical or inappropriate to use treatments found effective for majority populations on people of different cultural backgrounds or values (Zayas et al. 2010). Unique clients come with multiple needs and may provide imperfect information to professionals. The complexity and ambiguity of real-world mental health cases do not always allow for simple answers. Client values, preferences and actions vary widely. Professional expertise is always required.

Finally, on the political front, there is an image management issue as researchers are represented as knowledgeable and competent, having clear-cut answers contrasted with practitioners who are represented as uncertain or imprecise and therefore incompetent. Public perceptions may be actively shaped and manipulated as a part of the healthcare debate. Yet to frame professional mental health practitioners as incompetent in contrast to knowing researchers is a false and unhelpful dichotomy. EBP is a key part of the health-care industry where administrative control and cost management matter along with quality care. But to devalue practitioners may only undercut public perceptions of health-care professionals and may perhaps reduce service utilization by people in need. Accessible, high quality care must be an overall goal for mental health researchers and providers alike. Fewer labels and accusations and more engaged discussion, is a more appropriate course for professionals to undertake.

Summary

EBP provides a model for integrating the results of population level research into individual practice decision-making. It seeks to improve positive outcomes and reduce harmful or ineffective treatments. It should help clinical social workers be more confident in their recommendations and for clients to have greater confidence in their recommendations. Client values and preferences are a key part of EBP.

The contemporary EBP model emphasizes professional expertise as integrating knowledge of the clients' situation and needs with the best available research evidence as well as the client's values and preferences. Research evidence is one key part of the model, but not all there is to it. There are other efforts that seek to identify effective treatments that are similar to, but not identical to, EBP. One of these efforts is the empirically supported treatment (EST) model developed in psychology. Other efforts focus on outcome evaluation for single clients rather than populations. Differences in terminology are important but can be confusing.

Clinical social workers need to be knowledgeable about EBP. They need to use thoughtfully the EBP process in contemporary practice. Social workers must also include the client's values and social environments in appraising the clinical situation. Clinical social workers also need to read the literature carefully to understand the terminology and key ideas applied by researchers, administrators and policy planners. Further, clinical social workers must remain careful and critical consumers of articles and books on EBP.

From its foundations in the ideas of Dr. Archie Cochrane, EBM and EBP link research and practice at both policy and practice levels. Yet the information needs and interests, of clinical practitioners, researchers and policy makers may not always be the same. We will examine three different perspectives on EBP in the next chapter.

Chapter 2
Three Perspectives on Evidence-Based Practice

This chapter will examine evidence-based practice (EBP) from three different vantage points. As discussed in Chapter 1, there are several definitions of EBP, often shaped by the role the individual has within the EBP process. To clinical social workers, EBP is most often understood as a practice decision-making process. This is indeed one key application of EBP. But clinical social workers also understand the impact of EBP in other related contexts. We find it useful to think of EBP from three different perspectives: (1) its application in practice decision making, (2) its applications to health care policy and administration, and (3) its impact on research methods and research funding. To limit discussion of EBP solely to its practice application omits attention to other, broader, issues of interest to clinical social workers. The policies that shape practice delivery, the day-to-day administration of clinical social work practice, and the kinds of research evidence valued in making policy choices are also being affected by EBP. This is the context in which EBP is changing clinical social work practice.

In addition to guiding practice decision making, both evidence-based medicine (EBM) and EBP are being used at a policy level to reshape clinical practice. Cost containment, cost cutting and, in many cases, profit making are shaping the policies that orient health care practice. Beyond shaping policies, EBM and EBP are increasingly being used administratively. Improving the quality of care while reducing costs is the recent mantra of managed care providers. Large-scale research and EBM/EBP provide one valuable framework for examining service quality. At policy and administrative levels, however, EBP may conflict with client preferences and with professional autonomy. The methods of EBP may even be applied to evaluation of individual professionals. To understand EBP requires attention to the overall context in which it is embedded.

From a third perspective, EBM and EBP have begun to alter research priorities in ways that may restrict the variety of research approaches and methods used to understand and evaluate clinical practice. A key strength of EBM/EBP is its use of population level research results based on experimental (or RCT) research designs.

J. W. Drisko and M. D. Grady, *Evidence-Based Practice in Clinical Social Work*, Essential Clinical Social Work Series, DOI: 10.1007/978-1-4614-3470-2_2, © Springer Science+Business Media New York 2012

Yet overemphasis, or exclusive focus, on such research designs may undermine attention to other forms of research and inquiry that are also important to practice knowledge building. In this way EBM/EBP may serve to promote some types of research knowledge while limiting others. Relevant to clinical social work practice, research on understanding persons in situations, on identifying environmental factors that impact treatment effectiveness, and on the processes of clinical practice may be deemphasized in favor of large-scale outcome research. Social work researchers and educators who for the past 30 years have advocated for "many ways of knowing" (Hartman 1994) may find one method is favored, and funded, above all others. Issues of epistemology, ontology, values, and human diversity in research may lose traction while specific methods gain favor.

In this chapter we will explore how EBP is used beyond practice, but in ways that influence how practice is funded and provided. The four components included in the contemporary definition of EBM and EBP may not always be highlighted in policy level and research discussions. The roles of clinical expertise and of client values and preferences may become secondary or even marginal when EBP is viewed from these other perspectives. Our goal is to ensure the context in which EBP is located and shaped are part of how clinical social workers understand this social movement. In turn, clinical social workers may be better able to advocate for themselves and for their clients.

The Policy Level and Administrative Applications of Evidence-Based Practice

There is no question that high quality research evidence, drawn from large samples and appropriately applied in practice, can save lives and improve services. In medicine, efforts to apply evidence-based standards for acute coronary patient care, for sepsis in the use of respiratory ventilators, and even hand washing have all reduced illness and mortality. One study found that strictly following the guidelines for acute coronary care treatment might have reduced patient mortality by 22% after 1 year (Alexander et al. 1998). These guidelines addressed acute use of just three medications. Applying the results of large scale, population based, research can improve service outcomes in important ways. In 2002, large-scale epidemiological research established that the harms of estrogen replacement therapy for postmenopausal women were much more severe than first believed (Women's Health Initiative 2002). These harms were not apparent until a large-scale research project aggregated individual experiences. Routine treatment practices were quickly changed in ways that saved women's lives and reduced overall harm. Even what appear to be small changes, such as routine hand washing, can prove to be very important to improving aggregate outcomes and reducing risks. The importance of such efforts may only become clear when very large groups of people are studied and compared. How EBP is applied at the policy level shapes much of the health and mental health delivery system.

Both the EBM and EBP movements must be understood in the larger context of macro level models of health care delivery. In the United Kingdom, in Canada, and in the United States, many initiatives drawing on the EBM and EBP models now shape public and private health care funding and delivery. Each of these countries face the very real challenge of containing health care costs while providing services to a large and aging population. In each of these countries policies were developed to eliminate unnecessary health care services and to improve overall outcomes. Note that these macro level goals are fully consistent with the purposes of EBM set forth by Dr. Archie Cochrane. In the United States, a major part of this effort was the expansion of managed care in the 1970s and 1980s. Further, health care providers were viewed as having financial incentives for providing more services than might really be needed. A tension between the interests of health care organizations and profession providers became increasingly evident.

In 1984, a study by Wennberg revealed that the kinds of treatment provided by physicians around the United States varied widely in both diagnosis and in prescribed treatments. Other studies found similar variation in diagnosis and most prevalent treatments by geographic region. Epidemiological and actuarial studies would predict more or less consistent rates of diagnosis and comparable use of treatments across the country. Tanenbaum (1999, p. 758) states that these results were interpreted to mean "that physicians were uncertain about the value of alternative treatments and that their actions were consequently influenced by clinically extraneous factors such as tradition and convenience." In other words, physicians did not explore, weigh, and decide what treatment to use on the basis of the best evidence. Dr. Cochrane's earlier concerns seemed very well founded and still very relevant.

Reed and Eisman (2006) state that this perspective was adopted enthusiastically by the health care industry. "Health care professionals were portrayed as major causes of waste, inefficiency, needless expense..." (p. 14). This argument, combined with claims that physicians would gain financially from providing more services, even if unnecessary, made health care professionals a target for improved management and administrative control. In turn, health care organizations in the United States and also in the United Kingdom and Canada, began initiatives to transfer administrative authority from clinical providers to health plan personnel. These initiatives were intended to standardized care practices and reduce variation in delivered services. They also served to limit access to services and to reduce overall demand, which achieved cost savings for funders. In the United States, health care corporations will gain in profits by reducing service access and costs. This corporate financial incentive, which produced large profits, for for-profit health care companies, is not widely viewed as problematic.

Not only funders but governmental agencies took up this argument. A series of efforts by the United States National Institutes of Health in the 1990s began to promote the importance of teaching health care professionals to use research-based treatments. Emphasizing 'quality over numbers,' they also promoted the use of administrative strategies to ensure that such research-based treatments were used widely and consistently. Governmental support and funding promoted the

expansion of administrative control of professional practice in health care. During
these years, parallel efforts in the national health system of the United Kingdom
and Canada also took place (Trinder 2001c).

Tanenbaum (2003) states that managed care framed the debate over EBP into a
"public idea" contrasting good scientific research evidence against faulty clinical
judgment. To solve the problem of faulty practitioner judgment, research evidence
was used administratively to direct health care practice. A public idea (Reich
1988) is a form of marketing common in political campaigns and product promotion. Complex social phenomena, like drunk driving or health care, are simply
framed to highlight certain features of concern. In a public idea, a single, simple
summary is presented that includes an image of both the causes of the problem and
its optimal remedy. For drunk driving, the public image was one of repeat
offenders causing horrible accidents and the remedy was to put such offenders in
jail. The limitation of the argument is that, overall, many more drunk driving
accidents are caused by everyday people who drink too much—not repeat
offenders (though they do pose a problem). Preventive education would likely
reduce accidents more effectively than does jailing repeat offenders (Moore 1988).
Public ideas simplify complex social issues and may also distort them. Public ideas
may give undue credibility to specific approaches to solving complex problems,
rendering other useful solutions less prominent or less acceptable. They actively,
and politically, shape public opinion.

Tanenbaum (2003) calls EBP a public idea of great rhetorical power. Indeed,
who can argue with evidence? What scientific or rational approach remains for
those who would argue with 'evidence.' As Brush (January 11, 2010) states, EBP
can pit "competent researchers against clinicians." Those who define good evidence have great power and influence. In this instance, those who define the best
evidence also have both economic and political power over the services they fund.
"We only reimburse for services that are evidence-based" (Lehman 2010, p. 1)
provides a powerful rationale for payers to restrict or refuse services without full
regard for the needs, values, and choices of the individual client. The public idea
of EBP emphasizes only part of a very complex situation.

When clinical practice is simply seen as a product in need of repair, its complexity and its many merits are minimized or ignored (Schwandt 2005). While
controlling health care costs is an issue almost everyone would support, it can be
undertaken in a manner that does not divide funder and practitioner. As we shall
see, the image also suggests a great deal more certainty about 'what works' than
may be found in treatment outcome research.

It is also important to note that the policy level focus on EBP emphasizes
research results but does not address individual client needs and circumstances,
nor does it address client values and choices. It also omits attention to the pivotal
role of clinical expertise and first-hand clinical assessment. The policy and
administrative perspective on EBP appears to be based on a very different
understanding of EBP than is the practice decision-making model of the McMaster
Group. Population-based research results are widely applied to critique the individualized actions of clinical practitioners. Administrative judgment may also

replace the assessment of clinical social workers and other providers who have different training, qualifications, and much greater access to the individual client.

Mace (1999) states that the United Kingdom's National Health Services views EBP as a cornerstone of the effort to include quality assurance in the responsibilities of providers. While few would argue with quality services and professional accountability, funders, clients, and professionals may differ on what constitutes the best available services for a specific client in a specific situation. They may differ on what is the key problem, on what treatments and related services are appropriate to address it, and on what constitute suitable measures of treatment outcome. Administrative attention to the aggregate needs, and to cost cutting, may not always fit with ethical and appropriate client-specific decision making. There are important differences of perspective between people focused on large-scale, aggregate outcomes, and others focused on specific outcomes for a single client. Yet, at the same time, service costs and quality must be reviewed to control costs for all. There can be, at times, an understandable tension between the practices and goals of administrators and practitioners.

As we can see, EBP is actually a complex social movement. This means that the way EBP is understood, and the elements of EBP that are emphasized, will vary with the particular purposes of the author or speaker. It is important that clinical social workers bear mind that EBP can have a different 'look' depending on the focus of the speaker. Yet in practice, the key influence is the clinical expertise of the social worker who must integrate the client's clinical circumstances, particular values, and views with the best current research knowledge in making practice decisions.

Using Evidence in Evaluations of the Performance of Professionals

In addition to administrators potentially using EBP to influence and direct how services are delivered to clients, evidence-based arguments are being used politically and economically to evaluate, and hire or fire, individual professionals. For example, during the summer of 2010 the *Los Angeles Times* published a series of articles regarding the performance of public school teachers in Los Angeles (*Los Angeles Times*, undated). The series included the online, public, posting of the evaluations of approximately 6,000 teachers. The names of the teachers were also posted. These evaluations were paid for by the public school system and some people argued that they were open information. However, the teachers and their union officials stated they believed the evaluations were personal information to be used privately within the school system. Reputations were affected in a very public forum, with little opportunity for response by individual teachers.

Another aspect of the debate centered on a "value-added analysis," a research model that ranked teachers impact on student achievement (Dillon 2010).

The results of this statistical analysis were then used to decide whether or not teachers should be fired or rehired. In effect, teachers would retain or lose their jobs based on their evaluations, which were linked to the measured achievement of their students. Some people argued that teacher quality was crucial to student achievement. It is, of course, difficult to argue that some teachers are more effective than are others. Still, opponents of the model argued that many other factors, including student nutrition, degree of parental support, and prior 'social promotion' of students who had previously not demonstrated grade appropriate achievement all distorted the evaluations. They argued that to put all the responsibly for student performance on the teacher was neither valid nor fair. Here, outcome measures (the student's annual achievement) were interpreted and used as key measures of the teacher's competence, dedication, and effort. Notably, researchers spoke for both points of view (Dillon 2010).

Similar efforts to grade teacher performance using student test scores are underway in New York state (Otterman 2011). Teachers, using their political power, tried to expand the base from which judgments about their effectiveness were made. Noting that student performance was influenced by parental support, including adequate nutrition and sleep, they argued parents should also be evaluated. Florida state representative Kelli Stargel filed a bill that would require elementary school teachers to evaluate parents based on the quality of their involvement in their children's schools (Postal and Balona 2011). In parts of Alaska and in Pennsylvania, parents are fined if their children are frequently truant (Associated Press 2010; Levy 2011). There is considerable developmental research supporting the view that parental support is an important factor in child development and school performance. However, solutions to resolve these concerns often prove complex and multifaceted. More administrative oversight of professionals may not prove sufficient or effective in improving service outcomes. Nonetheless, the public idea of EBP may suggest such actions.

In mental health care, managed care companies sometimes profile individual clinical practitioners (Panzarino and Kellar 1994). The number of clients, types of disorders, number of sessions, and often the client's satisfaction are tracked and recorded. This information may be used to drop clinicians from company 'panels' and are, in effect, ratings of clinician performance or cost-effectiveness. It is not hard to imagine that the administrative use of EBP could both shape the nature of treatments clinicians can use and perhaps become a part of how a clinician's performance is evaluated.

States and some insurance providers are already establishing lists of what they consider to be empirically supported treatments or best practices. For example, the Minneapolis Veterans' Administration (VA) Health Care web site (2010) usefully lists evidence-based treatments for several disorders. Practicing clinical social workers also report their states and private insurance payers frequently suggest evidence-based treatments for specific disorders (Arnd–Caddigan and Pozzuto 2010). They also state that, in some cases, payers may refuse to authorize certain treatments for specific disorders due to what the payers claim is the lack of a sufficient evidence base for the proposed treatment.

It is important to note that neither lists of empirically supported treatments, nor best practices are necessarily based on kinds of evidence and methods used in EBP. How clinician effectiveness is conceptualized and measured will matter greatly to clinical social workers, much as it does to Los Angeles public school teachers. The administrative uses of EBP are an important driving force in its rapid adoption and promotion. EBP can also be used administratively and economically in ways that are still developing.

Of course, it *is* appropriate to use evidence in the evaluation of professional performance. No one would seriously argue that performance should not be tied to evidence. The issue is what kinds of evidence are most informative and how we understand them in context. To evaluate the quality of a teacher solely by the performance of his or her students may overrate the impact of a teacher. It surely diminishes the impact of social contexts including adequacy of space, materials and equipment not to mention the child's family supports and social circumstances. Similarly, clinical social workers often work with clients with multiple disorders and stressors that may directly impact the client's ability to engage in treatment and demonstrate 'success.' The appropriate use of research evidence requires fair and comprehensive models that fit with our best ideas about how complex systems work. Values, critical thinking, and theories all have a place in the optimal selection and use of research evidence (Gambrill 2000).

It is very important to consider how, and by whom, the term EBP is being used. Administrators, funders, researchers, and mental health clinicians may have different goals and information needs. Clinical practitioners may look for situation-specific treatment planning help, while researchers dispute what constitutes the 'best' methods to generate evidence, and payers seek to limits costs while maintaining service quality. Each of these endeavors has real merit. Each endeavor is also multifaceted and complex. Yet the view of EBP each perspective generates is somewhat distinct. Let us next consider the research perspective on EBM and EBP.

Evidence-Based Practice, Many Ways of Knowing and Qualitative Research

Tanenbaum (2003) argues that EBP is a public idea that purposefully shapes public perception. Several authors call EBM and EBP a social movement (Goldenberg 2006; Hansen and Rieper 2009; Trinder 2000a). We argue that a third perspective on EBP suggests it may also be an effort to shape, and perhaps to restrict, how science and research evidence are understood and valued. EBP may be the next research paradigm (Duggal and Menkes 2011; Guyatt et al. 1992). Paradigms shape how research is designed, funded, and taught. The impact of changes in research paradigms extends well beyond the university. Nespor (2006, p. 123) states that paradigms are results of "tensions and conflicts that stretch outside the university to state bureaucracies, pressure groups, big corporations, community groups." Paradigm debates may start within the academy, but their impact is much more widespread. As noted in the first section of this chapter, the impact of EBP may have profound economic and political consequences for mental health practice. To frame this perspective on EBP, we begin with some recent history on the debates regarding what Hartmann (1994) calls "many ways of knowing" that took place in social work and allied fields in the 1980s and 1990s. Note that this is the same time period in which EBM and EBP first became prominent.

Until the mid-20th century, there were few challenges to the centrality of the scientific method and knowledge as guides for the professions, including social work. In the early 1900s, a philosophy called logical positivism was promoted as a way to build mathematically based laws or models that accurately represented the world. In the hard sciences, such scientific laws had proved useful for over 200 years. However, the underlying justifications for the 'truth value' of scientific theories began to be challenged. In 1962, Thomas Kuhn published *The Structure of Scientific Revolutions*, a book that argued science was, in part, socially determined and did not progress solely through test and analysis. Kuhn argued that Western scientific knowledge had developed through a series of revolutions or 'paradigm shifts' where the framework through which scientists viewed the world changed radically. The newer paradigms routinely proved incompatible or incommensurate with the older ones. One widely cited example is the paradigm shift from a Ptolemaic or Earth centered view of the solar system to a Copernican or Sun centered view of the solar system. Scholars following Kuhn argued that human influences and power structures shaped scientific knowledge. Still more differing points of view about both *how* we know and the *value* of science arose during the 1970s and 1980s. The view that science is a social construction and is shaped by economic, political, and cultural forces became more prominent in both the social and hard sciences.

In the late 1980s and 1990s, the so-called 'science wars' contrasted science with other ways of knowing (see Flyvbjerg 2001; Nelkin 1979; Ravtiz 1997). The differences were both about epistemology—ways of knowing—and about research methods. Postmodernist scholars pointed to social knowledge as a social construction that is situated in a particular time and place, and shaped by the economics, politics, and social norms of the times (Foucault 1964; Lyotard 1984; Rorty 1979). They doubted that 'objective' methods could produce social 'truths' (Quine 1963). Feminist and cultural scholars noted how the interests and voices of women were often omitted or minimized in scientific scholarship (Belenky et al. 1986; Harding 1986; Nelson 1993). Indigenous scholars noted how the very different ways of knowing of aboriginal peoples was devalued and omitted in scientific scholarship (Tuhaiwai Smith 1999). Critical scholars noted how political interests shaped research funding and the application of research results (Foucault 1964; Habermas 1990). Some scholars advocated that research should include social action (Fals-Borda and Rahman 1991). For some, the kinds of work that constituted research expanded.

Arguments affirming the value of small sample, intensive research were also made during this time. Some scholars argued that clinically relevant and import research often used methods quite unlike those most valued in EBP. Rustin (2001) points out that a lot of valuable clinical and developmental research is small scale and intensive in format, rather than large scale and extensive. He points out how Ainsworth's Strange Situation test helped generate a typology of attachment styles that later proved to hold up in many different countries and cultures. Intensive study of a few mothers and children led the way to an innovative approach to understanding attachment and the consequences of its disruption. Rustin further notes how Stern's in-depth studies of babies and mothers pointed out that babies possess many more perceptual and meaning-making capacities than had previously been identified. Rustin argues for methodological pluralism and shows how clinical insights at the micro level can benefit many forms of research. EBP's focus on large-scale research has value, he states, but is not the only approach to productive clinical research.

Along similar lines, Tonelli (1998, 2001), a physician working with respiratory disease, argues that clinical experience and physiologic rationale are two types of medical knowledge that differ in kind from population-based epidemiological evidence. Tonelli believes their devaluation in EBP reflects a conceptual error. This is because clinical expertise, physiologic rationale, and epidemiological research are distinct kinds of knowledge that do not belong on the same graded hierarchy. Many kinds of evidence may have relevance to clinical decision making. Buetow and Kenealy (2000) and Buetow and Mintoft (2011) argue that EBM too severely limits the use of nonscientific knowledge, including patient intuition, that may complement, and enhance EBP decision making.

There are many kinds of research and knowledge that might extend, complement, or enhance EBM and EBP. Many of the more formal and well-developed forms of knowledge development are collectively known as qualitative research. Qualitative researchers argued for the merits of their approaches and methods in these 'science wars.'

During the 1990s many social workers advocated for greater attention to qualitative research (Gilgun et al. 1992; Popay and Williams 1994; Riessman 1994; Rodwell 1998; Shaw 1999; Sherman and Reid 1994). Qualitative research is frequently portrayed as a simple dichotomy contrasted with quantitative, statistical research in social work textbooks. More accurately, qualitative research consists of a wide-ranging family of related research approaches and methods. Qualitative research has many different purposes and draws on a range of different epistemological or philosophical premises (Drisko 1997). It emphasizes discovery, context, witnessing, understanding meaning, understanding process and can include social action, and even can aspire to liberation. Qualitative research is widely used to develop, refine, and even to test theory. Advocates for expanding attention to "many ways of knowing" (Hartman 1990) promoted the use of nonquantitative research approaches. In social work and allied fields, the number of publications using these methods increased dramatically during the 1990s and early 2000s.

More recently, Goldenberg (2006, 2009) argues that EBP is based on a dated positivist epistemology that promotes science as objective, despite many cogent critiques of positivism over the past 90 years. Specifically, she argues that the

methodological standards of EBP actually serve to obscure the inevitable subjective elements that shape all human inquiry. Citing the work of Kuhn and Quine,
she points out that theory is always underdetermined by data; meaning that our
backgrounds will always shape our observations. Further, she states that "our
theory choices are never determined exclusively by 'the evidence'." (2006,
p. 2623). She states that "orthodox empiricists" exclude any acknowledgment of
the historical, gendered, and locational differences among knowers in favor
of views that are disembodied and "distinctly androgenic" (2006, p. 2625).
Goldenberg notes that "In the current age where the institutional power of medicine is suspect, a model that represents biomedicine as politically disinterested or
merely scientific should give pause" (2006, p. 2621).

Whether or not, and if so, how, EBM and EBP will include different "ways of
knowing" is uncertain. Indeed, EBP hierarchies of evidence continue to locate the
results of case studies and qualitative research on the lowest levels of evidence.
As attention is directed to quantitative outcome studies, other research purposes
and methods are actively or implicitly devalued. In this way, EBM and EBP may
represent a social movement to restrict certain kinds of research and to privilege
other forms. Popay and Williams (1998, p. 35) call this the "Gingerbread Man
Threat"; that qualitative researchers will be gobbled up by their better funded and
more powerful quantitative colleagues. In effect, the EBP research hierarchy
resolves the science wars by omitting many kinds of research, mainly due to its
dependence on population based, quantitative, and experimental studies. In this
way, EBP may be viewed as a backdoor action in a long-term academic and
economic disagreement.

The choice to devalue qualitative research has both a clear rationale and some
serious consequences. The purpose of the research hierarchy is to promote research
results with strong internal validity, or the ability to make cause and effect claims.
This is one way to document the quality of research results. On the other hand,
it allows very little room for change and innovation as social needs, conceptual
systems, and diagnoses change over time. The EBM/EBP research hierarchy does
not address what innovations to explore when treatment prove ineffective or how
new treatment models would be created.

Greenhalgh (2010, p. 163) points out that qualitative research "is not just
complementary to, but in many cases a prerequisite for… quantitative research…"
That is, the concepts, diagnosis and treatment model tested for effectiveness in
EBM and EBP research are routinely developed and refined using qualitative
research designs and methods. Without openness to qualitative research, there is
no way for new ideas, new disorders, and new treatments to be developed. To
some authors, it is shortsighted to relegate qualitative research to the lowest levels
of evidence, especially because the results of such research may profoundly shape
the substance of later quantitative studies.

Popay and Williams (1998) argue that qualitative research may be viewed as
either "enhancing" EBM and EBP or as "different" from them. Black (1994)
points out several ways in which qualitative research can enhance EBM and EBP.
He states it: (1) can help researchers understand how and why interventions work,

(2) can help identify new variables and hypotheses for future study, (3) can help clarify unexpected results from quantitative studies, and (4) can help improve the accuracy and relevance of quantitative research. Yet, Popay and Williams see even greater potential in qualitative research's differences from quantitative research. They note it: (1) can help identify "taken for granted" aspects of health care and of potential risks, (2) can help professionals understand the experience and meaning of being a patient and of receiving a diagnosis, (3) can provide different sources of information and perspective from clients and important others (including subjective assessments of outcome), and (4) can explore the impact of agency practices and complex policies on clients. In this way, qualitative research helps identify what EBP may miss, omit, or render invisible. Qualitative research can complement EBM and EBP as well as enhancing them.

Trinder (2000) notes that the Cochrane Collaboration had begun a Qualitative Interest Group. She states that it is vital "that qualitative and other research designs be accepted and valued on their on terms, rather than fitted awkwardly and inappropriately into an existing framework" (p. 237). However, a decade later the role of qualitative research in EBM and EBP is still unclear (Nelson 2008). Greenhalgh (2010) points to standards for quality in qualitative research, but does not address how qualitative research fits with the larger EBM model. Gould (2010) argues for greater inclusion of qualitative research into EBP while pointing to the first two practice guidelines in the United Kingdom that integrate qualitative evidence. The Cochrane Qualitative Interest Group offers conference workshops on specific methodological topics, but the larger question of how qualitative research is valued and included in EBM and EBP remains unanswered.

In social work, Rubin (2008) states that qualitative research may be the appropriate source for answers about client's experience with illness or social challenges. This may prove to be one important use for qualitative research. Gilgun (2005a) points out that better conceptualization of patient values and patient preferences would help clarify key aspects of the EBM and EBP process. She adds that professional expertise and the personal experiences of the professional also deserve conceptual elaboration and further study. Petr (2009) offers a variation on EBP that emphasizes the voices and views of clients as the basis for determining effectiveness. His multidimensional approach to EBP expands the narrow focus on symptoms to include other areas of interest to clinical social workers and clients. Qualitative researchers, and many clinical investigators using qualitative research methods, make valuable contributions to the practice knowledge base.

The EBM/EBP hierarchy of evidence and research designs has many merits. It is one valuable way to enhance practice decision making and, in the aggregate, to make the best use of limited health care resources. Still, critical thinking is required to ensure that the assumptions embedded in the EBM/EBP model are fully understood and recognized. As a social movement, EBM and EBP advocate for the use of specific techniques and specific kinds of evidence. These merits have strong supporters as well as some cogent critiques. Clinical social workers must consider both the strengths and the limitations of EBM and EBP research methods as they impact on practice.

Summary

In this chapter we have explored how EBP is not solely a practice decision-making process. We argue that EBP can be viewed from three different perspectives that point out different aspects of the social movement that is EBM and EBP. The practice decision-making process is the core of EBP. From this first perspective, EBP adds to the responsibilities of clinical social workers. Yet from policy and administrative perspective, EBP is a way to increase accountability and reduce costs while improving service outcomes. At its worst, it may also restrict both client and professional autonomy, and replace them with administrative oversight. The large-scale methods of EBP may also be applied to the evaluation of individual professional performance. From a research perspective, EBP seeks to generate population level outcome studies that can identify effective treatments and reveal possible risks. Yet EBP may also reduce attention to important epistemological, value, and contextual issues that shape research. Qualitative research and other nonquantitative ways of knowing are devalued in the EBP evidence hierarchy and in related research funding. These methods may produce knowledge that can be useful to direct clinical practice and to administration and policy efforts. Critical thinking about the EBP model and its application is appropriate.

A Starting Point for the Mental Health Practitioner

A very useful starting point for mental health practitioners is to learn about the EBP practice decision-making process and to be able to use it to inform treatment planning. Still, practitioners must use this information in combination with professional expertise and critical thinking to meet the needs and interests of clients. Clients, too, must be active participants in the EBP practice decision-making process.

In the next chapter we will explore the several steps of the EBP practice decision-making model. This model organizes the practice application of research results to direct clinical social work practice.

Chapter 3
The Steps of Evidence-Based Practice in Clinical Practice: An Overview

We have seen that the evidence-based medicine (EBM) and evidence-based practice (EBP) movements follow the overall goals of Dr. Archibald Cochrane who sought to increase the use of effective treatments while reducing the use of ineffective and harmful treatments. In addition, EBP is usefully understood via three different perspectives in the social work and allied professional literature. As such, the focus of EBP discussion will differ based on the perspectives of (1) clinical practitioners, (2) researchers, and (3) funders or program administrators. While these different audiences all are key parts of the EBP movement, their specific purposes vary widely.

Many summaries of EBP begin by defining the steps of EBP as they apply to direct clinical practice. In turn, most clinical social workers view EBP as a set of steps that help structure treatment planning and decision making. Out of context, these seemingly structured steps of EBP decision making may feel like an imposition on professional expertise and autonomy. Their intent, however, is to help clinicians include the best research knowledge as one part of their clinical decision-making process. In the contemporary model of EBP, the client's clinical state and circumstances, research knowledge and the clients own values and preferences are all integrated using the professional expertise of the clinical social worker. The steps of EBP help guide and orient the use of research knowledge in clinical practice, but do not simply determine clinical choices. In other words, the EBP process will not lead the clinician to one clearly discernible 'right' answer. Clinicians must navigate through and incorporate many pieces of information for each client they serve. They must use their professional expertise and judgment to determine how best to weigh the various available clinical and research information.

It is important to keep in mind that the EBP model has been applied to other aspects of practice besides choosing treatments (Oxford University Center for Evidence-based Medicine 2009). It may also be used to select among preventive interventions or to examine the etiology or origins of medical disorders. In medicine

J. W. Drisko and M. D. Grady, *Evidence-Based Practice in Clinical Social Work*,
Essential Clinical Social Work Series, DOI: 10.1007/978-1-4614-3470-2_3,
© Springer Science+Business Media New York 2012

and psychology, EBM/EBP is also applied to the selection of differential diagnostic tests and procedures. In medicine, it is used to examine the prognosis of an illness, including survival rates over time. In administration and finance, the EBP model is even applied to economic decision making (Oxford Center for Evidence-based Medicine 2009). The EBM/EBP research approach can be applied to decision making in many areas of professional practice and practice management. Our focus in this chapter will be on using EBP as a practice decision-making process in clinical practice.

The Six Steps of EBP in Clinical Practice

The steps of the EBP practice model guide practice decision making. These steps must always be based upon a thorough assessment of the client and the client's circumstances. The assessment process allows the clinical social worker to learn both the foreground and background needs of the client. (Assessment will be the focus of the next chapter in this book.) Foreground needs usually become the priorities of interventions, while background needs provide the context that may influence if, and how, treatment is likely to proceed. In all cases, the intervention plans generated by the clinical social worker should be discussed with the client to determine if they are understood, are acceptable, are seen as appropriate, and likely to be effective. (We discuss this important step further in Chapter 9.)

Combining research knowledge, client needs and professional expertise starts with the identification of a priority practice issue and then moves through a sequence of steps. Scholars vary in the number of steps they name in the EBP process, but the core ideas do not vary.

The steps of the EBP practice decision-making process are:

(1) Drawing on client needs and circumstances learned in a thorough assessment, identify answerable practice questions and related research information needs;
(2) Efficiently locate relevant research knowledge;
(3) Critically appraise the quality and applicability of this knowledge to the client's needs and situation;
(4) Discuss the research results with the client to determine how likely effective options fit with the client's values and goals;
(5) Synthesizing the client's clinical needs and circumstances with the relevant research, develop a shared plan of intervention collaboratively with the client;
(6) Implement the intervention.

Note that these steps make the use of research a key part of practice decision making. This is a clear goal of EBP. Note carefully that the needs, values, and interests of clients are also actively included and may take precedence over research findings. Clinicians, therefore, must constantly consider how to understand the research findings given the unique situation of their client and how much of the research can be applied to that particular client, based on the client's unique presentation and context in which treatment will take place.

   Some authors add a seventh step to the EBP process (Gibbs 2002). This final step is to evaluate the effectiveness of the delivered intervention(s). We view this step as an integral part of all good professional practice. Most social work practice texts, CSWE's (2008) EPAS accreditation standards and the NASW *Code of Ethics* (2008) affirm this view. We do not, however, see practice evaluation as a part of the EBP process because it draws upon a very different research logic than does the EBP model. Practice evaluation is about determining the effectiveness of a treatment for a specific client, while the research model of EBP draws on the average results of research across large groups of clients. Because specific clients may not always match the average results of a large group of similar clients, the focus of practice evaluation is quite different from that used to rate evidence in the EBP literature. Still, evaluating the effectiveness of an intervention is an important part of good practice and should always be undertaken. When clinicians engage in quantitative practice evaluation, its purpose and design is quite different than is the core focus of EBP research as applied in the practice decision-making process. (We will discuss practice evaluation further in Chapter 10.)

   The six steps of EBP define the EBP practice decision-making process. Each step has a slightly different focus, but all demand specific—and varying—kinds of professional expertise. Client input from assessment serves to start and later to refine the EBP process. Research results substantiate the likely impact of intervention options. Integrating all these elements is the professional expertise of the clinical social worker. To more fully explore the EBP process, it is worth looking at each of its several steps in greater depth. Each step will also be further examined in later chapters of this book.

Step 1: Drawing on Client Needs and Circumstances Learned in a Thorough Assessment, Identify Answerable Practice Questions and Related Research Information Needs

To begin the EBP process, the clinical social worker must identify key practice concerns in interaction with the client. Note carefully that the EBP model is silent on just how these practice concerns are identified. Typically, clinicians identify such concerns through the intake and assessment processes. What constitutes a good enough client assessment, however, is not stated in the EBM/EBP model. The model simply assumes that professional practitioners will be able to make such an initial assessment. Indeed, good assessment is the hidden foundation of the optimal use of EBP (Drisko and Grady 2011). The pivotal role of a good assessment—the foundation of using EBP in practice—is left to the professional knowledge and expertise of the clinical social worker.

   The clinical social worker must carefully and thoughtfully determine what problems and needs are the priorities for a specific client in a specific set of social circumstances. The EBP model assumes the clinical social worker has the ability to make such assessments and has an institutional support system that allows careful and through assessment to be completed. In contemporary practice, many agency and funding influences may make a thorough assessment difficult to complete. Still, making a good choice about the client's priority needs is vital to applying the EBP model successfully. Professional expertise is very important to EBPs proper and successful application in practice.

One area in which clinical social workers may take a different stance than do other mental health professionals is the importance of social context. Clinical social workers often draw on the American Psychiatric Association's *Diagnostic and Statistic Manual of Mental Disorders* (2008) (DSM) as a resource for defining mental health problems. Yet clinical social workers also pay considerable attention to contextual factors (Kutchins and Kirk 1988; Probst 2011; Turner 2002). These may include whether or not basic concrete needs for food, housing, and medical care are available, if neighborhood and social supports for education and employment are adequate, and whether family and community supports are sufficient to encourage and sustain change. While clinical intervention may not be able to alter large-scale social circumstances, they strongly shape the context in which personal changes occur.

Another area of particular attention for clinical social workers is social diversity. Racial and ethnic factors may shape what kinds of intervention are acceptable to some clients. So too, religious beliefs and values may shape the kinds of interventions that are acceptable to some clients. Socially structured oppression through racism, sexism, ableism, and homophobia may influence how many actions and symptoms are understood. The impact of oppression may also influence the kinds of interventions that may be most effective in addressing them.

A thorough assessment will identify a number of factors that are concerns and challenges along with a number of factors that represent strengths and sources of active or potential support. Immediate risks to safety or of harm to self or others must be identified quickly. Assessment is a demanding process that requires professional expertise of several kinds. We will review assessments more completely in the following chapter.

Information Needs May Not Always Be About Selecting Treatments

The research information needs identified in the first step of the EBP practice decision-making process is not only about selecting treatment options (Oxford University Center for Evidence-based Medicine, April 2009; Rubin 2008). It may be that further differential diagnosis is needed. If so, research information about such differential diagnosis would be sought. In other cases information about prognosis might be needed, or about the likely course (progression) of a disorder. In some cases, policy planners and administrators use the EBP process to examine the cost-effectiveness of diagnostic procedures and treatments. The kinds of research information that arise during assessment may be widely varied and do not all center on treatment planning.

Table 3.1 The P.I.C.O.T. clinical question model

Patient, problem or population	What are the characteristics of a group of clients very similar to my client?
Intervention	What intervention do I wish to learn about?
Comparison	What are the main alternatives to this intervention?
Outcomes	What outcomes do I and the client hope for? (How exactly will outcome be determined?)
Type	What type of intervention question am I asking? (Treatment? Diagnosis? Prevention? Etiology? Prognosis?)

After Sackett et al. (1997)

A Model for Framing Clinical Questions: The P.I.C.O.T. Model

Sackett et al. (1997) developed a specific model for framing EBM questions. It is called the P.I.C.O.T., or P.I.C.O., model. To focus a clinicians' practice information needs, they suggest five steps. Each step is intended to help clarify a specific piece of the client's needs as it relates to EBM and EBP (Richardson et al. 1995). The full model is detailed in Table 3.1. 'P' stands for patient or problem, the 'who' you need to know about. The goal is to describe the key characteristics of your client and clinical situation. 'I' stands for intervention. Based on the client and clinical satiation, what are the key service needs? Do you wish to know about what works for a specific diagnosis or what preventative measures might avoid development of a full blown problem? The goal is to be clear about the kinds of interventions about which you wish to learn. 'C' stands for comparison. Is there more than one approach to treatment? If there are multiple approaches to intervening, do you want to learn if one is more likely to be effective than another specific alternative? 'O' stands for outcomes. To be clearer still, what specific kinds of outcome do you and your client seek? Is the goal reduction in certain symptoms or perhaps remission of the disorder as a whole? Are certain symptoms more important to address than others, at least at the beginning of interventions? Are there other issues or social circumstances to consider? Finally, 'T' stands for type of problem. Remember that EBM and EBP can address diagnostic issues, choice of treatments, choice of preventive interventions, even the etiology, and course of a disorder. What type of question do you have for which you need research information?

To illustrate the use of the P.I.C.O.T. model, let us look at the case of a specific client in brief. The client (P), Laticia, is an employed 26-year-old African–American woman in good physical health with no history of major depression but recurrent concerns about lack of energy and sleeping difficulties beginning in the fall. She reports similar feelings a year ago in the fall, and that the problems seemed to go away in the spring. These symptoms are aspects of Seasonal Affective Disorder (SAD). Bright light exposure has been reported in the news as one way to intervene for SAD. A useful clinical question might be (I) is light exposure therapy be more effective than (C) medication or (C) psychotherapy in (O) increasing energy level and hours of sleep per night? Note that there are very specific symptoms that define the client's desired treatment outcomes. This is an example of an (T) treatment question since the symptoms are currently evident. A key goal is to identify a number of likely effective treatment alternatives to address Laticia's needs. Assuming this summary includes all the key information that is currently relevant, the P.I.C.O.T. model both clarifies and focuses our information needs for treatment planning. Of course, it is always necessary to do a complete assessment. What might appear as SAD symptoms could alternately be a reaction to the anniversary of the death of a loved one. Understanding the problem fully and accurately is the foundation for selecting treatments and alternatives.

Remember that practice information needs are not always about the selection of treatments. In mental health, initial practice questions often center on (1) a need to develop a more productive relationship with the client, (2) a need for a more definitive diagnosis, or (3) the selection of the best treatment options. Less commonly used, but no less appropriate, is (4) the selection of preventive interventions. Rubin (2008) also suggests (5) understanding the etiology of a problem or (6) understanding how a client experiences a difficulty may also be an initial information needs in EBP. However, these last two information needs, while fully valid, have not been widely addressed in the mental health EBP practice literature. Similarly, questions about (7) the etiology and (8) the course of disorders is less commonly the focus of mental health practice information needs. In medicine, economic and even ethical decision making has become part of the evidence-based model (Snyder and Gauthier 2008). Any of these questions may be clarified through the use of the P.I.C.O.T. model. Let us next look further into some of these types of practice information needs.

Enhancing the Client–Practitioner Relationship

A good deal of research and a lot of practice wisdom indicate that establishing a relationship or alliance is important to good treatment outcome (Krupnick et al. 1996; Lambert and Barley 2001; Martin et al. 2000). Establishing a positive working relationship is also the first order of business for all clinicians who meet new clients. Without a positive working relationship, clients may not return for a second session, making effective treatment impossible. Yet how to develop a more productive working relationship has only recently become part of EBP. Castonguay and Beutler (2006a), reporting the work of four expert groups, empirically identified several factors that impact on the quality of the client-therapist relationship. These 'empirically based relationship' factors currently take the form of broad principles. For example, the group found that clients with greater levels of impairment or personality disorders are less likely to benefit from treatment than do other clients who are less impaired or without a personality disorder. The group also found that clinicians with secure attachments, who were able to tolerate intense affect and who could be open, informed, and tolerant about the client's religious views were generally more effective. While fitting this work into the EBP framework is only at an early stage of development, it may be possible to identify more specific approaches to intervention that guide specific interventions.

Improving Diagnostic Assessment

In medicine, identifying the necessary diagnostic procedures often is the first step of EBM (Ebell 2001). This emphasis on diagnostic procedures exists because particular kinds of information may be needed to be sure the diagnosis is thorough and accurate. Specific tests or procedures may be needed to ensure the correct diagnosis, and in EBM, there is often a direct link between a diagnosis and an intervention. In mental health practice, the link between diagnosis and intervention is often less specific and certain. There are fewer valid diagnostic tools available for differential diagnosis and the affirmation of possible diagnoses. Still, diagnostic and assessment tools social workers might utilize in EBP include neurological testing, learning disabilities testing, or psychological testing. At the level of risk assessment, protocols for suicide and self-harm risk potential are very common, as are assessments of homicide potential where indicated. Clinical social workers also routinely look for child or elderly abuse and domestic violence. Specific assessment for fire-setters may be required by some states as well as to complete referrals to certain services. Using the EBP process to sharpen or improve diagnostic assessment is a fully legitimate, and underused, part of EBP in mental health.

One complication in the use of diagnostic tests in EBP is that the lack of valid and reliable instruments often limits their utility in clinical social work practice. Most tests and assessment protocols in mental health add useful information but ultimately also require interpretation and judgment by the clinician. 'Certain' answers and conclusions are very rare. Simply transferring the EBM diagnostic process to mental health practice and EBP may give greater authority to the results of assessment tools than is warranted. Assessment and diagnosis based on invalid or unreliable instruments is not beneficial and does not fit with the premises of EBP or ethical clinical social work practice.

Assessment in today's mental health practice tends to be very brief and very focused. Assessing symptoms and risk takes priority over getting to know the whole person. Single session or very brief 'diagnostics' are commonplace in community mental health practice due to financial and other pressures. The merit of such focused sessions is that acute concerns and risks are systematically identified, such as suicide risk and substance use. The limitation of such an approach is that it may prematurely foreclose gaining and weighing other important diagnostic information. For example, as noted above, clients may not immediately share painful material such as histories of abuse. In other cases, obtaining accurate information about substance use, or even housing, may be difficult due to client anxiety or shame, despite direct requests for information. Without all of the information to consider, social workers can miss a critical factor influencing the diagnostic picture, and may begin the EBP process considering only part of the puzzle. Clinical social workers need to be sure they have a sound and complete assessment before moving on to selecting treatment options.

Selecting the Optimal Treatment

The focus of EBP in clinical social work practice is most often on the identification of potentially effective treatments for the client's concerns. Indeed, this question is the sole focus in many illustrations of the EBP process in the mental health literature. It is very important, but is not the only appropriate question for EBP. While funding and other supports make preventive services less common, identifying risk factors to get clients preventive supports may be clinical effective and cost-effective. Prevention may often be more desirable than treatment of full-blown problems.

Where thorough and credible information allows sound assessment, the first step of the EBP process is often to identify and prioritize the primary treatment needs of the client. This step involves several decisions. The key concern or diagnosis must be determined. Both psychological and social factors are often evident and important in client's presentations. Determining the priority concern may require the use of professional judgment to select one target concern from among several interrelated issues. Ideally, this priority concern will help the client make meaningful changes initially, while also helping to enhance the alliance with the practitioner and, as necessary, making effective treatment of other concerns more possible. For example, a client with an anxiety disorder, substance abuse issues, relationship issues, and work-related issues may benefit from first addressing the co-occurring substance abuse. Yet alternatively, some clients may find help with anxiety decreases substance abuse. Professional judgment is crucial to establishing treatment priorities in collaboration with the client. In some instances, clients are mandated for treatment for specific issues that may not appear to be the optimal starting point. Professional judgment is necessary to help the client work toward mandated changes while setting the stage for later efforts that more fully address their felt concerns.

The cases in the later chapters of this book detail how priority practice information is converted by clinical social workers into one or more answerable questions. The case examples also provide information on how clinician's use professional judgment to prioritize and direct assessment and treatment choices. While EBP emphasizes the use of research knowledge to guide treatment planning, there is very little research on how mental health practitioners make these expert choices. There are also no experimental studies of this process for ethical reasons. Use of supervision and consultation is always encouraged.

Once a researchable practice question is fully framed, the next step of the EBP practice decision-making model is to find research knowledge to guide practice decision making.

Step 2: Efficiently Locate Relevant Research Knowledge

Since a key part of EBP is to use research results to guide and affirm assessment and treatment choices, the second step is to find relevant research results to answer your practice question. This step requires a very different form of professional expertise than does identifying the practice question that begins the EBP process. Here the key expertise is more like that of reference librarians and information technologists than that of most mental health clinicians. Yet learning to do a literature search is part of professional social work training, and is familiar to most clinical social workers. This area of expertise may be off-putting to some clinicians, but the necessary skills can be updated and refined with a little practice. Turning to professional librarians for help and training may also be efficient, especially for beginners. In addition, there are also many print and online resources to help guide the location of useful research results.

It is important to note that the EBP process presupposes adequate and efficient access to current research results by mental health clinicians. This requirement often poses a new financial burden on mental health agencies and a new time burden on individual professionals. Many sources of very useful research information for mental health practice are compiled and made available by for-profit publishers and online data compliers. These publishers and online data providers have substantial costs to operate their services. In turn, access to current materials can represent a substantial new cost to clinics and clinical social workers engaged in the EBP process.

Still another important issue is 'information overload.' There has been an increase in the number of sources of clinical information, such as journals and books, as well as an expansion in technologies for accessing these materials. Some professionals find the number of materials they need to examine so vast that they quickly become discouraged. Simple searches using Wikis and Google can reveal staggering amounts of information. For example, the search term 'depression' yields over 197,000,000 'hits' on Google. Of course, some of this information may prove to be inadequate, commercial or based on dubious sources. Finding useful, high quality materials can be difficult despite apparent easy access online.

In response to the growth of EBM and EBP, a number of organizations, both professional and for-profit, have begun to develop summaries of research results. Books such as Carr's (2009) *What Works with Children, Adolescents and Adults?* and Roth and Fonagy's (2005) *What Works for Whom? A Critical Review of Psychotherapy* provide overviews of EBP and a summary of relevant research. These books are good starting points, and provide a background understanding for clinicians. Another useful volume, though recently more an online resource, is the British Medical Journal's (or BMJ) (2009/2010) *Clinical Evidence Handbook.* This work is organized like an encyclopedia, offering detailed information about psychological and psychopharmacological treatments for several common mental health disorders. It is a very practical resource for mental health practitioners. (More clinical practice information sources will be detailed in Chapter 5.)

Online resources are mainly 'foreground' resources that report summaries of research findings on a single specific disorder or problem. They frequently assume that the user has substantial background knowledge about clinical assessment, information searches, research design, treatment models, and statistics, which may be intimidating for some clinicians who attempt to read parts of the research methodologies and results. Online resources tend to be easier to access from multiple locations than are books and print resources. They do require some infrastructure such as computers, smart phones, personal data assistants (PDAs), or similar devices to use. Internet access is also required and can be expensive. In addition to ease of access, online resources can be updated frequently, unlike print resources and books. Many paid, subscription based, EBP resources are updated monthly or even more often. Thus they offer practitioners the latest research information. Beyond subscription options, there are also many excellent free online EBP resources.

The most rigorous online compilation of research evidence for clinical social work practice is the Cochrane Collaboration's Library of Systematic Reviews (www.cochrane.org). Named after Scottish physician Archie Cochrane, the Cochrane Library offers thoroughly reviewed summaries of research organized by diagnosis. Medical and mental health issues are both covered. Clinicians can find a concise report of the relevant available research concerning the diagnosis they are searching. For social service, criminal justice and educational programs, the Campbell Collaboration (www.campbellcollaboration.org) offers similar high quality research summaries. In contrast to the Cochrane Collaboration, the Campbell Collaboration targets social problems without using a medical model orientation. A wide, but somewhat spotty, collection of social service concerns are reviewed in detail. Both the Campbell Collaboration and the Cochrane Collaboration apply the same high standards to systematic reviews of research.

A different starting point is offered through online practice guidelines. Most are medically oriented and defined by diagnosis. Well-crafted guidelines provide a summary of research results for a specific disorder as well as a set of steps or principles of treatment for practitioners to follow or avoid. That is, not only a summary of the research, but an interpretation of the research by expert panels is offered. However, the standards used for establishing practice guidelines may not be as clear or as rigorous as from those used by the Cochrane and Campbell Collaborations. In contrast to the principles of EBM/EBP, expert opinion may heavily shape practice guidelines in some instances.

The United States government's Agency for Healthcare Quality and Research offers the online *National Guideline Clearinghouse*. Other practice guidelines are offered by professional organizations, such as the American Psychiatric Association's *Practice Guidelines*. The National Guideline Clearinghouse provides the most extensive collection of practice guidelines, drawing on international sources. Professional organizations also offer guidelines for common disorders, but generally offer many fewer guidelines than does the National Clearinghouse.

Many high quality research summaries and practice guidelines are readily available to those doing EBP. High prevalence disorders are often the focus of such summaries and guidelines. The research knowledge made available in such summaries and guidelines can be a very valuable way to ensure practice decisions are informed and guided by quality research. Online options make many resources efficiently available to practitioners as well as consumers. (URLs for many online resources are detailed in Chapter 5.)

Both summaries of research and practice guidelines have two limitations. First, they cover only a limited range of the many diagnoses in the DSM or World Health Organization's (2007) International Classification of Diseases (ICD-10). Second, available guidelines may not offer clear conclusions about what treatments or specific interventions are most effective. Many summaries note that rigorous research is simply unavailable, making it premature to draw conclusions about the effectiveness of any treatment for the target disorder. This lack of evidence may be very frustrating to the practitioner seeking to engage in the EBP practice decision-making process. A treatment that has not been researched is not necessarily ineffective. The lack of research exists because researchers have not studied all disorders in depth. This may be due to lack of funding, lack of agreement on the conceptualization of the disorder, lack of agreement on what constitutes a 'successful' outcome, or lack of participants for studies. The large number of disorders and their variations included in the DSM would make it impossible to fund and undertake large-scale experimental studies on all the disorders in any reasonable period of time. Still, seeking out available research evidence can help guide intervention planning in many cases where research is available and rigorous.

An Example: What the Literature Shows About Light Therapy

Drawing on the concerns of Laticia, the 26-year-old African–American woman described above, the clinical social worker wants to answer the practice question "Is bright light therapy as effective or more effective than are either medication or psychotherapy?" A Cochrane Library search for the term "light therapy" yielded a full systematic review done in 2004 showing light therapy as a promising treatment but only for *non-seasonal* depression (Tuunainen et al. 2004). This review is a bit off topic. No completed Cochrane Collaboration systematic reviews for treatments specifically for SAD were found. However, one review protocol was found, meaning a systematic review is in progress and two others are in the early planning stages. This will help in the future, but not right now.

A Google search reveals a published meta-analysis by Golden et al. (2005) reports that bright light therapy using specific lights in the morning was significantly more effective at the $p < 0.0001$ criterion level than was placebo intervention across eight randomized controlled trials (RCTs) including 360 people with SAD. The effect size for the bright light therapy was large (Cohen's

$d = 0.84$; 95% Confidence interval 0.60–1.08). This indicates a large and beneficial difference in outcomes for people who received treatment versus those who did not. (We will review the statistics and their interpretation in Chapter 7.) Four studies showed remission (ending) of SAD symptoms was three times more likely when using bright light therapy than by placebo alone. Another bright light therapy using a gradual dawn method was also significantly more effective at the $p < 0.0001$ level than was use of red lights or a rapid dawn intervention (Cohen's $d = 0.73$; 95% Confidence interval 0.37–1.08). This result aggregated five studies, including 69 patients with SAD. Light therapy as a treatment for SAD has some good research support.

However, looking a bit deeper, commentary by Terman (2006) indicates several studies on bright light therapy were mainly done by just one research team at a single university, and that the best designed study did not show a significant difference. Similarly, all the gradual dawn therapy research was completed by the same research team. This would suggest some caution in relying on the research conclusions due to possible bias. Nonetheless, the research supports the view that bright light therapy appears beneficial in reducing SAD symptoms.

Finally, Lam et al. (2006) report the results of a single experimental study (RCT) showing that both antidepressant medication and light therapy are equally effective in treating SAD. Both treatments yielded statistically significant improvements in measured depression. There was no significant difference in remission levels (i.e. no longer qualifying for a diagnosis of depression) between the two therapies (50% for light therapy vs. 54% for medication; $\chi^2 = 0.04$, $df = 1, p = 0.84$). Either bright light therapy or medication could be beneficial for the client, though this conclusion would be better supported if more studies had reported consistent results. Light therapy appears well supported and antidepressant medication also has some preliminary research support.

Comparison to psychotherapy alone was not found, so it appears psychotherapy was not studied as a treatment for SAD. This may mean simply that it has not been researched, but it does mean there is no strong empirical support for psychotherapy as a treatment for SAD. No information on racial or ethnic variation was included or mentioned in any of the reviews. Antidepressant mediations were reported to produce to unpleasant side effects for some patients (as is often the case). No harms or side effects were reported for bright light therapy. No practice guidelines for treating SAD were located.

Oddly, no mention of the types and range of skin tones included in the study samples was found in the outcome literature on light therapy. Since Laticia is African–American, and fairly dark in skin tone, it is unclear if the available research has included people with skin tone like her own. This may be a very important part of defining the patient—the P. in the P.I.C.O.T. model. Might African–Americans be differently responsive to light therapy than are whites? The information available in the literature simply does not address or answer this question.

In discussion with the client, the answer to the question "What treatments have documented effectiveness for SAD?" appears to be that light therapy has considerable research support. (The I. and C. of the P.I.C.O.T model.) Bright light therapy alone has the most consistent research support and little apparent risk. On the other hand, it is unclear if this research included African–Americans or more generally people with dark skin tones. It is possible that they may respond differently to light therapy or need different exposure time to bright lights. However, the best available research does not answer this question. The clinical social worker would next discuss and explore these options with the client to determine if either fits with her own values and preferences.

It is worth noting that this literature search took a well trained clinician with excellent access to resources about three hours to complete. This included preliminary searches to identify relevant articles and reviews, locating copies of the full text articles, and reviewing their content.

Today's electronic search engines can yield huge amounts of complex and detailed information on a selected topic. This is often (but not always) the case in searches for mental health topics. The quality of this information may vary widely, as does the quality of the sources. Different perspectives may be available, often framed by specific theories or points of view on the topic. For example, the views of consumers or clients, professional practitioners, and professional researchers may lead to different questions, study methods and results (Petr 2009). Researchers may also differ in their appraisal of the quality of results of findings of research studies. Thus, once you have located information about your practice problem, the next step is to appraise its quality and its relevance to your practice situation.

Step 3: Critically Appraise the Quality and Applicability of Located Knowledge to the Client's Needs and Situation

The third step of the EBP practice decision-making process is to appraise the quality and relevance of the research information you have found. This step requires a very different set of skills from doing a clinical assessment or locating research reports. Appraising the quality of research methods and reports may not be the strong suit of many clinical social workers. Yet with some practice, key issues in research quality can be identified and examined.

Scholars and practitioners with backgrounds in quantitative, epidemiological, research originally organized and promoted the EBM and EBP movements. Dr. Cochrane studied populations with pulmonary diseases from a strong quantitative perspective. Dr. Sackett et al. (1996) also promoted determination of research quality from a quantitative, statistical perspective. The EBM and EBP literatures clearly places the greatest value on research evidence derived from quantitative, experimental research designs. As discussed in Chapter 2, this type of research design has strong internal validity allowing cause-effect relationships to be established. In reports of RCTs, overall, less attention is directed to the conceptualization of problems and measures, or to comorbid disorders and social circumstances, than to research design and statistical analysis.

Table 3.2 The hierarchy of evidence (for treatment outcomes)

Level 1a	Evidence obtained from a systematic review evaluating and integrating the results of several experimental research studies (or RCTs) showing homogeneity (consistency) of results
Level 1b	Evidence obtained from a single experimental study (RCT) with a narrow confidence interval (showing high precision of results that are better than no treatment)
Level 2a	Evidence from a systematic review of several quasi-experimental or cohort studies (with no control groups or retrospective control groups) showing homogeneity of results
Level 2b	Evidence obtained from a single cohort study or low quality experimental study
Level 2c	Evidence obtained from 'outcomes research' or observational studies of treatment results based on a retrospective or after the fact matching of clients, lacking random assignment
Level 3a	Evidence obtained from a systematic review of 'case control' studies (not experiments) showing homogeneity of results
Level 3b	Evidence obtained from a single of 'case control' study (not experiments) showing homogeneity of results
Level 4	Evidence obtained from a 'case series' of observations made on clients with no control group or random assignment and poor quality case control or cohort studies. (Results of multiple single subject design studies would be Level 4 in this model)
Level 5	Expert opinion, bench research or first principles

The results of multiple studies of any type are considered as higher quality evidence than are the results of any single study of the same type. Note that it is assumed that the measures used to determine effectiveness are fully adequate (valid), reliable, and comprehensive. The populations studied are also assumed to be adequate in numbers and in relevant social characteristics. Further, it is assumed that treatments or interventions are fully specified and that, in experiments, no other factors influence treatment outcomes. Where reviewers have concerns about the quality of a study of a given type, the next lower grade may be assigned. That is, an RCT of questionable quality may be rated as a level '2' given concerns about its rigor. This table is adapted from the Oxford University Center for Evidence-based Medicine's Levels of Evidence (March 2009)

Researchers using the standard EBP model, drawing on EBM, endorse a specific hierarchy of quality in research evidence. This hierarchy of evidence categories is meant to help clinicians and researchers quickly appraise the quality of research knowledge. The recently updated hierarchy of research evidence developed by the Oxford University Centre for Evidence-based Medicine (2009) is presented in Table 3.2. An almost identical hierarchy is offered by the GRADE (undated) organization. The Oxford evidence hierarchy has several clear elements. Evidence obtained from comparisons across an untreated control group and a treated group are prioritized. Such comparisons help identify if a given treatment or intervention produces better results than no treatment at all. Since some mental health conditions appear to improve over time without treatment, these research designs help demonstrate that the treatment yields better results than does time alone. Further, by prioritizing random assignment of clients to the treated or untreated group, bias in group composition is limited. Random assignment minimizes any systematic bias in the assignment of clients to treated or untreated groups and is another asset of carefully done experimental research (RCTs).

Of course, even experimental research may have limitations. The lack of adequate criteria for including or excluding people in the sample selection process, overly narrow inclusion criteria, small sample size, missing data, and lack the statistical power necessary to detect differences may be limitations of experimental research. These limitations can undermine the ability of an experiment to detect differences in outcome or to allow generalization of results to larger client populations. (We will explore these issues of determining research quality in greater depth in Chapters 6 and 7.)

Note that the EBM/EBP hierarchy of research designs is intended to help practitioners quickly identify some key differences that impact on the quality of results. If no systematic review of experimental research or single experimental study is located, it is appropriate to look at the best available evidence based on other research designs. These lower levels of evidence are also determined by the specific research methods used. Comparisons that do not use random assignment of participants comparing treated versus control conditions, but do include a control or comparison group constitute level 2 and lower rated studies. Researchers often call these quasi-experimental or, in the medical literature, observational, research designs. Comparisons that do not use random assignment, nor a comparison group, are level 2 (or lower) rated studies.

This distinction is very important. Many observational program evaluations use only pre- and post-assessments of a single group of treated clients and do not include a formal comparison with untreated controls. This provides no basis for comparing gains due to treatment from gains due to other unidentified sources. Campbell and Stanley (1963) list several types of threats to interval validity, such as maturation and history, that are not accounted for in observational studies. Further, many program evaluations compare similar programs because random assignment may not be feasible due to legal or funding obligations. It may be unlawful and/or unethical to randomly assign clients to mental health programs or untreated control groups. In turn, level 2 studies have lesser internal validity than do level 1 studies that use comparison groups. That is, they do not show clearly that the treatment alone causes better outcomes than does no treatment.

The distinction between the lack of a comparison group versus the lack of random assignment of research participants to the treated or to the control group may take some careful study. Outcome studies of treatment programs, such as those that are used for substance abuse treatment or severe mental illnesses, often do not use random assignment of clients to treated or control groups. They often employ a comparison group, though it may not be an untreated control group.

Level 3 and 4 evidence is derived from all other *planned* research designs and methods. Levels 3 and 4 include studies such as surveys or 'case control studies.' These are studies in which people who have a disorder are retrospectively (after treatment) compared with people who did not have it to see what risk factors distinguish the two groups as time goes by. Level 3 and 4 research designs are often called descriptive, or exploratory, research designs. These designs are not intended to show cause-effect relationships as are true experimental designs or RCTs, but are often used to describe patterns or new concepts. Such patterns can serve as the foundation for future research projects aimed at exploring causal relationships among various factors.

Finally, level 5 knowledge is derived from expert opinions. Opinion and practice wisdom are not based on any planned research design. Note that all practiced wisdom is put into level 5, as are summaries developed by expert practitioners or researchers that are not specifically tied to research evidence as defined by the EBM/EBP model.

The levels of research evidence are a shorthand device meant to help practitioners and others quickly appraise the quality of available knowledge on a topic. In EBP, mental health clinicians are directed to look for level 1 systematic review or experimental results first, and to give priority to this knowledge over the other types. Thus an early step in an EBP appraisal of research is to determine which are derived from rigorous experimental research. In many situations experimental research will be located. However, for other disorders or concerns, no experimental research may be found. This is not necessarily a matter of an inadequate or incorrect search; it may simply reflect the lack of experimental outcome research on the chosen topic. In such cases, the EBP model directs practitioners to level 2, then level 3, then level 4 results. All these levels of evidence are parts of the EBM/EBP model, but the confidence one has in the quality of knowledge is higher when the optimal research designs and evidence are available. Level 5 is appropriate to use when no other research evidence is found. The EBP process calls for practitioners to use 'the best available evidence' in making decisions, which means use the best at whatever level of design quality is available.

Only level 1 results allow cause and effect to be determined; all other levels are suggestive but do not demonstrate that the treatment or intervention caused the change found. It may then appear that use of levels 3 and 4 results is only a poor approximation of the kind of research-guided decision making the EBP model promotes. However, research is developed incrementally, usually beginning with exploratory stages that clarify what constitutes a disorder and what constitutes a treatment. Case studies and personal stories can be of great value. Descriptive and correlational studies help clarify what other attributes may exacerbate or diminish the impact of a disorder, or mask it altogether. They may add to diagnostic profiles and to identifying risk factors. Such studies are also of great value.

In practice guidelines, groups of clinical and research experts go beyond apprising research results to rating specific practice interventions. That is, they establish a list of good practices, sometimes called practice parameters, and rank each component based upon the research support for it. Specific practice recommendations are then assigned a letter grade from 'A' to 'D' (see Table 3.3). The grade assigned to each recommendation is based upon the methodological quality of the available research evidence to support it. 'A' level grades are based on evidence from experimental research or RCTs. 'B' level grades are based on research that does not use random assignment (i.e. quasi-experiments). 'C' level grades are based on observational studies (no random assignment nor comparison groups). 'D' level grades are based on expert opinion. Clinical social workers are reminded that the professional groups assigning such grades, while themselves experts, are creating recommendations that

Table 3.3 Recommendation Grades (for Recommendations in Practice Guidelines)

Grade A	Assigned to specific treatment recommendations where at least one randomized controlled trial is found as part of a body of literature of overall good quality and consistency addressing the specific recommendation
Grade B	Assigned to specific treatment recommendations where at least one well-conducted clinical study without random assignments (a quasi-experiment) is found on the topic of recommendation
Grade C	Assigned to specific treatment recommendations where at least one observational studies that does not use either random assignment nor comparison groups are found on the topic of recommendation
Grade D	Assigned to specific treatment recommendations where only expert committee reports or opinions and/or clinical experiences of respected authorities are found on the topic of recommendation

Consistent research results over multiple studies of any type (experiment, quasi-experiment, observation, case study series) are viewed as more persuasive than is a single study of the same type. Where reviewers have concerns about the quality of a study of a given type, the next lower grade may be assigned. That is, an RCT of questionable quality may be graded as a 'B' given concerns about its rigor. A 'D' grade is assigned where no formal research has been completed on the issue. Adapted from the United States Department of Health and Human Services' Agency for Healthcare Research and Quality National Guidelines Clearance Center. Retrieved from http:// guidelines.gov/content.aspx?id–15647&search−major+depression (Not all grading rubrics use the same standards.)

might, ironically, appear to be expert opinion. Clinical expertise is always required in EBP to determine how appropriate treatment recommendations are, and how well they fit with each specific clinical situation and client preferences.

As an example, in the Michigan Quality Improvement Consortium's (2010) practice guidelines for major depression in adults, one major practice standard is to "initiate antidepressant medication following manufacturer's recommended dose." This practice standard is given an 'A' grade. An 'A' grade means that this recommendation is based upon evidence derived from RCTs or level 1 research designs. The next recommendation, "referral to, and coordination with, behavioral health specialist when [there is an] identified or suspected risk of suicide, or a complex social situation" is given a 'D' grade. A 'D' grade indicates the recommendation lacks research support and is based solely on expert opinion or level 5 practice wisdom. Of course, if primary care physicians had concerns about suicide risk, it is plausible that they might follow and manage this concern on their own or make such a referral. The grade alone is not a sufficient basis for making a clinical practice decision. It does, however, indicate whether or not the standard is supported by research evidence. As always, expert professional expertise is required to determine the best course of treatment for any particular client and circumstances.

It is quite likely that there are no experimental studies comparing the outcomes for patients with both major depression and suicide risk as treated by primary care physicians alone versus primary care physicians and behavioral health specialists jointly. This is why the 'D' grade is applied. It is important to bear in mind that the recommendation does not mean physicians should not make such referrals, only that there is no strong research evidence that it leads to better outcomes for such clients.

Yet, ethical and legal guidelines regarding the safety of clients are paramount in such a clinical situation, whether there is research to support such action or not. Professional expertise and critical thinking remain vital in all clinical practice.

Is This Research Applicable to My Client's Needs and Situation?

Once you locate studies based on strong research designs, the issue of their relevance to your particular client also arises. Experimental studies are planned to examine the impact of just one variable—usually the treatment—and its effect. This often means that clients with just one disorder are included and all others are excluded from the research. The yield of the research may, or may not, be informative about clients with multiple, comorbid disorders. Your client may also have medical conditions or other life circumstances that make the use of an otherwise effective treatment inappropriate. While the ability of experiments to demonstrate treatments cause a change is a real strength, experimental results may be only narrowly applicable.

Some scholars state that experiments may show effectiveness only in the laboratory (meaning tightly controlled circumstances, not use of a real laboratory). They draw a distinction between *efficacy studies* based on laboratory conditions, and *effectiveness studies* that are based in real-world clinical conditions. Effectiveness studies include people with comorbid conditions and varied circumstances, which reduces their internal validity (i.e. the ability to demonstrate that the treatment causes the change). The strength of effectiveness studies is that they can show a treatment produces change in real-world conditions. In this way effectiveness studies have a practical advantage over the more tightly controlled efficacy studies. However, interpreting their results, and to whom the results best apply, can be difficult.

It is always important to examine if the samples on which research is completed are similar to your specific client. Studies focusing on adults may have not automatic relevance to studies of children (though they sometimes do). Studies of adults may also yield different results that a study of elders (though not always). In addition, elders tend to be disproportionately omitted from clinical trials in medicine (Zulman et al. 2011). Most efficacy studies address just one diagnosis, such as major depression, and carefully exclude people with comorbid conditions. Such studies *do* show that a treatment is effective for a specific disorder (or is not). Yet they may not show effectiveness for persons with this disorder *and* other comorbid disorders. Comorbid social circumstances, despite being somewhat assessed under Axes IV and V of the DSM, may also impact upon a client's ability to undertake and complete a specific treatment or program. Research results may be generally or broadly applicable, but other factors may influence the outcome for any single client.

Other concerns about the applicability of research results center on racial and ethnic differences (Sue and Zane 2005; Zayas et al. 2010), gender differences (Levant and Silverstein 2005), sexual orientation (gay, lesbian, bisexual, and transgendered individuals) (Brown 2005), and disabilities (Olkin and Taliaferro 2005). Many otherwise well planned studies do not fully specify the composition of their sample beyond addressing the disorder under study. It is often very hard to assess from publications if people from diverse backgrounds and with varied belief systems were included in the available research. If the client you serve is a recent immigrant from a different culture, it may remain unclear if the research results fit with their belief systems and responses. Research reports may simply render other diverse populations invisible due to lack of clear details about study samples. It may also be unclear if the measures used to assess the mental health disorder are designed to reveal disorders in non-majority populations. Most measures of mental health disorders are normed or rated in comparison to middle class white populations. They may not adequately capture symptoms and behaviors expressed somewhat differently by non-white populations. These measures may not even include items related to disabilities or other sources of social difference. The mental health clinician must decide if the available research fits the ethnicity, social characteristics, and belief systems of each unique client. One important step in making this decision is to talk directly with the client about what the research shows and how they fit with the client's own goals.

In our example of Laticia, the 26-year-old African–American woman seeking help with her lack of energy and difficulties sleeping in the fall, two systematic reviews offered summaries of the results of multiple experiments. She reports no other disorders, so looking at research on SAD alone is appropriate. However, no information about the ethnic background of participants was included in Golden et al. (2005) systematic review. There might also be ethnic values, or other personal characteristics and needs of the client, that make bright light exposure an unacceptable treatment. Differences in sexual orientation might also matter, along with different abilities as appropriate. The clinical social worker and the client need to discuss how the client thinks and feels about the relevance of the research evidence to her specific needs and situation in the context of her culture, values, and goals.

Step 4: Discuss the Research Results With the Client to Determine How Likely Effective Options Fit With the Client's Values and Goals

Once the best available research is identified and appraised for quality and relevance to the client, the fourth step in EBP is to discuss the research results directly with the client. This step obligates the practitioner to synthesize and summarize the research results succinctly and clearly. Thus it helps the clinical social worker clarify what is known about the treatment options. This act of synthesis requires many forms of professional expertise and solid professional judgment.

Further, direct discussion allows the client to learn about, compare, and evaluate the various treatment options. Gambrill (2001) argues that this is also an ethical imperative for social workers. Fully informing clients is important to supporting their self determination and cooperative decision making. In today's practice world, it is often the case that clients have done their own searches of treatment options, or learned a great deal through discussion with others who have the same concern. Of course, these views may be very well informed or simply horror stories from others who have had bad treatment experiences. Direct discussion allows clients to share their views and interests, and allows the practitioner to help clarify any misunderstandings. Shared discussion enhances client understanding of their situation and options in the context of learning about what the best available research shows. It is also very helpful to developing a clear treatment contract.

Part of this discussion should always focus on how the research-based options fit with the client's belief system and expectations. For example, Castonguay and Beutler (2006b) report that there is empirical evidence that openness to the religious beliefs of clients can both strengthen the client–practitioner relationship and improve overall outcomes. The practitioner need not share personal beliefs with the client, but must show openness and support for the client's beliefs. Direct discussion of treatment options, and exploration of the client's views, facilitates understanding of the client's perspective. Research continues to demonstrate that successful treatment is heavily dependent on the client's agreement with both the explanation for the problem and proposed treatment approach (Wampold 2010). The explanation for why the problem exists and what to do about it must be aligned with the client's values, belief systems, and goals.

Clients may sometimes refuse treatment options that have good research support. Clients may find research supported options to be contrary to their cultural expectations, belief systems, or practical concerns like transportation and missing work. In such cases, alternatives that fit the client's views should be offered when available. In no instance should clients be pressured to participate in treatments that they find unacceptable. The EBP practice decision-making process can provide a forum for increasing client participation in treatment planning. This participation can increase motivation and help solidify the treatment alliance. To pressure clients into undertaking treatments they find unacceptable may undermine important elements that promote improvement. Such pressuring also contradicts the National Association of Social Worker's *Code of Ethics* (2008), and can undermine client dignity and self-determination.

There are situations in which courts or other authorities mandate treatment and require client participation in programs. It is fully appropriate to help clients understand the merits of programs supported by research evidence. It is also appropriate to help clients articulate their concerns about such treatments based on feelings of coercion or lack of motivation. Similarly, where publicly funded insurance programs or other payment-based limitations push clients to accept treatments they find unacceptable for any reason, direct discussion with the client must be undertaken. This should support the treatment alliance while helping the client state their concerns to the parties promoting specific treatment options they find objectionable. The clinical social worker may need to work with the client to advocate for alternate treatments.

Clients most often find discussion of treatment options a helpful way to increase their participation and sense of involvement in treatment planning. This shared process can aid understanding, can be empowering and can demonstrate the openness of the clinician to the client's views and beliefs. In addition, it is consistent with ethical social work practice principles of transparency and allowing clients to be partners in the treatment process.

Step 5: Synthesizing the Client's Clinical Needs and Circumstances With the Relevant Research, Develop a Shared Plan of Intervention Collaboratively With the Client

Once the client's views regarding the treatment options are understood, a final treatment or intervention plan is collaboratively developed. This plan will usually take the form of an oral or written contract with the client and a written note in the client's record. The written record should briefly reference the research information supporting the choice of treatment. Such a record would also document the use of the EBP model. Any concerns raised by the client regarding the treatment should also be formally documented.

Treatment goals should also be clearly defined and stated. Treatment models differ in the nature of their outcomes and in how they are assessed. This is why the P.I.C.O.T. model emphasizes specifically identifying the outcomes for treatment and looking carefully at the outcomes used by research studies. Before you and your client begin treatment, it is essential that there is agreement on the goals of treatment and the specific outcomes being sought. Different treatment approaches may emphasize different outcomes, and these various outcomes may alter what treatment approach you and your client ultimately chose to use. For example, cognitive-behavioral models will typically specify problem symptoms to be treated using a somewhat standard protocol. In contrast, solution focused treatments will make use of individualized treatment goals based on the specific strengths and capacities of the client. Psychodynamic models may look for repetitive dilemmas in relationships and specific behavioral changes that may be understood in the context of improved understanding and self-awareness. Some family therapy approaches seek to alter the typical style of interaction or equilibrium of the family rather than to change specific behaviors. Many other examples of different practice models exist. What is essential to consider with each approach is how does it fit with the needs and wishes of this client? How is it supported in the literature to address the specific goals identified by this client given her or his unique circumstances and characteristics?

Step 6: Implement the Intervention

The final step of the EBP process is to start the intervention. Documentation of session content and any evidence of changes should be included in the client's record. Such documentation helps demonstrate that the intended intervention was properly and fully delivered. It also provides a running record of the client's participation and progress or regression. Again, any concerns the client states about the treatment should also be documented in the client's record.

As we pointed out earlier, some authors include the formal evaluation of the intervention as a step of the EBP process. We take a different view. We think that evaluation of practice is an important and necessary part of any professional undertaking. Ongoing monitoring and evaluation of change, in addition to evaluation of improvement from the beginning to the end of treatment, is an integral part of a good clinical practice. However, quantitative evaluation of a single case is based on a very different research model than is the EBP. Single subject or single system research designs targets changes in a specific client system treated by a specific clinician in a specific manner. It is very useful to demonstrate and document change. The EBP model, however, is usually based on large numbers of clients with very carefully defined problems who are randomly assigned to treatment or control or comparison groups. Evidence derived from unique single cases is not highly valued in most EBP research models. Nor is it highly valued in the systematic reviews of treatment outcomes that identify level 1 and level 2 treatments. For this reason, we encourage evaluation of each client's progress as a regular part of good professional treatment, but do not include it as a part of the EBP model per se. (We will explore this issue further in Chapter 10.)

Summary

These six steps make up the EBP practice decision-making model. In many respects, the EBP model adds to professional practice the clear obligation to review the best research evidence as part of the treatment planning process. The EBP model also adds to professional practice the clear obligation to engage the client in discussion about the merits and limitations of a proposed treatment plan. The model further requires that the client's concerns about a treatment be fully explored and understood. This last requirement is very fitting in today's increasingly diverse world.

Note that several different forms of professional expertise are required to undertake the EBP model. These include competencies in clinical assessment, in problem formulation, in the literature search and retrieval, in appraising research methodology and quality, and in creating a treatment plan with strong client participation. At no point does evidence alone dictate a course of treatment. At no point is the client excluded from treatment planning model. In our view, EBP is not a simply top down practice model.

The EBP model can be used with any form of treatment, though currently much more research information is available to support cognitive-behavioral models than is available for most other treatments. Unfortunately, many treatment models have not yet been researched in a manner that fits with the EBP model. It is important to bear in mind that these treatment models have simply not been appropriately tested: lack of evidence does not mean such treatments are automatically ineffective.

The next chapter of this book explores the assessment models used in clinical social work practice. A good and thorough assessment is the foundation for applying the steps of the EBP practice decision-making model. The EBP model does not directly address assessment. Yet assessment starts and shapes EBP in practice and in research.

Chapter 4
Assessment in Clinical Social Work and Identifying Practice Information Needs

In order to know where to start using the evidence-based practice (EBP) decision-making model, you must first know what you are looking for. As discussed in the previous chapter, the assessment conducted by the clinician is the foundation of the entire EBP process. Although the utilization of research findings is one key part of EBP, the lynchpin of EBP actually rests with the question the clinician is seeking to answer. The development of the searchable question is based on the assessment the clinician conducts with the client(s). As such, an accurate assessment of the needs, situation, strengths, limitations, context, diagnosis, and much more is necessary to begin the steps of the EBP practice model outlined in the previous chapter.

Given the critical role of assessment in EBP, this chapter will be devoted to exploring how to conduct a thorough assessment through which a searchable question can be developed to start the EBP process. However, as noted in the previous chapter, there is very little evidence on what makes a strong assessment. Therefore, this chapter is based on the authors' own experiences with clinical practice, and in training and teaching social work students and practitioners. This chapter offers perspective on assessment, but is not intended as a 'how to' primer. We assume readers are familiar with several assessment models and related theories, and have some exposure to completing clinical assessments.

Defining Assessment

While most social workers have an image of what an assessment is in practice, the image or definition of an assessment varies a great deal depending on the role the social worker has with the client and with the agency, the skill set of the practitioners and the needs of the client. What actually takes place during the assessment phase can vary as much as it does during an intervention. Assessment can be very

J. W. Drisko and M. D. Grady, *Evidence-Based Practice in Clinical Social Work*, 55
Essential Clinical Social Work Series, DOI: 10.1007/978-1-4614-3470-2_4,
© Springer Science+Business Media New York 2012

standardized and can follow a set procedure if the setting promotes a stringent protocol. Alternatively, it may be more client-led, allowing the client to tell their own story in their own way, while providing considerable diagnostic information.

Some forms of EBM research specifically address how to make a diagnosis or an assessment, though this appears to be an infrequent focus in EBP practice (Baik et al. 2010). Such diagnostic questions often center on the quality of tests and procedures that are part of the overall assessment process. During the initial phases of working with a client, an assessment can involve making a diagnosis, or conducting a triage process where a client is assessed quickly and then referred on to a particular service. Assessment can also involve creating a working hypothesis or formulation that evolves into a treatment plan, and/or writing a formal document containing all of the above information—and more. Generally speaking, the scope of the assessment and the focus of any written documentation associated with the process will vary depending on three critical factors: "the role of the social worker, the setting in which he or she works, and the needs presented by the client" (Hepworth et al. 2010, p. 181). Therefore, clinical social workers must be clear about each of these aspects of their work when conducting an assessment to ensure that ultimately the needs of the client are met within the context of the setting and role that the social work has with the client.

Although the assessment phase is often associated with the beginning of treatment, in reality, good clinical practice involves an on-going assessment throughout whatever length of time the clinician is involved with the client. As such, "assessment is a fluid and dynamic process that involves receiving, analyzing, and synthesizing new information as it emerges during the entire course of a given case" (Hepworth et al. 2010, p. 181). Assessment should be an on-going process for social workers as they work with their clients. However, the aim of this chapter is to aid clinical social workers in how to conduct assessments in order to begin the EBP practice process.

Components of an Assessment

The elements included in an assessment are dependent on many factors. However, there are some common elements included in most clinical assessments. Obviously, individuals working on a macro or policy level would consider different factors in their assessments, such as organizational or neighborhood structures or policy influences. While these are also important for clinical social workers to consider, the focus of this book is on making clinically based practice decisions. We will, therefore, limit our discussion to components that most clinical social workers would need to consider in conducting an assessment.

There are several methods and guidelines that social workers can turn to help organize the assessment process (Brandell 2010). We will limit our discussion to five assessment methods used by clinical social workers. These are (1) the Person-in-Environment Classification System, (2) the Risk and Resiliency framework,

(3) Family Systems models, (4) Psychodynamic models, and (5) the descriptive diagnostic model based on the American Psychiatric Association's widely used *Diagnostic and Statistical Manual* (DSM). We will introduce each model briefly and describe how each model may be used in the EBP practice decision-making process.

We view many behavioral and cognitive behavioral models as defining specific target problems, rather than as wide-ranging assessment models. Such behaviorally focused models have great value and precision, but must follow a more comprehensive assessment of client and situation as a whole. At the end of this discussion, a case example will be used to illustrate how the assessment method chosen influences what clinical questions are asked to begin the EBP process. We also include as an appendix a synthetic social work biopsychosocial assessment outline.

The Person-in-Environment Classification System

Social work has one unique assessment model, the Person-in-Environment Classification System, or the PIE (Karls and Wandrei 1994). Developed by social workers, the PIE incorporates the person-in-environment perspective into the assessment process. The PIE model includes four domains or factors: Factor I is social role functioning and coping; Factor II is the influence of the social environment including institutions and access to resources, Factor III is mental health, and Factor IV is physical health and medical issues. (See Table 4.1.)

Using the PIE classification system, social workers develop a holistic view of the individual and to determine where within the client's system intervention needs to take place. Several domains of functioning and environment can be the focus of intervention, separately or in combination. If mental health problems are primary, then the initial focus of the treatment plan may target that domain. If social functioning problems are seen as primary, however, the social worker may focus more on an occupational issue that is creating the stress or difficulties reported by the client. Resource issues might lead to a concrete, environmental intervention. Similarly, environmental or policy-related problems might lead to a focus on advocacy or concrete, resource finding interventions. The decision about where and how to intervene is based on a wide-ranging assessment of multiple domains or aspects of the client's situation. The clinician must use professional judgment to determine which domain requires what level of attention. The domain that the clinical social worker views as most critical to the cause and resolution of the presenting problem will lead to the questions necessary to begin the EBP assessment.

For example, after preliminary assessment it might appear that the source of a client's depressive symptoms are driven primarily by the level of isolation and lack of power within the context of the family system (Factor I: Social Functioning Problems) rather than a mental health problem (Factor III: Mental Health

Table 4.1 Factors of the Karls and Wandrei PIE Assessment Model

Factor I: Social Functioning Problems

A. Social Role in which each Problem is Identified

1. Family (parent, spouse, child, sibling, significant other)

2. Other interpersonal role (lover, friend, neighbor)

3. Occupational (worker/paid, worker/home, worker/volunteer, student)

B. Type of Problem in Social Role

1. Power	4. Dependency	7. Victimization
2. Ambivalence	5. Loss	8. Mixed
3. Responsibility	6. Isolation	9. Other

C. Severity of Problem

1. No Problem	4. High Severity
2. Low Severity	5. Very High Severity
3. Moderate Severity	6. Catastrophic

D. Duration of Problem

1. More than 5 Years	4. 2 to 4 Weeks
2. 1 to 5 years	5. 2 Weeks or Less
3. 6 Months to 1 Year	

E. Ability of the Client to Cope with Problem(s)

1. Outstanding	4. Somewhat Inadequate
2. Above Average	5. Inadequate
3. Adequate	6. No Coping Skills

Factor II: Environmental Problems

A. Social System where Problem is Identified

1. Economic/Basic Needs 4. Health/Safety/Social Services

2. Education/Training 5. Voluntary Association

3. Judicial/Legal 6. Affectional Support

B. Specific Type of Problem within each Social System

C. Severity of Problem

D. Duration of Problem

Factor III: Mental Health Problems

A. Clinical Syndromes (Axis I of DSM)

B. Personality and Developmental Disorders (Axis II of DSM)

Factor IV: Physical Health Problems

A. Disease Diagnosed by a Physician (Axis III of DSM)

B. Other Health Problem Reported by Client or by Others

adapted from Corcoran and Walsh, 2006, p. 29; Karls and Wandrei, 1994

Problem). In turn, the question to begin the EBP process might then be "What are effective family therapy interventions that are aligned with the family context and cultural background of my client?" However, if the clinician thought that based on the client's family history of depression and the severity of the depressive symptoms that there was a potential biological or genetic component to the depression, the clinician's question might focus more on searching for interventions related to Factor III. As the social worker would not be one to prescribe medication, the question for this clinician might shift from finding effective interventions for a biologically based depression, to understanding when to make a referral to a medical professional. Therefore, the searchable question might be "What clients are appropriate for a medication consultation/referral?" Again, the social worker must be clear as to what role is taken on with the client, and what are the needs of the client. The clinician's assessment using the PIE will determine where to focus the search for likely effective treatments.

The PIE model is very comprehensive but is very rarely used in practice or as a required assessment for funding services. A PIE assessment is very time intensive. Further, the time required to complete a PIE assessment may not be acceptable to clients in some practice settings. The PIE model has not been used often for service outcome research. The main strength of the model is its comprehensiveness and its clear fit with the social work profession's defining person-in-environment perspective. It allows social workers to identify and address social, environmental, mental health, and physical health problems separately or in complex combinations. The comprehensive PIE assessment provides a solid basis for a wide range of potential interventions. It can point to multiple potential locations of intervention. Note that other forms of mental health and physical health assessment are components of a PIE assessment, so multiple assessment models may be used within the PIE assessment framework.

The Risk and Resilience Framework

Another framework that social workers use in assessment is the risk and resilience framework. This framework considers "the balance of risk and protective factors that interact to determine an individual's propensity toward *resilience*, or the ability to function adaptively despite stressful life events" (Corcoran and Walsh 2006, p. 4). *Risks* are seen as stressors or hazards either within the individual or in the environment that increase the likelihood of a problem occurring (Corcoran and Walsh 2006). *Protective factors* may provide a buffer against risk factors and act as a counterbalance to the risk factors facing an individual (Fraser et al. 1999). An assessment using the risk and resilience framework evaluates the risk and protective factors surrounding an individual and treatment planning is based on both factors. The social worker must decide to focus on the reduction of risk factors, such as poverty or access to medical care, or alternately to focus on creating or strengthening of protective factors, or both. As such, the assessment process involves identifying what risk and/or protective factors need to be targeted to reduce the problem as presented by the client.

In the context of EBP, the clinician must determine what interventions target the factor viewed as most critical to the resolution of the issue. This may be the removal or reduction of a risk factor, or to increase or develop a protective factor, or both jointly. Determining where the focus of the treatment (risk or resiliency or both) will help to develop the searchable question in the EBP process. For example, in the case of the individual with depressive symptoms, a clinician working from a risk and resilience framework might determine that a primary risk factor is the client's social isolation. According to the theory, an intervention plan would be to reduce or eliminate this risk factor to alleviate the depression. A searchable question for the EBP process might be, "What are effective interventions to reduce social isolation among similar clients?" Group therapy interventions may be one useful alternative, or other interventions focused on social skill development. If the same clinician determines in the assessment process that the lack of protective factors, such as the presence of an involved parent is missing and is the primary cause of the depressive symptoms, the clinician will have a different question to search. In thinking about how to increase the protective factor of an involved parent, the clinician might pose the question, "What are effective parent education programs to increase parent involvement?"

The risk and resiliency model potentially covers a wide range of social and environmental factors influencing the client's situation. It attends to both strengths and challenges. It can point to multiple potential locations for intervention. The model does not include a traditional medical model diagnosis, so it provides a framework for working with clients who have concerns about the medical model based on their beliefs or cultural concerns. The model may be time intensive, but preliminary determination of a focus on risk reduction or resiliency enhancement can help focus the assessment. This may reduce the time it takes to complete. That the model does not include a traditional medical diagnosis may fit well with some social work agencies and organizations, but may limit funding options in other settings. Outcome studies using this model are limited.

Family Systems Models

Family systems theory is an umbrella term for several different specific family therapy models used by social workers, such as Family Emotional Systems Theory (Bowen 1978), Structural Family Theory (Minuchin 1974), and Strategic Family Therapy (Haley 1971). While each of these models has a distinctive focus and techniques, they follow generally similar principles derived from systems theory (Hepworth et al. 2010; Walsh 2010). Systems theory is central to social work as a profession. It challenged the idea held in science that complex, interactive phenomena could be simplified to a linear cause and effect equation (Walsh 2010). Rather, systems theory argued that there is an interactive, circular pattern of causation, "in which all elements of a system simultaneously are influenced by, and influence, each other" (Walsh 2010, p. 92). Systems are assessed holistically.

While there are many variations of systems theory, including family therapy models that use a systems view, there are several common principles that are shared by these models, as outlined by Walsh (2010):

1. Connectedness: all parts of a system are interconnected and changes in one part will influence functioning of all other parts;
2. Wholeness: any phenomenon can be understood only by viewing the entire system;

3. Feedback principle: a system's behavior affects its external environment, and that environment affects the system. (p. 93)

Given these principles, the assessment process using a family systems framework involves assessing for factors that include "communication styles, culture, and family interactions and dynamics" (Hepworth et al. 2010, p. 244). In order to complete this task, there are many assessment tools designed to help practitioners determine the family structure, such as genograms (Carter and McGoldrick, 2004), others to understand the family's relationships with external resources and entities, such as the Ecomap (Hartman and Laird 1983), Still other tools help assess cultural considerations with a family, such as the Culturalgram (Congress 1994). Each of these tools is aimed at looking at families as a unit rather than as a collection of individuals. Each tool seeks to better understanding how the family system functions as a discrete unit, both internally and externally with outside phenomena.

The focus in a systems framework is to identify where the family is struggling, either internally as a unit and/or in their interactions with external groups or structures. For example, a family may be interacting well with other systems, but within the family, there is a lack of structure. In this case, the children may appear to make the rules and while the parents effectively communicate the rules, there is little structure to enforce or regulate the rules. As a result, the parents seek treatment because they are tired and frustrated and feel that they repeat themselves to their children to no avail. In such a family, an EBP based question may be, "What are effective interventions to help families enforce rules and consequences to increase compliance in the home?"

Family systems models are widely use in mental health settings. They do not focus on an 'identified client' and bring several components of the family system into the assessment and treatment process. Changing repetitive patterns of inter-action are a key target of attention. Family systems models may require an additional medical model diagnosis for funding purposes, though such a diagnosis is not always vital to family systems treatment planning. These approaches may attend to both risk factors and sources resiliency, but not all do so systematically. Family systems approaches may fit well with racial/ethnic groups who are more communal than individualistic in orientation.

Psychodynamic Models

Psychodynamic models of assessment and treatment draw on a number of related but distinct theories, as do the family systems models (Perlman and Brandell 2010). All psychodynamic models assume that some psychological processes may be unconscious, or unavailable to the purposeful awareness to the individual. Psychodynamic models also assume multiple determination; that personality structure and meaning develop from many sources rather than a single source. All these models also emphasize the importance of emotion (affect), the importance of repetitive patterns and themes, and the relationship between the client and the clinician as vital parts of assessment and treatment (Brandell and Ringel 2004).

Early psychodynamic models focused on conflicts among drives, subjective processes, and the internal structures that constitute personality (Gabbard 2010). Later psychodynamic models shifted focus to assessing psychic structures and capacities. These include the ego functions and defenses that individuals bring to bear to understand and tolerate internal experiences as well as to interact with others (Freud 1923; Goldstein 1995); and object relations or how interpersonal interactions become internalized into expectations of others and repetitive patterns of interaction (Berzoffet al. 2007; Mahler et al. 2000; Winnicott 1992). Still more recent models such as self-psychology focus on how people interactively make use of others to make up for internal deficits (Kohut 1977; Palombo 1985) and to intersubjective models that examine meaning making as a function of interaction (Brandell 2010a; Stern 2004). As with family systems models, each variant may be optimally revealing and informative for specific difficulties.

Psychodynamic assessment focuses on profiling the capacities of the individual to tolerate anxiety and manage it in socially effective ways, to self-regulate affect and cognition, to understand and to interact with others, to flexibly support others, and to non-coercively depend on others. Such an assessment includes components of identifying historical and enduring patterns of interactions with significant others and their meanings, along with description of interaction with currently significant people in the client's life, including the interactions with the clinician. The focus is both historical and current, with an emphasis on psychological factors. Medical conditions and other organic issues have long been viewed as potentially significant influences on psychological and social function within psychodynamic models (Gabbard 2010). Many social work authors point out that contemporary psychodynamic assessment models and theories considers the social environment as a shaping influence on personal capacities (Berzoff et al. 2007).

There are several models of psychodynamic assessment, from the child-oriented Hampstead Index (Sandler 1962) to the Blanck's developmental psychological profiles (Blanck and Blanck 1979, 1994). There is also a *Psychodynamic Diagnostic Manual* (Alliance of Psychoanalytic Organizations 2006). Generally, assessment involves a wide-ranging examination of internal conflicts, ego functions, object relations, and/or disorders of the self as expressed through internal experiences and in interactions with others. Attention to these features, in combination, will point broadly to ego supportive or ego modifying treatments. The specific form and content of the client's dilemma will lead to additional assessment of area of strength and challenge. Psychodynamic assessment may point to questions of differential diagnosis, but most often yields answerable clinical questions centering on "What kind of treatments are most effective for people with a long-standing character problem?" or "What kinds of treatments are most effective with mixed disorders?"

Some critics call psychodynamic assessment deficit oriented, though psychodynamic practitioners instead view it as appraising capacities that represent relative strengths and relative limitations (Berzoff et al. 2007; Goldstein 1995). Areas of strength must be known as they become assets useful for coming to understand areas of limitation. Psychodynamic assessment is lengthy and not intended to be completed in single or a few sessions. Critics argue it is too heavily weighted to the individual and pays too little attention to contextual factors. Its strengths are its focus on building self-awareness, enhancing self-regulation, and on examining how the individual makes meaning in life, including the meaning of emotions and relationships. There are several outcome studies on psychodynamic therapies consistent with the EBP/EBM research model.

American Psychiatric Association Guidelines: The Medical Model

The American Psychiatric Association's [APA] (2006) Psychiatric Evaluation Guideline is another format with which most clinical social workers are familiar. (See Table 4.2.) The format proposed by the APA is widely used in many medical and more traditional psychiatric settings. It leads to a multiaxial psychiatric diagnosis. It is also the underlying format for parts of the PIE assessment model and of some psychodynamic assessment models. This medically oriented model seeks to define disorders centering on individuals through a diagnostic assessment process. Diagnosis may involve interviews as well as laboratory or psychological tests. Diagnoses are then used for intervention planning as well as for payment purposes. The APA evaluation guidelines are available online for free on the APA's Web site (www.psychiatryonline.com/pracGuide/pracGuideChapToc_1.aspx). Online users of this site can click on the various headings for an expanded description for each of the content areas included in the assessment outline listed below.

The format has several parts, from an orientation to the types of assessment (general vs. emergency, etc.), to assessment location, to the specific domains of assessment, the process of assessment as well as several additional considerations and cautions. Part III., the domains of evaluation, are probably what most clinicians consider as most important, though the APA assessment format reminds users that purpose and setting may alter emphasis in assessment.

While this format appears to be quite comprehensive, it was developed by medical professionals and consequently has both strengths and limitations for social workers. The first limitation is that social workers cannot and should not perform physical examinations. As such, social workers who use this guide will need to include information obtained by a qualified medical professional. A second limitation is that these guidelines do not include a section on the strengths of the individual, either internal or external strengths. Social work is a strengths-based profession, meaning that we believe it is essential to identify, utilize, and empower our clients' strengths. The above guidelines do not include a section where the assessment of strengths can be specifically identified.

Table 4.2 Components of the American Psychiatrics Association's Psychiatric Evaluation Guidelines

I. Purpose of Evaluation
A. General Psychiatric Evaluation
B. Emergency Evaluation
C. Clinical Consultation
D. Other Consultations
II. Site of the Clinical Evaluation
A. Inpatient Settings
B. Outpatient Settings
C. General Medical Settings
D. Other Settings
III. Domains of the Clinical Evaluation
A. Reason for the Evaluation
B. History of the Present Illness
C. Past Psychiatric History
D. History of Substance Use
E. General Medical History
F. Developmental, Psychosocial, and Socio-cultural History
G. Occupational and Military History
H. Legal History
I. Family History
J. Review of Systems
K. Physical Examination
L. Mental Status Examination
IV. Evaluation Process
A. Methods of Obtaining Information
B. The Process of Assessment
V. Special Considerations
A. Privacy and Confidentiality
B. Interactions with Third-Party Payers and Their Agents
C. Legal and Administrative Issues in Institutions
D. Special Populations
VI. Future Research Needs
A. Interviewing Approaches
B. Rating Scales
C. Diagnosis and Formulation
D. Diagnostic Testing

An additional limitation of the medical model is the lack of emphasis on the social or cultural context. Item III. F does state that a socio-cultural history should be obtained, though its focus remains on the individual. There is some emphasis placed in the expanded description on assessing the values, beliefs, and cultural influences of the individual. There is not, however, consideration of the larger contextual issues that influence the presentation of the individual during an assessment, such as discrimination or homophobia. Social workers who use this guideline should therefore be conscious of this limitation and include the contextual issues into their assessment, along with the strengths of the client.

The APA evaluation has a key strength in its primary focus on one individual's mental health diagnosis. Using the guidelines, the ultimate goal is to determine the diagnosis of a mental health condition and to create the treatment plan based on this diagnosis. There has been a long-standing effort within the medical community to develop accurate diagnoses and link them with effective treatments. Since the APA format was developed by physicians, this goal is consistent with the format of the assessment. Related medical conditions are also given strong attention in this model. However, limited attention is directed to social context and to the potential situational and environmental conditions surrounding the individual. In the following section, a more in-depth discussion of diagnostic process will be provided. In considering how this framework fits with EBP, the searchable questions address primarily a diagnosis and the associated concerns with this diagnosis. Most often the concern is related to effective interventions, however, depending on the role of the social worker or the needs of the client, the questions could center on prognostic predictors or how the presentation of a disorder might manifest differently among varying cultural groups.

In thinking about the client with depressive symptoms, a searchable question might be "What are effective treatments for depression?" If the client is from another culture, or is bicultural, the clinician might want to determine that she or he is not making assumptions about how depression manifests among individuals from this culture. Therefore, the EBP question might be, "What does depression look like among Chinese-Americans?" in an effort to make sure that the clinician has an accurate diagnosis. Although the APA's focus on a diagnosis may ultimately seem simpler in terms of finding a searchable question, the clinician must still think through what it is that she or he wants to know about this client with attention to this client's situation and cultural context. The clinician must also consider the professional roles she or he plays with this client, in order to develop a relevant EBP question. Zayas et al. (2010) point out the diagnostic model may miss culturally specific disorders or inappropriately force them into pre-existing Western disorders. Clinicians must be careful to talk with their clients to be sure they have fully and correctly understood the client's needs in the appropriate contexts.

Assessment of Mental Health Disorders

The APA guidelines, as well as the PIE and psychodynamic models, include as part of assessment the development of a mental health diagnosis. One of the primary tasks in the assessment phase may be viewed as developing an accurate diagnosis of the client's difficulties. This phase helps narrow the clinical social worker's focus and may help develop an intervention plan. However, a focus on pathology or illness is historically associated with the medical profession and the medical model (Corcoran and Walsh 2006). Some social workers see a long-standing tension between social work's person-in-environment perspective and the medical focus on diagnosis (Corcoran and Walsh, 2006). The primary definition used to define a mental health disorder comes from the APA (2000a), which states that a mental disorder is a:

> significant behavioral or psychological syndrome or pattern that occurs in an individual and that is associated with present distress (e.g., a painful symptom) or disability (e.g., impairment in one or more important areas of functioning) or with significantly increased risk of suffering death, pain, disability or an important loss of freedom. (p. xxxi)

Regardless of the cause of the disorder, "it must currently be considered a manifestation of behavioral, psychological, or biological dysfunction in the individual" (p. xxxi). Given this definition, social causes or other factors outside of the individual are not to be considered mental health disorders, locating all of the pathology on the individual.

This medical, psychiatric, model that focuses on the source of the pathology on the individual is often times at odds with the social work world person-in-environment perspective. Therefore, for many social workers, using the *Diagnostic and Statistical Manual* (DSM) (APA, 2000a) to diagnose clients with a disorder is counter to social work values. Yet, the insurance industry, on which many social workers rely for their paychecks, largely bases its reimbursement system on a 'billable diagnosis.' This requires clinical social workers to diagnose clients as sick with a mental disorder, in order to obtain insurance reimbursement for their services. As a result, social workers must often diagnosis their clients, even if it is at odds with their professional values in order to support themselves and obtain services for their clients.

In addition, as discussed in Chapters 1 and 3, much of the research that is conducted on effective interventions is directly tied to the diagnosis of an individual. Therefore, for clinical social workers who are starting the EBP process, it is helpful to have a diagnostic label to use in searching the research. The vast majority of research outcome studies are also tied to specific diagnostic categories.

While social workers may feel a great deal of tension between the values of the medical model and their social work values, learning to accurately diagnose using the *DSM* is an essential skill that all clinical social workers must know (Probst 2011). This is required by state licensure laws, by the realities of making a living given the current reimbursement models, and to make use of many sources of EBP research knowledge. It is beyond the scope of this book to provide clinicians with all of the tools necessary to learn how to make an accurate diagnosis, or to discuss the other various debates surrounding diagnosing individuals. For a thorough review of the debates surrounding the use of the *DSM* and social work, readers are referred to Corcoran and Walsh (2007) and the work of Kirk and Kutchins (1988). Therefore, we will limit the discussion to the essential components of the *DSM*, some general guidelines, and provide the readers with a list of resources that will provide a more thorough review of the process of making a diagnosis.

Table 4.3 The multiaxial diagnostic system of DSM-IV-TR

Axis I	Clinical Disorders
	Other Conditions that may be the focus of clinical attention
Axis II	Personality Disorders
	Mental Retardation
Axis III	General Medical Conditions
Axis IV	Psycho-social and Environmental Problems
Axis V	Global Assessment of Functioning (GAF)

The Diagnostic and Statistical Manual of Mental Disorders

The *Diagnostic and Statistical Manual of Mental Disorders* (DSM) (APA, 2000a), is now in its fourth edition and is referred to as the DSM-IV-TR (the TR is for text-revised). It is the primary tool used in the United States to classify and diagnose individuals with a mental health disorder (Andreason and Black 2006; Corcoran and Walsh 2006; Grey and Zide 2008). The *DSM* uses a multiaxial system to diagnosis individuals, meaning that it utilizes a system "that characterizes patients in multiple ways so that the clinician is encouraged to evaluate all aspects of the patient's health and social background" (Andreason and Black 2006, p. 11). This allows for diagnosis of more than one disorder or comorbid disorders. The multiaxial system used by the current version of the *DSM-IV-TR* is outlined in Table 4.3.

The majority of diagnoses made by clinical social workers fall under Axis I. These include mood disorders (e.g., depression and bipolar disorder), anxiety disorders (e.g., panic disorder and post-traumatic stress disorder). Axis I disorders also include psychotic disorders (e.g., schizophrenia), pervasive developmental disorders (e.g., autism and Asperger's syndrome), substance abuse disorders, and many other relatively short duration disorders seen in practice.

Axis II disorders are more long-term challenges. Only personality disorders (e.g., borderline personality disorder and antisocial personality disorder) and mental retardation are classified under Axis II. Historically, these diagnostic categories were seen having a different source of etiology, and seen as more fixed or constitutional in nature (Corcoran and Walsh 2006). However, some critics argue that the distinctions between Axes I and II are not helpful or conceptually relevant (Corcoran and Walsh 2006).

Axis III disorders are limited to medical conditions that are diagnosed by a medical professional and not by a social worker. However, social workers completing a full five axis diagnosis should list the medical conditions reported by the client or found in the client's records to ensure that a complete diagnostic picture is presented and identify the source from which the information came. Where such information is not directly provided by a physician, it should be held as tentative or formally verified with the client's consent. Both the effects of medical conditions,

Table 4.4 Guidelines for general assessment of functioning (GAF) scoring

Step 1:	Start at the highest level, evaluate each range by asking "is *either* the individual's symptom severity OR level of functioning worse than what is indicated in the range description?"
Step 2:	Move down the scale until the range that best matches the individual's symptom severity OR the level of functioning is reached, *whichever is worse.*
Step 3:	Look at the next lower range as a double-check against having stopped prematurely. This range should be too severe on *both* symptom and severity *and* level of functioning. If it is, the appropriate range has been reached (continue with step 4). If not, go back to step 2 and continue moving down the scale.
Step 4:	Determine the specific GAF rating within the selected 10-point range, consider whether the individual is functioning at a higher or lower end of the 10-point range. For example, consider an individual who hears voices that to do not influence his behavior (e.g., someone with long-standing Schizophrenia who accepts his hallucinations as part of his illness). If the voices occur relatively infrequently (once a week or less), a rating of 39 or 40 might be most appropriate. In contrast, if the individual hears voices almost continuously, a rating of 31 or 32 would be more appropriate.

(from the American Psychiatric Association, 2000b, p. 46)

and medications used to treat them, may have serious impacts on mental health problems.

Axis IV is where psycho-social and environmental problems should be listed. Generally, this is a listing of factors in the individual's life that may play a role in his or her functioning within the last year. Examples of such factors include: recent job loss, risk of losing housing, homophobia, difficulties in accessing health care, or recent death of a parent. While Axis IV recognizes the importance of social influences, how such information is formally included in the diagnostic process is less clear. As noted, long-standing socially structured oppressions are not usually included in Axis IV.

Axis V provides a global assessment of functioning (GAF) summarized in a single number. It represents the overall level of functioning and psychological health of the individual. The GAF yields a quantitative score summarizing the clinician's assessment of the level of functioning of the client at any one point in time. Often, clinicians will give a score to represent the "current" GAF score or "highest in past month" to provide information regarding how the current level of functioning compares with other periods of time. The GAF score is based on a 0–100 scale that is divided into 10 ranges of functioning. The clinician is to identify a single score that "best reflects the individual's overall level of functioning" (APA 2000b, p. 44). The APA's guidelines for GAF scoring are presented in Table 4.4.

In combination, all five axes form the full DSM mental health diagnosis. Clients may not have specific diagnoses on all five axes. For example, a client may have no personality disorder or no significant medical conditions. In some circumstances where information is incomplete or unclear, tentative diagnoses on any axis may also be listed as 'rule outs' (R/O). Rule outs draw attention to areas lacking clarity and help clinicians bear in mind that other factors may also influence the client's situation. These other circumstances may also be important factors in treatment planning. The EBP model, however, assumes a complete and clear diagnosis and does not allow (in most cases) for comorbid or unclear assessments. This may make it difficult to apply the EBP practice decision-making method when some potentially important information is unknown or unclear. Again, the clinician's professional expertise must be applied in completing an assessment, and in making judgments about what disorder or problem is the priority concern.

The American Psychiatric Association's (APA) DSM-V is due to be published in 2013. This new manual proposes significantly revisions to many existing mental health diagnoses. One goal of the revision is to "expand the scientific basis for psychiatric diagnosis and classification" (APA 2011a). That is, key goals are to increase the empirical support for each distinct diagnosis, to improve the reliability or consistency of diagnoses, and to increase the clinical utility of DSM. Diagnostic categories will be significantly revised using a new 'meta-structure.' Bernstein (2011, p. 7) states that "the idea is to assemble existing disorders into larger clusters suggested by the scientific evidence and then to encourage researchers, granting agencies, and journal editors to facilitate research within and across clusters." Nineteen clusters of disorders are proposed to frame the diagnostic categories with a twentieth "other" category including those disorders that do not fit smoothly with the named categories. Each cluster will be presented in a "developmental, lifespan" manner, with disorders of infancy and childhood listed, then those of adulthood and finally those for elders (APA 2011b). The multi-axial approach of DSM-IV-TR will be continued. In addition, the concept of a disorder 'spectrum' is proposed for several diagnoses, including "schizophrenia spectrum" and "obsessive–compulsive disorders." Personality disorders are proposed to be reduced in number and diagnosed through appraisal of impairment of personality function, personality traits, and an overall assessment of severity of the disorder (APA 2011c).

Guidelines and Cautions Regarding Assessment and Diagnosis

As stated previously, it is beyond the scope of this book to train clinical social workers to diagnose using the *DSM* or any other assessment system. Our aim has only been to provide an overview of the essential components of each assessment system. We strongly encourage recent graduate and clinicians still in training to obtain formalized instruction in conducting mental health assessment and in making diagnoses. Such trainings are generally offered as part of the educational process in schools of social work, as well as reinforced as part of clinical internships. Individuals who did not receive such training are encouraged to obtain clinical supervision along with other formal training programs to ensure that they have been well versed in the language, process, and ethical challenges associated with diagnosing. The proposed changes planned for DSM-V will require additional training and a re-tooling by most mental health clinicians.

A mental health diagnosis label can have significant ramifications for individuals, including denial of benefits or discrimination. Therefore, it is essential that social workers understand and take seriously the process of diagnosing before taking on such a role with a client.

Diagnostic Tests and Measures

Another issue to consider regarding assessment and diagnosis is the use of standardized instruments. Many diagnostic tests and measures are widely used for both clinical and research purposes. These tests and measures may also be very helpful in making differential diagnoses of disorders. At face value, standardized instruments seem like as efficient way to streamline the diagnosis process and can "represent useful and expedient methods of quantifying data and behaviors" (Hepworth et al. 2010, p. 184). They are designed to allow the client to answer a set number of questions regarding a set of symptoms. Based on how the client answers each question or item, each client will receive a particular score placing her or him in a diagnostic category or range within a diagnostic category. Such tests and measures may either be specific to a single disorder or more comprehensive, including information about several disorders as separate subscales.

While there are many benefits to using assessment instruments, it is essential that clinicians understand both what the instrument is designed to measure and what it is not designed to measure. For example, some instruments may be designed to emphasize measurement of the cognitive changes associated with depression, but place less emphasis on the emotional, social, or physical changes that are also associated with depression. Individuals whose depression manifests mainly in a physical/somatic manner may score as only minimally or even not depressed on cognitive items. In turn, their depression may not be accurately assessed by such an instrument. Similarly, self-appraisal of cognition may not provide a full or accurate sense of an individual's interpersonal functioning.

An additional concern centers on what population the instrument was normed or standardized (DeVellis 2003). This means that an instrument that was created based on a specific population may, or may not, be representative for other groups including different ethnicities, gender expressions, ages, sexual orientations, or diagnoses. Many instruments are developed based on samples or groups of people that may not precisely match the demographic characteristics of the client you are trying to assess. Many are normed on relatively advantaged white populations (often on college students). As a result, the questions may not fit the cultural or class norms of the individual in front of you.

Table 4.5 Resources for social work assessment and diagnosis

American Psychiatric Association. (2000). *Diagnostic and statistical manual of mental disorders* (4th ed., text revision) (DSM-IV-TR). Washington, DC: Author.

Andreason, N., & Black, D. (2006). *Introductory textbook of psychiatry (4th ed.)*. Washington, D.C.: American Psychiatric Association.

Berzoff, J., Flanagan, L., & Hertz, P. (2011). *Inside out and outside in: Psychodynamic clinical theory and psychopathology in contemporary multicultural contexts (3rd ed.)*. Northvale, NJ: Jason Aronson.

Corcoran, J., & Walsh, J. (2006). *Clinical assessment and diagnosis in social work practice*. New York, NY: Oxford University Press.

Grey, S., & Zide, M. (2008). *Psychopathology: A competency-based assessment model for social workers (2nd ed.)*. Belmont, CA: Thompson/Brooks Cole.

Jones, R. (1996). *Handbook of test and measurements for black populations*. (2 vols.) Hampton, VA: Cobb & Henry.

Lukas, S. (1993). *Where to start and what to ask: An assessment handbook*. New York, NY: W.W. Norton & Company.

Using the example of depression again, there are many researchers who study depression who believe that men and women present differently when depressed (Nolen-Hoeksema 2001). An instrument that was standardized using men may not accurately capture the diagnostic picture of a woman being assessed for depression. Therefore, while standardized instruments can play a valuable role in assessment, it is essential for social workers to understand what the instrument is designed to measure, on which populations has it been tested, what role will it play in the assessment process being conducted, and how does the social worker plan to use the results in the context of the assessment.

There are a number of useful resources social workers can reference regarding the use of standardized measures, such as Corcoran and Fischer's (2007) *Measures for Clinical Practice and Research: A Sourcebook (4th ed.)*. Measures for populations of color are less easily obtained. One useful resource is Jones' (1996) *Handbook of Tests and Measurements for Black Populations*. Sadly, similar handbooks of measures for Latino, Asian, and Native American populations are not yet available.

A Social Work Assessment Format

An example of a traditional, wide-ranging, social work assessment outline can be found in Appendix A (Drisko and DuBois 2000). We believe that this outline includes many of the content areas included in the five models described above. It is an attempt to incorporate a social work perspective in its attention to environmental and social factors, as well as intrapsychic factors and family dynamics. As with all guidelines, it is meant to be a tool to help organize the material gathered in an assessment and provide a structure to the assessment process. However, the role of the social worker, the theoretical orientation of the clinician, the purpose of the assessment, as well as other factors will influence which factors are most salient for the worker to focus on during the assessment process. Clinical expertise and critical thinking must always be part of good clinical social work practice.

Many good texts can serve as background resources on clinical assessment. Table 4.5. lists several books that may be useful clinical resources on assessment and diagnosis.

Step 1 of EBP: Drawing on Client Needs and Circumstances Learned in a Thorough Assessment, Identify Answerable Practice Questions and related Research Information Needs

Within this chapter, we have provided some guiding principles around assessment and some examples of formats used to complete a clinical social work assessment. We have also described how these formats can lead to the searchable question used to begin the EBP practice decision-making process. The remainder of this chapter will focus on how to use such clinical information to develop a searchable question. Formulating a practice question through assessment leads to identification of your research information needs. This is Step 1 in the formal EBP practice decision-making process. We have emphasized the importance of good assessment. Now we will turn to using the results of the assessment to start the EBP process. In other words, now that you have gathered the necessary information, how do you create a good question using this information?

As we have emphasized throughout this book, the clinician's professional expertise is the glue that integrates the various pieces of information gathered during the EBP process. Gathering relevant information about a client, his or her wishes, the context of the client's situation, begins with the assessment and diagnostic processes. Possible interventions will also be shaped by the clinician's agency context, his or her designated role within the agency and the client's preferences and views. These also shape the assessment process. The conclusions that the clinician makes based on this information is where his or her professional expertise comes into play. The clinician must be able to take the information and put it into a funnel of sorts to come out with a succinct question that can be utilized in the EBP process. It is the role of the clinician to act as the funnel and prioritize what information is most relevant to the current clinical situation.

Recalling an earlier quote in this chapter, Hepworth and colleagues (2010) remind us that the scope and purpose of an assessment is dependent on "the role of the social worker, the setting in which he or she works, and the needs presented by the client" (p. 181). One way to begin the EBP process is to try to identify the priorities within each of these factors and work with your client to develop the question. None of these take priority over the others. Each factor acts as part of a three legged stool, each playing an essential role in creating a solid base for an assessment.

Beginning with the role of the social worker, you must first understand and determine what your role is with the client. Is your role to develop a treatment plan as you will be the primary provider of services for this client? Is your role to gather information so that you can make an appropriate referral as your agency does not provide services directly? Is your role to gather information and report back to a team that will make a collective decision regarding the needs of the client? Is your role to diagnose the individual to determine whether he or she is eligible for a research project or a service provided in your practice setting? Each distinct role will influence the questions you ask the client and then the question you will search using the EBP process. Finding clarity regarding what role you, the clinical social worker, have with the client is the first step in prioritizing what questions to ask.

Understanding the setting and contextual issues is also essential to being able to prioritize what research questions are most relevant to any search. Does your practice setting provide services? If so, what are they? Are you limited by those services or can you bring in others that are not currently offered? If you are able to bring in other services, what is the process to do so? What steps need to be taken? Is your agency a referral-based setting only? Does it serve clients matching the demographic characteristics of the client in front of you (e.g., children or Spanish-speaking clients)? Answering these questions regarding the practice setting will help you determine whether you need to be searching for treatment options that you can provide directly to the client in that practice setting; or whether you need to be exploring other options in the community by referral. Further, you may realize that you need to be trained in a new model that will better meet the needs of this client and others with similar needs.

The third leg of the stool is the client's needs and preferences. As discussed in Chapters 1 and 3, understanding the needs and goals of the client is paramount to EBP. A clinician must be able to leave an assessment with a clear picture of what it is that the client needs and prefers. What are the expectations that the client has for this meeting and their interactions with the agency? What are the hopes the client has for what you will do or say at the end of the assessment process? What are the priorities that the client has for their care? Do they want to address their housing conditions first or address their depressive symptoms first? Do they want to work with someone individually or as a family unit? Do they want to receive services from a clinician who is of a particular ethnicity, gender expression, or sexual orientation? Understanding the answers to these questions will help the practitioner begin to understand how to place the needs of the client in the context of the other areas of the assessment.

An important caveat to consider in regard is that sometimes the wishes or needs identified by the client do not align with the assessment of the social worker. For example, it may be that the client identifies that his primary goal is to have the department of social services out of his life, but he is not interested in following the plan that the child protective case worker has developed around safe discipline. Or a client that wants to cut back on her drinking so that she does not get another DUI conviction, but is not interested in stopping her drinking, despite that fact that she has a serious health condition that is directly affected by it. In these cases, the clinician must work with the client to develop goals that are consistent with the agency purposes, social work values, and meet the client where she or he is.

This process is not always easy. This part of the goal setting process takes patience and must be negotiated carefully in the context of a relationship that may not have had time to develop into a solid rapport. It is imperative that clinician and client have open conversations throughout the assessment and goal setting phase of an intervention. There are many situations where obtaining information from the client regarding his or her wishes is complicated further by the age of the client or the capacities of the client. For example, for clinicians who work with children, it is often a dilemma regarding whether to honor the parents' wishes or the child's. Another example might be a client who is in currently actively psychotic and does not seem to have the ability to make an informed decision about treatment. A further complication is whether the clinician believes the client is an accurate reporter of the situation or the facts surrounding why the referral was made. These situations add to the complexity of the goal setting process and it is during these times when seeking out supervision may be important for the social worker to help identify a clinically sound and ethical course of action.

Social workers who are unsure about whether the priorities that have been set by the client and the worker are compatible with social work ethical standards or the agency should seek consultation with a supervisor based within the agency or consult the local chapter of the NASW. Many chapters have an ethics consult available to members. Using the answers to these questions, the clinical social worker begins to funnel the information gathered in an assessment and determines how to prioritize the information to begin the EBP process. A case example follows to help illustrate this process more completely. The reader is also referred to the more extensive cases later in the book (Chapters 11–16) where the process is explored in greater depth.

An Example: Case of Samir—Identifying Practice Information Needs Through Assessment

Samir is a 16-year-old first generation male whose family is from India. He was born in the United States, but his parents are still very connected to India, as most of his extended family still lives there. He has an older sister who is in college in the United States. You work as a school social worker at a high school, and Samir was referred to you by one of his teachers due to concerns about recent changes in his academic performance at school. There were also some changes in his social behavior.

Before deciding which type of assessment format you will use in the assessment process with Samir, it is essential to first review the factors discussed previously. First, in your role as a school social worker in this institution, it turns out that you are not able to provide any ongoing treatment to students. The role of the SW is to provide crisis intervention or to refer out to an outside provider. Outside referrals are made if the student needs ongoing services of any kind that are not related to academic services, such therapy, medication, or ongoing supportive counseling. Second, the context of the setting is that the school is not equipped to provide ongoing therapy services to students. You are placed in multiple schools and do not have a consistent office each week where you would meet with students, even if this was an option. As such, the setting does not afford you with a consistent, private, location to meet with students during your time at their school. Finally, it is important to note before the meeting that Samir did not volunteer to come to meet with you. Although he may have agreed, he did not independently seek out services with the school social worker. It will be important to determine what his concerns and wishes are about meeting with you in order to understand how to begin the EBP process. This is also consistent with the EBP emphasis on honoring client values and preferences.

By reviewing the factors discussed previously, the assessment process is already somewhat streamlined. Your role with Samir, the limitations of the setting, and his role in the referral process are all better understood. Based on this information, you decide that your role with Samir will be to first determine if crisis intervention services need to be offered and if not, what ongoing services might be useful to him in the community. Second, you will need to combine this information with his wishes and needs in order to find what type of service will best align with his goals and needs. There is also the issue of what resources are available in the community.

In meeting with Samir, you learn from him that while he did not ask to come to see you on his own, he was "fine" with the referral. As you were trained using the PIE system, your assessment questions are derived primarily from that format. You ask a number of questions regarding the changes noted by his teachers, the changes he has experienced in himself, his own observations and what he hopes to gain from coming to see you. What you learn is that Samir has been a very strong student since starting high school. However, his grades have begun to drop within the past three months and he is starting to have panic attacks in association with big tests or examinations. These panic attacks are increasing. He feels like he is in a vicious cycle of worrying about his grades and then having a panic attack. This leads to more worry and more panic attacks.

In thinking through the PIE classification, you begin to ask questions about the four domains to better understand the potential source of these symptoms and stress he is experiencing. In speaking with Samir, you learn that recently his sister has had difficulties in college, has withdrawn from school, and has returned home for the semester. According to Samir, she was "partying too much and not paying attention to her school work." Their parents decided to withdraw her from school until she could "get her priorities in order." Samir reports that since she has been home, there is more conflict between his sister and his parents. Further, there is more conflict between his parents, who are now making more comments about his school work. They say that he will "not act like his sister and blow his educational opportunities." Using the PIE system, it appears that the main source of the difficulties falls within Factor I: Social Functioning Problems, specifically that the much of the tension comes from the current family situation.

In speaking with Samir about what he thinks would be helpful, he states that he would like help with finding better ways to "cope with the panic attacks" and "get back on track with my school work." When asked to elaborate, he states that he wanted someone who would work with him one on one to help him learn to "deal the panic" and give him some additional skills for managing stress. His stated goals and wishes were not in alignment with your assessment of where the origins of the problem lay. He placed the resolution of the problem with himself, and not within the context of his family.

Carefully, you explore with him whether he thought it would be useful to also involve his parents and sister in the meetings with such a person, since it sounds like life at home has become more stressful. Samir replied adamantly that he did not want to involve his family in this process, other than to have them see that he is seeking help to work on his academic performance. When asked if he could explain why he preferred this course, he stated that his family was very private and that they were also very stubborn. "You do not talk to people outside of the family about your problems, especially not non-Indians." However, he felt that if he saw someone and it was couched as an "academic coach" that it would be acceptable. A 'coach' might help take the pressure off him. His parents would see that he was actively seeking help around his academics, unlike what they perceive his sister is doing.

From this conversation, you learn that Samir is experiencing a great deal of stress due to changes in his family status. As a result of this stress, his school performance has declined, and he is experiencing panic attacks. His preferences are to meet with someone outside of the school individually to help him develop additional tools to manage his anxiety and stress, while helping boost his school performance. Although his wishes do not align with your assessment of the source of the problem, you defer to his wishes to get help individually at this time, rather than to involve his family. He states that their involvement would be a "dead end" as they would not engage in treatment surrounding a family issue due to their cultural beliefs about privacy. Keeping in mind your role and practice setting, the priorities outlined by Samir are consistent with your role as a school social worker and the limitations of the setting in which you practice. Your role now is to help Samir find an appropriate professional who can provide an effective intervention for his anxiety, while keeping in mind the family context and the recent changes within his family. Note that Samir's values and preferences are a key part of this decision-making process.

While you know many providers in the community, you want to make sure that you find a provider who is trained in an appropriate intervention that will most benefit Samir. As such, the research question that you develop to orient your EBP search is: What are effective interventions for addressing panic disorder and school performance anxiety in high school students? While ultimately you will not be conducting the final step of the EBP process of applying the intervention, it will be essential for you to follow the other steps outlined in Chapter 3 to determine the best match for Samir with a provider in the community. In addition, being informed of the available research, the intervention options, and being able to explain them and talk through them with Samir fits very much with your role as a school social worker. It may also be essential in helping Samir's parents support his desire to receive services.

Conclusion

It is through a careful assessment that social workers actually begin the EBP process. It is through the integration of the information they gather about the client, the context, the clients' wishes, the role they play in their agency and the context of the practice settings that clinical social workers use their professional expertise to organize the information into a searchable practice question. Step 1 of the EBP practice decision-making process begins, based squarely on how the clinical social worker interprets and synthesizes all of the available information. The assessment model used to gather that information will shape what questions are asked and what information is prioritized. It is essential therefore, for social workers to understand the limitations of each assessment format and any tests or measures used. Social workers must also be aware of the power that they hold when making an assessment, as these assessments determine the pathway taken by both clients and practitioners. They shape the EBP process, but simultaneously shape other processes and actions.

The next several chapters of this book explore each of the later steps of the EBP model in greater depth and detail. The next chapter shifts to a very different set of professional skills used in locating practice research, Step 2 of the EBP practice decision-making process.

Chapter 5
Locating Practice Research

Step 2 of the evidence-based practice (EBP) practice decision-making process centers on efficiently locating practice research. This chapter will offer a detailed introduction to the key print and online research information resources available for EBP. It will guide clinical social workers to finding specialized research for clinical practice. We will describe the key types of practice-related resources and identify many specific resources. We will also provide an introduction to effectively searching online resources.

Starting Points

After completing a thorough assessment and defining an orienting question, the second step of the EBP process is to locate the best available research relevant to your client's needs and specific clinical circumstances. There are many ways to begin locating useful research and practice information. The first choice may be between background information versus very specific information. If you are already familiar with a disorder, its diagnosis, and its treatments, a good starting point is to look for specific research information. On the other hand, if the issue is unfamiliar, or if you have reason to think your knowledge may be old or limited, starting with background information may be a better choice. Reviewing background materials will not only take longer, but will also prepare you for other clients with similar needs. Reviewing background materials offers a learning opportunity.

As discussed in Chapter 2, an initial choice will be between using print or online resources. Both have assets and liabilities. Both also have significant infrastructure costs. These costs are often borne by the professional user. Books are expensive, often very specialized, and must be updated as new editions are printed. Computers and Internet access also have significant costs for individuals and agencies

J. W. Drisko and M. D. Grady, *Evidence-Based Practice in Clinical Social Work*,   79
Essential Clinical Social Work Series, DOI: 10.1007/978-1-4614-3470-2_5,
© Springer Science+Business Media New York 2012

Table 5.1 Initial print resources for finding mental health research results

BMJ Clinical Evidence in Mental Health. The British Medical Journal (BMJ) offers very detailed summaries of outcome research in both print and online versions. It is organized by disorder and has extensive information on medications. Updated semi-annually.
Alan Carr's (2009) *What works with children, adolescents and adults?* offers a useful summary of psychosocial treatments for all age groups. It's strength and main limitation is that it addresses common ICD/DSM disorders and few less common ones.
Anthony Roth and Peter Fonagy's (2005) *What works for whom? A critical review of psychotherapy research* (2nd ed.) offers a useful summary of psychosocial treatments for adults. Its strength is that it reports both extensively studies treatments and also discusses treatments that are widely used but not yet well researched. Emphasizes common DSM disorders.
Peter Fonagy and colleagues' (2005) *What works for whom? A critical review of treatments for children and adolescents* offers a useful summary of psychosocial treatments for children and adolescents. Its strength is that both extensively studies and widely used but not well studied treatments are examined. Emphasizes common DSM disorders.
Alan Carr's (2002) *Prevention: What Works with Children and Adolescents?* examines outcome research on select prevention programs for children, adolescents and families.

Note carefully, print resources can become dated very quickly!

(Drisko 2010; Krueger and Sketch 2000). On the plus side, agencies and practices with electronic record systems may have much of the needed infrastructure on site.

The next choice will often be determined for users: between free and paid access to research materials. If your agency or an affiliated college or university has access to some of the many paid, password protected research data bases, you can access many more resources and gain much more detailed information. Free sites often offer just abstracts or summaries of full research studies. This means that if you need to explore research results in great detail, you may need to search paid sites. The good news is that a great deal of practice research is available online through free sources. For many practice information needs, these free sources are adequate.

Print Resources

Several excellent books offer summaries of practice research (see Table 5.1). They may not, however, be comprehensive enough if you need to search for information specific to elders or to disorders that appear infrequently in most practice settings (such as Reactive Attachment Disorder or Narcissistic Personality Disorder). Note that many books in mental health are organized by diagnosis. They are likely to follow a medical model approach to problem definition, with relatively little focus on the interpersonal and social aspects of client's situations. Alternative approaches to assessment, such as the Karls and Wandrei (1994) Person-in-Environment System or the Psychodynamic Diagnostic Manual (2006), are very rarely mentioned despite their important and useful efforts to expand the scope of mental health practice. Ethnically and racially diverse populations may also be inadequately addressed (Zayas et al. 2010). For example, the very different diagnostic system of other cultures is also very rarely mentioned. One such system, the Chinese Classification of Mental Disorders (2001), may help practitioners understand the unique needs and forms of expression used by populations who may appear in Western practice settings (Chen 2002). Further, disorders are usually addressed 'one at a time' in the literature. There is little recognition that clients often present with comorbid disorders or combinations of psychological and social challenges. This adds to clarity and validity for research purposes but may decontextualize research findings as guides to practice decision making. Bearing this in mind, these books are still valuable orienting resources for clinical social work practice.

Print materials can be very valuable background resources. They can provide an excellent way for clinical social workers to understand the conceptual and practical issues in practice research. They can also introduce clinicians into the complex world of evaluating research results and design. Print materials can also provide immediately useful foreground knowledge so long as they are recently published. Still, in many cases, online materials may provide more specific information and can help insure examination of the most current knowledge.

Online Resources

Due to the time constraints of clinical practice, online resources have great appeal. Information on a wide range of topics may be found quickly. Overviews of mental health disorders and practices are increasingly common online, though the quality of these resources varies widely. Be sure to examine the credentials and institutional affiliations of online resources. In general, look for well-known institutions and authors, ample use of citations, and specific results. Online resources with such detailed results, descriptions of the methods by which conclusions were drawn, and with ample and specific citations are likely to be better information sources for EBP. Still, be sure to apply critical thinking at all times. Use of Wikis is discouraged. Though Wikis may include quality information and may be a useful preliminary source, their information is of highly variable quality.

A general word of caution regarding URLs or web addresses: The web addresses of databases change and evolve very rapidly. This is largely due to consolidation among online publishing companies and among government agencies. If a web address listed below does not work, search the name of the resource and a current address is likely to be found.

Disorder- or Diagnosis-Specific Online Resources

Electronic access to research materials and practice guidelines is increasingly assumed by funders, program managers, publishers, and authors. This is because electronic resources can be accessed immediately and in a wide range of locations.

They can provide very focused summaries of relevant research to practitioners. For the ideal of EBP to be met, clinical practitioners need the best research information at all times to guide decision making. Up-to-date information provided electronically can be a major aid in going beyond simply relying on traditional practices.

Challenges to realizing this goal are found in infrastructure, funding, and training. Clinical social workers and other clinical practitioners would need technology to make use of online resources. Adequate access to computers, smart phones, or personal data assistants (PDAs) is expensive and not currently in place. Funding for such infrastructure might compete with funding for direct clinical services as well. Funding for the research needed to expand and update the practice knowledge base in mental health would also be challenging. Finally, if good access to technology was widely available, clinical practitioners would need to be trained in its optimal use and retrained or updated as new technologies emerge.

For psychiatric and mental health disorders, the Cochrane Collaboration Library is widely acknowledged as providing the highest quality systematic reviews of research. Many other sites link to the Cochrane Library, but many also offer systematic reviews using different (and often less rigorous) standards, as well as abstracts and full text reports of individual studies. These sites are generally organized by DSM or ICD diagnoses.

- *The Cochrane Library.* This is a database of very high quality systematic reviews (syntheses of available research) on single topics. The Cochrane Library is organized by disorder and medical model in orientation. Abstracts are available without cost. Cochrane reviews are widely considered to be the best sources of EBP research knowledge. This is because the Cochrane Collaboration includes a working group that set the most rigorous and transparent standards for systematical reviews of clinical research in medicine and psychiatry. Cochrane reviews also tend to be conservative, and may find less clear support for treatments than do other reviewing organizations www.cochrane.org.
- *The National Guideline Clearinghouse.* This is a compilation of treatment guidelines derived by expert panels but based on research results. It is organized by disorder and medical model in orientation. Guidelines are available without cost. The guidelines are often very detailed which can be useful in treatment planning and in insuring thorough assessment. Serious risks are often emphasized, pointing to medications or techniques to be avoided, or only used after very careful review of the client's unique satiation www.guideline.gov.
- *The United Kingdom's National Electronic Library for Health* is a resource to locate a wide range of mental health resources, some originally published on other web sites included here. The results are numerous, but point users to a mix of free publications and to sites that require subscriptions or payment for access to original documents www.library.nhs.uk/.
- *The Centre for Reviews and Dissemination Databases* at the University of York includes the *Database of Abstracts of Reviews of Effects (DARE).* DARE complies over 15,000 systematic reviews, including those of the Cochrane

Collaboration discussed above. The Center also provides access to papers examining the economic aspects of practice (through the UK's National Health Service Economic Evaluation Database or NHS EED) and papers on healthcare technologies (Health Technology Assessment or HTA) www.crd.york.ac.uk/crdweb/.

- *The Center for Evidence-based Medicine* provides summaries from the Cochrane Database and weekly updates of new additions and changes to the Cochrane Database (which includes many new titles at the beginning stages of research as well as newly completed systematic reviews http://cebmh.com/.
- *Evidence-based Mental Health* is a monthly print and online journal that "surveys a wide range of international medical journals applying strict criteria for the quality and validity of research." Relevance is determined by practicing clinicians who select the studies to be included. Print subscriptions are $193 per year and include online access. Online subscriptions are $108 per year http://ebmh.bmj.com/.
- *Clinical Evidence* is another subscription-based resource for medically oriented mental health results through the BMJ group. Searches yield results organized by age group or other relevant factors that delimit and focus results, a helpful feature http://clinicalevidence.bmj.com.
- *Evidence-based Mental Health Treatments for Children and Adolescents* has a strong cognitive-behavioral orientation. The site summarizes several forms of CBT and a few other treatments meeting American Psychological Association's definition of empirically supported treatments used to treat a range of childhood disorders. Oriented as much to families as to clinical practitioners, the site is very clear and well organized www.effectivechildtherapy.com/.
- *Physicians' Education and Information Resource.* The American College of Physicians created this resource of information on medical and mental health conditions. The mental health psychiatry module includes information on core mental health and substance abuse disorders. While free to members, non-members may subscribe at www.statref.com.
- The United Kingdom's National Health Service's *Clinical Knowledge Summaries* provide a source of evidence-based information about common conditions for the primary care practitioner. Includes both medical and mental health disorders http://www.cks.nhs.uk/home.
- *The Evidence-Based Psychiatry Center* of the Nagoya City University Graduate School of Medical Sciences in Japan "aims to accumulate and disseminate the currently available best evidence in the most clinically relevant way possible to practicing psychiatrists world-wide." Drawing on their own weekly case conferences, they assemble and critically evaluate materials on treatment, diagnosis, diagnostic tests, prognosis, and side effects. Easy to use www.ebpcenter.com/.

Program-Oriented Online Resources

While most medical model resources are organized diagnostically, by disorder, resources related to treatment programs are organized more generally by concern or problem type. That is, you can find information about programs for runaway teens or substance abuse treatment as a social need, not in terms of medical diagnosis. Some program-oriented reviews include information on specific psychosocial treatments (such as Multisystemic therapy or Solution-focused therapy).

- *The Campbell Collaboration Library.* This is a database of very high quality program reviews focusing on social welfare, education, and criminal justice. It is organized by topic. Full reviews are available without cost. The Campbell Collaboration Library is widely considered to be the best source for research knowledge about the effectiveness of programs. (While the "handbook" detailing Campbell Collaboration Guidelines is not available online at the time of writing of this book, Campbell systematic reviews draw on and closely follow the Cochrane Collaboration standards.) Campbell reviews tend to be conservative and thorough. The database is growing but may prove to be limited for any specific social need www.campbellcollaboration.org/library.php.
- The *National Mental Health Information Center* of the United States Substance Abuse and Mental Health Services Administration offers 'KITs' to translate evidence-based programs into practice. KITs contain information sheets for all stakeholder groups, orienting videos, practice demonstration videos, and workbooks or manuals for practitioners. Topics include integrated treatment for co-occurring disorders, assertive community treatment, illness management and recovery, supported employment and family psychoeducation. Additional topics are in preparation http://mentalhealth.samhsa.gov/cmhs/CommunitySupport/toolkits/.

General Online Resources Addressing Clinical Practice

The following online resources offer a wide range of materials. These include summaries and articles directly related to clinical practice and EBP, as well as materials on other topics.

- *Information for Practice* offers a free overview of new scholarship relevant to social work including journal articles, gray literature, infographics, and more. Developed and maintained by Dr. Gary Holden and others at the NYU Silver School of Social Work. Updated daily. Provides multiple RSS feed possibilities (for ongoing, active, 'push' of information to your web browser or smart phone) http://ifp.nyu.edu/.
- *Practicewise* offers subscription-based information including "on child-specific dynamic summaries of the best available research studies, clinical dashboards

for visualization of clinical progress and history, or clinical protocols and summaries." Online subscriptions for clinicians or organizations are $150 per year www.practicewise.com/web/.

- *Bandolier.* Bandolier provides monthly summaries of research articles on selected topics that are informative but that do not always meet the highest research quality standards. They are often useful as background information, though topics covered are selective rather than comprehensive. Topics include schizophrenia and depression as well as patient management issues and 'other stuff' such as cannabis use and mental illness and being sane in insane places www.medicine.ox.ac.uk/bandolier/.

When using any online resources, be sure to look for the dates when they were last updated. The research studies included in systematic reviews often span several years. However, the systematic reviews are done and updated from time to time as new results become available. Most reviews show the date of the last update in a very prominent location. When reviews are more than five-year old, as a rule of thumb it is wise to look for additional, more current information as an additional resource (Shojania et al. 2007).

If systematic reviews of research on any given issue are not found, the next option is to look for individual research articles on the topic. Many research articles are published commercially and will require subscriptions or payment for access.

Bear in mind that reviewing individual research articles takes a strong background in research methods to be done successfully. (More about doing this follows in Chapters 6–8.) The sheer number of choices that must be made to decide if the research is rigorous and relevant to your specific practice situation is demanding. The work done by professional reviewers in research compilations noted above now becomes the task of the clinical social worker. The strength of doing a review with a specific practice situation in mind is that you can weed out research that is not relevant much more accurately. You may also learn about issues that matter a great deal in your situation but were not so critical or widespread enough to be mentioned in the research summaries.

Databases of Individual Research Articles

Where systematic reviews of research on a topic are not available, the next option for clinical social workers is to look directly at individual research articles. The challenges in this task include locating the most relevant articles in the large volume of articles found on many topics (such as anxiety or depression), evaluating the relevance of the articles to your specific client and clinical circumstances, and evaluating the quality of the research articles located. The good news is that online resources make a vast array of materials available to clinicians and a wide range of articles are available for free (though some will require payment or subscriptions).

- *PubMed* is a useful interface to *Medline*, the vast online database of medical research articles maintained by the United States National Library of Medicine (part of the National Institutes of Health). Abstracts of articles are provided for free. Many, but not all, PubMed citations include links to full text articles for free. This is a major asset for clinicians. PubMed also includes prominent and easy to use search features that allow users to shift from a specific topic, say Borderline Personality Disorder, to a higher order topic such as personality disorders in general www.pubmed.gov or www.ncbi.nlm.nih.gov/pubmed/.
- *Agency for HealthCare Research and Quality.* This database offers "evidence reports" of research on depression and substance abuse as well as a few additional mental health topics. Medically oriented and spotty in results for mental health topics www.ahrq.gov/clinic.

Search Strategies

Searching online databases can be a complex task. Where possible, it is always a good idea to begin with some formal training from a research or reference librarian. Such training is routine for all levels of higher education. Introductory sessions can take an hour or two but are well worth the time. Librarians are familiar with the available database resources as well as knowledgeable in strategies for exploring them. Even if you are a skilled and persistent searcher, asking for librarian support when you are stuck or frustrated is strongly recommended.

To search for individual research articles, it is very helpful to use a specific database search strategy. This involves selecting keywords and some tips on using search engines efficiently. While a full tutorial on using search engines is beyond the scope of this book, there are some strategies that fit will with EBP needs and purposes.

Search keywords for EBP database searches start with the client's needs and situation. Very often the first keyword will simply be the name of the diagnosis, disorder, or problem that begins with the client's clinical need. There may be alterative terms for this disorder. For example, 'depression' might also be specified as 'major depressive disorder' if the criteria are met. 'Dsythymia' is a similar alternative, but is, of course, a different disorder and diagnosis. It is important to be as specific as possible when conducting searches, as your results will be much more targeted and directly related to your question. Use a thesaurus or a medical dictionary if you are unsure what alternate terms might be used. (Online thesauri and medical dictionaries are excellent for this.)

Commonly used medical search keywords are established by the National Library of Medicine's Medical Subject Headings list (www.nlm.nih.gov/mesh/MBrowser.html). This list of over 26,000 terms (as of 2011) is used to frame searches in Medline. Medline includes over 20,000,000 citations and is one of the largest EBM/EBP article databases. The Medical Subjects Headings (MeSH) list also provides sources of alternate search terms for clinicians and researchers. MeSH has a tree and branch format. Top level "Categories" include psychiatry and psychology, chemicals and drugs, and health care. These are followed by even more specific "Descriptors," such as 'mental disorders' or 'behavioral mechanisms.' Even more precise and narrow are "Qualifiers" that create specific subsets within topics. Qualifiers include 'CO' for co-occurring or associated disorders, 'DI' for diagnostic issues, and 'PS' for psychology. (There is no social work qualifier.) A search using the adverse effects qualifier 'AE' can locate adverse effects of treatments. Searches on a top level descriptor such as depression in Medline, with the qualifiers DI and PS, would target both diagnostic issues and psychological issues. This can speed up searches and limit the number of extraneous sources included in the search results.

PubMed, a useful interface to access Medline articles and citations, helps to organize your search. Pub Med starting pages ask for a category or descriptor to begin the search. The results pages often include click box options with suggestions to help you narrow and target your search.

Bear in mind, too, that reference librarians are also excellent sources of information regarding alternate search terms. They are skilled at finding the list of keywords and headings that are used by major professional groups and publishers to organize their materials in print and online. Do not hesitate to ask for search help from librarians.

A basic search tip is that any word placed in double quotation marks, such as "depression" will be searched for exactly as entered. This allows you to enter terms such as "generalized anxiety disorder" as a phrase and to have the full term used precisely as the focus of your search. This is a simple way to enter multiple word phrases as search terms. Commonly used words, such as 'a' or 'the' will be ignored by most search engines if not entered into a phrase using quotations marks to require a search for the exact phrase. (Google allows use of the '+' sign as well as double quotation marks to identify exact search phrases. By typing +depression+ Google will search for this precise term. Note that there are no spaces immediately before or after the search term.)

It is often useful to combine search keywords. This is most often done using Boolean logical operators. While the name might sound difficult, Boolean operators simply link terms to combine them in different ways. They are the foundation of most everyday Internet searches. Let us start with a two-term search example. The Boolean 'AND' operator gets all the information which includes *both* search terms. An 'AND' search yields all materials that include the overlap of both terms, but excludes materials with just one of the terms. For example, a search for "depression" AND "dysthmia" will locate materials including both terms, but not either one separately. Such results are generally large but focused. One might also search for "depression" AND "experiment" to get materials on depression that are only based on experimental research. By adding even more terms a still more precise search results. A clinical social worker might search for "depression" AND "treatment outcomes" AND "experiment" to locate articles on the outcomes of experimental studies on treatments for depression. Such combined searches can narrow the many materials to just those that are most likely to be clinically useful.

Another strategy uses the Boolean 'OR' search operator. The 'OR' operator gets all materials including *either* search term as well as *both at once*. That is, such a search includes the results for an 'AND' search as well as more materials about either term separately. A search for "depression" OR "dysthymia" would include all materials including either term as well as materials covering both terms. Such results can be overwhelming for common disorders. On the other hand, for less common disorders the 'OR' search operator may be a fine starting point. Searching for "pica" OR "eating non-food items" would yield a larger and wider set of results than a search for "pica" alone.

Finally, the Boolean 'NOT' operator will allow you to limit searches. That is, one might search for "depression" NOT "seasonal affective disorder" to narrow the search to exclude materials about SAD. Using the 'NOT' operator is a good way to limit searches to avoid materials on comorbid disorders (i.e., substance abuse, grief) when the other issues are not clinically relevant to the client's needs and situation. The 'NOT' operator may also be used to limit the population the search will target. For example, one might search for "depression" NOT "elders" to focus a search about a middle age client.

Search operators may also be identified by symbols. That is, depending on the search engine, an 'AND' search might be identified by a '+' plus sign or an '&' ampersand symbol. A 'NOT' operator might be symbolized as a '-' minus sign. The 'OR' search is often represented by 'OR/' where the slash indicates usage as a search operator. In Google the 'OR' operator must be typed in capital letters for the 'OR' to be understood as a search term. Also in Google, the '+' can be used to set up an 'AND' search by using spaces before and after the '+' sign. If the plus sign is used to surround a search term without spaces before and after, Google's search engine seeks the exact phrase. In effect, use of the '+' sign without spaces in Google is the same as using double quotations marks to specifically identify a search term.

In the illustrations used above several search operators can be combined into one phrase. One can also 'nest' search operations to give one priority over others. For example, one might search for (depression AND overeating) NOT grief. By placing the parentheses around (depression AND overeating) the search engine first examines these terms and then next combines the results with the information for the remaining terms not included in the parentheses.

The scope of thorough computerized searchers can be daunting. Lists of the Boolean search phrases used in some Cochrane Collaboration full reviews run to three full pages of single-spaced text. Keywords vary in subtle fashion and combinations of search phrases may yield different results. Still, for practice decision-making purposes, a few search combinations may point to a major fraction of the available research. In other cases, limited returns from searches may reflect a lack of available research, not a flaw in search methods.

While computerized searches can be terrific resources for finding clinically useful information, it is common to find many results or 'hits' that prove irrelevant. Search engines use very formal rules to find materials. They often include materials in which the search term is a very minor focus, or where the material simply states that it is excluding the topic from discussion! In all cases, careful human vetting of results is needed to ensure relevance to the clinical situation. Critical thinking is also needed to determine where results that are unusual are carefully evaluated for their potential relevance, credibility, and utility. Searches may expand our thinking and can help us generate new ways of looking at situations, but ultimately it comes down to how the clinician interprets what information she or he has found. The goal is to find the best available research for the clinical need that guides the EBM/EBP search process.

The Next Step in Evidence-Based Practice: Critically Appraising the Research Knowledge

It is very important to keep in mind that many print and online sources will make claims about 'best practices' and 'evidence-based treatments' using a wide variety of standards or, at worst, little systematic evidence. The EBP practice model emphasizes including research knowledge as one vital part in the development of assessment and treatment plans. EBP equally emphasizes the client's clinical needs and situation, as well as the goals and values of the client. Using the professional expertise of the clinical social worker, the best available research is integrated into intervention planning. The goal of EBP is to help make treatment (or diagnostic, or preventive) decisions that are likely to be most effective with the least potential for ineffectiveness or harm. Clients need to participate in EBP treatment planning in order to fully meet their needs and ensure their active involvement in treatment processes. More than one treatment (or diagnostic test or prognosis) may be relevant and supported by strong research evidence.

One challenge for clinical practitioners is that many terms have developed around EBP. As we have pointed out in Chapter 1, books and articles claiming best practices or empirically supported treatments or interventions may use standards that are not the same as those promoted within the EBP movement. Keep in mind that best practices has no standard definition. It may be claimed by authors whose work has little or no solid research support. Best practices is also used by funders or working groups who develop lists of services they will fund or endorse. Further, as we noted in Chapter 1, some states have defined lists of treatments or services they will fund that are called best practices. Such lists are often developed using standards quite different from those used more widely in the EBP movement. Empirically supported treatments and programs usually have at least one outcome study, but this research may not be experimental or of high quality. Many authors use the term 'empirically supported' when only a single study has been completed showing positive outcome, with or without a clear research design or a clear definition of the treatment used. "Empirically supported treatments" under the American Psychological Association model must have at least two experimental outcome studies or ten or more single subject design studies to use this label (Chambless and Hollon 1998).

Once suitable research information has been found on the clinical question, the third step in the EBP practice decision-making model is to appraise this information for relevance and for quality. The focus shifts from finding information to critically evaluating it. Different kinds of professional knowledge and skill are applied in this appraisal process. The next three chapters will explore how to appraise and evaluate research reports and results. The first step is to identify the research design used by each study.

Chapter 6
Evaluating Research: Research Designs in Evidence-Based Medicine/Evidence-Based Practice

Once you have located some research reports that can help answer your practice question, Step 3 in the evidence-based medicine (EBM) and evidence-based practice (EBP) decision making model is to appraise the quality and relevance of this research. An initial inspection of materials should help differentiate those that are relevant for your purposes from those that are not. Relevance may often be determined by examining the research question that each study addresses. Studies should have clear and relevant research questions, fitting your practice needs. That is, the topics should fit your clinical question, and the sample should be similar in age and other background criteria. Once these 'apparently relevant' studies are identified, the appraisal shifts to issues of research methodology. Even studies that appear be quite relevant initially may later on prove to have important limitations as the details of their methods are explored.

Evaluating the quality of individual research reports can be a complex process. It involves several components. This chapter will review the research designs that orient studies used in EBP. While many of these designs should be familiar to social workers, they may be described using different terminology in EBM and EBP research reports. Yet research designs are one key aspect of establishing research quality. When clinical social workers have to review individual research articles, determining their research design will be a key aspect of establishing their quality and rigor. Chapter 7 will review several other methodological steps in appraising individual research reports (sampling, defining the treatment or other intervention, tests and measures, and statistics). Together Chapters 6 and 7 provide a basis for assessing the quality of *individual* research studies. These same methodological issues are also vital to the aggregation of multiple research studies on a particular topic like depression. In Chapter 8 will we examine how multiple studies are aggregated for review in EBM/EBP through meta-analysis and systematic reviews. Both of these aggregation methods build upon specific quality standards for individual research reports. This is why we will begin our review of research methods at the level of appraising the individual research report.

J. W. Drisko and M. D. Grady, *Evidence-Based Practice in Clinical Social Work*,
Essential Clinical Social Work Series, DOI: 10.1007/978-1-4614-3470-2_6,
© Springer Science+Business Media New York 2012

Research design is the first methodological issue a clinical social worker must identify in appraising the quality of a research study. A research design is the orienting plan that shapes and organizes a research project. Researchers use different research designs for projects with distinct goals and purposes. Sometimes this is a researcher-determined choice, and other times practical and ethical issues force the use of specific research designs. In EBM/EBP, research designs are one key part of appraising study quality.

While all clinical social workers are introduced to research methods as part of their required course work, most do not make much use of this knowledge after graduation. EBP, however, will require clinical social workers and other mental health professionals to make greater use of their research knowledge in evaluating research for practice. Therefore, we will review several types of research designs in considerable detail.

Research designs are so important to EBM/EBP that this chapter will focus on them exclusively. (As noted, we will examine other very important–and very closely related–aspects of research methods will be examined in the next chapter.) Our goal is to provide a useful refresher and reference for clinical social workers. For readers who have a basic grasp of research designs and methods, this chapter can serve as a brief review and resource. Some terminology, drawn from medicine, will no doubt be unfamiliar. For other readers, who need only an update on research methods, this chapter offers it. We will identify many excellent follow-up resources in each section of the chapter. We also remind readers that there is an extensive glossary at the end of this book.

Research Designs

This review of research designs has three main purposes. First, it will introduce the variety of terminology used in EBP research, which is often drawn from medical research. Much of this terminology differs from the terminology used in most social work research texts that draw on social sciences research terminology. Second, the strengths and limitations of each research design are examined and compared. Third, the research designs are rank ordered from 'strongest' to 'weakest' following the EBM/EBP research hierarchy. This allows readers to quickly understand why some research designs are favored in the EBM/EBP literature.

Thyer (2011) states, quite accurately, that the EBP practice decision-making process does not include any hierarchy of research designs. This is indeed correct. The EBP practice decision-making process states that clinicians should use the best available evidence. It does not state that only the results of research with certain types of research designs are to be valued. That is, it is entirely appropriate to use the results of case study research, or even practice wisdom when no better evidence is available. Yet many organizations and institutions make quite explicit that there is a *de facto* hierarchy of evidence within EBP. This hierarchy is even clearly stated in the early writing of Dr. Archie Cochrane (1972), who promoted the use of experimental research knowledge to inform contemporary practice decision making. Littell (2011) notes that the Cochrane Collaboration publishes, 'empty reviews' that report no research results deemed to be of sufficient quality to guide practice decision making. This practice contradicts the idea of identifying the best available evidence. In effect, the best available evidence is limited to evidence generated by experimental research designs. This practice creates confusion about what constitutes the best available evidence for clinicians, policy planners, and researchers. Such authors do not report the best available evidence, but instead report only experimental evidence that they deem worthy of guiding practice. They make this choice because only well-designed experiments allow attribution of causal relationships; to say that an intervention caused observed changes with minimal error. Still, this practice represents some academic and economic politics within EBP research summaries. As discussed in Chapter 2, there are good arguments for and against this position, but it is not entirely consistent with the stated EBM/EBP practice decision-making model. Clinical social workers should be aware that this difference in viewpoints about the importance of research design quality is not always clearly stated in the EBP literature. Critical, and well-informed, thinking by the clinician is always necessary.

Research designs differ markedly. They have different purposes, strengths, and limitations. Some seek to explore and clarify new disorders or concerns and to illustrate innovative practices. Others seek to describe the characteristics of client populations. Some track changes in clients over time. Still others seek to determine if a specific intervention caused a specific change. While we agree that the EBP practice decision-making process states that clinicians should use the best available evidence, and not solely evidence derived from experimental results, we will present research designs in a widely used hierarchy drawn from the Oxford University Centre for Evidence-based Medicine (2009, 2011). This hierarchy does very clearly give greater weight to experimental, randomized controlled trial (RCT) research results. It should be seen as representing a specific point of view, applied for specific purposes. At the same time, such research designs do provide a strong basis for arguing that a treatment caused any changes found, so long as the measures are appropriate, valid and reliable and the sample tested is of adequate size and variety. Due to the strong interval validity offered by experimental research designs, results based on RCTs design are often privileged in EBM/EBP reports.

We will begin this listing with the experimental research designs that allow causal attribution. We will then progress from experiments, to quasi-experiments, and then move to observational or descriptive research and end with case studies. The organization of this section follows the research evidence hierarchy of the Oxford University Centre for Evidence-based Medicine (2009, 2011).

Types of Clinical Studies

Part I: Experimental Studies

EBP researchers view properly conceptualized and executed experimental studies (also called randomized controlled trials or RCTs) as providing very strong empirical evidence of treatment effectiveness. They are prospective in nature as they start at the beginning of treatment and follow changes over time (Anastas 1999). Random assignment of participants symmetrically distributes potential confounding variables to each group in the study. Probability samples provide a suitable foundation for most statistical analytic procedures.

The key benefit of an experimental research design is that it minimizes threats to internal validity (Campbell and Stanley 1963). This means the conclusions of well-done experiments allow researchers to say an intervention caused the observed changes. This is why experiments are so highly regarded in the EBM/EBP model. The main limitation of experiments is their high cost in money, effort, and time. Further, they may be ethically unsuitable for some studies where random assignment is not appropriate. A final disadvantage is that volunteers willing to participate may not reflect clinical populations well. This may lead to bias in external validity, or how well results from controlled experiments can be generalized to less controlled practice settings (Centre for Evidence Based Medicine 2009).

In the European medical literature, experiments and quasi-experiments may be called *analytic studies*. This is to distinguish them from descriptive studies that, as the name implies, simply *describe* clinical populations. Analytic studies are those that quantify the relationship between identified variables. Such analytic studies fit well with the P.I.C.O. or P.I.C.O.T. treatment decision-making model (Center for Evidence Based-Medicine, undated).

A. Randomized Controlled Trial

A prospective, group-based, quantitative, experimental study based on primary data from the clinical environment (Solomon et al. 2009). Researchers randomly assign individuals with the same disorder or problem at the start to one of two (or more) groups and the outcomes for each group are compared at the completion of treatment. Since researchers create the groups by random assignment to generate very similar groups, the RCT is sometimes called a *parallel group design*. Usually one group is treated and the other is used as an untreated control group. Researchers sometime use placebo interventions with the control group. However, researchers may alternately design experiments comparing two or more different treatments where one has been previously demonstrated to produce significantly better results than were found for an untreated control group. Pre- to post- comparisons demonstrate the changes for each group. Comparison of post- scores across the treated groups allows for demonstration of greater improvement due to the treatment.

Follow-up comparisons may also be undertaken, but this is not a requirement of an experiment.

The experiment or RCT can be summarized graphically as:

$$\mathbf{R} \quad \mathbf{O_1} \quad \mathbf{X} \quad \mathbf{O_2}$$
$$\mathbf{R} \quad \mathbf{O_1} \quad \quad \mathbf{O_2}$$

where $\mathbf{R}$ stands for random assignment of participants, $\mathbf{O_1}$ stands for the pretest assessment (most often done using a standardized measure), $\mathbf{X}$ represents the intervention, and $\mathbf{O_2}$ stands for the post-test, done after treatment, using the same measure (Kazdin 2002). There may also be additional follow-up post-tests to document how results vary over time after treatment ends. These would be represented as $\mathbf{O_3}$, $\mathbf{O_4}$, etc. Frequently, more than one measure of outcome is used in the same experiment.

In medical studies, particularly of medications or devices, it is possible to *"blind"* participants, clinicians, and even researchers to their experimental group assignments. The goal is to reduce differences in expectancies that might lead to different outcomes. In effect, either conscious or unconscious bias is limited to strengthen the validity of the study results. A *"double blind"* experiential study keeps all group assignments unknown to participants and to the treating clinicians. *"Single blind"* experiments keep only the participants unaware of group assignments. Blinding is more possible where placebo pills or devices can be used to hide the nature of the intervention. Blinding is much more difficult in mental health and social service research where interactions between clients and providers over time are common. In mental health research, interactions between client and provider make double blinding very difficult.

While blinding is common in EBM studies of medications and devices, it is rare in mental health research. There is, however, research that shows that clinical practitioners and researchers may act consciously or unconsciously to favor treatment theories and models that they support (Dana and Loewenstein 2003). This phenomenon is known as *"attribution bias,"* in which people invested in a particular theory or treatment see it more positively than they do other approaches. Attribution bias may work consciously or unconsciously to influence study implementation and results. In turn, it is stronger research evidence if clinicians and researchers who do outcome studies are not the originators or promoters of the treatment under study. The American Psychological Association standards for empirically supported treatments (ESTs) require that persons other than the originators of a treatment do some of the outcome studies used to designate an EST (Chambless and Hollon 1998). That is, at least one study not done by the originator of a treatment is required for the EST label. How clinician and researcher biases are assessed in the EBM/EBP model is less clear. Similarly, Cochrane Collaboration and Campbell Collaboration systematic reviews do assess and evaluate the potential for bias when the originators of treatments are the only sources of outcome research on their treatments (Higgins and Green 2011; Littell et al. 2008). All Cochrane and Campbell Collaboration systematic reviews must include a statement of potential conflicts of interest by each of the authors.

It is important to keep in mind that experiments based on small samples may have serious limitations despite their use of a 'strong' research design. Sample size is one such issue. Many clinical studies compare small groups (under 20 people in a group). Studies using small samples may lack the statistical power to identify differences across the groups correctly and fully. That is, for group differences to be identified, a specific sample size is required. The use of an experimental research design alone does not mean that the results will always be valid and meaningful. (We will examine issue beyond research design that impact of research quality later in the Chapter 7.) Still, done carefully, the experimental research design or RCT has many merits in allowing cause-effect attribution.

The CONSORT Statement (2010) established standards for the reporting of RCTs. CONSORT is an acronym for "CONsolidated Standards of Reporting Trials." The people who make up the CONSORT group are an international organization of physicians, researchers, methodologists and publishers. To aid in the reporting of RCTs, CONSORT provides a free 37 item checklist for reporting or assessing the quality of RCTs online at www.consort-statement.org/index.aspx?o=2964. The CONSORT group also provides a free template for a flow chart of the RCT process and statement online at www.consort-statement.org/index.aspx?o=2966. These tools can be very helpful to the consumer of experimental research since they serve as guides for assessing the quality of RCTs. The CONSORT flow chart is often found in published reports of recent RCTs.

B. Randomized Cross-Over Clinical Trial

A prospective, group-based, quantitative, experimental research design based on primary data from the clinical environment. Individuals with the same disorder, most often of a chronic or long-term type, are randomly assigned to one of two groups and treatment is begun for both groups. After a designated period of treatment sufficient to show positive results, groups are assessed and a "wash-out" phase is begun in which all treatments are withheld. After the washout period is completed, the treatments for the groups are then switched so that each group receives both treatments. After the second course of treatment is completed, a second assessment is undertaken. Comparison of outcomes for each treatment at both end points allows for determination of treatment effectiveness on the same groups of patients/clients for both treatments. A comparison of active treatment outcomes for all patients is possible. However, if the washout period is not sufficient, there may be carry over effects from the initial treatment that in turn undermines the validity of the second comparison. Used with many medications, there are often lab tests that allow determination of effective washout periods. Secondary effects, such as learning or behavior changes that occur during the initial treatment may continue and not 'washout.' Similarly, it may not be possible to washout learned or internalized cognitions, skills, attitudes or behaviors.

The merit of cross-over designs is that each participant serves as his or her own control which reduces variance due to individual differences among participants. This may also allow use of smaller sample sizes while generating a large enough sample to demonstrate differences. This is known as statistical power. All participants receive both treatments. Random assignment provides a solid foundation for statistical tests. Disadvantages of cross-over studies include that all participants receive a placebo or less effective treatment at some point which does not benefit them immediately. Further, washout periods can be lengthy and curtail active treatment for the washout period. Finally, cross-over designs cannot be used where the effects of treatment are permanent, such as in educational programs or surgeries.

Cross-over trials may also be undertaken with single cases rather than groups of participants. These are called *single case cross-over trials*. The basic plan of the single case cross-over trial mimics that used for groups of clients, but is used with just a single case. The cross over trial may be represented graphically as:

$$\mathbf{A_1} \quad \mathbf{B_1} \quad \mathbf{A_2} \quad \mathbf{B_2} \quad \mathbf{A_3}$$

where $\mathbf{A_1}$ stands for the initial assessment, $\mathbf{B_1}$ represents the first intervention given, $\mathbf{A_2}$ represents the next assessment which is made at the end of the first intervention and $\mathbf{B_2}$ stands for second type of intervention or the cross-over. Finally, $\mathbf{A_3}$ represents the assessment of the second intervention done when it is completed. Note that a wash out period is not specifically included in this design, but could be included. Comparison of treatment outcomes for each intervention with the initial baseline assessment allows determination of the intervention effects. More than one measure may be used in the same study.

Since random assignment is not possible with single cases, the results of single case cross over studies are often viewed as 'weaker' than are group study results. However, each individual, each case, serves as its own control. Since the same person is studied, there is usually little reason to assume confounding variables arise due to physiologic changes or social circumstances.

It is possible to aggregate the results of single case designs. This is done by closely matching participants and replicating the single case study over a number of different participants and settings. This model is known as *replication logic*, in which similar outcomes over many cases builds confidence in the results (Anastas 1999). It is in contrast to *sampling logic* used in experiments in which potentially confounding variables are assumed to be equally distributed across the study groups through random assignment of participants. In replication logic, repetition over many cases is assumed to include potentially confounding variables. If treatment outcomes are positive over many cases, the general effectiveness of the treatment may be inferred.

In EBM single case studies are not usually designated as providing strong research evidence. Yet consistent findings from more than 10 single case study outcomes are rated as strong evidence in the American Psychological Association's designation of empirically supported treatments (ESTs) (Chambless and Hollon 1998).

C. Randomized Controlled Laboratory Study

A prospective, group, quantitative, experimental study based on laboratory rather than direct clinical data. These are called *analog studies* since the lab situation is a good, but not necessarily perfect, replication of the clinical situation. Laboratory studies are widely used in the so-called 'basic' research since all other variables or influences except the one under study can be controlled or identified. This allows testing of single variables, but is unlike the inherent variation found in clinical settings. Randomized controlled laboratory studies are often conducted on animals, where genetics can be controlled or held constant. Ethical issues, of course, limit laboratory tests on humans. Applying the results of laboratory studies in clinical practice has some limitations, as single, 'pure' forms of disorders or problems are infrequent and contextual factors can impact of treatment delivery and outcome.

Effectiveness Versus Efficacy Studies: Experiments Done in Different Settings

In mental health research, a distinction is drawn between clinical research done in real-world clinical settings and that done much more selectively for research purposes. Experimental studies done in everyday clinical practice setting are called *"effectiveness studies."* Such studies have some potentially serious limitations in that they often include people with comorbid disorders and researchers may not be able to ensure that treatments are provided fully and consistently to all clients. This reduces the interval validity of effectiveness studies for research purposes. On the other hand, using real-world settings enhances their external and ecological validity, meaning that the results fit with real-world practice and generalize to everyday clients and settings quite well. In contrast, more carefully controlled studies that ensure experimental study of just a single disorder are known as *"efficacy studies."* Efficacy studies carefully document that a fully applied treatment for a single, carefully screened disorder are effective (or are not effective).

One well-known example of a clinical efficacy study is the NIMH Cross-site Study of Depression (Elkin et al. 1989). This study rigorously compared medication and two forms of psychotherapy for depression. Strict exclusion criteria targeted only people with depression and no other comorbid disorders. Medication washouts were required of all participants. Such efficacy studies emphasize internal validity; they focus on showing that the treatment alone caused any change. The limitations of applying efficacy studies results are that real-world practice settings may not be able to take the time and effort needed to identify only clients with a single disorder. Such efforts might make treatment unavailable to people with comorbid disorders, which may not be practical or ethical in many clinical settings. Further, the careful monitoring of treatment fidelity required in efficacy studies may not be possible to provide in many clinical settings. This is often for practical reasons of funding, staffing, and time.

Efficacy studies are somewhat like laboratory research, but the similarity is not quite exact since they are done in clinical settings, just with extra care. Efficacy studies add an extra measure of rigor to clinical research. They do show with great precision that a treatment works for a specific disorder. However, results of efficacy studies may be very difficult to apply fully in everyday clinical work given the ethical, funding, and practical limitations of clinical work.

D. The Quasi-Experimental Study or Cohort Study

In studies of clinical practice in mental health, it is sometimes unethical or impractical to randomly assign participants to treated and control groups. For example, policy makers may only fund a new type of therapy or a new prevention program for a single community, or only certain types of insurance pay for the new therapy. In such situations, researchers use existing groups to examine the impact of interventions. Where pre- and post-comparisons are done on both groups, such a research design is called a quasi-experiment. The key difference from a true experiment is the lack of random assignment of participants to the treated and control groups.

The quasi-experiment can be summarized graphically as:

$$O_1 \quad X \quad O_2$$
$$O_1 \qquad\quad O_2$$

Once again, O_1 stands for the pretest assessment (most often with a standardized measure), X represents the intervention, and O_2 stands for the post-test, done after treatment using the same measure (Kazdin 2002). There may also be additional follow-up post-tests to document how results vary over time after treatment ends. More than one measure may be used in the same quasi-experiment. Note carefully that the key difference from a true experiment is only the lack of random assignment of participants.

The lack of random assignment in a quasi-experiment introduces some threats to the internal validity of the study. That is, it may introduce unknown differences across the groups that ultimately affect study outcomes. The purpose of random assignment is to distribute unknown variables or influences to each group as equally as possible. Without random assignment, the two groups may have important differences that are not equally distributed. Say, for example, that positive social supports interact with a treatment to enhance its outcome. Without random assignment, the treated group might be biased in that it includes more people with strong social supports than does the control group. The interaction of the treatment with the impact of social supports might make the results appear better than they might have been if random assignment had been used. Thus in some EBM/EBP hierarchies of research evidence, quasi-experimental study results are rated as 'weaker' than are the results of true experiments. That said, quasi-experiments are still very useful sources of knowledge. They are often the best available research evidence available for some treatments and service programs. To reduce potential assignment bias, quasi-experimental studies use "matching" in which as many characteristics of participants in each group are matched as closely as possible. Of course matching is only possible where the relevant variables are fully known at the start of the study.

Advantages of cohort studies include their ethical appropriateness in which participants are not assigned to groups. Participants can also make their own treatment choices on an informed basis. Cohort studies are usually less expensive in cost than are true experiments, though they may both be costly. Disadvantages of cohort studies are potentially confounding variables may be operative but unknown. Further, comparison groups can be difficult to identify. For rare disorders, large samples are required which can be difficult to obtain and may take a long time to complete.

E. The "All or None" Study

The Center for EBM at Oxford University (2009) includes in its rating of evidence the "All or None" research design. This is a research design in which, in very desperate circumstances, clinicians give an intervention to a group of people at high risk, usually of dying. If essentially all the people who received the intervention survive, while those who do not receive it die, the inference is that the intervention caused the life saving change. This is actually an observational research design, but the all or none results are viewed as strong evidence that the treatment caused the change. However, given their very important life saving effects, such research results are highly valued—so long as all or a large fraction of people who receive the intervention survive after treatment. Such designs fit crisis medical issues much better than most mental health issues, so all or none design are extremely rare in the mental health literature. They do have a valuable role in informing practice in some situations.

Part II: Observational Studies, Including Non-interventive Studies

Not all practice research is intended to show that an intervention *causes* a change. While EBM/EBP hierarchies of research evidence rank most highly those research designs that can show an intervention causes a change, even these studies stand on a foundation built from the results of other types of research. In the EBM/EBP hierarchy, clinicians are reminded that exploratory and descriptive research may not be the best evidence on which to make practice decisions. At the same time, exploratory and descriptive research designs are essential in setting the stage for rigorous and relevant experimental research. These types of studies may also be the best available evidence for EBP if experiments are lacking or are of poor quality. Critical thinking is crucial to determining just what constitutes the best available evidence in any clinical situation.

F. Observational Studies

Are prospective, longitudinal, usually quantitative, tracking studies of groups of individuals with a single disorder or problem (Kazdin 2002). Researchers follow participants over time to assess the course (progression) of symptoms. Participants may be either untreated or treated with a specified treatment. People are not randomly assigned to treated or control groups. Because participants may differ on unknown or unidentified variables, observational studies have potential for bias due to the impact of these other variables. That is, certain variables such as genetic influences or nutrition or positive social support may lead to different outcomes for participants receiving the same treatment (or even no treatment). Some scholars view observational studies as a form of descriptive clinical research that is very helpful in preparing the way for more rigorous experimental studies.

G. Cohort Study (Also Called Longitudinal Study or Incidence Study)

A prospective, quantitative and/or qualitative, observational study ideally based on primary data, tracking a group in which members have, or will have, exposure or involvement with specific variables. For example, researchers might track behavioral problems among people following a specific natural disaster or the development of children living in communities with high levels of street violence. In medicine, researchers might track people exposed to the SARs virus. Researchers use such studies to determine the incidence of specific responses to the initial variable. While such variables are often stressors, cohort studies may also be used to track responses to positive events, such as inoculation programs or depression screen programs.

Graphically a cohort study can be represented as:

$$\mathbf{X} \quad \mathbf{O_1} \quad \mathbf{O_2} \quad \mathbf{O_3} \quad \mathbf{O_4} \quad \mathbf{O_5} \quad \mathbf{O_6} \quad \mathbf{OR}$$
$$\mathbf{O_1} \quad \mathbf{O_1} \quad \mathbf{O_2} \quad \mathbf{O_3} \quad \mathbf{O_4} \quad \mathbf{O_5} \quad \mathbf{O_6}$$

Here the $\mathbf{X}$ stands for exposure to a risk factor and $\mathbf{O}$ stands for each assessment. The exposure or event $\mathbf{X}$ may either mark the start of the study or may occur while assessments are ongoing. Participants are not randomly assigned which may introduce biases. Note, too, that there is no control or comparison group though studies of other people without the target exposure can serve as rough comparison groups.

In contrast to experimental studies with random assignment, participants in cohort studies may be selected with unknown strengths or challenges that, over time, affect the study results. Thus confounding variables can influence cohort study results. Over time, loss of participants may also bias study results. For instance, if the more stressed participants drop out of a study, their loss may make the study results appear more positive than they would be if all participants continued to the study's conclusion. Because cohort studies are prospective in design, rather than retrospective, they are often viewed as stronger than are case–control studies. Cohort studies do not demonstrate cause and effect relationships, but can provide strong correlational evidence.

H. Case-Control Study

A retrospective, usually quantitative, observational study based on secondary data (or data already collected, often for different initial purposes). Looking back in time, case–control studies compare the proportion of cases with a potential risk or resiliency factor against the proportion of controls who do not have the same factor. For example, people who have very poor treatment outcomes for their anxiety disorder might be compared with a closely matched group of people who had very positive outcomes. A careful look at their demographic characteristics, medical histories and mental health histories might identify risk factors that distinguish most people in the two groups. Rare but important differences in risk or resiliency factors are often identified by such studies. Case–control studies are relatively inexpensive but are subject to multiple sources of bias if used to attribute cause to the risk or resiliency factors they identify.

I. Cross-Sectional Study (or Prevalence Study)

A descriptive, quantitative, study of the relationship between disorders or problems and other factors at a single point in time (Kazdin 2002). Cross-sectional studies are used descriptively in epidemiology. They can provide useful baseline information on the incidence of disorders in specific geographic areas. Cross-sectional studies are very valuable in a descriptive manner to policy planning, but do not demonstrate cause and effect relationships. An example of a cross-sectional study would be to look at the rate of poverty in a community during one month of the year. It is simply a snap shot picture of how many individuals would be classified as living in poverty during that month of the study. Comparing the number of persons in poverty with the total population of the community gives *prevalence rate* for poverty in this community.

J. Case Series

A descriptive, observational study of a series of cases, typically describing the manifestations, clinical course, and prognosis of a condition. Both qualitative and quantitative data are commonly included. Case series can be used as exploratory research to identify the features and progression of a new or poorly understood disorder. They can be very useful in identifying culture-bound or context-specific aspects of mental health problems. Case series are inherently descriptive in nature. They are most often based on small and non-random samples. The results of case series may not generalize to all potential patients/clients. Despite its limitations, scholars point out that the case series is the most common study type in the clinical literature. It may be the type of study closest to real-world practice and the type of study practitioners can undertake easily.

In some EBM/EBP research design hierarchies, the case series are among the least valued form of clinical evidence, as they do not demonstrate that an intervention caused a specific outcome. They nonetheless offer a valuable method for making innovative information about new disorders or problems and new treatment methods available at an exploratory and descriptive level. One example of this type of research design in the Nurses' Health Study (Colditz et al. 1997). This study examined female nurses who worked at Brigham and Women's Hospital in Boston and who completed a detailed questionnaire every two years on their lifestyle, hormones, exercise, and more. Researchers did not intervene with these women in any way beyond the survey, but used the information compiled over several decades to identify trends in women's health. These results can then be cautiously generalized to other women or used to provide information on health trends that could be explored further through more intervention-based research (Colditz et al. 1997).

K. Case Study (or Case Report)

This design centers on use of descriptive evidence drawn from a single case (Kazdin 2002). Case studies may be the best research design for the identification of new clinical disorders or problems. They can be very useful forms of exploratory clinical research. They usually include the description of a single case, highlight the manifestations of the disorder, its clinical course, and outcomes of intervention (if any). Because case studies draw on the experiences of a single case, and often a single clinician, some researchers call them "anecdotal." This term is used to differentiate evidence based on multiple cases from that based on just a single case. It also implies that case study reports often lack the systematic pre- and post-assessment found in single case research designs. The main, and often major, limitation of the case study is that the characteristics of the single case may, or may not, be similar to other cases in different people and circumstances. Another key limitation is that reporting of symptoms, interventions, course of the problem, and outcomes may be piecemeal. This may be because the disorder is unfamiliar or unique in some way (making it worth publishing about). Yet since there are few widely accepted standards for case studies authors provide very different kinds and quality of information to readers (Spence 1982).

Case studies offer a valuable method for generating innovative information about new disorders or problems, and about new treatment methods on an exploratory or formative basis. These ideas may become the starting point for future experimental studies.

We note again that case studies may be best available evidence found in an EBP search. If research based on other designs is not available, case study research may be used to guide practice decision-making.

L. Expert Opinion or Practice Wisdom

The EBM/EBP research design hierarchy reminds clinicians that expert opinion may not (necessarily) have a strong evidence base. This is not to say that the experience of supervisors, consultants, and talented colleagues has no valuable role in practice. It is simply to point out that they are not always systematic and may not work well for all clients in all situations. As research evidence, unwritten expert opinion lacks systematic testing and control for potential biases. This is why it is the least valued form of evidence in most EBM/EBP evidence hierarchies. Such studies may still be quite useful and informative to clinicians in specific circumstances. They serve to point out new ways of thinking and intervening that may be useful to specific clinical situations and settings.

Research Designs: Section Summary

This chapter has reviewed the range of research designs used in clinical research. The different types of research designs have different purposes and different strengths. These purposes range from exploratory, discovery-oriented purposes for the least structured designs like case studies, to allowing attribution of cause and effect relationships for highly structured experimental designs. This chapter has also explored the research design terminology used in EBM/EBP. Some of this terminology draws heavily on medical research and may be unfamiliar to persons trained in social work or social science research. Still, most key research design concepts can be identified despite differences in terminology.

The EBM/EBP research design hierarchy places great emphasis on research designs that can document that a specific treatment caused the changes found after treatment. This is an important step in determining the effectiveness or efficacy of a treatment. Many documents portray experiments, or RCTs, as the best form of evidence upon which to base practice decisions. Critical consumers of research should pay close attention to the kind of research designs used in the studies they examine.

Key reviews of outcome research on a specific topic, such as those from the Cochrane Collaboration and the Campbell Collaboration, use research design as a key selection criterion for defining high quality research results. That is, where little or no experimental or RCT research is available, the research summary may indicate there is inadequate research knowledge to point to effective treatments.

Some so-called 'empty' summaries pointing to *no* high quality research evidence on some disorders are found in the Cochrane Review database. This reflects their high standards and careful review. It also fails to state just what constitutes the best available evidence for practice. Empty reviews do not aid clinicians and clients in practice decision-making. They simply indicate that clinicians should undertake an article-by-article review of research evidence on their clinical topic. Clinicians must bear in mind that the EBP practice decision-making process promotes use of the best available evidence. If such evidence is not based on experimental research, it should be used, but used with caution. Still, it is entirely appropriate in the EBP framework to look for descriptive or case study research when there is no experimental evidence available on a specific disorder or concern.

Even when experimental or RCT research designs set the framework for establishing cause and effect relationships, a number of related methodological choices are also important to making valid knowledge claims. These include the quality of sampling, the quality of outcome measures, the definitions of the treatments used, and the careful use of the correct statistical tests. Adequate sample size and representativeness is important to generalizing study results to other similar people and settings. Appropriately conceptualized, valid, reliable, and sensitive outcome measures document baseline status and any changes. How treatments are defined and delivered will have a major impact on the merit and worth of study results. Statistics serve as a decision-making tool to determine if the results are unlikely to have happened by chance alone. All these methods work in combination to yield valid and rigorous results. These issues will be explored in the next chapter on appraising some additional methodological issues in practice research.

Chapter 7
Evaluating Research: Other Issues of Research Methodology in Evidence-Based Medicine/Evidence-Based Practice

Appraising the quality of research studies for practice use is Step 3 of the evidence-based practice (EBP) practice decision-making process. It can be a difficult task and requires professional expertise quite distinct from doing clinical assessment (Step 1 in EBP) or locating research resources (Step 2 in EBP). Chapter 6 addressed the key role of research design in appraising research quality. While research design is one very important aspect of evaluating evidence-based medicine (EBM) and EBP research reports, it is hardly the only important methodological issue. In addition to research designs, a number of related methodological choices also are important to making valid claims about treatments, diagnostic tests, or prognosis. These include the quality and comprehensiveness of the sample, the validity and sensitivity of the outcome measures, the definition of the treatment under investigation, and the careful use of the correct statistical tests. These methods work in combination to yield valid and rigorous results in quantitative clinical research. In this chapter, we will review each of these issues in order.

For clarity and simplicity, we will focus on treatment outcomes in the examples used in this chapter. Readers are reminded that EBP methods can also be applied to diagnostic protocols, determination of prognoses, and even to cost-effectiveness studies. Our focus on treatment is meant to be representative of, and of interest to, most clinical social workers. It does not mean that the other concerns are any less important applications of EBP. We will also focus on the appraisal of individual research reports in this chapter. Chapter 8 will examine how individual research reports are aggregated using meta-analysis and systemic reviews—two key tools for summarizing multiple research studies used in EBM/EBP.

J. W. Drisko and M. D. Grady, *Evidence-Based Practice in Clinical Social Work*,
Essential Clinical Social Work Series, DOI: 10.1007/978-1-4614-3470-2_7,
© Springer Science+Business Media New York 2012

Sampling Issues

Just who is included in a clinical study shapes how well its results will reflect the range of persons with a particular disorder or problem. Even an experimental research design will be limited as a resource for treatment planning if it covers very few people or only people with very limited demographic characteristics.

There are three key components to look for in sample selection: Representativeness, size, and randomization. In quantitative research, a sample should be *representative* of the persons and setting of interest. That is, if researchers want to study a particular genetic disorder, they would target people with the disorder. They might also include other people without the genetic disorder for comparison purposes. If there were environmental factors or cultural factors that might interact with the genetic disorder, such as diet or exposure to toxins, groups would be sought that vary in diet and exposure to toxins. This would represent the variety of populations impacted by the genetic disorder as well as we can conceptualize them. Of course, money, time, and access might not be available to study all subgroups at once, so researchers might choose to study a smaller subset of this larger population. In this case, several studies would be necessary to obtain a sample that is representative of the genetic disorder and the factors we think that exacerbate or minimize it.

In clinical mental health studies, there may be a wide range of factors that could influence the effectiveness of a treatment or diagnostic test. Clinical social workers look for a wide range of bio-psycho-social-spiritual factors that help understand human problems. These include differences in gender, race, cultural or ethnicity, sexual orientation, class, age, ability, religious beliefs, legal status, genetic makeup, and geography. At times additional factors may also be important. This makes representativeness a very challenging issue for mental health researchers. Practical limitations also mean that fully representative samples may not be easy to obtain. Researchers, with input from clients and clinicians, must carefully conceptualize both their study problem formulations and the nature of their samples.

Compromises are common in sample size and representativeness due to limitations in time, funding, access, and client participation. For example, Wilt et al. (2008) report that very few RCTs on treatments for prostate cancer have been completed. No type of prostate cancer treatment has been demonstrated to be more effective than 'watchful waiting.' Side effects of the treatments were also not well identified. One reason was that men were unwilling to participate in the randomization process needed to compare different treatments. In this case, useful clinical research was limited due to the active choices of men who sought, quite understandably, to get what they believed were the best personal outcomes. Wilt and colleagues also note that differences in definitions and methods made the synthesis of findings across the available studies difficult.

Where samples are drawn from may impact study representativeness. Glickman et al. (2009) point out that many drug trials are being outsourced to developing countries. They note that this raises ethical issues regarding subjecting people in these countries to the risks of research participation, and allows companies to offer lower payments as incentives to participants. They also note that it is unclear whether the living conditions of persons in developing countries create an appropriate sample for comparison with those in developed countries. In effect, persons in developing countries may be an inappropriate population for sample selection in drug tests when the consumers of the drugs live in different circumstances. Other researchers argue that including a wider range of people in drug tests may benefit the clinical trial participants and others in their country as well. Selecting samples for clinical trials is complex, and may raise important ethical, practical, and representativeness issues.

The size of a sample is also very important. A larger sample is more likely to represent the population from which it was selected fully and effectively than is a smaller sample. Larger samples tend to produce less sampling error in representing an entire population. Larger samples also allow for more variety in background factors than is possible in very small samples. Further, when looking at the sample as a whole, the influence of a few 'outlier' cases with extremely high or low scores is also reduced as the size of the sample increases. Unfortunately, there is no simple way to estimate what is a large enough sample without considering the research question, design, sample, measures, and intended analysis type (Dattalo 2008). Still, it is probably a fair rule of thumb that studies with less than 40 participants in total employ what researchers call small samples. This would allow comparison of 20 persons in both treated and control groups in an experimental research design. On the other hand, some of these small-scale studies may have samples that are quite adequate to document clinical effects. Where small samples are used, having equal numbers in each group is very helpful when some statistical tests are used. Specifically having equal sized groups in an experimental comparison reduces standard error terms in these statistical analyses.

Probability samples are samples in which each member of the population or sampling frame has an equal chance of being selected. A *sampling frame* is a list of potential participants used to make concrete the larger conceptual population the study seeks to address. Probability samples are intended to limit active selection bias by the researcher. Selection bias is an active tendency to exclude certain cases (also called elements) from a sample. For example, persons with very severe levels of anxiety might be excluded while persons with low or moderate levels of anxiety are included in the sample. In this example, a selection bias yields a sample which excludes persons who may make up a substantial part of the population of persons with anxiety. Such a bias is also called a *non-response bias*, as persons with high levels of anxiety are excluded from the study sample. Their responses will remain unknown. The results of a study, based on such a sample, will not apply well to all people who may be found in clinical practice. In other words, the result is not easily *generalized* or applied to the larger population of people with anxiety disorders. Generalization is a key goal of most experimental research.

Nonprobability samples, oriented by theory or a specific research purpose, emphasize certain characteristics of sample members but do not insure equal chance of selection from the sampling frame or population. Nonprobability samples may be representative, or may be very unrepresentative, of the sampling frame or population (Dattalo 2008). When used in quantitative studies, probability samples provide a better mathematical basis for defining and limiting selection biases and nonresponsive bias than do most nonprobability samples.

There are a number of different methods for selecting probability samples. These include single or independent random sampling, systematic sampling, stratified sampling, and cluster sampling. *Simple random sampling* begins with assigning a number to each case or element in the study sampling frame. Sampling frames, however, are often not entirely inclusive of all the cases in the population of interest. A sampling frame might be the list of NASW members used as a way to define the larger, and not perfectly known, population of all social workers in the United States. The next step in single random sampling is to use an unbiased method to select cases from the sampling frame. This is usually done using a software generated list of random numbers to select cases from the sampling frame. Selection continues, using numbers from the random listing, until the desired number of cases are selected.

Systematic random sampling is a similar method, which begins with the random selection of a case from the sampling frame. Then every third or tenth or hundredth case is selected until the desired number is selected. *Stratified sampling* begins with dividing the sampling frame into groups with no shared members. For example, groups might be distinguished by ethnicity or age. These distinct groups are known in sampling as strata. Random sampling is then undertaken within each 'strata.' The purpose of stratified sampling is to ensure adequate sampling of subgroups that are few in numbers and might not be sufficiently sampled by simple random sampling methods. Some strata may be disproportionately sampled in order to ensure inclusion of enough cases from each subgroup to represent the population successfully. Finally, *cluster sampling* is used for very large populations. Cluster sampling uses existing subsets of a population to define subgroups. Random sampling is then completed on these subgroups to generate a probability sample. One common example is to use geographic areas defined by a government to identify neighborhoods. Neighborhoods may then be selected randomly. From within each neighborhood, cases are then selected on a random basis. Techniques to ensure probability proportionate to the size of each subgroup can be used to ensure equal chance of selection for each case.

For further information about probability sampling, clinical social workers may turn to most social work research texts (Anastas 1999; Grinnell and Unrau 2010; Rubin and Babbie 2011). However, very few social work texts offer detailed information about sampling issues related to qualitative research (Drisko 2003). Patton (1990) and Kuzel (1999) both offer solid introductions to several varieties of qualitative sampling and their purposes.

Probability samples are used in clinical experiments or RCTs to maximize representativeness. They are often required for the appropriate use of statistical tests. Finally, probability samples allow appropriate generalization from the sample to the larger populations from which it was drawn. Probability sampling can be a vital part of quantitative clinical research.

Increasing Statistical Power: Sample Size and Other Influences

Sample size also influences statistical analysis. Dattalo (2008, p. 16) states "a study should only be conducted if it relies on a sample size that is large enough to provide an adequate and prespecified probability of finding an effect if the effect exists." That is, specific sample sizes are needed to generate adequate statistical power. If a sample is too small, no significant effect can be found. If it is too large, undue and unnecessary burdens are placed on participants. The costs of completing the study also increase.

Statistical power is the probability of falsely accepting a null hypothesis when the research hypothesis is actually true (Cohen 1988). It is defined mathematically as 1-ß, where ß (beta) is the probability of accepting the null hypothesis falsely, also called Type II error. Statistical power is a function of the statistical significance criterion level (or a level) set for a specific test, the precision of measures, the type of research design, the magnitude of the effect under study, and the sample size (Dattalo 2008).

In using inferential statistics, a criterion or a level of <0.05 (<1 chance in 20) is a commonly used standard for rejecting a null hypothesis. This standard is set conservatively in order to avoid making an incorrect, '*false positive*,' decision, also called Type I errors. Researchers can increase the a level to <0.10 in order to be more likely to obtain a significant result. However, in doing so the chance of false positives, or Type I errors, is increased. Although there is no simple standard for statistical power, a value of 0.80 is widely accepted. In effect, researchers accept a 4 to 1 tradeoff in making a 'false negative' decision, or a Type II error, versus a Type I error. If the magnitude of an effect is very large, a small sample might lead to a correct decision to reject the null hypothesis. But if the magnitude of the effect is small to moderate, a small sample may not be adequate to reveal it. Some samples are simply too small to generate adequate statistical power. This renders the result of a statistical test invalid regardless of the research question and design to which it is connected. Increasing the sample size may be an easy and effective way to increase statistical power.

There are several methods for determining statistical power and related sample sizes (Aberson 2010; Dattalo 2008; Kraemer and Thiemann 1987). These methods differ by the nature of the measures used (discrete versus continuous) and the statistics employed. There are also several computer software programs to calculate statistical power and to identify the specific sample sizes needed for adequate statistical power (Dattalo 2008).

Another important way to increase statistical power is to use more structured research designs, particularly experimental and observational designs (Cook and Campbell 1979). Such research designs reduce the number of extraneous factors that can influence the study results, and thereby reduce unknown, systematic errors. Use of measures with high validly and reliability can also increase statistical power. This is because such measures reduce measurement error compared to less precise alternatives.

Overall, strong samples for EBM/EBP research will be (1) representative of the population of interest, (2) will be selected using probability sampling techniques, and (3) will be large enough in number to ensure adequate statistical power. These factors are especially important in experimental or RCT research designs. Very small sample sizes (under 20 per group) warrant careful scrutiny. This is because small samples may lack the statistical power to reveal important but modest differences in outcomes between groups. Inadequate statistical power is a greater concern when tests or measures of uncertain validity and reliability are employed. Researchers using small samples should state clearly how they determined that the sample had adequate power to produce meaningful results. This should be evident in the Methods section of the research report.

The Human Diversity Included in Study Samples

Clinicians should look carefully at the social diversity included in a study's sample. Researchers may not report many details about the social demographics of their sample beyond age and gender. Even racial and ethnic differences may be minimally detailed. This may make it unclear whether the sample used in an article was representative of a specific minority client whose care you are planning. It would be very helpful for clinical practice use if researchers and publishers provided greater detail about samples in research reports.

Another issue relates to attrition of participants as a research project continues. While study attrition is not exactly a sampling issue, it can influence the nature of the final study sample. Excellent sampling plans can be undermined when people drop out of a study, creating unequal group sizes and reducing the number of participants. Readers of research reports should look for the number and characteristics of the original, planned sample. Next, the characteristics of the researcher's final, obtained sample should be compared to the initial 'intent to treat' sample. Where follow-up measures are used, researchers should carefully document any attrition during follow-up periods. A common concern is that dropouts and clients who cannot be found for follow-up measures reduce the overall sample size, and may alter the equivalence of groups compared in experimental research. Dropouts may also reduce the social diversity in a study's sample.

In mental health research there is one final complicating issue regarding sampling. Many clients who apply for mental health services discontinue, or drop out of services after only a few sessions. Many do not complete even planned, short-term treatments. The challenge for researchers is that it is unclear whether clients who drop out have actually gotten better, gotten worse, were disappointed in the services, or left for other reasons. Knowing the reasons for dropping out could inform the research, but is generally unknown and unexamined. Dropouts can produce unequal group sizes, smaller samples that undermine statistical power, and limited information about the actual effects of treatment. This can reduce the validity of experimental comparisons in mental health studies.

After a research design has been selected and the study sample defined, researchers must select tests and measures to assess key concepts. These tests and measures may specify both the grouping variables that define who is treated or untreated, as well as the outcome or dependent variables that define what changes might occur.

Standardized Tests and Measures of Biopsychosocial Issues

Identifying and Locating Standardized Tests and Measures

To scientifically test whether a treatment or a diagnostic protocol is effective, it is vitally important to have content appropriate, valid, and reliable measures of the client's situation before and after the intervention. These measures may include observations, frequency counts of behaviors, spoken statements, reviews of client records, and/or standardized tests. Each data collection method has somewhat different strengths and limitations (Anastas 1999). Standardized tests and measures are widely used in EBM/EBP research. They provide a known and replicable approach to assessing and summarizing client status and behavior.

Standardized tests and measures are developed and refined through a series of steps that helps define their validity and reliability. These characteristics are known as the *psychometric properties* of a test or measure. There are literally thousands of tests and measures that could be used in clinical social work practice. It is sometimes difficult just to understand the abbreviations used to refer to these tests, and to learn their intended uses. Most standardized tests and measures are protected by copyright. Copyright provides protection for the intellectual property of the test creator, as well as some payment for their work. Researchers also keep some tests away from potential test takers to ensure they cannot be studied and reviewed by test takers in order to influence, or even to fake, test results. One consequence of copyright protection is that the full text of test and measures may be difficult to obtain, even for practice or teaching purposes. However, some standardized tests are available in full for clinical and research uses (see Corcoran and Fischer 2007; Hudson 1982).

An extensive database of tests is available online, without cost, from the Educational Testing Service TestLink web site at http://1340.sydneyplus.com/ETS_Test_Collection/Portal.aspx. The TestLink database provides abstracts of educational tests but includes many for mental health and counseling as well. It is a fine resource to learn the basics about psychological tests. The limitation of the Testlink database is that it does not provide psychometric information to help clarify the validity and reliability of each test. Another database of tests and measures, the Health and Psychosocial Instruments (HaPI) database, is available through paid subscription or purchase only. Many large agencies, hospitals, and social work programs have access to the HaPI database. HaPI includes links to publications about the development of psychosocial tests and measures which may provide more detail than is available through Testlink. Still, neither database provides psychometric information about listed tests and measures. Neither database provides full copies of tests; both are nonetheless very useful for initially identifying tests and their intended uses.

The Buros Institute's *Mental Measurements Yearbooks* provide much more information about specific tests and measures. Currently in its 18th edition, these print reference books may be found in academic libraries and even in some larger public libraries. The limitation of print copies is that they may not include the latest versions of tests. (They are not exactly yearbooks; new editions appear about every 3 years.) The strength of the Buros yearbooks is that they provide details on the purposes, norming samples, range of scores, assessments of validity and reliability, as well as commentary on the test. Buros Test Reviews Online allows purchase of reviews of individual tests and measures included in the print yearbooks. The test reviews online are available at http://buros.unl.edu/buros/jsp/search.jsp. Costs for purchase of individual reviews are modest.

Identifying the Specific Properties of Tests and Measures

Once you have located an appropriate test or measure, the next step is to examine its psychometric properties. These details are available in the Buros' yearbooks or some online reviews. They are also found in the manual available for most widely used copyrighted measures. Researchers typically provide few details about tests and measures in research reports. However, psychometric information helps readers establish the degree of confidence they should place in specific tests and measures. It also provides information about whom the test was designed to assess. This includes whether or not the test was normed on socially diverse samples and any age-related limits on use of the test. Next we will review the attributes of tests and measures.

Sound tests and measures must be both valid and reliable. *Validity* refers to whether the measure fully captures what it is intended to measure. *Reliability* refers to whether the measure produces consistent results. Together, validity and reliability make up the key components of the *psychometric properties* of the tests and measures used in mental health research. A third factor, the *sensitivity* of a test refers to how well it can capture the type and magnitude of changes. A sensitive measure can capture small changes effectively. This is especially important in tracking changes in brief interventions. Sensitivity is often difficult to assess, but may be very important to clinical research. Complete research reports will include the psychometric properties of all tests and measures they employ. Medical research typically focuses on nonpsychological variables using biological and physiological measures that should have strong validity and reliability.

Validity of Measures

Validity as it relates to tests in mental health research has several aspects (Campbell and Stanley 1963). The first is *face validity* or whether or not the items (questions) that make up a test appear to address the construct of interest. For example, a test of marital conflict should include items that directly address different types and forms of marital conflict. A similar term is *content validity*. Content validity refers to how well the content of a test reflects the content of a multifaceted construct. For example, measure of child maltreatment should include items about the domains of neglect, verbal abuse, sexual abuse, and physical abuse. *Construct validity* refers to the extent to which a test reflects the entire construct of interest. For example, we would expect a test of depression to include items on mood, diminished interest in activities, sleeping patterns, feelings of worthlessness, inability to concentrate, suicidal ideation and actions, psychomotor retardation, and weight loss. These items reflect core DSM criteria for depression. A valid test must examine all of these component parts to fully cover the construct of depression as defined by DSM criteria. To exclude any one of them would reduce the construct validity of a test of depression. Note that these three aspects of validity are conceptual and require critical thinking to appraise. They also require a look at the actual items included in the measures. The absence of an important component of a construct from a measure is not (usually) captured by quantitative psychometric summaries. Clinicians need to find and look for the actual content of tests and measures to evaluate face, content, and construct validity unless the report author includes discussion of them.

Other forms of validity are based on quantitative methods. These are collectively known as *criterion validity*. In criterion validity, the results of one test are compared with the results on another, similar, test or measure. Most texts suggest a greater than 70%, or greater than 0.70, criterion for establishing strong criterion validity. This is consistent with the way most correlation statistics are interpreted. Correlation values from 0.00 to 0.30 are generally labeled "weak" correlations, values from 0.31 to 0.70 values are labeled "moderate" correlations, and values from 0.71 to 1.00 are "strong" correlations.

In *concurrent validity* the results of similar tests are correlated with each other or to another established criterion. For example, a researcher might correlate the scores of people at similar points in time on the Beck Depression Inventory, revision II, and the Hamilton Depression Inventory. Both are measures of depression based on DSM criteria. If the results correlated highly ($r > 0.70$) the researcher could state there was good concurrent validity between the two measures. Developers of new tests often correlate their new results with the results on a more widely used test to establish concurrent validity. *Predictive validity* refers to how well performance on a measure at one point in time predicts future performance on another measure or criterion. A researcher might find that high school grades are predictive of staying in a certain treatment program. This information might be used to screen out people with low high school grades, or to examine whether the program's model and language are pitched to a higher level than is truly necessary. *Discriminant validity* refers to how well a test distinguishes between groups of different people. For example, a screening test for anxiety disorders should be able to distinguish between people likely to have an anxiety disorder from those who are unlikely to have one.

Reliability of Measures

Researchers and psychometricians (psychological test developers) determine the reliability of test and measures through quantitative tests. In *test-retest reliability* assessment, researchers give the same test to the same group of people at two different times. Results of the two administrations of the test are then correlated with each other to provide a measure of test–retest reliability. The assumption is that the characteristics of the group will change very little in the brief time between two test administrations, and that exposure to the test items will have limited impact on the results. In *internal consistency reliability* assessment, researchers correlate items within the measure with each other. This is done by comparing results from the first half of the test with results from the second half of the test, called, *split-half reliability*. Split half reliability assumes items are included in the test more than once, and/or that both halves appropriately reflect the full content of interest. Other models involve complex correlations of all test items to all other items. Researchers often report internal consistency reliability using the coefficient alpha (a) statistic. Finally, *inter-rater reliability* compares the results of assessments made by two or more researchers to assess their consistency. This might include comparison of diagnoses or ratings made by several different clinicians. Researchers also use percentages of agreement, correlation statistics, and the kappa statistic to report inter-rater reliability based on the characteristics of the test or measure.

Reporting Validity and Reliability Assessments

Due to space limitations in journal articles, many research reports provide only summary information about the psychometric properties of the measures they employ. Some include only abbreviations for tests names and cite only the test developer's manual in regard to a measure's psychometric properties. Such limited information makes it very difficult for a practicing clinician to determine whether the outcome measures used in a study are valid and reliable, or truly applicable to any specific client's needs. Critical thinking is always necessary in interpreting such reports.

Clinical social workers should expect brief but detailed description of the psychometric properties of standardized tests used in EBP research. Tests should be named in full with any abbreviations clearly stated. At a minimum, a citation to the test manual or other resources describing the tests purposes and psychometric properties should be clearly cited for follow-up. For example, Telch et al. (2001, p. 1072) describe each standardized test they use in a sentence and followed by a full citation for further review: "Questionnaires used in this study include the Binge Eating Scale (Gormally et al. 1982), a measure of severity of binge eating problems…" This is a useful start. We would argue that the validity and reliability of each test should also be described in more detail to guide the reader more fully. This is often done in a very brief summary such as "the XXX depression scale has $r = 0.81$ concurrent validity when correlated to results of the widely-used ABC depression measure. The mean test-retest reliability is 0.76 over 4 trials with different samples including a total of 220 people." In such a summary, it is clear that the tests in use have documented validity and reliability.

Detailed information about validity and reliability is often omitted when widely used standardized tests are employed. These include tests such as the Symptom Checklist-90, the Achenbach Child Behavior Checklist (CBCL), the Beck Depression Inventory, and the Hamilton Rating Scale for Depression. The drawback of this practice is that it assumes readers are familiar with the tests and measures, which is very often not the case for clinical practitioners. Note that even this summary information does not specify whether a standardized test has been normed on minority population groups, or with people who have comorbid or co-occurring disorders.

Interpreting Reports of Clinical Standardized Tests and Measures

One obvious but tricky issue in treatment outcome research is to be sure the people included in a study all share the same challenge. Standardized tests are often used to verify the diagnosis of participants in research studies. For example, the Structured Clinical Interview for DSM-III for Axis II [SCID-II] (Spitzer et al. 1990) was widely used to define operationally many personality disorders. The reliability of the SCID-II was tested in several studies with kappa values ranging from $k = 0.02$ to 0.98 (Columbia University Biometrics Research Department, undated). The kappa values for each diagnosis included several studies with $k > 0.70$, but results were not consistent across the measures. These extremely varied results mean that across different DSM diagnoses, and evaluated using different methods, the measured reliability of the SCID-II varies widely. It may be understood as a good enough, but far from perfect, method to determine DSM diagnosis.

A related issue is how standardized diagnostic tests fit with current diagnostic standards. That is, research based on DSM-III criteria may not be fully valid and applicable when compared with the same DSM-IV diagnosis if the criteria have changed. DSM-V, for example, proposes to remove several personality disorder diagnoses listed in DSM-IV. DSM-V criteria for personality disorders will also be based on very different criteria than those used in DSM-III and DSM-IV. Clinical social workers must critically appraise how research using older measures and diagnoses is applicable under newer standards. There is also an inevitable time lag between when new diagnostic standards are published and when new standardized diagnostic measures become available. In turn, research based on new standards will not be available in the first years after new diagnostic standards are published.

There is a wide range of tests and measures to assess client status before, during, and after treatment. For example, Binks et al. (2009, pp. 5, 6), in their systematic review of psychological treatments for borderline personality disorder, were interested in concerns such as anxiety, depression, self-reports of self-harm, mental states, service outcomes, substance use, and frequency of admission to psychiatric hospitals or incarceration. They report these outcomes in 15 categories, including (among others) behavior, global state, mental state, substance use, economic cost, and recidivism. They go on to detail 77 specific types of outcomes, such as no change, no clinically important change, average changes, etc. (pp. 5, 6). Such a wide range of variables requires a number of different techniques to assess. Further, some of these variables are more directly applicable to practice decision making and immediate client needs than are others.

It is very important that measures be clearly defined and fully specified in reports. Marshall et al. (2000) found that use of poorly defined and unstandardized measures was a major limitation in their research on services for people with schizophrenia. Poorly defined outcome measures, with unknown validity and reliability, will not produce the high quality experimental results sought in EBP. While not all service outcomes can be understood in advance, it is very important that the outcome or dependent variables in an experiment be assessed using valid and reliable methods.

Some measures of status, such as length of an inpatient stay, are direct measures leading to frequency counts. Other measures employ scales and indices to cover a wider range of content and to get at internal states, cognition, and feelings. In all cases, the process of measurement should be defined and standardized to ensure accurate assessment when used in experimental research. This enhances the reader's ability to compare results across different clients and settings. Even a simple count of days of inpatient hospitalization requires a definition of just what constitutes a 'day.' Similarly, scales of depression or anxiety require careful construction to produce valid and reliable measurements.

Clinical rating scales come in two main types: measures of global function and measures of specific disorders (Ogles et al. 1996). For example, some studies included in the Binks et al. (2009) systematic review used the Global Assessment Scale (GAS) (Endicott et al. 1976) of overall psychological well-being. The GAS, completed by the clinician, rates client well-being on a 0–100 scale. Higher scores are positive results. The GAS is a global measure of functioning covering several domains of the patient's well-being. The Brief Psychiatric Rating Scale (BPRS) (Overall and Gorham 1962) was also used to assess mental state on several dimensions or subscales. Some of these 18 subscales are somatic concerns, depression, anxiety, suspiciousness, hallucinations, and grandiosity. The BPRS is scored from 18 to 126, with higher scores representing greater overall symptom severity. The BPRS, as a global standardized test, assesses both prominent and unspoken concerns. Global standardized tests can help clinicians and researchers identify comorbid disorders or sources of resilience and challenge that shape the client's specific clinical presentation.

To complement the results of global standardized tests, more narrowly focused tests are used. Tests of specific disorders or concerns are often more comprehensive on the dimensions they cover (have greater construct validity) and are often more sensitive to small differences. Thus, they are useful both to pinpoint specific client concerns and to reveal small changes that occur during treatment. The Beck Depression Inventory-II (Beck et al. 1996) is disorder specific standardized test that measures depression largely in terms of patient's cognitive views. Binks et al. (2009, p. 13) describe the BDI as measuring "supposed manifestations of depression," pointing up the importance of critical thinking and of appraising content validity! The BDI rates depression severity from 0 to 63 with higher scores indicating greater severity of depression. The Inventory of Interpersonal Problems, Circumplex Version (Horowitz et al. 2000) also known as the Interpersonal Circumplex, measures interpersonal behavior and motives on two axes. One dimension assesses power, dominance, and need for control while the other assesses friendliness and warmth. It is a 64-item self-report questionnaire on which items are rated from 0 to 4. Higher scores indicate greater difficulty in interpersonal functioning. Many other disorder-specific rating scales are available for common mental health problems such as anxiety, eating disorders, and thought disorders.

Standardized tests further differ on the source of information—who fills them out—and on what information they are based. Self-report questionnaires are quite common. These tests are efficient and cost-effective, but allow respondents to enter misleading or false information. Providing socially acceptable but inaccurate information is a widely known phenomenon (Ogles et al. 1996). Other widely used tests are clinical rating scales based on a diagnostic interview. Such interviews must include specific content for the clinician's appraisal to be valid. Ratings made by clinicians may miss specific content that questionnaires might capture. On the other hand, clinician ratings may capture subtleties of communication and nuances missed by questionnaires. These forms of data collection are complementary.

Standardized tests also differ in sensitivity. Some are meant more as screening tools, but are also used in clinical research to measure outcomes. One example is the Achenbach CBCL. The CBCL is a widely used screening test, and comes in different versions for pre-school (Achenbach and Rescorla 2000) and for school-aged children (Achenbach and Rescorla, 2001). It is based on rating specific behaviors as 'not true' or not evident, 'sometimes true,' or 'always true.' As a result, important changes in just one or two key behaviors may not be immediately evident in an overall CBCL score. Its use as an outcome measure must be carefully appraised. Optimal outcome measures have strong sensitivity to small changes. This is especially important when they are used to assess change in brief interventions.

All tests and measures used in clinical research should be reported in detail. The complete names of standardized tests should always be reported, with citations for sources. Many measures have more than one version, and multiple editions are common. At what point(s) in time the measures are completed should also be stated clearly. As noted above, the basic psychometric properties of a measure, including assessments of its validity and reliability should be included. Limitations to the use of the measures, by age range, gender, intellectual ability or other factors should be clearly stated. The use of adult measures with adolescents and with persons over age 65 may be invalid. Different versions of measures for children of different ages are also common. For progressive disorders such as Alzheimer's disease, different version of measures may be available for persons with different functional abilities. The scoring range of each measure, and whether high scores represent positive or negative results should always be stated.

Increasingly, standardized tests are available in versions geared toward persons for whom English is not the first language. Bit by bit, versions of standardized tests normed for different racial and ethnic groups are being developed or identified. However, not all standardized tests have been normed on non-white or multicultural populations.

For further information, most social work research texts offer good introductions to tests and measures. More detailed information about psychometrics may be found in texts by Furr and Bacharach (2007) or Rust and Golombok (2009).

Defining outcomes is another challenging process. There are many test and measurement technologies available to both researchers and clinical practitioners. Still more complex is clearly defining and distinguishing among treatments and their active components.

Defining Treatments

Standardized tests assess the baseline state and outcome of interventions. They are the dependent or outcome variables in EBM/EBP research. The independent variable, or the factor that leads to change in an experiment, also needs careful definition. The goal is to learn whether a specific treatment causes specific changes. There are many models of biopsychosocial interventions. Interventions also vary in modality, with individual, dyad, couple, family, group, and even community interventions available (Ogles et al. 1996). Mental health and social service treatments also vary in complexity and in specificity. Some treatments involved several components, often delivered in a specific sequence. Some treatments may be described using a curriculum-style manual, while others are based on a set of principles but are intentionally individualized in application. Defining treatments is a very difficult undertaking. However, if the delivered treatment is not well-defined, one key foundation for making cause and effect attributions is absent (Ogles et al. 1996).

To illustrate the challenges of defining biopsychosocial therapies, we will examine Binks et al. (2009, p. 4) definitions of psychological treatments for people who have borderline personality disorder (BPD). These definitions are drawn from a careful systematic review, and are meant to illustrate how thoughtful researchers address the challenges of defining treatments. The authors report that they faced a "huge" number of distinct treatment types making an exhaustive listing "almost impossible" to develop (p. 4). They ended up defining six key treatment types, including cognitive behavioral, behavioral, psychodynamic, group, miscellaneous, and standard care categories. They defined cognitive behavioral treatments (CBT) as follows:

> A variety of interventions have been labeled CBT and it is difficult to provide a single, unambiguous definition. Recognizing this, we constructed criteria we felt to be both workable and to capture the elements of good practice in CBT. In order to be classified as 'well defined' the intervention must clearly demonstrate that a component of the intervention: (1) involves the recipient establishing links between their thoughts, feelings and actions with respect to the target symptom; and (2) the correction of the person's misperceptions, irrational beliefs and reasoning biases related to the target symptom. In addition a further component of the intervention should involve either or both of the following: (i) the recipient monitoring his or her own thoughts, feelings, and behaviors with respect to the target symptom; and (ii) the promotion of alternative ways of coping with the target symptom. All therapies that do not meet these criteria but are labeled [by the original authors as] 'CBT' or 'Cognitive Therapy' will be included as 'less well defined' CBT. (p. 4).

Here the definition of the treatment is based on a few reasonable, but broad, principles that look for the application of CBT theory in practice. Note that some actual CBT studies may not include enough information in their reports to be classified as CBT even if they did actually meet these standards. Note too, that it would be difficult to completely replicate CBT treatments in other agency settings using this definition. Other agencies might be doing CBT according to this definition, but other factors not covered in the definition, might interact to make the treatment more or less successful.

Binks et al. (2009, p. 4) defined psychodynamic therapy in a similar fashion:

> In order to be classified as psychodynamic, the intervention must not focus on a specific presenting problem (such as aggression) but rather on the unconscious conflicts that repress the individual and need to be confronted and re-evaluated in the context of the people' [sic] adult life. The following two components had to be documented in the therapeutic intervention for the therapy to be included: (a) it must explore an element of the unconscious, and (b) emphasises the importance of the patient's relational interaction with the therapist.

In some measure this definition appears to define psychodynamic therapy by an absence of attention to the presenting problem, which might surprise some psychodynamically informed clinical social workers. Further, sole attention to repression seems an odd choice for treating people who have BPD. Uncovering unconscious conflicts would actually be contraindicated for people who have BPD in contemporary psychoanalytic theory and practice; supportive interventions are instead recommended (Goldstein 1995, 2001).

The authors' intent, it seems, is to again define the therapy by how its defining theory is evident in real-world practice. Yet, identifying unconscious conflicts and patterns of interpersonal interaction might look in practice very much like establishing links among thoughts, feelings, and actions in order to change irrational (or no longer relevant) perceptions and beliefs about the target symptom. This is the same language used to define CBT.

Finally, group therapy is defined. Group therapy of course, is actually a modality of treatment that can be informed by several different theories, including cognitive-behavioral and psychodynamic theories. Binks et al. (2009, p. 4) define group therapy as "any intervention that extends beyond the individual and specifically uses a group format in this category (e.g. family therapy and psychoanalytic group therapy). We would have included studies of therapeutic communities in this category..." Here the modality of therapy defines its key features. How specific theories are evident within the content of the group sessions is not the defining feature for group therapy, though it is for the definitions of CBT and psychodynamic therapies. The format of the treatment, not the theory or premises that inform it, is used instead as its defining properties. Note that this definition would be quite inadequate if used to replicate any particular group therapy in a new setting.

To add further clarity to the definition of treatments, researchers often report the number and duration of sessions, the qualifications of the clinicians doing the treatment, and how often supervision was provided. This information does help describe the treatments used. These descriptive efforts, too, fall short of defining treatments in a manner that allows equivalent replication in other settings. Defining mental health treatments can be very difficult.

It is interesting to note that the two therapies Binks et al. (2009) found to be effective in treating BPD, a psychodynamically informed partial hospital program and dialectal behavior therapy (DBT), both include highly structured treatment programs with several components such as individual and group therapy. These shared features of the two models found to be effective were not specifically highlighted in Binks and colleagues' systematic review. Instead their different theoretical foundations were emphasized. (No disrespect to Binks et al. is intended. We view them as going much further than most authors in these treatment definitions.)

Another effort to further clarify the definition of treatments or other biopsychosocial intervention processes, including diagnostic procedures, is the treatment manual. Researchers often use treatment manuals to add greater specificity to the definition of treatments.

Treatment Manuals

Treatment manuals seek to set forth the components of treatments in detail. Some go so far as to offer a curriculum, defining the tasks and activities to be completed in each session. One goal of the treatment manual is to improve the quality of treatment definitions in order to enhance the validity of clinical mental health research. Researchers view treatment manuals as an important way to increase the integrity of the intervention that causes change in experimental trials. This requires enough detail to be able to replicate the same treatment in different locations. As LeCroy (2008, p. 3) states, "treatment manuals move us closer to treatment fidelity." *Treatment fidelity* means that clinicians deliver the treatment fully as intended. It also means that different clinicians in different settings deliver the same treatment fully and consistently. This enhances replicablility. Such replicablility is useful in research to ensure a treatment was fully delivered. In practice, manuals may also be promoted administratively to allow less well-trained, and less costly, providers to deliver a service.

Some clinicians state that treatment manuals may undermine the individualization of therapies and other interventions to fit unique client needs, situations, and values. Ollendick et al. (2006) argue that treatment manuals might lead to mechanical interventions, stifling creativity and innovation. Smith (1995) called treatment manuals "cookbooks" and Silverman (1996) called them "paint by number approaches." In effect, these clinicians argue that treatment manuals omit professional expertise, a core component of EBM/EBP according to Haynes et al. (2002a). There is a clear tension between individualizing therapy to specific and perhaps unique client needs, versus enhancing fidelity of treatment for research purposes.

In mental health, Sanderson and Woody (1995, 1996) define a treatment manual as materials that provide sufficient detail to allow a trained clinician to replicate the treatment. They leave unclear whether sufficient detail is provided by description of broad psychological principles, or whether much greater detail is necessary. Sanderson and Woody also point out that treatment manuals are inadequate if the clinician lacks solid theoretical grounding or lacks supervised experience in the particular approach they apply. Specifically, they point out that workshop training alone, without supervised experience, does not constitute adequate training in any therapeutic model. This view is countered, however, by manuals that claim to provide "step-by-step instructions for conducting individual and group sessions" (Center for Substance Abuse Treatment, 2007). In such manuals, detail is substituted for professional expertise, contrary to the goals of EBM and EBP. There appear to be different views on both the definition and optimal use of treatment manuals.

What do treatment manuals cover? Trepper et al. (undated) offer a treatment manual for solution-focused therapy (SFT) with individuals. Their manual details the basic tenets of SFT, how goals are set via conversations with clients, and the specific active ingredients of SFT. These ingredients include (1) a collaborative interaction between clients and clinician, (2) a positive, solution-focused stance, (3) looking for previous solutions, (4) looking for exceptions to problems, (5) using questions rather than interpretations, (6) maintaining a present time focus rather than a focus on the past, and (7) using compliments. Within sessions, pre-session changes are appraised, goals are framed in terms of desired outcomes to current problems, goals are numerically scaled, and the miracle question technique may be used. The manual also includes vignettes of interactions within sessions as illustrations of these active techniques.

In the SFT manual, a broad description of the therapy is combined with specification of certain techniques that make it possible to determine if the treatment was delivered in a valid and complete manner. A supervisor or a researcher could review a videotape or a transcript of a SFT session and determine if this therapy had been fully applied. Left a bit unclear is how many of these features must be present for the therapy to be called valid SFT for research purposes. For example, using many more interpretations than questions would not fit with SFT, but it is probably fine that the miracle question is not used in a specific therapy session.

Other manuals are still more detailed and prescriptive. Stark et al. (2010) offer a manualized treatment for girls ages 9–13 and their caregivers called the ACTION program. They set forth a number of plain language themes for the program, including (1) "If you feel bad and you don't know why, use goals skills;" (2) "If you feel bad and can change the situation, use problem solving;" and (3) "If you feel bad and it is due to negative thoughts, change the thoughts" (p. 94). Structurally, the program consists of 20 sessions of 45–75 minutes delivered in school to small groups of girls ($n = 2$–5). Parent training involves once-a-week meetings with the same therapist but for only 10 sessions. Skills emphasized in the girl's groups include affective education, goal setting, coping skills training and mood monitoring.

These skills are further broken down into a session-by-session format. Meeting 1 (p. 97) centers on "Introductions and discussion of pragmatics." The objectives of meeting 1 are to: "Discuss parameters of meetings. Introduce counselors and participants. Establish rationale for treatment. Discuss confidentiality. Establish group rules. Build group cohesion. Establish written group incentive system." We may assume that setting of parameters is not so unlike any other small group, but the specific rationale for the ACTION program may be. Note that building group cohesion is a universal issue for new groups, but one that is very difficult to specify fully and may include some idiosyncratic components that vary from group to group.

Later meetings have different goals and progressively more focused objectives. Meeting 6 centers on "Cognition and emotion introduction to cognitive restructuring." The objectives of Meeting 6 session are to: "Demonstrate the role of cognition in emotion and behavior. Introduce connection of thoughts to feelings. Enactment of coping skills activity within session." Over the course of the ACTION program, the group leaders teach the girl clients to be "thought detectives;" to consider if there are alternative ways to look at a problem and to assess the evidence on which a thought is based. Several techniques fill out the objectives for Meeting 6. One such technique in the ACTION program is talking back to the "Muck Monster." The group leaders label being unable to let go of a negative way of thinking as "being stuck in the muck monster." In turn, the muck monster creates distance from the negative thoughts and the whole person of the client and creates a suitable opponent to challenge. The enactment within Meeting 6 is likely a direct exploration of being stuck in the muck monster and ways to move out of this stuck position. Later session-by-session content is also outlined and linked to related ACTION techniques. Many of the later meetings (12–20) include practice of the program techniques within the group setting.

It is not clear that treatment manuals fully achieve their goal of making bio-psychosocial therapies more fully replicable, but they may help. Treatment manuals can make more explicit the principles and tenets, the distinguishing characteristics and the key techniques of a treatment. This alone, however, may not allow a therapy to be fully replicated by others in a different location. Therapeutic principles and techniques overlap considerably despite differences in theory and even across treatment modalities. Individual differences in client needs, style, and comfort may require adaptations of carefully described treatment procedures. Still, treatment manuals take a useful step toward improving the validity of complex biopsychosocial interventions to enhance the validity of research claims made about them.

Treatment manuals are not limited to behavioral and cognitive-behavioral approaches, though they are more common for these therapies. Treatment manuals are available for certain psychodynamic psychotherapies (i.e., Clarkin et al. 2006), for many behavioral and cognitive behavioral therapies (i.e., Reilly and Shopshire 2002; or Andrews et al. 2002), and for certain family therapies (i.e., Lock et al. 2002). Treatment manuals for specific disorders may also include sections or chapters on different age groups or other subpopulations that are likely to be affected by the disorder (see, for example, Benedek and Wynn 2011 on PTSD).

The last component of appraising a research report centers on methods of analysis. For quantitative research, statistics are a vital method for decision making. The final section in this chapter offers a review of key statistics and issues in their appropriate use.

Statistics

Statistics do not tend to be the greatest strength of most clinical social workers. While statistics are required content in most social work programs, many students do not often retain a good grasp of their use after graduation. There are many statistics, each with limiting assumptions that shape their appropriate use. We will review a number of premises for the appropriate use of statistics and point out a few key issues in interpreting statistics in research reports. It is, however, beyond this book to provide a thorough introduction or review of all statistics. Many good introductory statistics texts are available such as Weinbach and Grinnell (2009) or Abu-Bader (2006); along with review books such as Norman and Streiner (2003).

This chapter has examined how research designs shape clinical research. In interpreting research results, readers should always be clear on whether the study seeks to show differences between groups or seeks to measure associations among characteristics of clients. Experimental and quasi-experiment research designs explore differences between groups. Observational research designs generally explore correlations among the characteristics of group members. In a similar fashion, statistics fall into the same general categories: those that examine differences and those that examine correlations or associations.

Where differences are being studied, it is important that the groups being compared are as similar as possible. Comparing group differences is best achieved by using an experimental research design, but readers should further be sure the demographic characteristics (ages, ethnicities, religions, etc.) and levels of functioning of the groups being compared are similar. Researchers often report and compare the characteristics of each group in a clinical trial at the start of treatment, also called at baseline. Statistics are often used to show that there is no significant differences on important variables between the groups being studied. This documents that they are similar before treatment.

Data may be either *discrete* or *continuous*. Discrete data comes only in certain finite values. If we think of "number of children," answers such as '3' or '0' make sense but 1.5 does not. On the other hand, income is continuous data. It makes sense to have an annual income of $23,453.72, even if the cents might not matter all that much. Similarly, a scale of depression might range on a continuous scale from '0' for no depression to '20' for severely depressed. A group mean score of 12.32 for several depressed clients makes sense and allows comparison to another group with a mean score of 18.65. Most (but not all) outcome measures draw upon continuous data.

Levels of Measure

The next issue to review is the nature of the data the researchers have examined. Researchers use different statistics to examine different kinds of data. Numbers can be used to define categories with no rank order, such as '1' represents the treated group and group '2' represents the untreated control group. Statisticians call measures with mutually exclusive categories and without a hierarchical ranking *nominal level measures*. Numbers can also be used to establish a rough hierarchy with clear but imprecise differences among the ranks. We could use '0' to represent no formal schooling, '1' to represent some grade school, '2' to represent finished grade school and '3' to represent some middle schooling and so forth. The higher numbers do represent more school completed, but the numbers do not reflect years of school completed in a precise and consistent manner. Statisticians call measures with mutually exclusive categories and a rough hierarchy but without equal intervals between values *ordinal level measures*. We can also use numbers to establish a more precise hierarchy in which the interval between the numbers represents some measured dimension. It is meaningful to distinguish between a body temperature taken by mouth of 98.6° and one of 102.4°. The intervals between the tenths of a degree are all the same, and provide a scale or metric for comparison. Statisticians call measures with mutually exclusive categories, a clear hierarchy of values, and equal intervals between values *interval level measures*. If the scale includes a nonarbitrary zero point, we gain even more information. A body temperature of 0.00° has no everyday meaning (and is not included in the range of most fever thermometers). But having zero dollars of annual income has a very real meaning and is much less desirable than an income of $30,000. Each dollar represents an equal and consistent increase (or decrease) in annual income. Statisticians call measures with mutually exclusive categories, a clear hierarchy of values, equal intervals between values and a non-arbitrary zero point *ratio level measures*.

These differences in levels of measure are important for selecting appropriate statistics. Researchers select different statistics in part based on the level of measure of the available data. Generally speaking, using interval or ratio level provides more detailed information and allows use of more powerful statistical tests. In experiments, the independent or grouping variable must be constituted by at least nominal level non-overlapping categories. The dependent or outcome variable is most often interval or ratio level data that conveys a meaningful scale of severity. Interval and ratio level measures also allow for more precise scaling. While interval and ratio level data is more 'information rich' than are nominal and ordinal level data, any level of measure can be used as a clinical outcome (dependent) variable. For example, nominal categories (i.e., meets criteria for a DSM diagnosis or does not meet criteria) and ordinal level data (i.e., low, moderate or high pain severity) would be appropriate outcome variables.

Parametric and Nonparametric Statistics: Differences in Population Distributions

Another issue that influences the selection of statistics is the nature of the distribution of values or scores in the target population. All statistical tests are either parametric or nonparametric. *Parametric data distributions* assume that the population from which the researchers collected the sample data was a particular kind of distribution. Most often, this is to assume a normal distribution of data in the population. A normal distribution is symmetrical around the mean value, with equal 'tails' on each side. Most textbooks call this the bell curve, though normal distributions can vary in look when graphed. A normal distribution means that there are roughly equal numbers of very low scores and very high scores. *Nonparametric data distributions*, on the other hand, assume no specific form of population distribution. In general, parametric statistics are more powerful and researchers should use them when possible. This is because nonparametric statistics are calculated using rank order information only, which includes less specific information than do the parametric statistics.

Once the data are collected, researchers must examine the nature of the obtained sample's distribution. Data collected from a population that is assumed to be normally distributed population may prove to have different characteristics. The collected data ideally should have few outliers (very extreme high or low scores). In studies of small samples, a few outliers can alter the results of statistical comparisons profoundly as they increase or decrease group mean scores. In some studies, outliers are purposefully excluded from the final data analysis to avoid their strong influence on the overall results. Authors should clearly state whether outliers are present and how outliers were interpreted and handled.

Researchers should also review the distribution of scores in the obtained data. Distributions may be skewed, or have many high or low scores, shifting them from a symmetrical normal shape. The problem with skewed distributions is that comparing skewed and nonskewed groups may lead to results that are inaccurate. Statisticians can often transform non-normal distributions of data into a near normal form by doing logarithmic transformations or other procedures. These transformations do not alter the relative values of scores, only the shape of their distribution. If transformations of the data distribution are undertaken, they should be clearly reported in the research report.

The Five Uses for Statistical Tests

There are five main uses for quantitative or statistical data analysis. These uses or purposes are (1) describing the characteristics of a sample or population, (2) testing for differences among groups, (3) testing for associations among variables, (4) testing for group membership, and (5) examining structure of a theory or of a measure (Tabachnick and Fidell 2007). The first purpose is descriptive; the other four are inferential in nature.

Descriptive statistics, as the name implies, seek to (a) describe the typical or most common member of a distribution and to (b) describe the spread or dispersion found within a distribution of scores. Descriptive statistics therefore come in two types: *Measures of central tendency* and *measures of dispersion*. Descriptive measures of central tendency seek to tell us about the typical member of the distribution we are studying. That is, of all the cases we have, what are the most common features and what would the typical member of the distribution look like? Descriptive measures of dispersion tell researchers about the variation within a distribution or how much cases differ one from the other.

Statisticians apply descriptive statistics differentially based on the target variable's level of measure. Among descriptive statistics of central tendency, only the mode can be used with a categorical or nominal measure. For an ordinal, hierarchal measure, both the mode and the median may be used. The median conveys information about both category and place in the hierarchy so it is a bit more 'information rich' than is the mode, and therefore a somewhat more useful measure of central tendency. For an interval or scaled level measure, any measure of central tendency can be used (mean, median, or mode). This is because with interval measures we can perform mathematical operations on the data legitimately. With an interval variable, the mean is called the preferable measure of central tendency because mathematical operations are used in its calculation, requiring equal intervals along the hierarchy it measures.

Measures of dispersion are all calculated using mathematical operations so they may be used only with interval or quantitative measures. No measure of dispersion can be used with nominal or ordinal level data. Key measures are the range (maximum value minus minimum value), the variance and the standard deviation. Skewness and kurtosis also provide information about how similar, or how different, a given distribution of scores is compared to a calculated normal distribution.

Inferential statistics, as the name implies, are used by statisticians to make inferences and decisions about statistical significance. They are all based upon probability theory and compare actual, observed results with a mathematically constructed model that presumes no difference or no association between/among the variables under study. *Inferential statistics tell us how likely it would be to obtain a specific result if there was no difference or no association among the variables under study.* If the result is quite unlikely to have occurred by chance alone, we may say there is a statistically significant difference or connection among the variables under study. Yet, statistics only provide probabilities and never 'prove' anything absolutely. Instead they can only be said to 'support' or to 'fail to support' specific hypotheses about relationships among variables being studied. Still, statistics provide a very useful technology for making decisions, especially about large groups of people.

Inferential statistics are available in many named types. Researchers select specific inferential statistics based on (a) the kind of research question being asked (about difference or association/correlation), (b) the level of measure of each variable of interest, (c) the nature of the sample (independently selected or paired/correlated selection), (d) whether the sample distribution is parametric or non-parametric, and (e) the number of variables under study. This makes it imperative to think out carefully which inferential statistic best meets your decision-making needs.

Inferential statistics come in two main types: *tests of difference* and *tests of association. Tests of difference* help us decide if two or more groups differ on one or more outcome measures. Note there must be both an independent, or grouping variable to establish the groups under comparison *and* another dependent, or outcome, variable that reveals the extent of differences across the groups. That is, do women and men differ on average annual income? The groups are the values of gender (usually female and male). The dependent variable that shows difference is income. For example, the values of income establish whether the groups differ through the application of statistical tests.

In *tests of association* researchers take another approach. The goal here is to see whether two variables are related, and if so, how strongly. That is, if one variable increases one value, will the other variable's value also increase, or might it decrease instead? To determine whether two or more variables are associated, treatment and control groups are not needed, only values on both variables for all participants. Say a researcher measures the number of hours studied before a test and also the grades received on the test. If there is an association between the variables 'hours studied' and 'grades,' people who studied for more hours studied will likely score higher than people who studied fewer hours.

Tests of association are often reversible, meaning there is no clear independent variable and no clear dependent variable. For example, the association between height and weight can be viewed from either direction. This is most common with bivariate (two variable) questions. However, with several variables under study in tests of association, we tend to think of independent variables as those that precede the dependent variable in time. For example, SAT scores precede college grades (even though they do not have much direct impact on them). Thus, we might label SAT scores the independent variable and grades the dependent variable—though the terminology gets awkward at times.

It is also very important to keep in mind that even a statistically significant association does not necessarily indicate that one variable *causes* the other to change. Association or correlation does not imply cause and effect.

Multivariate statistics, based on inferential statistics, are also used to *predict group membership* and to *examine the structure of a theory* using quantitative data. *Predicting group membership* requires a large sample and interval level data on several variables. We might want to study whether certain teens fall into 'high risk' or 'low risk' groups based on information about drug use, sexual activity, and basic mental health problems. Statistical techniques such as discriminant analysis help us predict which group one would fall into based on our data.

Finally, techniques such as factor analysis and principal component analysis use interval level data on several variables and a large sample to *explore the structure of theory and measures.* Say we wanted to create a test for depression, knowing it has several component parts such as mood problems, sleep problems, and psychomotor problems. We might collect data from people who have depression and see whether these 'parts' actually are elements of a general depression or if they differ enough to help identify different forms of depression. These different forms of depression might include a predominantly sleep disturbance type which does not have much apparent mood change to it. Factor analysis takes data on each of the component parts of a theory and examines which elements (factors) maximally differ one from the other. This allows factors with similarities and distinct differences to be identified.

Choosing a Statistical Test

So, what statistical tests can researchers use and how do they select them? First, examine the nature of the research question we are asking: is it descriptive, or a question of difference or of association, or one of group membership or of theoretical structure? This is the first choice point. Next, look at the number of variables under study. Third, look at the level of measure of each variable. It may also be important to distinguish the independent and dependent variables. Fourth, review the nature of the sample. Was there independent selection versus paired or correlated selection? Fifth, for interval or ratio level, scaled, data, determine the nature of the data distribution. Is it a normal distribution or not? If not, can it be mathematically transformed into a near normal distribution? From this review, researchers select a statistic that fits the mix of variables under study.

There are many charts to help researchers and statisticians pick the correct statistical test. Table 7.1 is adapted from Leeper's (undated) "Choosing the Correct Statistic" and is provided to help clinical social workers review the requirements for selecting among several widely used statistical tests (see Table 7.1). Note that appropriate use of these tests is constrained by several factors, including the level of measure of each variable, the number of variables under study, and the nature of the distribution of the collected data.

The Misuse and Misinterpretation of Statistics in Published Reports

It should be clear by now that the correct use of statistics is a complicated process. There is a small but important literature on the misuse of statistical tests in social work and in allied mental health fields. Cowger (1984) initially described the misuse of statistical tests in the social work literature. Huxley (1986) profiled errors in the use of statistics in the *British Journal of Social Work*, Volumes 1 through 14, finding over half of the articles using statistics contained errors. Dar et al. (1994) found several repeated misuses of statistical tests in their review of the psychology literature between 1968 and 1988. These include inappropriate use of null hypothesis tests and p values, neglect of effect sizes, and inflation of Type I error rates through multiple comparisons. Cowger (1984) and Huxley (1986) reported similar concerns in the social work literature. Thompson (2001) provides an extensive list of articles pointing to concerns with the use of tests of significance in several fields. We point out these concerns to make clear to clinical social workers that statistics should not be taken simply at face value. Researchers, like all human beings, sometimes make mistakes. Critical thinking and careful attention is always required in professional endeavors.

Reporting Statistics

Statistical tests should always be reported in detail. This begins with providing enough information to allow the reader to fully determine the specific hypothesis under study. Since statistical tests actually examine the null hypothesis of no difference between groups or no association between variables, the reader should also be able to determine the null hypothesis under study. Null hypotheses are

Table 7.1 Choosing a statistical test: Number of independent and dependent variables, required levels of measure and required types of data distribution

Number of dependent variables	Nature of independent variable(s)	Nature of dependent variable(s); and data distribution	Appropriate statistical test(s)
One	0 IVs (One population)	Interval; normal	One-sample t test
	0 IVs (One population)	Ordinal or interval; any distribution	One-sample median
	0 IVs (One population)	Nominal (only two categories); any distribution	Binomial test
	0 IVs (One population)	Nominal; any distribution	Chi-square goodness-of-fit
	One IV with two levels (independent groups)	Interval; normal	Two independent sample t test
	One IV with two levels (independent groups)	Ordinal or interval; any distribution	Wilcoxon-Mann or Whitney test
	One IV with two levels (independent groups)	Nominal; any distribution	Chi-square test
	One IV with two levels (independent groups)	Nominal; any distribution	Fisher's exact test
	One IV with two or more levels (independent groups)	Interval; normal	One-way ANOVA
	One IV with two or more levels (independent groups)	Ordinal or interval; any distribution	Kruskal-Wallis
	One IV with two or more levels (independent groups)	Nominal; any distribution	Chi-square test
	One IV with two levels (dependent/matched groups)	Interval and normal	Paired t test
	One IV with two levels (dependent/matched groups)	Ordinal or interval	Wilcoxon signed ranks test
	One IV with two levels (dependent/matched groups)	Nominal; any distribution	McNemar test
	One IV with two or more levels (dependent/matched groups)	Interval and normal	One-way repeated measures ANOVA
	One IV with two or more levels (dependent/matched groups)	Ordinal or interval	Friedman test
	One IV with two or more levels (dependent/matched groups)	Nominal; any distribution	Repeated measures logistic regression

Table 7.1 (continued)

Number of dependent variables	Nature of independent variable(s)	Nature of dependent variable(s); and data distribution	Appropriate statistical test(s)
	Two or more IVs (independent groups)	Interval and normal	Factorial ANOVA
	Two or more IVs (independent groups)	Ordinal or interval	(None)
	Two or more IVs (independent groups)	Nominal; any distribution	Factorial logistic regression
	One interval IV	Interval; normal	Correlation
	One interval IV	Interval; normal	Simple linear regression
	One interval IV	Ordinal or interval; any distribution	Non-parametric correlation r_S
	One interval IV	Nominal; any distribution	Simple logistic regression
One	One or more interval IVs and/or one or more nominal IVs	Interval and normal	Multiple regression
	One or more interval IVs and/or one or more nominal IVs	Interval and normal	Analysis of covariance
	One or more interval IVs and/or one or more nominal IVs	Nominal; any distribution	Multiple logistic regression
	One or more interval IVs and/or one or more nominal IVs	Nominal; any distribution	Discriminant analysis
Two or more	One IV with two or more levels (independent groups)	Interval and normal	One-way MANOVA
Two or more	Two or more	Interval and normal	Multivariate multiple linear regression
Two sets of Two or more	0	Interval and normal	Canonical correlation
Two or more	0	Interval and normal	Factor analysis

Adapted from "Choosing the Correct Statistic" by James Leeper of the University of Alabama College of Community and Health Sciences. Retrieved from http://bama.ua.edu/~jleeper/627/choosestat.html

almost never stated in published reports, but they can be inferred from statements of the research hypothesis. This may take some effort in unpacking a complex table, but should be made a bit easier by descriptions in the text as well. Note that it is almost always the case that the null hypothesis is obviously incorrect; the issue is *how unlikely* a result is to occur by chance alone. Second, after stating the hypotheses, the levels of measure for all variables should be stated if not obvious. Readers should not expect to have the level of measure for gender specified, but it should be stated for unusual tests or measures. Third, the nature of the obtained data distribution should be clearly stated. A normal distribution is required for many statistical tests. If a normal distribution is not obtained, or generated by transformation, only nonparametric statistics may be used. Fourth, the criterion level to be used to determine whether results are statistically significant should be selected *before* data are collected, analyzed, and reported (Dar et al. 994). This criterion level should be clearly stated in research reports, but is often just a footnote in a table, and is often mainly represented by an asterisk. This is an acceptable, if perhaps confusing, space-saving convention in publications. Readers should expect that a consistent criterion level is used throughout a study unless changes in the criterion level are explained in detail. It is inappropriate for researchers to change criterion levels without providing a rationale for such changes.

By American Psychological Association (2009) standards, a particular format for reporting the results of statistics is widely used. These conventions apply to both tables and text-based reports. First, the names of the variables under analysis should be clearly stated or evident in the table. Second, the name or symbol for the statistic is stated. Publishers assume that journal readers will understand the names and abbreviations for most common statistical tests. Any unusual statistical test should be explained in some detail and a citation for more information should also be provided in the report. Third, the numerical value of the statistic is reported. Fourth, the sample size or degrees of freedom for the statistic is reported. Finally, the probability of the result is reported. It is good practice to state exact probabilities for all statistics, rather than to simply note that some are "not statistically significant." For example, the results of an analysis of variance or F test used to compare to groups might be reported as: "A statistically significant difference on level of general anxiety was found between the treated and control groups, $F = 5.681$ (1, 85), $p = 0.001$." Here the value of the F statistic ($F = 5.681$) is clear, as are the degrees of freedom (1 and 85), and the probability value. Since probability levels vary with both the value of the statistic and the degrees of freedom (or sample size), both are reported to allow readers to verify that the probability level is correct for this information.

The probability level or p value for each statistic is used to determine whether the null hypothesis is to be accepted or rejected. If the p value is less than (smaller than) the criterion level in use for the study (i.e., $p = 0.003$ compared to a criterion level of $p < 0.05$), the null hypothesis is rejected. Researchers may then state that a statistically significant difference exists. Readers are often confused that reports do not directly address the null hypotheses but instead simply move on to what it implies about the research hypothesis. This too is a convention used to save space based on the assumption that professional readers should have a basic understanding of statistics.

Bear in mind that statistical tests are influenced by sample size. As noted above in regard to statistical power, small samples may not be able to reveal significant differences between groups. On the other hand, large samples may yield significant associations even when the strength of the association is small. Readers should not confuse statistical significance with substantive or clinical significance.

To assess the magnitude of changes, effect size statistics are often reported along with tests of statistical significance. Effect size statistics complement tests of significance by more directly summarizing the magnitude of differences between groups in experimental research (Dar et al. 1994). Effect size statistics will be examined in the next chapter.

Finally, where group differences are reported, as is common in outcome research, a confidence interval should be presented along group means and probabilities. Most statistical results are presented as point estimates that appear quite exact. *Confidence intervals* [CI] estimate the chance that the same study, repeated with another sample taken from the same population, will yield the same results. Usually the confidence interval is established at a 95% chance that replicating the same study on a different sample will yield the same results. If the CI is narrow, the study results are more likely to be consistent when replicated. If the CI is wide, the study results are less likely to be consistent when replicated. CI ranges help the reader assess the confidence that should be placed in study results when generalizing from a single sample to the larger population. However, a confidence interval does *not* predict that the unknown, true, value of the population parameter has a defined probability of being within the confidence interval.

Chapter Summary

This chapter has examined several issues of research methodology that join with research designs to influence the validity of clinical research. Research, like clinical practice, is a complex process involving many decisions. While use of an RCT research design allows for claims of cause and effect relationships, such claims are only valid and useful if they are predicated on many other interconnected choices. The other choices include the quality and comprehensiveness of the sample; the type, validity, and sensitivity of outcome measures; the quality of the definition the treatment under study; and the careful use and reporting of the correct statistical tests.

To aid practitioners, many individual research reports may be aggregated or synthesized to provide a summary of available research on a specific topic. The research designs used in individual studies may become a criterion for the inclusion or exclusion of studies from such aggregate reviews. Indeed, many summaries of several research studies include only studies using experimental or RCT designs.

Two useful resources for clinical social workers in the EBP process are meta-analysis and its elaboration into the systematic review of research studies. Examining systematic reviews that combine the results of many individual research reports will be the focus of the next chapter.

Chapter 8
Meta-Analysis and Systematic Reviews: Aggregating Research Results

Step 3 of the evidence-based practice (EBP) decision-making process is to critically evaluate the relevant research on your topic. In the previous two chapters, we have examined the role of research design and other methodological issues in evaluating individual practice research reports. These chapters explored how researchers design and report individual research studies in a rigorous manner. Yet in many circumstances, multiple research studies are available on a specific practice topic. In this chapter, we will explore how researchers undertake studies that aggregate the results of several separate studies on a single topic.

Clinical social workers who have located research for use in EBP will often find compilations of several research studies on their topic of interest. Researchers call such compilations "meta-analyses" or "systematic reviews" (Littell et al. 2008). Both can be very useful to the clinician seeking to evaluate research for use in practice. Both methods help the clinician appraise and compare the results of multiple studies on the focal topic. It is important to understand how meta-analysis and systemic reviews are similar and different. It is also important to understand their strengths and limitations for evidence-based medicine (EBM) and for EBP.

Meta-Analyses as a Method of Research Synthesis

Researchers first developed the method of meta-analysis, which introduced several important concepts and methods for aggregating research results. These steps may seem quite familiar to clinical social workers and others learning EBP. Meta-analysis begins with (1) clearly formulating and stating the focal question, followed by (2) a thorough and reproducible search of the literature. Next, researchers (3) evaluate the relevant literature using specifically stated quality criteria, leading to identification of the best research reports for inclusion in the aggregate analysis. Finally, studies are (4) compared statistically using specified procedures that vary

J. W. Drisko and M. D. Grady, *Evidence-Based Practice in Clinical Social Work*,
Essential Clinical Social Work Series, DOI: 10.1007/978-1-4614-3470-2_8,
© Springer Science+Business Media New York 2012

somewhat to accommodate different kinds of data. The process, in its outline, is parallel to the initial steps of the EBM/EBP practice decision-making process. The purpose of meta-analysis, however, is to aggregate study results and provide a general, summary, conclusion.

Pratt et al. (1940) completed one of the earliest meta-analyses on the topic of extrasensory perception (ESP). They located and reviewed over 50 studies on ESP using similar methodologies. A full 61% of the studies endorsed ESP. Pratt and colleagues noted, however, that published reports with positive results had much more influence than many more unpublished studies with negative results. This is important because, they believed, the unpublished studies might have been refused publication due to their negative results. In today's EBM/EBP context, early meta-analyses demonstrated how important it is to search thoroughly the relevant published and unpublished literature, and to have a solid method for aggregating results.

In the 1970s and 1980s researchers developed more sophisticated models of meta-analysis. Many of these pioneers addressed mental health topics. Smith et al. (1980) completed a meta-analysis entitled "The Benefits of Psychotherapy" that found similar, positive, effects for several therapies for adults with depression or anxiety drawing on different theoretical premises and using different measures. A key innovation from Glass in this same article was a statistical method for aggregating studies that used different tests as outcome measures. This statistical technique, called meta-analysis, is in wide use today in EBM/EBP.

Meta-Analysis as a Statistical Technique

It may be confusing that meta-analysis refers to both a research process with many steps as well as to a statistical technique. Meta-analysis set the stage for still more detailed systematic reviews of research. However, they also had some important limitations. Today's more rigorous systematic reviews have set new quality standards for aggregating individual research reports. Yet current articles may be entitled "A meta-analysis of..." referring to either a systematic compilation of studies on a specific topic or to the use of meta-analytic statistical methods. Careful reading and critical thinking is required since authors may use the same terms quite differently.

Over time, wide variation in the quality of studies included in, or excluded from, published meta-analyses proved a serious problem. Researchers might use very different standards to appraise research quality and very different methods to report how they had searched the literature. Issues of undisclosed biases, methodological flaws, and lack of reproducible results raised questions about the quality of many meta-analyses. Further, the methods used to locate studies were often described poorly or inadequately. These problems required the development of new standards that would make compilations of research results fully reproducible by other researchers. Researchers sought more complete and transparent research results.

In EBM, the Cochrane Collaboration began in 1993. This international organization works to develop and promote standards for reviewing and synthesizing medical research results. Their standards added many details to the meta-analysis process, but continued to use meta-analysis as a specific statistical technique.

The current, more refined, approach to research synthesis is called the systematic review. The Cochrane Handbook for Systematic Reviews of Interventions (Higgins and Green 2011; 1.2.2) defines a systematic review as an

> attempt to collate all empirical evidence that fits pre-specified eligibility criteria in order to answer a specific research question. It uses explicit, systematic methods that are selected with a view to minimizing bias, thus providing more reliable findings from which conclusions can be drawn and decisions made.

A systematic review should have clearly stated objectives and eligibility/inclusion criteria for studies defined *before* the researchers begin the review. The methodology of the systematic reviews should be reproducible; including full details about the literature search strategy that produced the set of individual studies for inclusion. Researchers should document the validity of included studies and make extensive efforts to limit bias. The final presentation of the systematic review results should also be structured to provide details of the included studies (1.2.2).

The *Cochrane Handbook* further points out that many (but not all) systematic reviews contain meta-analyses. Meta-analysis here refers to only the statistical technique for aggregating the results of separate studies. "Meta-analyses can provide more precise estimates of the effects of health care than those derived from the individual studies included within a review… [by identifying] the consistency of evidence across studies, and the exploration of differences across studies" (1.2.2).

In summary, meta-analysis introduced an approach to aggregating the results of research studies that was further refined and elaborated with the systematic review. Yet meta-analysis, as a statistical technique, is still widely used as a component of a systematic review. Reports of systematic reviews can be a valuable resource for clinical social workers doing EBP. We will now explore the systematic review in detail.

Systematic Reviews

A systematic review is an aggregate summary of almost all research on a single topic and based on clear and transparent methods. Systematic reviews may focus on either quantitative or qualitative research studies (Sandelowski and Barroso 2007). At best, a systematic review is a special form of research synthesis, guided by a thorough literature review and an extensive set of rules all leading to both plain language and highly technical reports. These rules are intended to insure transparency of methods so that the review could be fully repeated, or replicated, by others. The rules establish procedures to locate, evaluate, and integrate the research results. Both the focus of the systematic review and its procedures must be defined before the review is begun. These practices are all steps to minimize bias and build transparency in the review.

The Cochrane Collaboration's *Handbook for Systematic Reviews of Interventions* (Higgins and Green 2011) is the key resource for planning and implementing quantitative systematic reviews. The Campbell Collaboration also uses these standards as the two organizations work cooperatively. The *Handbook* is a book-length and very detailed document. It is updated from time to time to include new methods and improve the transparency of review procedures. The *Handbook* is available for free review online at http://www.cochrane-handbook.org/ and also for purchase as a hardcover book.

Methods for systematic reviews of qualitative studies are less standardized. Noblit and Hare (1988) developed meta-ethnography, which pioneered the core methods of qualitative systematic reviews. More recent methods with a specific clinical focus are offered by Sandelowski and Barosso (2007) and Dixon Woods and colleagues (2006a, b). While qualitative systematic reviews have considerable merit, the focus of the remainder of this chapter will be on quantitative systematic reviews.

It is useful to understand what goes into a systematic review, even if most clinicians may not often review the full, technical versions of such reviews. More often, clinicians will use the much shorter plain language summary that provides the key information in a condensed form. The format of the plain language summaries follows that used for full systematic reviews.

We remind readers that systematic reviews are not mentioned in the practice decision-making process of EBM/EBP. Systematic reviews are a process that groups of professionals have developed to summarize research results with rigor and consistency. Professional expertise and judgment must be used to decide whether a systematic review offers more relevant and clinically useful information than do other sources of the best available evidence for practice decision making.

Specifying the Systematic Review Topic

To start a systematic review, the topic it will cover must be clearly stated (Cochrane Handbook 2011). This step is a guide to the researchers, but also keeps the review focused. It also sets boundaries on what topics, and what kinds of research, will be studied from the outset. Its purpose is to keep systematic reviews focused and to limit alterations to the review to include material of interest to the authors but not quite on topic, or not using high quality methods.

Applications to register systematic reviews at both the Cochrane Collaboration and the Campbell Collaboration require a clear statement of the review focus. Scholars and researchers must apply to register a proposed systematic review before it is started. A team of peer reviewers evaluates each application. Peer reviewers are a 'jury' of equally knowledgeable and skilled researchers. The peer reviewers look for a clear focus and a detailed research plan consistent with the *Handbook* standards. Only proposals that meet the quality standards are accepted and registered. Clinicians may find some reviews in their preliminary stages listed online as "registered" or "in progress." Such reviews do not (yet) include any results. This can be frustrating as it does not help in practice decision making, but it shows such knowledge may be available in the near future. It also tells other researchers that the topic is taken.

Cochrane and Campbell systematic reviews are team efforts (Littell et al. 2008). Several people, ideally including at least one consumer, constitute the review team (Cochrane Handbook 2011; Sect. 2.3.4.1). Not only researchers, but also policy makers and clinicians may be included. This range of review team members should bring in some diversity of viewpoints about the purposes of the review and serve as some check on its final report. It also allows for more than a single researcher to assess each piece of research, again as an effort to limit bias.

Researchers undertaking a systematic review must also declare their "interests and commercial sponsorship" to set forth any potential conflicts of interest. Sponsorship of Cochrane reviews by any commercial interest in prohibited. Noncommercial sponsors of Cochrane systematic reviews, such as foundations offering research funding, must agree to have no influence over its process and final report content (Cochrane Handbook 2011; 2.6).

Locating Research Studies for a Systematic Review

Once a topic is selected, the literature is next reviewed extensively. What literature is included in the review must be fully specified. It is common to see a listing of several electronic databases used as the starting point in quality systematic reviews. Each electronic database (such as PubMed, PsychINFO, or Social Work Abstracts) will include many journals and articles. The point of detailing how the literature search was done in great detail is to make it replicable by other researchers. This means that other people could repeat the review process fully, and should come up with the same results. Steps to insure quality and transparency are included in each part of the systematic review process.

Not only the databases that are searched for the study are detailed; the search strategies used to locate relevant studies within each database are also reported. These often include a combination of search terms or keywords that represent variations on the topic (i.e., depression, depressive, major depressive episode) but also types of research designs (i.e., experiments, RCTs, outcome studies). Further, the dates of the studies included in the review and the range of countries or languages searched are often stated. Again, the purpose of specifying the search strategy is to make the process both transparent to readers and replicable by other researchers.

Finally, systematic reviews include active efforts to locate unpublished research. There is a bias in journal publications that favors studies with positive results (Dickersin 1990; Hopewell 2009; McGauran et al. 2010; Sridharan and Greenland 2009). "Positive results" are those that show a significant difference between a treatment and a control group, or that one treatment is better than another. This means that research studies that do not show significant differences often go unpublished. Researchers call this the "file draw problem" (Scargle 2000). Research that is completed but unpublished may simply end up in a researcher's file draw, unknown to others. This can create a bias in favor of making it seem that a treatment is better than it would appear with the nonsignificant results also examined. Further, there have been cases where businesses and other groups that do not want negative results published have actively undermined the publication of negative results. One such case involves the active intervention of drug companies to limit publication of results that make their products look bad—even if they are not effective. Carey (2008) reports that makers of antidepressant drugs did not publish up to one-third of their research results, but only those that were unflattering. Carey also notes that a similar incident had occurred previously in 2004.

Authors of systematic reviews seek out unpublished reports by contacting the author of published studies to ask whether they have unpublished research on the topic. They also ask the published authors whether they know of other researchers who might have unpublished studies. These efforts also uncover works in progress that have not been formally published, such as evaluations funded by state agencies. Occasionally the researcher is near completion of a study in progress. Such as yet unpublished results may be included in the systematic review as well, whether positive or negative. Efforts to locate unpublished results must also be specified in the systematic review methods.

The entire process of the literature search can be presented in summary form using a Quorom Flow Chart (see Fig. 8.1). In the 1990s, a group of physicians called the Quorom Group began to establish standards for reporting meta-analyses (Moher et al. 1999). Quorom is an acronym for the "Quality of Reporting of Meta-analyses." A Quorom flowchart summaries the number of relevant items found at each stage of a literature search process. It starts with the total number of relevant articles or reports located, and then identifies all the criteria for including or excluding reports in the review process. The flowchart identifies both why materials were included or excluded and how many reports were included or excluded. In the figure, we see that 9,676 reports were located, but 8,538 proved to be off topic. In the end, only 14 reports met all of the study's inclusion criteria and were not duplicates. A Quorom flowchart provides a quick and visually effective way to summarize the search process of a meta-analysis or a systematic review. They are beginning to become common in the social work literature (see, for example, Litschge et al. 2010).

Another approach to reporting systematic reviews is called PRISMA (Moher et al. 2009). This 21 point checklist examines how systematic reviews are reported, seeking further clarity about potential sources of bias. The authors argue for the use of PRISMA standards as an improvement over QUORUM standards.

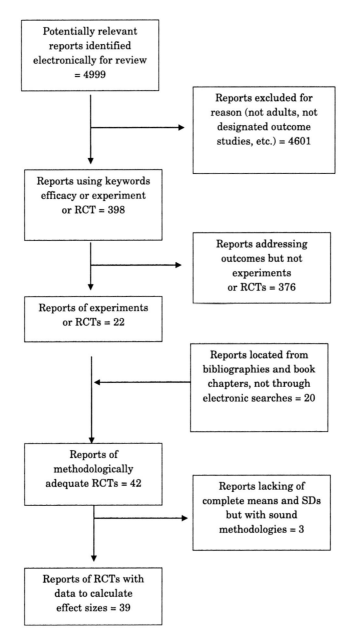

Fig. 8.1 A Quorom flowchart

Evaluating the Methodological Quality of Research Reports in Systematic Reviews

The next activity in a systematic review is once again parallel to the steps of the EBP process. Once research on the review topic is located, its quality must be evaluated. Some systematic reviews only include studies based on experimental or RCT research designs. This is an acceptable choice for inclusion in a quantitative systematic review. It makes the rationale for including or excluding individual studies quite clear. On the other hand, it does not fully conform to the EBM/EBP standard of using the best available research evidence whether there is little or no experimental research on the topic. This may be the case where a topic is not well conceptualized, such as chronic fatigue syndrome or reactive attachment disorder, or is not so common as to be extensively researched. The EBM/EBP practice decision-making process takes into account that not all topics are well studied by multiple RCTs. EBM/EBP process then points clinicians to use thoughtfully the results of research derived from other research designs, following the research design hierarchy.

While Cochrane systematic review standards clearly reflect a privileging of results from RCTs, there is also some ambiguity in the *Handbook*. The *Cochrane Handbook* includes a brief section on including qualitative research results in systematic reviews (Chapter 20). This brief chapter states that qualitative research can address questions beyond those examined by quantitative research and may be helpful in explaining the results of RCTs. Here we find an instance where the hierarchy of research evidence used by both the Cochrane and Campbell Collaborations seems limited, and other forms of research are explicitly acknowledged as valuable. Non-randomized studies "may" be included in Cochrane reviews, but are to be "interpreted with caution" (*Cochrane Handbook*, Chapter 13). At the same time, qualitative studies are devalued as sources of evidence in other sections of the manual. Systematic reviews are social constructions and may have some inconsistencies despite a great deal of work by many people to make them internally consistent. Researchers differ in how they understand and prioritize research designs and methods. Systematic review standards may also apply a hierarchy of evidence that leads to results that are *less* inclusive of useful research knowledge than is called for by the core definitions of EBM and EBP.

The *Cochrane Handbook* emphasizes attention to reducing bias and ensuring clarity of methods in all reviews. This is a very worthy and important goal. Note carefully that much less attention is directed to the initial conceptualization of disorders, to the quality of measures, and to the definition of treatments. Experimental research has great strength in the attribution of cause–effect relationships, but is only meaningful if the disorder of interest is quite well understood and the measures used to assess it are valid, complete, and reliable. Further, the populations included in the experimental research must be very similar to those of interest to clinicians. Attention to social diversity, and to socially structured oppressions, is not emphasized in the *Cochrane Handbook* criteria though it is heavily emphasized in social work.

Criteria for including or excluding studies in a systematic review may also be based on issues such as sample size, the clarity of the description of the treatment, the fidelity, or care shown in insuring the treatment was delivered as described, and the kinds of statistical information provided. The various components of each study must be carefully assessed and coded as warranting inclusion in the systematic review or as warranting exclusion from it.

Coding Study Components and Results

All decisions regarding inclusion and exclusion from Cochrane and Campbell systematic reviews must be made by at least two reviewers. The reviewers work independently but then compare their results for quality control purposes. This ensures discussion where the reviewers are not fully in agreement regarding their views of a study's quality. How these differences were resolved, and the final inclusion/exclusion standards, must be stated in the full systematic review. All later quality appraisal decisions are also made by at least two reviewers.

Summaries of the quality appraisal process may be presented in a Quorom flowchart in reports of systematic reviews. These flowcharts can illustrate succinctly the inclusion and exclusion criteria used in the review, as well as other criteria used in data extraction and assessment of study quality. As noted above, Quorom flowcharts specify the numbers of studies found in the literature search and the numbers included or excluded at each step in the review process. In most cases the number of research studies found on the topic is large and the final set of included studies is very much smaller.

Statistical Meta-Analysis

Meta-analysis refers to a set of statistical techniques employed to combine the quantitative results of prior research. The yield of these statistics is usually a measure of effect size, a weighted average of the magnitude of difference between groups. This statistical usage will be our focus in this book. The other usage of meta-analysis as a method for aggregating research now overlaps with the process of a systematic review. Indeed, meta-analyses were the precursors of today's systematic reviews. Meta-analyses, as publications, are research reports that locate, evaluate and combine statistically the results of prior research. Systematic reviews expanded on the original methods of locating and evaluating research literature created for meta-analysis. Systematic reviews often use the statistical techniques of meta-analysis to combine the results of prior quantitative research. One key difference is that the procedures of Cochrane and Campbell systematic reviews are more fully detailed and better documented than is common in most meta-analysis reports. This increases the clarity and transparency of systematic reviews. Systematic reviews are also examined by methodologically sophisticated peer reviewers, which may not be the case for some published meta-analyses.

The idea of a meta-analysis statistic is to develop a common measure (also called a metric) to allow the combination of statistical results across several studies on a topic. Research results on a given topic often differ and may include discordant results. Meta-analysis provides a technique to combine results despite use of different tests and measures in the individual reports. For example, in a meta-analysis of depression treatments the goal is to combine the results of studies on people who have depression treated by different professionals, using different treatment models, and whose depression was assessed by different measures. This might include people treated for depression with cognitive behavioral, interpersonal, short-term psychodynamic, and multisystemic therapies all combined. The goal is to find out the overall effect of depression treatments and often to determine whether the specific treatments have different results. Suppose it turns out that the available studies use different measures to assess depression levels. Some use the Hamilton Rating Scale for Depression and others use the Beck Depression Inventory. This may appear to be a major 'apples and oranges' problem where the varied treatments and different measures do not seem to allow comparison. Solving this problem is the strength of meta-analysis. Meta-analysis allows the creation of a common measure of change or difference, using the same units despite any differences in the original tests and measures used in each study. Thus it allows for fair comparison of treatment outcomes despite initial differences.

Statistics Used in Meta-Analysis

The most widely used meta-analysis statistic is Cohen's d (Ellis 2008), also called a standardized mean difference (SMD). Cohen's d is a measure of the standard mean difference across two groups. This statistic shows the magnitude of change in an experimental comparison. Researchers calculate it by subtracting the mean score for the control group from the mean score of the treated group and then dividing the result by the pooled standard deviation of both groups. Cohen's d is a measure of the magnitude of the difference between the treatment and control groups, taking into account the variation of scores within both groups.

Cohen's d scores range from 0.0 to about 2.0. Cohen (1988) established rough benchmarks to help interpret these scores in plain language. Cohen's d values between 0.00 and 0.49 are "small" effects. Values from 0.50 to 0.79 are "moderate," and values larger than 0.80 are "large" effects. This means that the magnitude of the difference between two treatments can be called "small" if Cohen's d is 0.48 or lower, and "large" if the Cohen's d value is 0.80 or larger. Lenth (2008) cautions that all effects size statistics should be interpreted in context and with careful attention to operational definitions.

The purpose of Cohen's d is to assess the magnitude of differences between groups. This is not the same as establishing the statistical significance (usually reported with a p = value). However, it is *usually* the case that moderate and strong effect sizes are found where significant differences between groups are found using probability tests. Effect size measures complement probability statistics.

Cohen's d is best when used with large samples. With smaller samples (roughly 20 or fewer participants in each treatment), the Hedges' g statistic is usually a better choice. This is because in a small sample one or two outliers, or extreme scores, can have a large impact on the value of the d statistic. In addition, Hedges' g employs a different calculation of the pooled standard deviation than does Cohen's d. It includes a correction factor when used to make population level estimates. Thus, Hedges' g yields more conservative estimates of the magnitude of group differences for small samples. Some critiques of mental health meta-analyses target the use of Cohen's d with small samples as a methodological concern (Thombs and Jewett 2009). Hedges' g does not make any statement about whether or not the difference found is likely to reflect that in the larger population, as probability statistics do. The Hedges' g statistic is rarely covered in current social work research and statistics texts.

Other measures of effect size include correlations and odds ratios. Correlations are used as measures of effect sizes in observational studies. Correlations statistics can serve as their own measures of effect size, with a range from -1.0 (a perfect negative correlation, through 0.0 (no correlation) to $+1.00$ (a perfect positive correlation). Cohen (1988) states that a correlation of 0.10 may be interpreted as "small," a correlation of 0.25 or larger as "medium," and a correlation of 0.40 or higher as "large."

Researchers use odds ratios (OR) where both measures are binary (such as 'Meets DSM diagnostic criteria' or 'Does not meet DSM diagnostic criteria' and 'Female' or 'Male'). Another statistic, relative risk (RR), also known as the risk ratio, measures the risk of an event relative to an independent variable. Relative risk is a ratio of the probability of the event occurring in a treated or 'exposed' group versus an untreated or 'non-exposed' group (Sistrom and Garvan 2004). The frequency, or count, of how often the event occurs in the treated group is divided by the frequency of the event observed in the untreated group. For example, the number of smokers who develop lung cancer might be compared over a 20-year period to the number of nonsmokers who develop the same illness. A RR ratio value of 1.0 indicates no difference in risk between the two groups. A RR value of less than 1.0 indicates that the outcome event is less likely to occur in the treated group than the control/comparison group. A value of more than 1.0 indicates the outcome event is more likely to occur in the treated group than in the control/comparison group. OR and RR are epidemiological statistics that are rarely covered in social work research and statistics texts. They are, however, quite commonly found in systematic reviews.

Relative risk statistics may be reported along with "Number Needed to Treat" (NNT) statistics. NNT is a measure used in epidemiology to assess the effectiveness of a treatment (Christensen and Kristiansen 2006). It is the number of people who need to be treated to prevent one additional negative outcome. In others words, how many people would need to be treated for one person to benefit more than was observed in the control/comparison group. A NNT value of 1 is ideal since it means everyone who is treated benefits from the treatment while no one benefits in the comparison group. Low NNT values indicate that the treatment is more effective compared to the comparison group. The higher the NNT value, the fewer people benefit compared to the comparison group in the study. McQuay and Moore (1997) note that NNT values of 2 or 3 are rare, but indicate that the treatment is highly effective.

Researchers use many statistics with meta-analyses depending on the nature of the data relevant to the clinical question. A more complete overview of these statistics may be found in Littell et al. (2008). The Children's Mercy Hospital and Clinics (Simon 2008) offers very accessible online information about several statistics used in clinical research at http://www.childrens-mercy.org/stats/.

Meta-analytic statistical analyses are not possible when only one or two studies are found on a topic. This is why meta-analysis may not be appropriate for all systematic reviews. Such a small number of studies does not allow for appropriate use of the meta-analysis statistics. Of course, meta-analysis statistics are not used in qualitative systematic reviews.

Meta-analysis is a very helpful part of a quantitative systematic review. The procedures of the systematic review structures the identification of high quality studies that meet the stated inclusion criteria for the review. A meta-analysis provides a statistical measure of the magnitude of differences between the tested groups. It also provides a general way to articulate the statistical differences in plain language.

Integrating Results and Identifying Limitations and Cautions

Meta-analysis is one very useful statistical method for integrating the results of several studies on a topic. Published Cochrane and Campbell Collaboration systematic reviews generally include meta-analysis statistical results. In addition, most systematic reviews also point out the limitations of the available research and some cautions about its application. For example, a systematic review might note that while two treatments are effective, the outcome for one treatment was measured by rates of rehospitalization and the other was measured by a standardized test of symptoms. Clearly, helping a client stay out of the hospital is a general good, but it may not be the main concern of the client or the client's family. The client may be more directly concerned about reducing symptoms. In such a situation, the systematic review may help the clinician recommend to the client the treatment that demonstrated symptomatic improvement, while noting an alternative treatment was also effective but that it was measured by rates of rehospitalization. Here, the details of the review can be useful in helping the client understand the differences in evidence that may matter to them and to their interests.

Systematic review summaries may also point out the relative limitations of the available research they summarize. For example, review authors may state that samples sizes for all of the included treatments were small. This might suggest that while the treatments were effective, it is not yet unclear whether this will generalize to other clients and settings. Cochrane and Campbell systematic reviews also point out potential biases in the available research. One key area is to identify when the researchers who study a treatment are also the originators of the treatment model under investigation. Considerable research suggests that when the developer of a treatment model tests the effectiveness of their model they may, unconsciously or consciously, introduce attribution biases in favor of their own model. It is helpful for readers to keep in mind what kinds of biases might influence studies done by researchers who might favor one model over another. Economic influences, such as sources of funding, may also shape research results in a nonscientific, biased manner.

An Example of a Cochrane Collaboration Systematic Review

One disorder of considerable interest to clinical social workers is borderline personality disorder (BPD). Clients with BPD may be confusing and can generate a wide range of reactions in clinicians. Some scholars question the validity of the BPD diagnosis, and others note it often co-occurs with childhood abuse and Post-traumatic Stress Disorder (PTSD). It is, however, a defined disorder in the DSM-IV-TR and in the international ICD-10.

Binks et al. (2009) completed a systematic review of psychological treatments for BPD registered with the Cochrane Collaboration.

The plain language abstract of this systematic review is available free online at http://www2.cochrane.org/reviews/en/ab005652.html. A Spanish language version of this abstract is also available. Binks and colleagues report in the plain language summary that:

> People with borderline personality disorder are often anxious, depressed, self-harm, in crisis and are difficult to engage in treatment. In this review of the talking/behavioural therapies for people with borderline personality disorder, we identified seven studies involving 262 people, over five separate comparisons. Dialectical behavior therapy (DBT) included treatment components such as prioritizing a hierarchy of target behaviors, telephone coaching, groups skills training, behavioral skill training, contingency management, cognitive modification, exposure to emotional cues, reflection, empath, and acceptance. DBT seemed to be helpful on a wide range of outcomes, such as admission to hospital or incarceration in prison, but the small size of included studies limit confidence in their results. A second therapy, psychoanalytic orientated day hospital therapy, also seemed to decrease admission and use of prescribed medication and to increase social improvement and social adjustment. Again, this is an experimental treatment with too few data to really allow anyone to feel too confident of the findings. Even if these are trials undertaken by enthusiasts and difficult to apply to everyday care, they do suggest that the problems of people with borderline personality disorder may be amenable to treatment. More well-designed studies are both justifiable and urgently needed (2009: p. 2).

Both DBT and psychoanalytically oriented day hospital treatments "seemed" helpful, but the small samples and "experimental" treatments on which this conclusion is based limit its credibility. It is also noted that persons who were viewed as "enthusiasts" for the treatments they studied, a potential source of positive attribution bias, completed the research. Indeed, both researchers were also the developers of the treatments under investigation.

The longer Abstract (2009: pp. 1–2) of this review states its background and objectives in single sentences. The review's search strategy, selection (inclusion) criteria, and methods of data analysis are also very briefly reported. The search strategy centered on "a systematic search of 26 specialist and general biblio-graphic databases," followed by searches of "relevant reference lists for further trials" to uncover unpublished research. Criteria for inclusion were "all relevant clinical randomised controlled trials involving psychological treatments for people with BPD." Psychological treatments only "included behavioural, cognitive-behavioural, psychodynamic and psychoanalytic" models.

Overall, this systematic review included seven studies involving 262 people, and five separate statistical comparisons. Specific results are reported on a study-by-study basis, including detailed statistics. For example, "comparing (DBT) with treatment as usual, studies found no difference for the outcome of still meeting SCID-II criteria for the diagnosis of BPD by six months ($n = 28$, 1 RCT, RR 0.69 CI 0.35–1.38) or admission to hospital in the previous three months ($n = 28$, 1 RCT, RR 0.77 CI 0.28–2.14)" (2006: pp. 1–2). In other words, there was no difference between DBT and "treatment as usual" in that persons with BPD in both treatments still met SCID-II diagnostic criteria after 6 months of treatment. This conclusion was based on one RCT with 28 participants, with a risk ratio (RR) of 0.69 and a confidence interval (CI) from 0.35 to 1.38. This means more people in the treatment as usual group were more likely *not* to meet diagnostic criteria for BPD at six months, a favorable outcome. However, the result was not statistically significant. There was no difference in hospital admissions as well. This conclusion was based on one RCT with 28 participants, with a risk ratio of 0.77 and a confidence interval from 0.35 to 1.38. This means hospital admissions were somewhat less likely in the treatment as usual group. However, the result was not statistically significant.

In another example, "one study detected statistical difference in favour of people receiving DBT compared with...treatment as usual for average scores of suicidal ideation at 6 months ($n = 20$, MD -15.30 CI -25.46 to -5.14)" (2006: p. 2). While it is not stated here, we can assume the "one study" was an RCT since only RCTs were included in this systematic review. Including 20 participants, a mean difference of -15.30 was found. Note that no effect sizes, nor the exact probability of this difference, were reported in the systematic review abstract, though many other details were included. DBT produced a considerable reduction in symptoms compared to that found in the treatment as usual comparison group.

Binks colleagues (2009) also found that psychoanalytically oriented partial hospitalization yielded better outcomes on hospital readmissions then did "general psychiatric care." Persons with BPD who received this treatment "were less likely to be admitted into inpatient care" when measured 18 months after treatment ended "(n = 44, with a RR of 0.05, CI 0.00–0.77; NNT 3 CI 3–10)." "Depression scores were generally lower" in the partial hospitalization treated group (n = 44, 1 RCT, RR >/=14 on BDI 0.52 CI 0.34–0.80, NNT 3 CI 3–6). "More people in the control group took psychotropic medication by the 30–36 month follow-up... (n = 44, 1 RCT, RR 0.44 CI 0.25–0.80, NNT 3 CI 2–7)" (all quotes from Binks et al. 2009: p. 2). This means people in the psychoanalytically oriented partial hospitalization treatment took less medication at the 30–36-month follow-up, which may also be interpreted as a positive outcome for the treatment. The NNT statistics (number needed to treat) statistics also indicate an effective treatment. NNT values of 2 or 3 indicate an effective treatment, which is reported by Binks and colleagues for the psychoanalytically oriented partial hospital treatment.

Based on these results, as well as the relatively small number of studies, the small samples sizes included in the studies, and the involvement of the originators of the treatments in the outcome studies, the Binks and colleagues (2009: p. 2) state in conclusion that:

> Some of the problems frequently encountered by people with borderline personality disorder may be amenable to talking/behavioural treatments but all therapies remain experimental and the studies are too few and small to inspire full confidence in their results. These findings require replication in larger 'real-world' studies.

This is mildly affirming language that indicates that both DBT and the psychodynamically oriented partial hospitalization program have preliminary research support as effective for some aspects of BPD. It is very cautiously worded, and appears to promote further research as much as it makes a clear statement about which treatments are effective treatments for BPD. Nonetheless, the Binks et al. (2009) systematic review does provide evidence that these two treatments have the best available evidence to support their use in clinical practice.

Evaluating Systematic Reviews

We have noted that systematic reviews and meta-analysis reports are terms that may be applied to publications of varying methods and overall quality. Working groups have made efforts to establish ways to assess the methodological quality of systematic reviews. One such effort is AMSTAR, developed by an international group of epidemiologists and public health specialists (Shea et al. 2007). AMSTAR is an acronym for Assessment of Multiple SysTematic Reviews. AMSTAR is an 11 item rating scale for assessing systemic reviews, including meta-analytic content. The full checklist is available free online at www.biomedcentral.com/content/supplementary/1471-2288-7-10-s1.doc. It summarizes several quality issues necessary for producing a strong systematic review. These include having an a priori review design (stating the review question at the start) and clear study selection criteria. Other criteria address standards for "scientific quality" assessment of each included study and for appraising the quality of meta-analyses used to synthesize multiple studies. Finally, the use of a range of efforts to identify and reduce bias in the systematic review are assessed. Cochrane and Campbell systematic reviews generally conform to the AMSTAR criteria very well.

The AMSTAR checklist provides a useful way for clinicians to frame their assessments of systematic reviews. Its main limitation is that the 11 items are quite general. For example, specific elements of scientific quality assessment are not provided, but must be determined by the user. This leaves many technical issues to the knowledge and skills of the user. On the other hand, the AMSTAR checklist provides a very helpful framework for assessing the overall quality of a systemic review.

A final caution about systematic reviews is in order. Shojania et al. (2007) did a survival analysis of 100 systematic reviews in medicine. They found that significant changes in research results on at least one key outcome indicator were very frequent. Specifically, within 1 year, 15% of systematic reviews warranted revision. Within 2 years, 23% of systematic reviews studies warranted revision. By 5 ½ years, half of the systematic reviews warranted revision. Note carefully that these results were not specific to mental health and psychiatry where research is less prolific. Still, careful review of research findings must include consideration that systematic reviews more than a year old may warrant revision based on newer studies.

Chapter Summary

This chapter has reviewed systematic reviews as used in clinical research and in EBM/EBP. It has also introduced the Cochrane and Campbell Collaboration systematic review process and requirements. One part of this process is the statistical technique known as meta-analysis. Meta-analysis statistics provide a way to combine the quantitative results of several different research studies. Clinical social workers are reminded, however, that not all reports claiming to be systematic reviews meet the strict standards of the *Cochrane Handbook*. Similarly, many publications called meta-analyses vary in scope and quality.

The reports of Cochrane and Campbell systematic reviews include both a plain language summary of key results and a much longer technical report giving much more detail about each study and the review process. In the United States, only the abstracts of Cochrane Collaboration systematic reviews are available free online. The full technical reports, however, are only available on a subscription basis. (This is due to United States funding policies; specifically, lack of United States funding for the Cochrane Collaboration). In most other countries, the full versions of the Cochrane systematic reviews are available free. Still, the abstracts of systematic reviews include considerable detail. There are both print and online resources that can help clinicians interpret these details as needed.

While the EBM/EBP practice decision-making model makes no mention of systematic reviews or meta-analyses, the standards of Cochrane and Campbell reviews make them a key resource for clinicians. Still, clinical social workers must apply their professional expertise and critical skills in determining just what constitutes the best available research evidence for their unique practice needs.

Appraising the quality of research reports and systematic reviews requires skills quite different from the core skills of clinical practice or the skills used in locating practice research. It can be a complex, multi-faceted process. Yet, bringing the results of high quality research into practice decision making should improve outcomes and reduce harm. It is an important part of EBM and EBP.

Step 4 in the EBP practice decision-making process is to discuss the best available research with the client. Step 4 brings the best available evidence back to the client to better inform the client's active participation in treatment planning. This shared process is the focus of the next chapter.

Chapter 9
Shared Decision-Making with the Client

Step 4 of the evidence-based practice (EBP) practice decision-making model centers on developing a shared, collaborative, treatment plan with the client. The goal is to determine how the most likely effective options fit with the client's goals, values, and preferences. This requires the clinical social worker to summarize the results of the literature search, and to summarize it in language that the client can understand. It also requires the client's active participation in the collaborative development of a treatment plan. This step of the EBP process fits well with social work's professional values. However, it may pose some challenges in practice.

In 2001, Gambrill wrote an article titled "Social work: An authority-based profession." In this article, she argues that in order for social workers to uphold the values of the profession, they must be transparent in their work with clients and include the "clients in making decisions that affect their lives" (p. 166). Step 4 of the EBP practice decision-making process addresses the concerns raised by Gambrill (2001). It is a crucial step in diminishing the potentially authoritarian stance clinicians may take with clients. It is also a step that distinguishes EBP from traditional medical models, and hierarchical 'expert' approaches.

In Step 4 of the EBP practice decision-making process, the clinician discusses the research results with the client to determine how the research supported treatment options fit with the client's values, preferences, and goals. We believe that clinicians from many professionals often overlook or minimize this step in EBP. It may be interpreted as involving a *presentation to the client*, rather than *a collaborative dialog with the client*. We hope that after reading this chapter, readers will have a stronger appreciation for importance of having a conversation with the client before making a shared decision regarding a treatment approach.

J. W. Drisko and M. D. Grady, *Evidence-Based Practice in Clinical Social Work*, 155
Essential Clinical Social Work Series, DOI: 10.1007/978-1-4614-3470-2_9,
© Springer Science+Business Media New York 2012

Reasons to Include the Client in the Decision-Making Process

Consistency with the Code of Ethics

There are many reasons to include the client in the decision-making process in EBP. One of the reasons is that social work's *Code of Ethics* (National Association of Social Workers [NASW] 2008) states:

> Social workers should use clear and understandable language to inform clients of the purpose of the services, risks related to the services, limits to services because of the requirements of a third- party payer, relevant costs, reasonable alternatives, clients' right to refuse or withdraw consent, and the time frame covered by the consent. Social workers should provide clients with an opportunity to ask questions. (1.03)

While individuals can interpret this part of the *Code* in multiple ways, informed consent does not limit the worker to simply stating or explaining a proposed treatment plan. We view this ethical standard as calling for a shared, interactive dialog with the client. Gambrill (2001, p. 169) states that social workers are "in violation of our code of ethics" if they use an authoritarian approach in which the clinician informs the client about a treatment approach that is 'best' without including the client in the decision-making process. A true dialog with the client about treatment options should continue until a unified decision has been made regarding an intervention plan that is agreeable to both the clinician and the client.

The Importance of a Shared Approach

In addition to adhering to the *Code of Ethics*, psychotherapy research has demonstrated that "if a client is not attuned to the approach being offered and shows resistance to the treatment, persistently and insistently offering the same approach is not therapeutically helpful and probably is harmful" (Wampold 2010, p. 54). Therefore, before the intervention process can begin, it is essential that the client and the clinician be in agreement about the approach that will be used. Without agreement at the start of the intervention, the intervention is less likely to be effective (Wampold 2010).

Including the Client Strengthens the Alliance

Another reason to include the client in the practice decision-making process is because such action will help to foster a collaborative relationship. Collaborative relationships have been shown to be a critical component in the formation of a strong therapeutic relationship (Horvath and Bedi 2002). A strong therapeutic relationship or therapeutic alliance has been consistently shown to be one of the most critical factors in producing positive outcomes in treatment (Horvath and Bedi 2002; Horvath and Symonds 1991; Hubble et al. 2010; Norcross 2010; Orlinsky et al. 2004; Wampold 2010). Given the depth of research on the importance of the therapeutic alliance, it is imperative that the clinician work to strengthen it throughout the course of treatment. The therapeutic relationship may be especially important at the beginning of the treatment process. A collaborative relationship that actively includes the client in the decision-making process can strengthen the therapeutic relationship. It may also increase the likelihood of a positive outcome in treatment.

The Shared Decision-Making Model

Along with the rise of evidence-based practice, another social movement, patient centered health care has developed. The United States Agency for Health Care Research and Quality (2002, p. 1) states that "health care has been evolving from a disease centered model to a patient centered model." They state that in the disease-centered model physicians and professionals made decisions based on clinical experience and data from tests. In the patient-centered model, "patients become active participants in their own care and receive services designed to focus on their individual needs and preferences, in addition to advice and counsel from health professionals" (p. 1). Such a patient-centered model fits well with the current model of evidence-based practice that combines clinical presentation with client views and preferences, research evidence, and professional expertise (Haynes et al. 2002a, b). As described above, it also fits well with social work values and ethics (NASW 2005a, b; 2008). The patient-centered model of health care directly acknowledges the active role of the whole person in health services. Patients bring information, expectations, and preferences. They have their own goals. They also have their own approaches to healthcare needs and services.

Differences in Client Approaches to Healthcare Decision Making

Groopman and Hartzband (2011a, b) describe some differences in the way clients approach healthcare services. They state there are those maximalists "who want to be very proactive, ahead of the curve, to do everything possible to prevent or treat an illness. And then on the other hand you have minimalists, and to them less is more" (2011b, para 5 and 6). Groopman and Hartzband (2011b, para 9) add there are also "people who are more oriented towards natural approaches... And then there are people who are very oriented towards technology, and they believe that the answers are in procedures, technology, scientific, laboratory-based products." Finally, there are believers and doubters. To Groopman and Hartzband (2011b, para 11)

> believers are convinced that there's a good solution for their problem, and they just want to go for it. Sometimes they are believers in technology, sometimes believers in more natural remedies, but they believe. And then the doubters are the people who are always skeptical, worrying about side effects, worried about risks, and that maybe the treatment will be worse than the disease.

Given the variation in approaches to client decision making, healthcare providers must actively explore client views and goals for services. The objectives of Step 4 of EBP and of shared decision making are the same.

Towle and Godolphin (1999, p. 766) introduced the concept of "informed, shared decision making" in health care. They note that contemporary ethical and legal requirements obligate a high standard of disclosure about informed consent. They argue that this amounts to a principle of informed choice for people seeking health care. Towle and Godolphin also point out that there is evidence that treatment adherence and outcomes both improve when clients are more involved in decision making. They use the term informed shared decision making to describe

> decisions that are shared by doctor and patient and informed by best evidence, not only about risks and benefits but also patient specific characteristics and values. It occurs in a partnership that rests on explicitly acknowledged rights and duties and an expectation of benefit to both. (p. 766)

Towle and Godolphin argue that informed shared decision making implies responsibilities for both parties. That is, both client and professional have something to gain and to contribute in their interaction. Finding common ground—together—is a key goal.

Towle and Godolphin (1999) also note that the informed, shared decision-making process requires explicit attention to, and discussion about, the client-professional relationship. This expectation fits well with Step 4 of the EBP practice decision-making model.

For clients, challenges include identifying their preferred form of client-professional relationship, limitations in their ability to articulate key concerns and goals in a clear and systematic manner, and lack of health information or access to such information (Towle and Godolphin 1999). We would add that client anxiety about health concerns and any history of unhelpful interaction with authority figures might also shape a client's comfort and ability to share health-related information. This may be a particular concern for people with major mental illnesses, substance use, history of trauma, or history of discrimination. Lack of trust, shame, and anxiety can undermine the most knowledgeable client's ability to share information, wishes, and goals.

Furthermore, Swenson et al. (2004, p. 1069), in a RCT study of 250 U.S. medical patients, found that patients preferred "a patient-centered versus a biomedical communication style." Patients who preferred a patient-centered approach were younger, more educated, used complementary and alternative medicine, and had a patient-oriented provider. They also rated a 'doctor's interest in you as a person' as 'very important.' No information on ethnic variation in client preferences was reported. Their study further supports the premise that participatory, shared decision making is preferred by most medical patients.

Challenges to informed, shared decision making for professionals include lack of time, lack of predisposition and skill, and client's inexperience with making decisions about treatment (Towle and Godolphin 1999). We would add that payment structures that limit the contact between professional and client actively undermine efforts toward truly informed decision making. Despite these challenges, Murray, Pollack, White, and Lo (2007) found in a study of over 1,000 U.S. physicians that 75% endorsed shared decision making, while 14% endorsed paternalism in decision making, and 11% endorsed consumerism.

Mental Healthcare Providers Support Shared Decision Making

Barrett (2008, p. 407) states that despite evidence of improved outcomes, stated support from physicians, and a strong ethical foundation, shared decision making "remains limited in practice, particularly outside academic and tertiary health care centers." Légaré et al. (2008, 2011) have begun international efforts to implement and evaluate shared decision-making processes in practice. The model is new, but of growing interest and importance.

In mental health, Patel et al. (2009) state there have been few studies of shared decision making in mental health (24 articles from 1990 to 2007). They add that this is so despite literature indicating shared decisions making can play a useful role in all phases of the treatment process from engagement to recovery, and that both patients and providers express an interest in it.

There may be some ethnic variation in client participation in shared decision making. A study by Patel and Bakken (2010) found that Hispanic patients took a more passive role in treatment decisions making around anxiety and depression than did persons from other ethnic groups. Cortes et al. (2008) found Latinos in community mental health agencies could be reluctant to participate actively in decision making out of concerns about offending their providers. Specifically, valuing 'personalismo,' the regard and respect for the individual provider or attitudes toward the provider as an all-knowing authority figure, limited their active participation. Cortes and colleagues note, however, that this result is based on a small sample and must be regarded as preliminary.

The shared decision-making approach would appear to fit well with the involvement of the client in the EBP practice decision-making process. Clinical social workers must be active to ensure full, informed, and shared decision making in EBP.

Factors to Consider During the Conversation

After completing the literature review process, it is imperative that the clinician consider how the various treatment alternatives are "compatible with the attitudes and values of the client. If not, the client is likely to be resistant to what is being presented" (Wampold 2010, p. 53). In order to reduce resistance, research suggests it is important for clinicians to match therapeutic approaches to individual characteristics of the client. These include personality, cognitive abilities, and coping styles. Such matching addresses the fit of the treatment alternatives to the client rather than to the disorder (Wampold 2010). As such, when a clinician presents the results of a literature search to a client, the clinician must consider how the various interventions align with the individual characteristics of the client. In fact, one of the guiding principles of EBP for social workers published by The Institute of the Advancement of Social Work Research (2008) is that the EBP process must be adapted and personalized for clients based on their culture, interests and circumstances. Social workers do not view clients merely as 'diagnoses'.

To that end, we offer the following points for clinicians to consider when presenting the options found in the practice research literature. These points are not meant to be an exhaustive list, but rather a number of starting points to help clinicians think about the unique characteristics of their client. These questions help clinicians appraise how well the alternatives under consideration match with the client or client system.

Guiding Questions to Consider:

- What is the composition of the client system and how does that effect the definition of the client or client system?
- Where does the power lie within the client system or family?
- Is the identified client a minor? If so, with whom do you discuss the options? Does the age of the minor influence this decision? Who gets to make the decision about treatment?
- What are the client's cognitive capacities?
- What are the client's beliefs about what helps in treatment?
- What are the values of the client regarding issues that may shape treatment? Culture? Race or ethnicity? Gender? Identity and sexuality? Class and opportunity? Special abilities or limitations?
- What are the client's views about religion and spirituality? How do these views influence the client's understanding of the problem? How do these influence the client's views about healing and how it occurs?
- Are there any language barriers that might impact either your ability to effectively communicate with your client? Are there any language barriers regarding homework or other tasks within the treatment?
- Are there any external factors that might influence a client's ability to participate in treatment, such as financial status, immigration status, access to services, disabilities, transportation, child care, employment responsibilities, care-giving responsibilities, or other such factors?

- What were the client's previous experiences with treatment (if any)? What worked and what did not? Was any aspect of treatment unacceptable to the client?
- What is the severity of the presenting problem? How able is the client to engage in the potential treatments due to the current challenges?
- Are their multiple disorders or presenting problems with which the client is struggling? What is main priority of the client?
- How motivated is the client? Is the client eager to participate in treatment or feeling forced to participate? How well do the treatment requirements match with the client's level of motivation?
- What is the client's view of a helper? An expert? A partner? An enemy? How are you the clinician viewed within this framework?
- Are you the clinician seen a trustworthy individual? As an expert?
- How is the system in which you work viewed by the client?
- What influence might personal history or cultural beliefs have on the client's views regarding how acceptable it is to receive help from an individual outside of the family?

Additional Questions to Consider Regarding the Clinician and Setting:

- Are there aspects of your personal values and beliefs that shape your interpretation of the information? Are they in tension with professional values?
- Do you have any values or significant personal experiences that influence your view of this particular client? The client's age? Race/ethnicity? Gender? Sexual orientation? Class? Other factors?
- What is your level of expertise regarding the various alternatives you are suggesting?
- Are you able to present the information clearly and concisely?
- Can you or others at your agency provide each of the proposed evidence-based alternative treatments?
- Is there appropriate supervision and support to for you to deliver the treatment alternatives fully?

Discussing treatment alternatives with the client involves many considerations. Most of these issues are addressed in the assessment process and should be somewhat familiar to the clinician. However not all points of sensitivity and concern will be identified during the assessment process. New issues and specific concerns may arise as client and clinician dialog about treatment alternatives.

Key Dimensions of Client Input in Clinical Decision Making

Client Preferences and Goals

As discussed in Chapter 4, it is possible that the practitioner and the client may have different views regarding what to address in treatment or what alternatives may be most effective and appropriate. It is also possible that there are times when both the client and the clinician agree on the presenting problem, but have different views on how to address it. In other words, it is possible that the treatment alternatives proposed by the clinician based on the review of the literature are all incompatible with the values and preferences of the client. For example, for a client with an anxiety disorder, a clinical social worker determines through a thorough literature review that a cognitive behavioral treatment (CBT) has the strongest empirical support for addressing the client's concerns. However, this particular client has had a prior CBT treatment. She did not find it effective and does not believe it will be useful to her at this time. At this point, the clinician must make several important decisions based on professional expertise and knowledge of the client. Is more information needed? Should the clinician ask for more information about the prior treatment and its quality? Should treatment alternatives with lesser research support be offered to the client? Could a modified version of CBT be used to accommodate the client's concerns? Would such modifications undermine the evidence base supporting this treatment alternative? Are such modifications appropriate and ethical? Should the client be referred to another therapist who can give her what she wants? Is this ethical and clinically appropriate?

Unfortunately, there is no definitive answer as to what to do in this situation. We offer the following recommendations to help guide clinical social workers in this process.

1. Ensure that you have a completed and thorough assessment. Obtain more information as needed.
2. Listen to the client's concerns and see what she or he feels would be most helpful.
3. Ask additional questions regarding the client's concerns about the proposed model to better understand in what ways the model is, and is not, helpful.
4. Discuss other treatment options based on the literature search and discuss the evidence or support of these models. Repeat the literature search if more options need to be identified. (But be sure to explain the differences in research support for the effectiveness of each option.)
5. Decide in discussion with the client what treatment alternative has the best combination of evidence, 'buy in' from the client, and fits within your expertise to deliver it competently.
6. If you and the client cannot agree on an approach that (1) fits with the views of the client, (2) that you believe will be effective based on your understanding of the literature, and (3) that you are competent to deliver, then you and the client must discuss if you are the best professional to provide services. If the answer to this question is no, then ethically, you are responsible to refer the client to another agency or professional who is more qualified to provide the type of treatment the client is seeking.
7. Document the conversation in the client's record.

We believe it is essential that the decision-making process with the client be transparent (Gambrill 2001). Treatment alternatives must be discussed with the client using language that the client can understand (Walsh 2010). The client must be able to provide various kinds of feedback about the proposed treatment alternatives, and how they fit the client's values, goals, and preferences. Discussing treatment alternatives in the EBP practice decision-making process should engage the client, provide hope, and increase motivation for the treatment process (Wampold 2010).

Safety Concerns

There are times when a client may suggest a treatment that poses risk of harm or has been shown to be ineffective for the presenting problem. In this situation, social workers are bound by the *Code of Ethics* to refuse to provide such a service. "Social workers should base practice on recognized knowledge, including empirically based knowledge, relevant to social work and social work ethics" (NASW 2008, 4.01.c). While it is important to listen to the client, and their preferences, the *Code* also states

> When generally recognized standards do not exist with respect to an emerging area of practice, social workers should exercise careful judgment and take responsible steps (including appropriate education, research, training, consultation, and supervision) to ensure the competence of their work and to protect clients from harm. (1.04.c)

A social worker's primary duty is to his or her client. Therefore, if after reviewing the literature and evidence, the client proposes treatments options that are known to be ineffective or potentially harmful, the social worker must refuse to provide such services. The social worker must also explain the reasons behind the refusal. Such conversations must also be documented in the client's record.

What if the Client Refuses all the Interventions with Strong Research Support?

We have emphasized that Step 4 of EBP centers on active and shared decision making between client and professional. Yet since the focus of services is the client's well-being, the client retains the option to refuse any and all treatment options even if they have clear, high quality research support. The only clear limitations to refusing services would be based on safety and legal issues of harm to self and others. Such concerns define the boundary between client choice and society's obligations to limit harm.

If a client refuses all the treatment options uncovered in an EBP search, the clinical social worker should document this decision and the reasons for it in the client's record. A description of the clinician's best sense of how this decision may be harmful to the client should also be stated to the client and documented in the client's record. Such situations are difficult, but clients retain their autonomy and power to make choices regarding their health care. Neither research evidence nor clinical expertise overrides the client's self-determination unless serious harm to self or others is imminent.

Conclusion

"It is the client who makes therapy work" (Wampold 2010, p. 103). This is a simple but powerful statement illustrating the important role each client plays in the success of a treatment intervention. To increase the client's willingness to work and engage in the work of treatment, the client must believe in and feel part of the intervention process. A simple yet powerful way clinicians can engage clients early in treatment is to undertake informed, shared practice decision making. Step 4 of EBP makes active discussion of treatment alternatives with the client a key part of the treatment planning process. In shared decision making, clients partner with professionals to develop the treatment plan. By doing so clients will understand all of their options and feel that the treatment they committed to is one in which they had an active role in choosing.

Some authors frame this step of the EBP practice decision-making process in a more 'top-down,' authoritative manner. We believe this step of the EBP process can be critical to maximizing client motivation and participation in treatment. We also believe an active and thorough dialog with the client fits well with social work values and ethics. We encourage informed, shared decision making within EBP. Without the client's active participation, and expression of goals and preferences, the process of EBP is not complete. The client's preferences, goals, and voices must be a key part of EBP in clinical social work practice.

Chapter 10
Finalizing the Treatment Plan and Practice Evaluation

The Steps 5 and 6 of the evidence-based practice (EBP) model are (Step 5) to finalize the treatment plan and (Step 6) to implement it. Authors of books and articles on EBP frequently address these two steps only minimally as they mark the shift from making practice decisions back to 'doing' practice. We think these steps warrant some further exploration and discussion. We also think that practice evaluation, sometimes included as a step in EBP, deserves some further discussion. These issues will be the focus of this chapter.

Discussing Treatment Options with the Client and Finalizing the Treatment Plan

There is no clear line that distinguishes discussing treatment options with the client (Step 4 of EBP) from finalizing and implementing a shared, collaborative treatment plan (Step 5). The purpose of the discussion with the client is to avoid unacceptable options and to find acceptable ones. It is to insure the treatment options are clear to the client and that any concerns they have are articulated and taken into account. We hope that the discussion also enhances client motivation and enhances the working alliance between the clinical social worker and client. The goal is to integrate the views, values, and preferences of the client into the treatment plan in order to maximize its potential effectiveness and to minimize misunderstandings that will lead to early termination or failed treatment. We assume an interactive, shared effort between clinician and client. This aspect of EBP is different from the hierarchical, or expert, model sometimes apparent in EBM descriptions of the practice decision-making model. In the EBP model, clients are invited to be active participants, rather than passive and compliant recipients, in shared treatment planning. This allows for enhancement of the curative factors of client motivation, of the therapeutic alliance, of shared

J. W. Drisko and M. D. Grady, *Evidence-Based Practice in Clinical Social Work*, 165
Essential Clinical Social Work Series, DOI: 10.1007/978-1-4614-3470-2_10,
© Springer Science+Business Media New York 2012

treatment goals, and a shared view of what will lead to change to become active (Lambert 1992). Not just specific therapies or technique, but a variety of common factors, leads to positive outcomes (Cameron and Keenan 2010; Drisko 2004; Frank and Frank 1991).

To clinical social workers, such an interactive approach to treatment planning should be quite familiar. It is important to understand, however, that it is not consistently applied in all book and articles about EBM/EBP. The early model of EBM, and some current descriptions of EBP, so heavily emphasized the use of research findings as a guide to practice that they often omitted or minimized attention to the client's view and preferences. For example, Grey (2004) in his book *Evidence-based Psychiatry,* labels the fourth step of EBP as "Applying the Evidence" (p.186) or "Apply the Results to Your Patient" (p. 12). He states that "where valid evidence is found, the next step is to apply it to the care of your patient, which is where your clinical expertise is most important" (p. 12). He goes on to note that "this step is where we often falter…The most important question to ask here is whether your practice is becoming more evidence based (p. 186). Grey does not mention interactive discussion of results with the patient or client, nor efforts to understand their views and values. Such discussion is not excluded, but it is certainly not emphasized. This approach reflects a more hierarchic, medical model of treatment decision making. Clinical social workers generally take a more participatory approach, actively including client views and values in the treatment planning process.

Critical thinking is required to distinguish more authoritarian approaches to EBM/EBP from more collaborative and less hierarchic ones. The requirement to locate the best available evidence is shared by both approaches, but most social work models are more likely to take a collaborative approach to treatment planning. Emphasis on client views and values and also on clinical expertise is much more explicit in the contemporary model of EBM/EBP, but is still not universal.

Documenting the Treatment Plan

One action that marks the end of treatment planning is the formal documentation of the treatment plan in the client's record. There do not (yet) appear to be standards for documenting the use of EBP steps in all mental health records. It is appropriate to briefly summarize the search process you have completed and briefly document its key results in the client's record. A few sentences should be adequate. For example, "I reviewed the Cochrane Collaboration Library and PubMed for systematic reviews on Panic Disorders. There was research support for the use of cognitive behavioral therapies or medication for these disorders. After discussion with the client, she preferred the therapy as a first choice and expressed concern about medication side effects." In this example, considerable high quality research evidence was located, with good support for the proposed treatments. The clients concerns were clearly stated, and led to selection of a preferred option that was feasible to deliver.

Where clients have religious or cultural concerns about treatments with strong empirical support, we suggest a more detailed summary be included in the client's record. This would clarify how and why a treatment plan was developed that might not employ a treatment with the strongest research support. It provides useful information for future healthcare providers, as well as documenting the rationale for using treatments that may have less research support. As always, client records may be part of legal actions, and such documentation clarifies the basis for treatment selection. Similarly, justifications to payers for the use of treatments without strong empirical support may be increasingly required, where client values and preferences lead to the use of alternative treatments.

Clinical social workers must carefully attend to the reporting and documentation requirements of their agencies and their funders. Public and private funders have begun to develop lists of treatments that they argue have "demonstrated empirical support." The treatments included on these lists may—or may not—meet the standards for empirically supported treatments (ESTs), interventions (ESIs), or programs. However, they may not be consistent with the results of an EBP search using the (often more rigorous) *Cochrane Handbook* standards.

To argue for use of a treatment not on a list of approved treatments, clinical social workers are encouraged to carefully document the results of an EBP search on the client's need. Where payers limit funded treatment options to a specific list, they may not allow for consideration of client preferences and values. This may run counter to key participatory aspects of the EBP practice decision-making model. It may also run counter to both clinical expertise and the client's views. In some cases, clients may be unwilling to accept any treatment on the funder approved list, keeping them from treatment and posing a serious ethical issue for the clinical social worker. In the current system of health care in the United States, clients are not entitled to treatment. Yet funders are frequently willing to make exceptions for clients they cover where a clear rationale for the use of alternative approaches is made on the basis of good research evidence and client participation.

Implementing the Treatment

Step 6 of EBP appears quite simple: Implement the treatment. Clinical social workers know that implementing a treatment can be challenging, with many twists and turns. First, implementing a treatment assumes that it is available to the client, financially and practically. For persons with borderline personality disorder, the Cochrane Library (Binks et al. 2009) reports preliminary support for two treatments: Linehan's (1993) Dialectical behavior therapy (DBT) and Bateman and Fonagy's (1999, 2001) psychodynamically informed partial hospital program. To implement either therapy requires that the client has reasonable access to a program. This assumes these treatment programs are available in one's geographic area and funded by the client's payer or otherwise subsidized. It also assumes the client's family and employer are supportive of the client's undertaking such an extensive therapeutic process. In fact, geographic variation in treatment availability can be a serious obstacle to locating effective treatments. Even if located and feasible, funding may be another obstacle to obtaining treatment.

One important aspect of both discussing treatment options with a client (EBP Step 4) and finalizing a shared, collaborative treatment plan (EBP Step 5) must be a realistic appraisal of feasible options. It is often unclear that the specific treatments found to be effective by high quality research are actually available in many areas. Sometime qualified and trained providers are not immediately available.

Where effective treatments are located but local options or expertise is lacking, clinical social workers are obligated to make difficult choices about alternative options. The NASW *Code of Ethics* (2008) argues that social workers should only provide services that they fully are competent to deliver. Section 1.04a states that social workers should only provide services "...within the boundaries of their education, training, license, certification, consultation received, supervised experience, or other relevant professional experience." Further, social workers should only provide services that "...are new to them only after engaging in appropriate study, training, consultation, and supervision from people who are competent in those interventions or techniques" (2008, 1.04b). Professional expertise dictates that clinical social workers should only provide services that they are well qualified to deliver. This may mean treatments and other services with good research support are not available to clients in areas where no fully trained providers can be located. In such circumstances, referral to other providers is warranted.

Finally, the NASW *Code of Ethics* (2008) states that clients must be protected from harm. Professionals have an active obligation to be educated about treatments and services that may be useful to their clients. We believe that this obligation to learn new skills should be shared by, and actively promoted by, their agencies and their funding sources. However, the obligation to learn new knowledge and skills is more often made by an individual cost, enforced through continuing education requirements for licensure and certification. Clinical social workers must remain current and renew their professional knowledge and skills regularly.

In implementing new treatment models, note carefully that a key obligation is to protect clients from harm due to the intervention. Clinical social workers must always be sure that their service efforts provide the least, or no, harm. Dr. Archie Cochrane's vision of EBM as reducing the number of harmful and benign but ineffective treatments should be a routine and ongoing part of clinical practice.

Practice Evaluation

Some authors make practice evaluation a formal step in the EBM/EBP process (Gibbs 2002). We take a different position. First, we believe that evaluation is a vital part of any professional practice effort. That is, we view practice evaluation as an essential part of routine good practice. The NASW *Code of Ethics* (2008) and many social work textbooks also support this position. Clinical social workers have long expressed this viewpoint (Hollis 1964) and the National Association of Social Workers (2005a, b) standards for clinical practice and in healthcare practice specifically endorses this position. This position is not in conflict with EBP, it simply distinguishes the steps of practice decision making from practice monitoring and evaluation as distinct processes.

Second, we believe that the best practice evaluation is an ongoing process, from assessment through to termination. We also believe that the best practice evaluation addresses not just outcomes but also monitoring the processes of treatment. This process provides feedback to both the clinical social worker and to the client. It helps clarify if treatment is working or not. That is, evaluation includes ongoing formative discussion of how the client perceives the treatment, what parts seem helpful or unhelpful, and what other influences may be influencing the progress of the treatment. It allows for changes in the treatment plan. It also maximizes client participation in the treatment process. At several points in treatment, a summative evaluation of progress should also be routine.

Third, it is imperative that evaluation of practice directly address the client's view of the clinical problem. This may sound obvious, but measures of success or effectiveness may use standards that are a bit different from the client's stated concerns. Sometimes this is mandated. For example, a court mandated client may have to come to sessions and have 'clean' urine tests. These are surely measures of progress or even success, but they may not fully reflect the motivations or goals of the client. In addition to the mandated measures, the client's own goals should be monitored and evaluated. If the client views drug use as self-medication, the court mandated goals, while appropriate, may not address all the important concerns in the client's life. Both mandated and client-specific measures of progress and outcome should be evaluated. Both should also be regularly documented in the client's record.

Practice evaluation also allows payers and administrators to have confidence that clinical services actually work. If published as case reports, practice evaluations can contribute to our professional knowledge base. However, this knowledge is very different from the population scale experimental research used in the EBM/EBP practice decision-making process.

There are several models of practice evaluation. These models are intended to be easy to incorporate into practice, but they do take some planning and effort to complete. They range from informal to formal methods. All such evaluation efforts should be documented in the client's record.

Models of Practice Evaluation

There are both qualitative and quantitative models of practice evaluation. It is beyond the goals of this book to describe them all, but a few key points are worth exploring. Qualitative models based on client self-report are the traditional form of practice evaluation used for many years in clinical social work practice (Chambon 1994; Davis 1994; Gilgun 2005b; Lang 1994; McDowell 2000; Nye 1994; Ruckdeschel et al. 1994; Shaw and Lishman 1999) as well as in psychiatry (Campbell et al. 2000) and clinical psychology (Amedeo 1997). There are both informal and formal approaches to qualitative practice evaluation (Drisko 2004; Greene et al. 1988; Shaw and Lishman 2005). Qualitative methods are flexible, allow for individually tailored client input, examine both behaviors and internal experiences, and can address both issues of process and outcome. They can capture complex and unexpected results. Critics of qualitative practice evaluation state that it lacks replicablility and precision. Further, critics argue its data analysis procedures may be unclear or prone to bias.

Quantitative practice evaluation methods have been widely used over many years in behavioral and cognitive behavioral practice. A wide range of research designs may be used in quantitative practice evaluation (Drisko 2011). The most common method of quantitative practice evaluation centers on a pre- to post-comparison of client functioning on one or more target issues. This model of evaluation is known as the single case or single system research design. This model was widely used in social work during the "Empirically based practice" movement of the 1980s and early 1990s. (Note carefully, this is not the same as the current "Evidence based practice" movement). The effort to increase usage of single case evaluation was part of an attempt to demonstrate the effectiveness of social work services. The single case method is very useful in documenting client changes, but does not clearly demonstrate that the treatment or services caused the change. That is, in contrast to true experimental research designs, the single case design has limited interval validity. Others argued that the logic of the single case design did not fit well with psychodynamic or family systems approaches (Dean and Reinherz 1986).

Clearly, there are a wide variety of practice evaluation methods for use with clinical practice. Yet given the foundation of the EBM/EBP movement in quantitative epidemiology, single case evaluation methods are most often suggested for evaluation of client progress and outcomes. This is one reasonable choice for clinical social workers to use. On the other hand, they should understand that single case evaluation differs from the overall logic of EBM/EBP in important ways.

Single Case Evaluation and Evidence-Based Practice

Several models of single case evaluation are available for clinical social work and clinical psychology (Barlow et al. 2008; Kazi 1998; Thyer and Myers 2007). Single case practice evaluation is based on a different logic, and a different model, than is other EBM/EBP research. EBM/EBP places great emphasis on experimental (RCT) research designs for individual studies and systematic reviews that combine the results of multiple high quality studies. Random assignment of cases to treated and control condition is also very highly valued. Quantitative practice evaluation emphasizes pre- to post-comparison of status for just one client using pre-experimental research designs. Each method is appropriate to its purpose, but the purposes and methods are quite different.

In addition, many models of single case evaluation use unique, situation specific measures. This is a strength of the single case model. Self-anchored outcome measures can be developed collaboratively with the client and tailored to specifically address their concerns (Nugent 1992). Such measures may include counts of thoughts or observation of behaviors that are simply not replicable by others. In some instances, self-anchored scales are employed to measure quantitatively the severity or intensity of a client's concern (Nugent 1992). Such measures are, again, specifically tailored to the client, and may not be replicable or even relevant to other clients with similar concerns. Both the nature of the research designs used in single case evaluation and the nature of the measures used in it differ considerably from those most valued in EBM/EBP research. Both are useful, but they have different purposes and are based on different logics.

Finally, the analytic methods for single case evaluation and large-scale EBM/EBP experimental research differ (Jagaroo et al. 2008). Single case designs may be analyzed using visual inspection methods that document pre- to post-changes. These visual methods do provide a reasonable accounting of the client's situation, but lack precision and a clear basis for deciding if the changes described are truly significant. They are very helpful in documenting change in a clear manner for use directly with the client.

There are statistical methods for estimating statistically significant changes for use with single case evaluation designs. These include the "Two standard deviation method" in which improvement from pre-treatment baseline status is interpreted as statistically significant (Jagaroo et al. 2008). This is an application of a well defined logic, and a reasonable way of estimating significance, so long as the measures are valid and the data was collected in a reliable manner. Further, statistics specific for use with single cases and time series data are also available for single case data analysis (Jagaroo et al. 2008; Jayaratne 1978).

Single case evaluation offers one valuable method for documenting change in clinical practice. It may be easy to incorporate in some forms of clinical practice. In terms of limitations, incomplete results are common in single case evaluation using self report measures. Biases in the data are difficult to rule out. Well-defined analytic methods are available for single case evaluation, but, as always, are only as good as the data upon which they are based. Making cause and effect claims from single cases is usually inappropriate.

We encourage all clinical social workers to monitor and to evaluate all their practice efforts. There are many useful models of practice evaluation from which to choose. Some of the models apply more smoothly to specific models of practice. We view practice evaluation as an integral part of good clinical practice, but we leave open to the clinician, the agency, and the circumstances the selection of an appropriate model of evaluation.

In summary, practice evaluation is based on such a different logic than is EBM/EBP that we have chosen not to include practice evaluation in the EBP process. Reasonable people may hold different views on this issue. We believe distinguishing between the two approaches helps make understanding the logic of the EBP model easier. We believe our view is more internally consistent than are models that advocate for practice evaluation as a part of EBP. Both are worthy; they are just different.

Instruments and Procedures for Practice Evaluation

In recent years, researchers have created several different instruments designed to monitor and evaluate the success of treatment. One such instrument is Miller and Duncan (2000) Outcome Rating Scale (ORS). The ORS was designed to be a briefer alternative to the Outcome Questionnaire 45.2 (Lambert et al. 1996). The ORS was designed in an effort to create an instrument that could be completed in less time and was simpler for clients to use (Miller et al. 2003). The ORS addresses three areas of functioning: individual, relational, and social. The ORS has undergone extensive testing regarding its reliability and validity, and has been found to have strong psychometric properties (Bringhurst et al. 2006; Campbell and Hemsley 2009; Miller et al. 2006, 2003). Further, in a large study involving 75 therapists and 6,424 clients over a two-year period, there was a high rate of use among therapists. These findings appear to counter concern that therapists felt it was cumbersome to use (Miller et al. 2006).

A second instrument also developed by Miller and colleagues (Johnson et al. 2000) is called the Session Rating Scale (SRS). As its names implies, it is a measure intended for use on a session-by-session monitoring basis. This instrument is a

> brief, four-item, client-completed measure derived from a ten-item scale originally developed by Johnson (1995)...The scale assesses four interacting elements, including the quality of the relational bond, as well as the degree of agreement between the client and therapist on goals, methods and overall approach of therapy (Miller et al. 2006, p. 8)

Miller and colleagues (2006) report from previous research on the psychometric properties of the SRS that it has strong reliability with a Cronbach alpha coefficient of 0.96 based on a sample of nearly 15,000 administrations (Duncan et al. 2003). In addition, they tested concurrent validity through correlations with another valid instrument that yielded Pearson correlation coefficients averaging $r = 0.48$. Subsequent evaluations of both instruments psychometric properties have yielded similar results (Campbell and Hemsley 2009). Both of these instruments and related documents can be found on Duncan's web site, The Heart and Soul of Change Project, online at http://heartandsoulofchange.com/.

Research on the ORS and the SRS has not only examined its psychometric properties and its rate of use, but also how its use impacts the outcome of treatment. The same study by Miller et al. (2006, p. 14) found that:

> Ongoing feedback to the therapists regarding clients' experience of the alliance and progress in treatment results in significant improvements in both client retention and outcome… At the same time, clients of therapists who failed to seek feedback regarding the alliance as assessed by the SRS were three times less likely to return for a second session and had significantly poorer outcomes.

Similarly, in a RCT conducted with 46 heterosexual couples in therapy, the results indicated that those couples whose therapists administered the ORS and SRS had significantly better outcomes compared to those couples receiving treatment as usual, without monitoring feedback (Reese et al. 2010). Those couples in the treatment that utilized the instruments were more likely to experience significant clinical changes (48.1%) compared to those in the control group (26.3%). While the authors state that much still needs to be understood regarding the mechanism of change to which feedback contributes, they conclude that this study lends further support for the importance of incorporating such feedback into the therapeutic process in order to improve outcomes in clients (Reese et al. 2010).

Lambert (2010) has explored the use of another monitoring system in routine psychotherapy practice. Using the Outcome Questionnaire (OQ-45), developed by Lambert and Burlingame, clients completed weekly measures of therapeutic status (Lambert et al. 2010; Lambert and Vermeersch 2008). Clinicians were given weekly 'green light' indicators where OQ scores showed clients were improving, 'yellow light' indicators where clients were not improving, and 'red light' indicators where clients were regressing. These simple indicators, completed by staff, helped clinicians change their interventions when progress was not noticeable. Dropout rates were reduced, though early changes did not necessarily predict later changes consistently. Further, decelerating rates of improvement cannot be taken for granted (Percevic et al. 2006). The course of psychotherapy is highly variable, but simple quantitative monitoring can be useful in shaping clinical practice.

The OQ-45 is available in several languages. It has been researched on white, African-American, Asian/Pacific Islander, Latino and Native American clients, making it useful with many diverse populations (Lambert et al. 2006). The OQ system allows for routine practice monitoring and outcome evaluation.

Still another approach to evaluating practice outcomes has been developed by Chorpita and colleagues. Their evaluation model is called Dashboards (Chorpita et al. 2008). Dashboards are a computer-based quantitative method that was designed to link specific outcomes with specific intervention strategies. Chorpita is known for developing the Common Elements (CE) approach, in which clinicians build treatment plans for clients using specific techniques that have been used previously in empirically supported treatment models. These elements include, for example, exposure or cognitive restructuring (Chorpita et al. 2007). Dashboards are an evaluative method that tracks changes in clinical progress over time as recorded quantitatively on an Excel spreadsheet. The dashboard allows the clinician to graph where there are improvements and declines in specific target areas. In addition, the progress made is also linked to the specific elements the clinician has chosen to implement during the treatment.

For example, an adolescent client presents with depression, which manifests in the client's self-report of depressive symptoms, a reduction in social activities and missing school or going to school late. The goals for treatment are (1) to improve mood based on self-report on a 1–10 scale, (2) to increase the number of social activities each week from the baseline of 0, and (3) to increase on-time school attendance from 3 to 5 days per week. Using the CE approach, the clinician identifies that for this particular client's age, race, and gender, the treatment elements included should be: Psychoeducation; cognitive coping; activity scheduling; and problem-solving. On separate spreadsheets within the case Excel computer file, the therapist enters in data on the three target goals. On one spreadsheet, the therapist enters in a score for each outcome measure during each session. On a second spreadsheet, the therapist enters which treatment element was covered during each session. On a third spreadsheet, Excel tracks the progress for each outcome graphically to illustrate the changes being made on the indentified outcomes. The third spreadsheet also includes a table aligned with the outcome graph. This spreadsheet summarizes which element of treatment was linked to improvement, no change or regression (Chorpita et al. 2008). The result of this process is a graphic report that shows how the client improves or declines over time. The graphic report also shows how those changes are linked with the specific elements included within each session.

Returning to the case example, in studies of depression psychoeducation and cognitive coping are elements of treatment that appear in the highest percentage of studies. In theory, these common elements should have the highest likelihood of positively impacting on the client's depression. However, in tracking the case using the dashboard method, the clinician sees that it was not until activity scheduling was introduced into the treatment that there was improvement for this specific client on the outcome measures. The dashboard provides an immediate method for documenting how different interventions impact the progress on each identified outcome measure. This makes changes and their sources clear to both client and clinician. It also allows changes in the choices of interventions to be altered relatively quickly within the course of the intervention.

Note that this evaluative model demonstrates what helps a specific client. It documents the association between common elements and specific outcomes. However, as a single case evaluation tool, the dashboard model does not demonstrate conclusively that each element causes the change observed. Like other single case evaluation methods, it employs a logic different from the large scale, experimental research most valued in EBM and EBP. The use of self-anchored rating scales also can produce measures of uncertain validity.

Chorpita and his colleagues have now created multiple templates of dashboards (PracticeWise 2008) including the common elements with some empirical support for various disorders already programmed into the Excel spreadsheet. For example, there are dashboard templates for depression, anxiety, and trauma. There are also blank ones so that clinicians can build their own unique dashboards using elements identified through the CE approach. All of the templates for the dashboards are available on the PracticeWise web site at www.practicewise.com/web. However, access to these resources, and others, are restricted to those who have paid a subscription fee.

Many models for monitoring practice and documenting single case outcomes are available for clinical social works to use. These models and measures offer a fine complement to the EBP practice decision-making model.

Summary

Steps 5 and 6 of EBP center on finalizing the treatment plan and implementing it. In these steps, the clinical expertise of the clinical social worker is crucial. Finalizing the treatment plan decided in conjunction with the client's values and preferences allows for formal documentation in the client's record. It is also appropriate to document the research evidence that supports the plan in a succinct manner. Clinicians should also document any client-specific values and preferences that shape the treatment plan. This is especially important when treatments with limited research support are chosen.

Monitoring of progress and summative evaluation are key components of good clinical social work practice. These practice components draw on single case evaluation logic which differs from the premises of population-based experimental research used to guide EBP. Still, qualitative or quantitative evaluation of practice should always be part of good clinical social work practice. Single case evaluation methods offer one widely used approach to practice evaluation. More recent innovations employ session-by-session progress monitoring using convenient standardized measures. The dashboard model of progress monitoring and evaluation links outcomes to specific common elements of practice.

In Part I of this book, we have introduced EBP and explored three perspectives useful to understanding its application to clinical practice, policy, and research. We have also explored the six steps of EBP in detail. In Part 2 of this book we will examine several cases to illustrate the EBP process in action. Both the strengths and some challenges of doing EBP come to life when the model is applied to clinical social work practice.

Part II
Case Examples of Evidence-Based Practice

Introduction

In the following section, six case illustrations of the EBP process are provided to show how the process is integrated with clinical decision-making. The cases also show the complexities involved in the EBP process. They illustrate how the process is dependent on (1) the client's clinical presentation, (2) the client's values and preferences, (3) the best available research evidence and (4) the professional expertise and judgment of the clinical social worker. These constitute the four elements of the EBP practice decision-making process.

The cases are reported in the same structured format. Each case opens with a brief summary of the client's presentation and concerns. Next, each of the six steps of the EBP practice decision-making process is described, leading the reader through each part of the EBP process. In some instances, several empirically supported treatment alternatives are identified; in others, the research offers less clear guidance. The match of the best available research to the specific case needs varies, as does the quality of the research located during the search process. Further, in some instances treatments with strong research support are easily accessed; in others, research supported options are not readily available.

The EBP process says very little about the clinical assessment process and how the clinician determines the target problem on which the entire search process is based. It is assumed that professionals have the required 'professional expertise' to complete an appropriate and thorough clinical assessment. In clinical social work practice the types, severity and number of challenges faced by clients can be daunting. Traditional mental health problems warranting DSM diagnoses as well as social problems are common among the clients that clinical social workers encounter in their work. The cases illustrated in this text were chosen to reflect the diversity of clients that social workers see in a variety of real world practice settings. Below is a brief description of the cases and the clinical concerns raised within each case.

Chapter 11—Sam: Sam is a 68 year old white gay male who has suffered a series of losses in recent years and is reporting symptoms of grief and depression to an outpatient therapist.

Chapter 12—Ray: Ray is a 27 year old single white male who is suffering from panic attacks. He does not appear to have any other mental health issues, so these attacks are very distressing and confusing to him.

Chapter 13—Sally: Sally is a 12 year old biracial (African–American/white) girl who has been diagnosed with Reactive Attachment Disorder, disinhibited type. Sally was adopted by a biracial couple 2 years ago. Her parents are concerned about her lack of connection to them and her apparent willingness to turn to anyone for comfort and guidance.

Chapter 14—Loretta and Newman: Loretta and Newman are the parents of Arthur, who is a 36 year old African–American male who has been diagnosed with schizophrenia, and who has had a recent decline in functioning. The parents are seeking services through a hospital program for patients with schizophrenia and their caregivers. The parents report increased feelings of stress about their own age-related health issues, the strain of caring for Arthur and their fears of his future when they are not around to care for him.

Chapter 15—Jin: Jin is a 16 year old Korean–American male who was referred to an outpatient clinic after he was found for the second time passed out after drinking alcohol. His family is involved and they are very concerned about his behavioral changes and his pulling away from his family and the Korean community.

Chapter 16—Jennifer: Jennifer is a white 23 year old homeless female who has Borderline Personality Disorder. Her immediate mental health and social service needs highlight the difficulties faced by persons with multiple challenges and few supports.

Chapter 11
Sam: An Older, Gay Man
Who Appears Depressed

Sam is a 68-year-old Caucasian male with bright white hair. He has an athletic build, and stands just over six feet tall. Despite his apparent excellent physical health, he walked into the therapy room slowly and looked very tired. He stated his primary care doctor referred him to this small group psychotherapy practice after his doctor ruled out a physical reason for his symptoms. According to Sam, about four to six weeks ago, he began feeling "very tired," had difficulty in concentrating and stopped exercising, which he had done on average of five times a week for as long as he could remember. Although he had stopped exercising, he had lost about 10 lbs. over the last several months, which he stated was because "I just don't have the energy to eat." In addition, Sam said that he had been staying home more, and not attending social functions or dinners with friends. He states that the activities he used to enjoy are "just not the same and it feels like such an effort to go and pretend I am having fun when I am not." When asked about any recent changes in his life, he could not think of any immediate changes. However, during the history gathering stage of the interview, he discussed several significant changes that had occurred in the last 5 years.

Five years ago, he moved his mother into a nursing home near to his home and became primarily responsible for her care. Although he has three other siblings, they are estranged from him, and have been since he came out as gay almost 25 years ago. He described his family as a very conservative 'Bible Belt' family. They would not accept his sexual orientation. After his father died about 10 years ago, his mother began to reconnect with Sam and they worked on rebuilding their relationship. Nine months after his mother's move near him, she died quite suddenly and he felt cheated since he felt like it was "finally [their] time together," while at the same time some relief since her care was quite exhausting.

About 3 years ago when he turned 65, Sam decided to retire. He looked forward to spending time with his partner of 17 years who was about 7 years older and who was already retired. For 2 years, they traveled, attended concerts and shows that they "had been meaning to see." They did other activities together that they had

J. W. Drisko and M. D. Grady, *Evidence-Based Practice in Clinical Social Work,*
Essential Clinical Social Work Series, DOI: 10.1007/978-1-4614-3470-2_11,
© Springer Science+Business Media New York 2012

"never gotten to because we were both working so much." However, about 2 years later, his partner suffered a stroke, and went into a coma and died 2 months later.

Sam feels he coped well at the beginning. He stated that his friends and his community were a wonderful source of support for him. However, it has been over a year since his partner died and he now is experiencing the symptoms described above that led him to seek consultation from his doctor. He and his partner, while connected to friends in their community, still lived a relatively "solitary life." They had no children and both of their families had distanced themselves from them decades previously. Many of his peers are now not around in the same way that they were 10–15 years ago. Many have retired and moved closer to their grandchildren, frequently travel or have moved to warmer climates. Without work in his life, Sam feels like he has "no purpose." He cannot find the motivation to even get up some days, as he often questions "what is the point?"

Sam is seeking services to help him "at least feel some energy" and interest in some of his previously enjoyable activities, such as running, traveling, and enjoying the arts.

He stated that this was the time he had planned to "really enjoy life," but now he states he cannot find the joy he once had.

Applying Steps of Evidence-Based Practice to Case

As you will recall from Chapter 2, the steps of Evidence Based Practice (EBP) are:

(1) Drawing on client needs and circumstances learned in a thorough assessment, identify answerable practice questions and related research information needs.
(2) Efficiently locate relevant research knowledge.
(3) Critically appraise the quality and applicability of this knowledge to the client's needs and circumstances.
(4) Discuss the research results with the client to determine how likely effective options fit with the client's values and interests.
(5) Synthesizing the clinical needs and circumstances with the views of the client and the relevant research, develop a plan of intervention considering available options.
(6) Implement the intervention.

We will use each of these steps as the outline for examining how to apply the EBP practice decision-making model in clinical practice.

Step 1: Drawing on client needs and circumstances learned in a thorough assessment, identify answerable practice questions and related research information needs

In the first step of EBP, the clinician must work with the client to identify the primary clinical issue around which to focus the EBP process. As discussed in Chapter 4 on assessment, it is essential to work with your client to identify the issue that the client feels is the highest priority. This preliminary step of assessment is the hidden foundation of the EBP practice decision-making process.

The client must be actively engaged in the assessment process. Therefore, in working with Sam, it is essential to discuss with him what his personal priorities are, and what does he feel he is most motivated to address in treatment. In Sam's situation, he has several areas that could be the focus of the clinical work with him, including grief work around the losses of his partner and his mother, his depressive symptoms, his life transition from working to retirement, his estrangement from his family, and his social isolation. In conversations with Sam, he identifies that his depressive symptoms are the highest priority for him at this time. He states that while he knows that the other areas are caused by his grief, including his isolation and all of the other previously identified problem areas, he does not feel he has "the energy right now to tackle" those until he can "get some energy back." As such, he and the clinical social worker agree that the primary treatment goal will be to help him increase his coping strategies to manage more effectively his depressive symptoms. Therefore, the practice question is: What are effective treatments for depression with older gay males?

In the **P.I.C.O.** model, the **P**opulation is older gay men with depression. The **I**nterventions under consideration are psychotherapies and similar psychosocial interventions as well as medications. **C**omparisons would be between different therapies or psychosocial interventions as well as among medications and combinations of mediations and psychosocial therapies. The **O**utcomes would be increasing Sam's energy and social involvement. The focus for Sam is on determining likely effective treatment options.

Step 2: Efficiently locate relevant research knowledge

The search process began with web sites that provide summative knowledge regarding mental health and effective treatments. Starting with the Cochrane Collaboration Library (www.thecochranelibrary.org), the first search used the following key words in the search engine: older, gay, men/man, and depression. However, no results were returned by this search. A second search using the terms depression, older adult, and males, returned several unrelated articles; oddly none were specific to depression though one addressed sleep problems. While the worker attempted to conduct a search that combined the multiple aspects of Sam's identity and needs, these searches did not immediately lead to systematic reviews that directly corresponded to his situation and characteristics.

However, by broadening the search further using the terms depression and older adults, numerous articles were identified by the web site's search engine that appeared to address older adults with depression, the primary clinical question. One review was on antidepressant medications (www.cochrane.org/reviews/en/ab000561.html) that provides a summary of research comparing antidepressants and effectiveness in the aging population with depression. This article concludes that antidepressants are more effective than placebos. In this review, Wilson et al. (2001) review, tricyclic antidepressants (Odds Ratio 0.32; 95% CI: 0.21–0.47), as well as SSRIs (OR 0.51; 95% CI: 0.36–0.72) and MAO Inhibitors (OR 0.17; 95%

CI: 0.07–0.39) and found that they were all more effective than placebos. This review leads the social worker to consider that a referral for a medication consult would be one possible course to take with Sam.

A second review finds that there is no enough research on Electric Convulsive Treatment (ECT) to recommend it as a treatment of depression in older adults (www.cochrane.org/reviews/en/ab003593.html). Finally, there was a systematic review of the literature on psychosocial treatments for depression in older adults (http://www.cochrane.org/reviews/en/ab004853.html). This review of treatments by Wilson et al. (2008) included nine trials that compared cognitive behavioral therapy (CBT) and psychodynamic psychotherapies. These two types of therapies were the only ones included as there were no available studies on other forms of psychotherapy to include in the review. Seven studies compared CBT versus controls but none of the psychodynamic trials used untreated control groups:

> Based on five trials (153 participants), cognitive behavioural therapy was more effective than waiting list controls (WMD −9.85, 95% CI −11.97 to −7.73). Only three small trials compared psychodynamic therapy with CBT, with no significant difference in treatment effect indicated between the two types of psychotherapeutic treatment. Based on three trials with usable data, CBT was superior to active control interventions when using the Hamilton Depression Rating Scale (WMD −5.69, 95% CI −11.04 to −0.35), but equivalent when using the Geriatric Depression Scale (WMD −2.00, 95% CI −5.31 to 1.32). (Wilson et al. 2008, para 9)

The Wilson et al. (2008) review indicates that there is good research support for both CBT and psychodynamic intervention with older depressed males. These are important options to discuss with the client.

A second search using the SAHMSA web site led to sections from the Surgeon General's report on mental health (U.S. Department of Health and Human Services 1999, ch5, sec3). This material outlines prevention strategies and risk factors about which clinicians should be aware. This web site also provides information on psychopharmalogical treatments for depression and concludes that.

> There is consistent evidence that older patients, even the very old, respond to antidepressant medication (Reynolds and Kupfer 1999). About 60–80 percent of older patients respond to treatment, while the placebo response rate is about 30–40 percent (Schneider 1996). These rates are comparable to those in other adults... Treatment response is typically defined by a significant reduction—usually 50 percent or greater—in symptom severity. (para. 33)

Note that specific details of the studies on which these conclusions are based is not clearly reported, raising questions about its quality and completeness.

In addition, there is a section entitled: *Psychosocial Treatment of Depression* that provides the following information:

> Most research to date on psychosocial treatment of mental disorders has concentrated on depression. These studies suggest that several forms of psychotherapy are effective for the treatment of late-life depression, including cognitive-behavioral therapy, interpersonal psychotherapy, problem-solving therapy, brief psychodynamic psychotherapy, and reminiscence therapy, an intervention developed specifically for older adults on the premise that reflection upon positive and negative past life experiences enables the individual to overcome feelings of depression and despair (Butler 1974; Butler et al. 1991). Group and

individual formats have been used successfully. A meta-analysis of 17 studies of cognitive, behavioral, brief psychodynamic, interpersonal, reminiscence, and eclectic therapies for late-life depression found treatment to be more effective than no treatment or placebo. (Scogin and McElreath 1994, para. 46–47)

Again, the studies on which this conclusion are based are not fully detailed, and differ somewhat from the Cochrane Library systemic review of psychological treatments for depression.

Neither of these research summaries directly explored any potential differences for gay men. It is not clear whether psychological treatments would, or would not, be differentially effective for gay men. However, the impact of societal oppression for gays is evident in Sam's family life and may influence the psychosocial sources of resilience and risk even in his later life. These earlier studies most likely used less stringent review standards than do current Cochrane Collaboration systematic reviews.

A general search on the web site GoogleScholar using the key words depression older gay males brings up several books that address this question, such as *Gay and Lesbian Aging: Research and Future Directions* by Herdt and de Vries (2004). However, if these books are not easily accessible, they may not be immediately useful. In addition, without very careful review, the quality of the evidence on which such books base their conclusions is unclear. Therefore, it appears that the core EBM/EBP summative web sites are the most fruitful in the search for information on how to best help Sam address his depression.

Step 3: Critically appraise the quality and applicability of this knowledge to the client's needs and situation

In conducting step 3 of the EBP process, it is essential to go back and see if the clinician can look to see the quality of the research provided in these summative studies. The Wilson et al. (2008) systematic review on the Cochrane Library site provides full details on all included and excluded studies—in the full review (which in the United States requires a paid subscription to access). For the psychotherapy interventions, the authors state that their findings are based on a meta-analysis of seven studies, yet the meta-analysis included a small number of trials and that the "review shows that there is relatively little research in this field and care must be taken in generalising what evidence there is to clinical populations" (para. 7). Samples sizes are also small, and there is no mention if any older gay men were included in the studies.

The information from the SAHMSA web site is less specific. The report summarizes study findings, but does not provide details on each included study. As a result, there is not much information on which to base a critical appraisal about the quality of the studies included in the report. It is an expert summary of research, compiled by a credible source and includes a large number of studies, but it is not fully transparent in its methodology. Such summaries might be considered Level 5 expert opinion, the lowest grade of evidence in the EBM/EBP hierarchy. On the other hand, the conclusions of these experts are at least partly based on research. The lack of full detail undermines their credibility and makes them less useful as guides for clinical practice. Transparency and detail is a real strength of systematic reviews.

While it is difficult to find specific information on the design quality of some of these studies, the participants included in the studies are similar to Sam in terms of age and primary presenting issue. On the other hand, they do not specifically identify unique characteristics or challenges associated with being gay. That is, the populations included in these studies are not an exact fit with Sam's personal characteristics. Given what is available, it appears that this research may be a relatively good fit for Sam, albeit limited in the number of studies and in information on gay older adults.

Step 4: Discuss the research results with the client to ensure they fit with the client's values and goals

In the next session with Sam, the clinical social worker would then provide him with a summary of the information found and offer some approaches for consideration. The two forms of psychotherapy and medications found in the searches would need to be described in sufficient detail for Sam to understand his options, their likely benefits, and their potential costs and side effects.

In addition to the information on psychotherapy research, it is also in Sam's best interest for the therapist to share with him the information on the use of medication and discuss his feelings and thoughts about this type of intervention. In this conversation, he says that he is willing to try medication. He states he would rather work with his current primary care doctor rather than starting over with a new psychiatrist.

Finally, although support groups and social supports were not specifically listed in the research, based on the clinical social worker's experiences, she believes that expanding his social network in an effort to decrease his isolation would be helpful to him in further alleviating his depressive symptoms. This is consistent with Sam's concerns about social isolation, although this issue was not specifically addressed in the outcome research. The clinical social worker therefore suggests a group therapy or support group intervention, providing him with an array of options regarding the focus and/or composition of the group. For example, he may want to have a support group that is focused on grief and loss or one that is specifically targeted toward individuals who identify as GLBTQI or one that is aimed at older adults in general, or a combination of any of the above. Sam says that he is open to this idea and the clinical social worker and Sam agree that both will do some searching for group options. After further discussion, Sam can then decide which one feels is the best fit for him.

It would be important to point out that the studies did not include gay men, and to ask Sam what he thinks of this omission. The goal is to be sure the client views the best evidence as truly applicable to him or her. It is not clear that the effectiveness of these treatments is different for gay men or lesbians, but one of the points of EBM/EBP is that differences we may not consider important may prove to have significant impact when rigorously researched.

Step 5: Synthesizing the client's clinical needs and circumstances with the relevant research, finalize a shared plan of intervention collaboratively with the client

Given the available research, it appears that psychopharmacological treatments and/or psychotherapy are the best options for helping to address Sam's depression. The next consideration is the expertise of the clinician and the availability of services one cannot personally provide. This aspect of planning involves whether to not the clinical social worker is trained and competent to provide the appropriate services, or has them available within the agency or through consultation arrangements. If the services are available, treatment may begin immediately. Clinicians must make a referral to a provider with appropriate expertise if such services are not directly available. In some cases, making such a referral will involve locating providers of the service.

In Sam's case, the assessing clinical social worker has expertise in both cognitive behavioral therapies and in psychodynamically based psychotherapies. She also has experience working with individuals around depression and loss.

Based on this conversation, the following treatment plan emerges and is agreed upon by both Sam and the clinical social worker.

1. Sam will attend weekly brief psychodynamically oriented psychotherapy, contracting for 3 months. Within the therapy, the focus will be initially on his depressive symptoms, his understanding of their origins, and helping him to develop more effective strategies to cope with the depressive feelings.
2. Sam will set up an appointment with his doctor and discuss the potential of starting him on an antidepressant, taking into consideration his age and the side effect profile. The social worker will consult with the doctor on a regular basis regarding possible side effects, medication efficacy, and changes in symptoms. (Sam signs the consent forms to authorize this communication.)
3. Sam and the social worker will both ask others they know about group therapy or support group options in the community. From the available options, Sam will pick one of the groups that he feels would most suit his personality and comfort level.

Step 6: Implement the intervention

Sam and the clinical social worker identified a start date for the interventions to begin and the parameters around the treatment, including a targeted termination date. Sam and his clinical social worker agreed to monitor his energy level and social involvement on a session-by-session basis. They agreed that if progress is not apparent in a month, a more formal tracking of his progress would be initiated.

Alternately, Sam's depression could have been quantitatively assessed using a standardized measure of depression completed at regular intervals. This would allow for quantitative evaluation of progress using a single case evaluation approach. Sam was comfortable with an ongoing, narrative assessment of his situation.

Chapter 12
Ray: A Man Fearful of Panic Attacks

Ray is a 27-year-old single white man. He sought mental health services due to panic attacks and increasing concern that they would reoccur. This is despite the fact that he has had only four attacks in all, each occurring in the past six months. "The attacks are horrible, but now I am even more worried that they will come back." He has only had panic attacks in his apartment. He notes no precipitant or sensations that might warn of an oncoming attack. "It's such a mystery—they just come on me—this just makes it harder." During the attacks he sweats and trembles; he says he feels "like there's electricity running through me." He feels faint, but only once felt that he was choking. "Only one time did I fear I was going to die... I couldn't really catch my breath. It was the worst. That's why I'm here today." He denies any numbness during or after the attacks, any chest pains, or any fears he is going crazy. "It just takes me over."

Ray is a computer and network installer and repair technician. He is college-educated. He runs a small business with a college friend, begun four years ago. Their business has been successful and his income is "good enough" and "steady." He has no legal issues. Still, his concern about more panic attacks is making it harder for him to do on-site service work for customers. "I'm doing the work visits but I am worrying more and more. I can't get the fear out of my head." Despite the attacks, he has done his work appointments. "Recently it has become harder, 'cause I worry more and more about having an attack, but I still do my job." He shows only hints of potential agoraphobia.

Ray has had no prior mental health concerns and has had no medical issues; including a physical examination two months ago which revealed no cause for any concern. He denies changes in mood other than concern about more attacks. He denies changes in weight, eating, or sleeping habits. Ray denies any suicidal ideation other than wondering if he did have been better off dead after his worst attack in which he thought he would die. This ideation did not continue. He has no identified plans for suicide or passive self-harm, and seemed truly puzzled he was asked about this. He notes no family history of mental health issues or undue

J. W. Drisko and M. D. Grady, *Evidence-Based Practice in Clinical Social Work*, Essential Clinical Social Work Series, DOI: 10.1007/978-1-4614-3470-2_12, © Springer Science+Business Media New York 2012

anxiety, which makes him feel all the more different. His parents run a family florist business that employs his older brother and sister; he says "I can always work there if I want to." He likes his sibs and knows he could work in the family business, but instead wanted to try his hand at his own business. The family was supportive of his decision but teases him at times about "going his own way." Ray says it is only teasing: "there is no doubt I'd be there if they really needed me. They have too many people for the amount of work they do." His beloved grandfather died 18 months ago, which was a significant loss of a life-long caregiver and source of support, but Ray does not see this as related to his panic attacks. Ray has a circle of friends from work and college, with whom he plays softball and "sometimes drinks too much." He says he used pot and tried cocaine in college but denies current use. He has had two relatively long-term sexual relationships with women, including an engagement that did not work out just after college. He wishes he could "find the right girl" but is not worried it will happen.

Ray is able to identify his own strengths: as persistent, "pretty smart," willing to take risks (such as in starting the business), loyal-always there for my family and friends, having a sense of humor, and being tolerant of different ideas. He sees himself as well supported by family and friends, who have both attributes he likes and enjoys as well as small flaws that bug him at times.

Beyond the panic attacks and worry, which he says "is only recent," Ray thinks his limitations are "I'm kind of sloppy," "I should put more time into learning the technical side of the business, but instead I watch sports on my own or with my friends," and "my mother says I should be around more." He does not seem overly self-doubting or unable to view himself and other people in a flexible and balanced manner.

Step 1: Drawing on client needs and circumstances learned in a thorough assessment, identify answerable practice questions and related research information needs

Ray fits DSM-IV criteria for a panic disorder. Ray was actively involved in his assessment and appeared to be forthcoming if sometimes a bit puzzled by questions about family and history. He has had unexpected panic attacks and over a period of over a month his worry about them has become persistent and intensified. His behavior has not (yet) changed due to the attacks, but this has become a source of some concern for Ray. His panic attacks do not appear related to substance use or medication use. He does not appear to fit criteria for either social or specific phobia, obsessive–compulsive disorder or post-traumatic stress disorder as alternative sources of his symptoms. Ray does not appear to fit criteria for either an Axis II personality disorder or Axis III medical condition. He reports that he has had a recent physical exam showing no medical concerns.

Ray's life circumstances have not changed significantly in the past few years beyond the death of a beloved grandparent. His overall social and employment functioning appear essentially unchanged over the past few years, though his panic attacks are raising the possibility of future withdrawal which might impact on both areas. He has several sources of support and resilience and very few other challenges.

Panic disorder is associated with increased risk for agoraphobia and for depression. Onset for panic disorder often occurs in young adulthood, specifically during the 1920s. It is a low prevalent disorder at 2–3% of the population, but common in prevalence for mental health disorders.

In the P.I.C.O. model, the Population is adult males with panic attacks or, more formally, panic disorder. The Interventions under consideration are psychotherapies and similar psychosocial interventions as well as medications. Comparisons would be between different therapies or psychosocial interventions as well as among medications and combinations of mediations and psychosocial therapies. The Outcomes would be reducing the frequency of Ray's panic attacks and worries about them, as well as ideally ending the panic attacks.

Step 2: Efficiently locate relevant research knowledge

A visit to the Cochrane Collaboration web site (www.thecochranelibrary.org) reveals at the time of writing two systematic reviews related to panic disorder (Furukawa et al. 2007; Watanabe et al. 2009). Both are recent, and current through 2009. The reviews note that panic disorder can be treated with pharmacotherapy, with psychotherapy, or with both in combination. However, the systematic review abstracts indicate that the relative merits of combined therapies were previously not well established. Advantages of the different types of therapy might differ over time. That is, while one therapy might be most helpful initially, another might prove more helpful over an extended period of time. Thus, both short- and long-term effectiveness should be appraised.

The reviews found just three high quality studies comparing behavioral therapies with benzodiazepines for panic disorder, and another 23 studies comparing mainly behavioral or cognitive-behavioral therapies with antidepressants for panic disorder. Watanabe et al. (2009, Abstract) found there was no statistically significant difference between combined use of benzodiazepines and therapy compared to therapy alone during the intervention period (relative risk (RR) for combined therapy 1.25, 95% CI 0.78–2.03, $p = 0.35$). Nor was there any difference at the end of intervention (RR 0.78, 95% CI 0.45–1.35, $p = 0.37$). Both conclusions were based on two studies involving 166 patients. There was also no statistically significant difference between combined therapy compared to treatment by benzodiazepines alone during the intervention (RR 1.57, 95% CI 0.83–2.98, $p = 0.17$) in one study involving 66 patients. There was also no statistically significant difference at the end of treatment (RR 3.39, 95% CI 1.03–11.21, $p = 0.05$) or at seven-month follow-up (RR 2.31, 95% CI 0.79–6.74, $p = 0.12$). (The authors called the end of treatment result $p = 0.05$, "borderline significant." However, since statistical significance requires a result of $p < 0.05$ this is *not* a statistically significant result.) Watanabe et al. (2009, Plain language summary) state there is a "paucity of high quality evidence investigating the efficacy of psychotherapy combined with benzodiazepines for panic disorder. Currently, there is inadequate evidence to assess the clinical effects of psychotherapy combined with benzodiazepines for patients who are diagnosed with panic disorder." Yet this preliminary evidence, to Cochrane Collaboration standards, indicates that *either* behavioral

Analysis 1.10. Comparison 1 Psychotherapy+Benzodiazepine vs Psychotherapy alone, Outcome 10 Global/Avoidance/Panic severity at the end of the intervention.

Review: Combined psychotherapy plus benzodiazepines for panic disorder

Comparison: 1 Psychotherapy+Benzodiazepine vs Psychotherapy alone

Outcome: 10 Global/Avoidance/Panic severity at the end of the intervention

Study or subgroup	PT+Benzo		PT		Std. Mean Difference	Weight	Std. Mean Difference
	N	Mean(SD)	N	Mean(SD)	IV,Random,95% CI		IV,Random,95% CI
1 Behaviour therapy							
Marks 1993	28	2.3 (1.1)	24	1.8 (1)		37.4 %	0.47 [-0.09, 1.02]
Wardle 1994	24	81.46 (23.99)	23	77.43 (29.42)		34.9 %	0.15 [-0.42, 0.72]
Subtotal (95% CI)	**52**		**47**			**72.3 %**	**0.31 [-0.09, 0.71]**
Heterogeneity: Tau² = 0.0; Chi² = 0.62, df = 1 (P = 0.43); I² =0.0%							
Test for overall effect: Z = 1.54 (P = 0.12)							
2 Cognitive-behavioural therapy							
Auerbach 1997	18	0.33 (0.83)	20	0.09 (0.27)		27.7 %	0.39 [-0.25, 1.03]
Subtotal (95% CI)	**18**		**20**			**27.7 %**	**0.39 [-0.25, 1.03]**
Heterogeneity: not applicable							
Test for overall effect: Z = 1.19 (P = 0.24)							
Total (95% CI)	**70**		**67**			**100.0 %**	**0.33 [0.00, 0.67]**
Heterogeneity: Tau² = 0.0; Chi² = 0.66, df = 2 (P = 0.72); I² =0.0%							
Test for overall effect: Z = 1.93 (P = 0.053)							

```
        -1    -0.5    0    0.5    1
     Favours PT+Benzo    Favours PT
```

Fig. 12.1 A forest plot comparing the effectiveness of psychotherapy versus psychotherapy plus benzodiazepine medication on panic severity at the end of treatment. From Watanabe et al. (2009, page 37) Figure of a Forest plot entitled "Analysis 1.10 Comparison 1...". Reprinted with permission from John Wiley and Sons

therapy alone *or* in conjunction with benzodiazepines have empirical support for use with panic disorders.

Figure 12.1 displays a Forest plot of the comparative effectiveness of behavioral and cognitive behavioral therapies with and without benzodiazepine medication on global anxiety scores at the end of treatment (Watanabe et al. 2009, p. 37). Note that the box and whisker plots are largely on the right hand side of the dividing line. This indicates that the results favor psychotherapy alone. The key to this interpretation is provided at the bottom of the chart ("favors PT" = favors psychotherapy alone). However, each of the box and whiskers plots and the summary diamond plots touches the dividing line. This indicates that the advantage of psychotherapy over psychotherapy and medication is a relatively small one. Both treatments can be effective as noted in the plain language summary reported above. Note, too, that the plain language summary also incorporates effectiveness on other outcomes, not only reduction in global panic severity at the end of treatment.

Furukawa et al. (2007, Abstract) found that in the early "acute" phase of panic disorder treatment, the combined use of antidepressants and psychotherapy was superior to either antidepressants alone (RR 1.24, 95% CI 1.02–1.52) or to therapy alone (RR 1.17, 95% CI 1.05–1.31) in 23 comparison involving 1,709 patients.

However, the combined therapy lead to more drop outs due to unpleasant medi-cation-related side effects than did the psychotherapy alone (NNH about 26). After therapy at follow-up, the combined treatment was "as effective" as therapy alone (RR 0.96, 95% CI 0.79–1.16) and more effective than antidepressants alone (RR 1.61, 95% CI 1.23–2.11). Furukawa et al. (2007, Abstract) conclude that "either combined therapy or psychotherapy alone may be chosen as first line treatment for panic disorder with or without agoraphobia, depending on patient preference."

Three studies also appeared relevant and pointed to additional types of treat-ment for consideration. Having alternatives is important if Ray proved unwilling or uncomfortable with some potential treatments. They also allow Ray to make informed decisions about alternative treatments. Wiborg and Dahl (1996) com-pared a psychodynamic psychotherapy and antidepressant medication for panic attacks over an extended follow-up period. They cited prior work indicating that panic disorders, treated by medication alone, had variable but potentially very high rates of reoccurrence [20–30% at the low estimate, 70–90% at the high estimate according to Ballenger (2003)]. They sought to reduce relapse rates by combining brief psychodynamic psychotherapy adapted from Davenloo (1978) as well as Strupp and Binder (1984) coupled with medication. The issue of relapse rates would be an important piece of information to communicate to Ray as part of his treatment planning process. Milrod et al. (2007) studied psychodynamic psycho-therapy separately and in combination with medication for panic disorders. Berger et al. (2004) studied the effectiveness of antidepressants combined with interper-sonal treatment for panic disorder, but in a population of person with comorbid personality disorders, that did not fit with Ray.

Wiborg and Dahl (1996) studied people with DSM-III criteria panic disorder. They randomly assigned 20 patients to clomipramine therapy for 9 months and another 20 patients to combined clomipramine for 9 months combined with 15 weekly sessions of brief dynamic psychotherapy. Outcomes were measured by patient reports of panic attacks and by the Hamilton Rating Scale for Anxiety and the Panic Attack and Anxiety Scale. They followed the patients for numbers of panic attacks and levels of both anxiety and depression at 6, 12, and 18 months after beginning treatment. The relapse rate was significantly higher after nine months for patients treated with medication alone (panic attacks $M = 0.8$, sd $= 0.8$ versus $M = 0.0$, sd $= 0.0$ for the therapy and medication group; effects size $d = 2.07$ for medication alone versus $d = 3.20$ for medication and therapy). There were no significant differences on the Hamilton Rating Scale for Anxiety scores between groups.

Milrod and colleagues found that across a racially mixed sample, the 26 clients receiving panic focused psychodynamic psychotherapy completed therapy with significantly lower Panic Disorder Severity Scale scores ($M = 5.1$, sd $= 4.0$ to $M = 9.0$, sd $= 4.6$; $t = 3.30$, df $= 47$, $p = 0.002$; Effect size $= 0.95$; no CIs were reported) than did 13 clients receiving relaxation therapy. However, scores on the Hamilton Anxiety and Hamilton Depression Rating Scales did not differ signifi-cantly. One person in the relaxation group worsened significantly and was dropped from the study and offered medication. This is a point worth mentioning as a possible risk to track carefully for Ray and any other person with panic attacks. This study was impressive for its inclusion of racially diverse patients, which might prove very relevant in some clinical situations.

Overall, it appears that the combination of therapy and medication is likely to be effective in treating Ray's panic disorder. There are alternatives for Ray to consider in regard to treatment by psychotherapy alone versus psychotherapy in combination with medication. While this discussion would be between Ray and his prescribing physician, it appears that antidepressants more often generate unpleasant side effects than do anti-anxiety medications. Ray does not appear depressed, so anti-anxiety medications may also fit better with his clinical presentation. On the other hand, anti-anxiety mediations have potential for abuse and/ or over-use, though Ray does not seem to have a significant history of abuse of substances or mediations. Given his panic and level of desperation, however, caution is in order. It would also be a reasonable choice to consider psychotherapy without medication.

Step 3: Critically appraise the quality and applicability of this knowledge to the client's needs and situation

In terms of psychotherapies, cognitive and cognitive–behavioral therapies have been well studied and demonstrate good effectiveness with panic disorders. They appear to be a strong choice for Ray to consider. If Ray is uncomfortable with these treatments, there is some evidence in support of brief psychodynamic psychotherapy as an effective treatment for panic disorder, but the evidence base for this recommendation is less well developed than is the evidence base for cognitive-behavioral treatment.

The study samples are not limited to men only, though there is no clear reason to think that these therapies would be contraindicated for Ray based on his age or gender.

Step 4: Discuss the research results with the client to ensure they fit with the client's values and goals

Ray chose a behavioral therapy (Barlow et al. 1989) after discussion of these alternatives with his clinical social worker. He had only a few questions, but had some clear preferences regarding medication. He was not interested in taking medication at first, though he was happy that medication could be a "back up plan" if therapy alone did not work well enough. He clearly did not like the idea of possible mediation side effects of any kind. He understood the general idea of cognitive-behavioral therapy and was open to it. It was clear his outlook on the therapy was positive.

Step 5: Synthesizing the client's clinical needs and circumstances with the relevant research, finalize a shared plan of intervention collaboratively with the client

Cognitive-behavioral therapy for panic disorder was immediately available for Ray through his community mental health clinic. The clinic would also make access to a psychiatric consult for medications possible should it become appropriate.

Step 6: Implement the intervention

The main challenge of the treatment planning was the lack of an obvious precipitant. Ray's concerns were general and difficult for him to pin down as specific cognitions. It took some time for Ray to think of his fear of the next panic attack as a way of thinking he could address. Once he caught on to this idea, he was able to combine relaxation techniques and breathing exercises with increasing exposure to thoughts of another panic attack. He concluded therapy after eight sessions over 10 weeks. Eight weeks later he reported having no further panic attacks and much lower worry about them reoccurring.

Given the apparent effectiveness of the treatment, no additional structured evaluation of outcome was undertaken. Ray's descriptions of the reduction in both number of panic attacks and worries about them were formally documented in his clinic record. His reports on the frequency of his panic attacks over the 10 weeks were also recorded. This would have allowed for a single case evaluation, but the clarity of his improvement did not make such a formal evaluation model appear necessary. Ray was quite satisfied with his treatment and its results.

Chapter 13
Sally: A 12-Year-Old Who has Reactive Attachment Disorder

Sally is a 12-year-old biracial (African-American/white) child. She is tall and lanky with very neat cornrows. Her adoptive parents in conjunction with her adoption social worker referred her for services. Sally seems comfortable living in her adoptive home, with her African-American father, her white mother, and her younger biracial biological sibling. Sally has been in the home for just over two years and her adoption was legally finalized eight months ago. She interacts smoothly with the family but her parents say that "something's missing." Sally does not turn to her parents for comfort or guidance. Her parents have offered considerable daily life structure to help her become more connected, but she does not seem to look for their care and support. They fear she will turn to "just anyone" and as a near teenager this could mean others might take advantage of her. "She doesn't think at all about her safety." From the parent's perspective, it is difficult "to get so little response" from Sally, though they are quite aware they are "in it for the long haul." "We are committed to her." They find it difficult to understand her nonverbal cues and, even after they encourage her to talk, Sally seems puzzled about her feelings and needs.

Protective services had placed Sally in several different foster homes due to parental neglect between ages four to nine. They returned Sally to her mother after each out of home placement, some lasting up to a year. Her single parent biological mother worked long hours and, at times, left Sally alone for extended periods. During the foster placements she was described as "a very eager to please child," who "treated everyone as a friend," was "very open" and "had lots of friends." There was no evidence of physical or sexual abuse during the placements, though other children would sometimes verbally tease Sally. Her first child protective worker noted she was "attractive and pleasant," but also noted she "did not seem to discriminate among people, seeking what contact she could get from just about anyone." She has limited self-care skills and would "get lost" in TV shows if given the chance. She loved "Disney films" which it seemed to be used as surrogate babysitters. Sally was two years behind academically in school at age

J. W. Drisko and M. D. Grady, *Evidence-Based Practice in Clinical Social Work*,
Essential Clinical Social Work Series, DOI: 10.1007/978-1-4614-3470-2_13,
© Springer Science+Business Media New York 2012

nine, had a limited vocabulary, and limited math and reading skills. None of these learning issues had any apparent organic basis based on physical and neurological examinations. She behaved well in school and "was never a behavior problem." "People like her."

The local courts terminated parental rights after the mother's boyfriend got into several fights with her. The final straw was that he hit Sally in the back of the head with a frying pan, which seemed to be a one time occurrence. Sally was unconscious for several hours, and had a very small laceration where she was hit. She was treated for swelling around her brain over the next few days. She was diagnosed with a closed head trauma from the incident. The organic effects of the incident are unclear, both in terms of any learning-related challenges or changes in self-regulatory functions. Still, her neurological and learning testing did not indicate any significant issues beyond lagging beyond grade level. Her biological mother said she seemed "different" after the trauma, but was never able to pin point just how Sally had changed.

Sally's adoptive parents have a biological child and wanted to adopt. They were "taken" with Sally immediately upon seeing her: She had the skin tone and hair color of their biological daughter. "She seemed to fit right in" her father said. Early visits and her moving in seemed to go well. Sally showed no hesitancy in engaging with the family, which then seemed to be a pleasant surprise. "We knew she should be more careful, but we were glad she seemed to accept us." "There was no honeymoon; she was just part of the family."

The problems emerged when Sally got involved in school and in activities beyond the core family. "She treated everyone like family!" In consultation with the adoption worker, the family increased their daily structure and actively kept Sally within defined limits. "This wasn't hard, and we only seldom got upset, but it took vigilance." The limits seemed to provide some order for Sally but did not decrease the indiscriminate contact with others, including passers-by, the delivery man, and dog walkers. "We weren't sure she'd always be safe, you know, and she's almost a teenager." Her parents also noted they did not see how Sally got cared for when she seemed down or hurt. They would have to seek her out and actively question Sally about her emotional state; which seemed to confuse Sally. "At first we thought we were too pushy, but then we realized she didn't really know how she felt or at least wouldn't easily share it."

Sally has lots of acquaintances, but no real friends. She easily connects with people but does not sustain interaction and most are brief. She makes good eye contact. She displays a wide range of emotion. She has been oddly resistant to organized sports activities or clubs, which her parents thought might be of interest to her. Her concern is that "the kids will tease me." She has never stuck with a sport or club for more than a few weeks, though her parents are now encouraging her to pick one activity to pursue based on her skills and interests.

Sally appears to meet DSM-IV-TR criteria for reactive attachment disorder, disinhibited type. She displays diffuse attachments, as evident through indiscriminate sociability and a marked lack of selective attachments (to her biological mother or foster caregivers in the past and to her adoptive parents currently). This pattern began before age five, can be reasonably viewed as the cause of her current attachment problems (what is called "pathogenic" care in DSM-IV-TR terminology). The attachment issues do not appear to be related to specific trauma as neither physical nor sexual abuse were reported in the past. Neglect predominated. (Given her multiple placements, the possibility of such abuse is real, but it had not been not substantiated by her caregivers or by Sally herself at this point.) There is no evidence of autism spectrum disorder or pervasive developmental delay; in fact, Sally has very good motor skills and eye-hand coordination even after her head trauma. The effects of her head trauma are unknown but do not appear to account for the attachment challenges. Alexithymia should also be ruled out given Sally's difficulties in identifying her feelings.

Attachment is an interpersonal process that occurs between people. It is quite unlike a bacterial infection or depression that may be viewed as "located" within a person. The consequences of a lack of attachment, or a disinhibited attachment, may be observed in behaviors such as indiscriminately turning to known or unknown people for care and support, and failing to use a known caregiver for support when hurt or emotionally upset. The behaviors require at least two people in interaction, and the quality of their interaction is crucial to identifying attachment problems. The interactive quality of attachment disorders makes evident some of the shortcomings of medical model diagnosis. The lack of attachment opportunities before age five are assumed to have a significant internalized effect on a child's development, but for attachment to develop, other people must offer "good enough" sources of care on a consistent basis. Diagnosing reactive attachment disorder is a difficult endeavor. Clinicians use different diagnostic standards and protocols for children of different ages (Zilberstein 2006). Children who have received poor care from adults are expected to respond appropriately to any unknown adult, across a variety of contexts, as if such interactions should not be expected to be untrustworthy and stressful.

Due to the interpersonal nature of attachment problems, it is difficult to develop valid standardized measures for them. For non-clinical populations of preschoolers, the Ainsworth Strange Situation Test (1978) is often used to identify different types of attachment. However, the Strange Situation Test is not a scaled measure, and is not intended to be used as an outcome measure. For school-age children and teenagers, there is no widely used measure of attachment. The Randolph Attachment Disorder Questionnaire [RADQ] is often used as an outcome measure, though it was intended as a general screening tool for broad attachment problems. The RADQ has only face validity and emphasizes problems with conduct more than attachment quality per se. Smyke and Zeanah's (1999) Disturbances of Attachment Interview also generates a typology and is rarely used in outcome research. Other measures, particularly the Achenbach Child Behavior Checklist [CBCL] (1991, 1992), are widely used as proxy outcome measures in studies of treatments for RAD, but do not include any direct measures of attachment. Instead, the CBCL's conduct and learning disorder subscales are used as proxies for attachment quality. The problem with this use of proxy measures is that conduct or learning problems may, or may not, be related to attachment quality. These conduct and learning issues may represent distinct but comorbid disorders rather than representing a core aspect of attachment.

These key problems with conceptualizing and measuring RAD have not stopped researchers from preliminary outcome studies. They do seriously limit the confidence that clinicians and researchers can put in their results. What is measured may not fairly and comprehensively reflect the dimension of RAD nor measure it effectively. The conceptual, diagnostic, and measurement problems become crucial in identifying and applying high quality research to Sally's needs.

Step 1: Drawing on client needs and circumstances learned in a thorough assessment, identify answerable practice questions and related research information needs

Sally does not identify any problems with her behavior or her interactions with her parents. She says her parents and teachers are "overreacting" (a word she also says is used by her parents about her sister's behavior). Sally's parents are concerned about her disinhibited social interactions that could increasingly be unsafe and risky. They are also concerned that Sally does not turn to them for support when she is hurt or anxious, though this vulnerability is clearly a lesser concern. It does not seem to be the driving force behind their referral of Sally for assessment and possible treatment. The family's adoption worker has been a steady support since Sally's adoption and agrees that Sally's indiscriminate or disinhibited interaction has been consistent, and views the parents concerns as reasonable. Both the parents and the adoption worker believe there may be some subtle medical issue related to her head trauma, but both view her prior workup as through. Her parents do not report concern about possible sexual abuse, though both the adoption worker and the clinical social worker doing the assessment think it should remain an open question.

In the **P.I.C.O.** model, the **P**opulation is school-age children with Reactive Attachment Disorder, Disinhibited Subtype. The **I**nterventions under consideration are psychotherapies and similar psychosocial interventions or programs. Medication is not under consideration. **C**omparisons would be between different therapies or psychosocial interventions or programs. The **O**utcomes would be increasing Sally's attachment to her parents as most clearly demonstrated through turning to them for support when she is worried or fearful—to be her parental attachment figures. Reduced indiscriminate social relations are another important outcome from the parent's perspective.

Step 2: Efficiently locate relevant research knowledge

At the time of writing, a search of the Cochrane Collaboration Library (www.thecochranelibrary.org) for the keyword "reactive attachment disorder" reveals only a provisional application to undertake a systematic review of research on "disorganized infant attachment and preventive interventions: a review and meta-analysis." A similar search for social service programs at the Campbell Collaboration Library (www.campbellcollaboration.org/library.php) returns the phrase "search gave no hits." There appear to be no systematic reviews of treatments for RAD.

RAD is a relatively low incidence disorder and one that child clinicians may not understand in depth. Limited research is available on treatment outcomes for RAD. According to O'Connor and Zeanah (2003, p. 233), "no treatment method has been shown to be effective for children with attachment disorders." Further searches of individual research studies are the next approach to locating the relevant research literature.

A search for research articles using PubMed (www.ncbi.nlm.nih.gov/pubmed/) reveals no outcome studies for children with RAD of this age group. Further paid subscription searches of PsychInfosss (http://www.apa.org/pubs/databases/psycinfo/index.aspx) and Social Work Abstracts (through EBSCO Host) reveal only a few pre-post treatment outcome studies for RAD among a wide range of conceptual articles, case studies, and opinion articles. None of the outcome studies is a true RCT (experiment). Myeroff (1997) and Myeroff et al. (1999) report that Levy and Orlans' (undated) holding therapy produced significant reduction in aggression and delinquency as measured by subscales of the CBCL for 11 adolescents receiving therapy (Aggression subscale, paired $t = 4.26$, df $= 10$, $p = 0.001$; Effect size Cohen's $d = 1.33$. Delinquency subscale, paired $t = 2.37$, df $= 10$, $p = 0.04$; $d = 0.77$) while a comparison group of nine adolescents showed no change. No significant change in RADQ scores was reported (and this information was simply not reported in the 1999 article). No evidence that the adolescents met criteria for a DSM-IV-TR RAD diagnosis was offered. It is unclear if the authors or other provided the treatment. In another study, Wimmer et al. (2009) report a single group pre-post study using a combined 10 h therapy including family counseling, behavioral management training, and holding therapy as taught by Children Unlimited of South Carolina (2004). All the children had received diagnoses of RAD. They report significant gains on RADQ scores ($t = -3.65$, df $= 21$, $p = 0$ 001; Effect size by Cohen's $d = 0.71$) and on the Child and Adolescent Functional Assessment Scale (Hodges et al. 2004) for general behavior ($t = -2.61$, df $= 22$, $p = 0.02$; Cohen's $d = 0.65$). It is important to note that holding therapy has been heavily challenged on safety and ethical grounds due to deaths of several children treated with it or variants of it (American Academy of Child and Adolescent Psychiatry 2005).

While these findings might appear promising, holding therapy (also called rebirthing therapy) has been deemed inappropriate and potentially dangerous by the American Professional Society on the Abuse of Children and the American Psychological Association, Division 37 (2006) and the American Academy of Child and Adolescent Psychiatry (2005). It should not be used due to risk of severe harm or death. Note carefully that finding significant research results does not automatically mean that the treatment is appropriate or without substantial risk of harm. Such harms are unlikely to be noted in the original articles, or necessarily, in later research reviews.

Becker-Weidman (2006a, b) reports a quasi-experimental comparison of Hughes' (2004) Dyadic Developmental Therapy [DDT] versus treatment as usual.

All the children included in the study met criteria for DSM-IV-TR RAD diagnosis. Pre-post comparison demonstrated significant improvement for the DDT group ($n = 34$) on five CBCL subscales for aggression, withdrawn, social problems, rule-breaking, and thought problems (t values ranged from 4.38 to 12.81, df = 0 33, all p values were $p < 0.001$; d values ranged from 1.01 to 2.78). In addition, significant improvement on the RADQ was reported ($t = 12.82$, df = 33, $p = 0.001$; $d = 2.70$). Only results on the CBCL subscale anxious-depressed were not significant. The treatment as usual group ($n = 30$) showed no significant pre-post improvement.

Step 3: Critically appraise the quality and applicability of this knowledge to the client's needs and situation

Research on the effectiveness of treatments for RAD is very limited. The measures used to assess attachment are also very limited and of questionable validity. Some research findings support a therapy that has been essentially banned due to several deaths associated with its use and very high potential for harm. Overall, the best available evidence points to Hughes' (2004) DDT. The evidence is not an RCT but is Level 2 quality. However, the researcher was also the provider of the therapy, which may be a source of attribution bias. Note that the effect sizes are extremely large, near their practical limits. Yet even taking into consideration that Cohen's d effects sizes may be inflated when applied to small samples sizes, the effect sizes are very large. In context, this treatment model includes many components also endorsed by observational studies and practice wisdom.

A summary of a wide range of non-experimental studies completed by Drisko (2009) documents that many studies of RAD address single treatment components or issues that might better be viewed in combination to generate a much more comprehensive treatment package. For example, one excellent clinical report stated that parents under-estimate the levels of anxiety of children with RAD and might do better to take a more active and preventive or preemptive approach to caring for their children (Lieberman 2003). On the other hand, this detailed article did not mention that without a safe, enduring, and consistent family placement, a child with RAD might have a great deal of difficulty making continued progress. It is as if the many components of RAD treatment are stated one by one, with few comprehensive models. This may reflect the interest or expertise of the many researchers. They may be knowledgeable enough to focus on specific treatment components, and assume that other conditions are already in place. One comprehensive approach is Hughes' PLACE model (see Hughes, undated). This model was used in the Becker-Weidman study reported above.

In the diagnosis and treatment of RAD, the clinical social work person-in-environment perspective proves very useful. Clinical social workers should consider the child's placement situation, its safety, empathy, potential longevity, and appropriateness as a foundation to child and family psychotherapy per se. Treatment is best understood as a package of many interventions. These interventions may have different purposes and even different auspices. Drisko and

Zilberstein (2006) report that parents attribute improvement by their children with RAD to a combination of factors. These include the (1) constant parental presence and supervision, (2) parental bonding and strong commitment, (3) providing clear and consistent daily life structure, (4) steady behavioral management, (5) acute empathic attunement to interpret the child's often odd or confusing messages, (6) responding to an intuitive or empathic grasp of the child's needs, (7) using social supports for the parents and the child, (8) therapy for the child often related to managing the effects of trauma, and loss, (9) promoting the child's active involvement in community life, and (10) intervening to support their social activities. Finally, parents and children both had long-term access to prolonged relationships with child welfare/adoptive workers, clinical social workers, and networks of parents of children with similar needs. Treatment of RAD might best be understood as taking an entire childhood and required extensive efforts by parents and professionals together. Yet no RCTs are available to compare such a package of interventions to alternatives. The best available evidence is still quite limited for RAD.

Sally is a biracial child with mixed race adoptive parents and a biracial biological sibling. The research literature on attachment rarely specifies the races of children and parents included in outcome studies. It is not clear that race is a major influence in Sally's situation. It was not raised as a concern by her parents. Still, the limited detail on sample characteristics offers no information on this topic should it be a concern.

Step 4: Discuss the research results with the client to ensure they fit with the client's values and goals

There is no specific evidence base for treatment of RAD, disinhibited type RAD. Outcome studies for RAD, based on children with clear DSM-IV-TR diagnoses, are very few. Sally's parents must be informed that holding therapy, which is widely discussed in the media and on internet sites, presents a great potential for harm and should not be undertaken. Several professional groups prohibit its use for safety reasons.

The best available evidence suggests treatment using the Hughes' (2004) DDT. The evidence base for this therapy is quite limited, but it appears to yield good results on several attachment and behavioral issues. One practical concern might be if any professional trained in the DDT model is available in the geographic location of the family.

Sally's limited motivation for treatment might be an obstacle to her participation. Ironically, her lack of motivation is offset by her disinhibited attachment. Sally, like many children, may be brought for treatment "against their will" with a very strong chance that her investment will build over time.

Step 5: Synthesizing the client's clinical needs and circumstances with the relevant research, finalize a shared plan of intervention collaboratively with the client

After discussion with the parents and Sally, a plan centering on Hughes' DDT model was selected. Both Hughes publications, and many reports of the effective components of treatment for children with RAD and their families, indicate this will be a long-term effort. The DDT model emphasizes work with parents to provide safety and security with attention to the parent's own attachment strategies. In parent work and conjoint work with the child, parents work to increase attunement to the child, to help understand the child's subjective experiences and to address inevitable misattunements and interpersonal conflicts. Attachment facilitating and cognitive behavior interventions are also used in day-to-day interaction. The parents were pleased with this plan, though they were not happy or encouraged by the limited research on effective treatments. They found the lack of strong support for any treatment to suggest their therapeutic work might be ineffective. Sally was willing to be involved but her understanding of the treatment was uncertain.

No therapist trained in Hughes' DDT was found in the family's local region. However, a therapist with expertise in treating RAD, who had attended training workshops by Hughes and others, was available nearby. The family was open to a referral and understood that they might be making a long-term contract to work with a clinical social worker.

Step 6: Implement the intervention

After 18 months of treatment, Sally's parents reported she had made some progress in reducing her indiscriminate social contacts that they viewed as important. They continued to be concerned that as she entered adolescence, her lack of discrimination and social judgment might increasingly put her safety at risk.

On the other hand, their therapeutic work had helped them better interpret Sally's signs of stress and anxiety. This allowed them to intervene preventively, as well as to help a relationship in which Sally felt them as supportive, tuned in, and nurturing. They understood this as reflecting changes in Sally's attachment to them, as well as in their own behavior toward Sally.

In individual therapy, Sally had begun to explore and mourn the loss of her biological mother. Sally's repertoire of affect remained limited, but sadness was more apparent and connected to appropriate content. No indications of sexual abuse were evident, though alexithymia remained a relevant rule out.

Sally's clinical social worker asked her parents to rate her behavior using the CBCL on an annual basis. Over the course of one year, Sally's scores on the CBCL subscales for withdrawal increased, reflecting less disinhibited behavior. At the same time, her CBCL subscale scores on social problems decreased. Visual inspection of the scores was another source of documentation of Sally's improvement.

Chapter 14
Newman and Loretta: Parents of Arthur, a Man Who has Schizophrenia

Arthur was brought to the hospital by his parents, Newman and Loretta, after Arthur reported that he was hearing voices that were telling him to hurt himself. This is not the first time that Arthur has heard such voices, but this time his parents felt that he was "taking them more seriously" than he has done in the past. They were concerned that he would listen to the voices and actually take action to hurt himself.

Arthur is a 36-year-old African–American male who lives with his parents, Newman (64-years-old) and Loretta (63-years-old). He has an older sister, Mary (age 39) who lives out of state with her husband and three children. He attends a day treatment program in their local community, where he participates in a vocational program for individuals with severe and persistent mental illnesses. Arthur was diagnosed with schizophrenia, paranoid type, approximately 15 years ago while he was attending college in another state. Over this time period, he has had several hospitalizations. His presenting symptoms at the time of hospitalization included hearing voices, questioning the motives and actions of his close friends, ceasing to attend classes and complete required assignments, decline in ability and/or interest in personal hygiene, and withdrawing from all social connections. His parents withdrew him from school in the middle of his junior year after his third hospitalization and he has been living with them since that time.

Upon his return home, his parents got him involved in a program through their local hospital for people who have been diagnosed with schizophrenia. The clinical social worker is a staff member on an interdisciplinary team that works with Arthur on an ongoing basis. Through this program, he has received medication management services through a physician, case management and vocational training referrals through a social worker, as well as individual therapy and group therapy to help manage his symptoms and increase his functioning in the community provided by different team members. Although the clinical social worker has met Arthur's parents before on several occasions, she has not worked with them lately due to Arthur's symptom stability and the fact that she is a relatively

J. W. Drisko and M. D. Grady, *Evidence-Based Practice in Clinical Social Work,*
Essential Clinical Social Work Series, DOI: 10.1007/978-1-4614-3470-2_14,
© Springer Science+Business Media New York 2012

new member to this unit. The clinical social worker's role on the team is to focus on the family members, providing a combination of case management and psychotherapy, including supportive therapy and/or family therapy among others, depending on the needs of the family.

His parents report that lately Arthur's symptoms seem to be increasing. They are worried about him and his future. Some of their concerns stem from the health problems he has, some of which are attributed to the medications he takes to manage his delusions and hallucinations. He has developed diabetes, and now has several health problems related to smoking, a habit his parents state he started when he joined the day treatment program where "everyone smokes like chimneys." He has a "terrible cough that won't go away" and has high blood pressure as well. They state they have tried to talk to him about changing his diet, exercise, and smoking habits, but that he has not done so. (It is also clear from his chart that several team members have promoted similar efforts with Arthur with no success.)

Newman and Loretta state that their primary concern is that this is the first time Arthur has taken the voices "seriously," and that this is an indication that his symptoms are getting worse. However, upon further questioning, it is clear that other stressors are also present for the family. Newman is close to retirement age, but does not feel like he can afford to retire given the care that they provide for Arthur and its costs. Although Arthur receives disability benefits, Newman states "it doesn't even come close to covering all that he needs." Loretta stopped working as a teacher when Arthur came home from college, but had not worked long by that time, as she stayed home while the children were young. Loretta had just recently reentered the work force when Arthur came home. As a result, she has very little pension of her own as she has devoted much of her time to caring for Arthur.

They also report that they personally are facing increased medical costs as they age, leading to more financial stress and are worried that their stress is what is causing the increase in Arthur's severity of symptoms. Their daughter lives across the country and is involved with her own family. Newman and Loretta are starting to feel more pressure to work out a long-term plan for Arthur. They feel that they have to "continue on as long as we can" since they do not think they can afford to retire or move. Another concern about moving is that Arthur's care providers and all other issues related to his care would also have to change. Loretta states she feels "trapped" and really worried about what will happen to Arthur when they are "too old to care for him or dead."

As a result of this stress, Loretta states she is having difficulty sleeping at night, spends most of her days worrying, has lost weight, and has started to separate some from her friends, as she feels that she is becoming a "broken record" by relaying all of her worries and does not want to be "such a downer." Newman reports similar symptoms, but also states that he is worried about Loretta as well. They feel very isolated and feel that they need help in managing all of the stress they are experiencing.

Despite their financial concerns and worries about Arthur's current and future care, Newman and Loretta's love and commitment to their son is obvious. Other staff members and a psychiatrist have mentioned to the social worker how fortunate Arthur is to have such devoted and caring parents.

While Arthur is having significant personal struggles that we will be addressed by his individual therapist, the clinical social worker's role in this case is to focus on helping Loretta and Newman with their identified issues. In speaking with them, they have two primary goals for coming. The first goal is to find more effective ways of managing their stress so that they can be better caregivers for Arthur and for each other. Their second goal is to identify a long-term plan for Arthur. They are worried about him, practically and physically, such as where he will live, about his health, and about his financial situation once they are gone. Given these priorities, the clinical social worker thinks that it would be most helpful in addressing their first goal to look for information on interventions for families who are experiencing stress related to a family member with schizophrenia. In regard to the long-term plan for Arthur, the social worker could take the lead in calling a team meeting so that all members can help brainstorm about resources and plans to support Arthur. The clinical social worker proposes this initial focus. Loretta and Newman agree to this plan. The clinical social worker also arranges a date for a team meeting among program staff.

Step 1: Drawing on practice questions, identify research information needs

Using the concepts outlined in the Chapter 4 on Assessment to develop the searchable question, there are many points to consider. The first point to consider is the role that this social worker has with the family. In this case, the worker's role is to help support the family. In this case, the family has asked for help in managing the high levels of stress they feel as they age and their son's needs increase.

In the **P.I.C.O.** model, the **P**opulation is parents of individuals with schizophrenia or stress in older adults. The **I**nterventions under consideration are psychotherapies and similar psychosocial interventions, as well as medications. In addition, interventions to help Newman and Loretta develop a plan for Arthur's long-term care is also a key long-term need. **C**omparisons would be between different therapies or psychosocial interventions as well as among medications and combinations of mediations and psychosocial therapies. The **O**utcomes would be increasing Loretta and Newman's capacities to manage their stress, as well increase their hopefulness and confidence in a plan for Arthur's future.

Step 2: Efficiently locate relevant research knowledge

To find effective interventions, the social worker first conducts an initial search on the Cochrane Collaboration's web site. However, there is little helpful information, as most of the materials address how family therapy can help the identified patient, rather than how different interventions may be useful in helping the family of the patient.

The social worker then searches the National Alliance of the Mentally Ill (NAMI) Web site (www.NAMI.com), using the search term "family support." One group treatment called "Family to Family" is identified. From the Family-to-Family site, links to several studies are found. These studies report that for family members, the group increased their sense of empowerment and decreased stress levels, including subjective feelings of burden and worry. The group treatment also increased their capacity to cope, and improved self-care (Dixon et al. 2004). Further, a link was found to a report regarding a 2010 study that found parents of adult children with mental illness who participate in education and support groups experience more positive outcomes and fewer burdens than those who do not participate in such groups   (http://www.nami.org/Content/ContentGroups/Press_Room1/20102/ June17/New_Study_Support_Groups_Help_Parents_of_ Adult_Children_Living_ with_Mental_Illness,_Create_Advocates.htm).

Despite numerous searches on Psychiatricguidelines.com, NAMI.org, Cochrane, NIMH.gov, and SAMHSA.gov, no individual treatments or family interventions were found beyond the family support groups discussed above. The searches all yielded studies discussing interventions aimed at helping the individual with schizophrenia, rather than their family members. Multiple family group interventions might be a source of support for family members, but the outcome studies located focus more on the seriously mentally ill family member rather than the family member. Searches of the Campbell Collaboration Library using several different terms also led to no hits.

In searching the same web sites then for stress management, no empirical studies have been conducted around their specific issues. However, Cochrane conducted a review in 2008 on using relaxation techniques for managing depression   (http://www2.cochrane.org/reviews/en/ab007142.html).   While   the study found that it was better than no intervention, it was not as effective as other therapies such as cognitive-behavioral therapy. Using Google, a Mayo Clinic site was located that discusses stress management. This site lists many different strategies and options for reducing stress (http://www.mayoclinic.com/health/ stress-management/MY00435).

Step 3: Critically appraise the quality and applicability of this knowledge to the client's needs and situation

After conducting this search, it appears that a support group designed for parents of children with schizophrenia is the most promising treatment option for Loretta and Newman. One such program is the Family-to-Family group sponsored by NAMI. The research on these groups and the information found on the NAMI Web site that discussed the topics covered in the group appear to align well with the areas that the parents would like to address in treatment (http://www.nami.org/ Template.cfm?Section=Family-to-Family&Template=/TaggedPage/TaggedPage Display.cfm&TPLID=4&ContentID=32973).

There is very little outcome research on these groups. Given the lack of alternative interventions, the social worker views this program as fitting the EBP practice decision model's requirement to locate the best available research. No alternatives with stronger research support were located. The program fits with the couple's needs and interests quite well.

In a further search of NAMI's Web site, the social worker learns that there is a Family-to-Family group that is run by the local chapter. She prints out this information to give to the parents. While there appears to be generic information on stress reduction, very little research has been done to determine how effective these strategies are in reducing stress. However, based on the practice knowledge of the clinician who has worked on stress reduction in other settings, she feels confident in recommending stress reduction strategies to the parents. In reviewing the Mayo Clinic's web site listed above, she feels that it provides a nice summative list and a good place for the parents to begin. As such, she prints out the Mayo Clinic guide to stress management before meeting with Loretta and Newman.

At the present time at the hospital clinic, there is not a group running locally for parents like Loretta and Newman. While the clinic has held similar programs in the past, there is currently not one available. In addition, the social worker who is working with them has never run one herself. As a result of this lack of experience, she does not feel qualified to modify such a curriculum and work with them individually and feels that this is a service that they would need to seek elsewhere. She has worked with individuals on self-care strategies, and does feel relatively comfortable in helping the parents learn and practice additional behavioral techniques to help manage their stress. In the past, she cofacilitated a mindfulness group intervention program at a local hospital, where she worked with individuals on a psychiatric unit. While the population was different, she feels she can take those techniques and modify them to meet the needs of these parents.

Step 4: Discuss the research results with the client to ensure
they fit with the client's values and goals

In the meeting with the parents, the social worker explained the search process and the process she followed. She then shared with the parents with the information about the support groups and about the research on how they appear to be effective in reducing the symptoms like theirs. Newman and Loretta state that they went to a similar group many years ago when Arthur was first diagnosed, but that they can barely remember the group as it took place almost 20 years ago. They were a bit "shell shocked" and they admitted to not feeling like they were very attentive at the time. They stated they were open to attending another one as they feel that they could use some help from others who understand their struggles "in a personal way." They take the information about the next group and state that they will follow up.

In addition, the social worker gives them the information from the Mayo Clinic. They both smile and say that these are all "things that we know we should be doing," but admit that they have not been following through. The social worker and the parents talk through different ideas on how to incorporate many of the strategies into their daily routine, such as prayer or meditation and consistent exercise. They both agree that these will be important steps for them, along with trying to reconnect to their church community, which Newman firmly states that they will do, "even if I have to drag her there!"

Step 5: Synthesizing the client's clinical needs and circumstances
with the relevant research, finalize a shared plan of intervention
collaboratively with the client

After discussing other options with them, such as exploring other therapies for depression or anxiety, they decide that they would first like to try to increase their self-care to manage their stress on their own and then attend the NAMI group. They state that if these do not help, they will return to explore what other "more intensive" interventions might be worth considering. In addition, the social worker reports back on the scheduling progress in coordinating a team meeting to help with long-term planning as well as crisis management and Arthur's acute care needs. The parents report they feel better having "a plan" and say they are committed to start working in these areas to begin to address their needs. The social worker will also actively maintain regular contact with Newman and Loretta. She will also poll other staff to see if there are other couples who might take part in a Family-to-Family style group.

Step 6: Implement the intervention

In this situation, Newman and Loretta decided not to begin formal therapeutic services at the hospital clinic. They did agree to call the clinical social worker and "check in" after a month. The social worker also agreed to contact them if she did not hear from them in a month to ensure they maintain regular contact. Newman and Loretta also agreed to allow her to call them in about three months to schedule a second check in session. They were pleased to know they could share this responsibility.

In this case, the social worker's role is one of providing support, case management, and referral. Her increased contact with Newman and Loretta is documented. Informal monitoring and check in sessions are used to evaluate the intervention. Additional services will be offered as indicated.

Chapter 15
Jin: A 16-Year-Old Korean–American Male with Drinking Issues

Jin is a 16-year-old Korean-American male who was referred to your clinic after his parents found him "passed out and dead drunk" for the second time in two months. His parents report that they are very concerned about his drinking and that he has "changed recently," which includes a decline in his grades at school. He is also "more disrespectful" to his parents. Further, according to his parents, Jin is more interested in his friends than his family. His parents report that they have always been a close family and believe very strongly in having protected family time. Jin appears to be less interested in this and states that he would rather spend time with his friends rather than attend family gatherings.

In speaking to Jin, he is quiet, and appears irritated that he is being asked to come to the clinic. When questioned about his feelings about being at the clinic, he shrugs and states, "Well I didn't have much of a choice, did I?" Jin does admit that his grades have fallen, but quickly adds that his parents' expectations are "over the top, so any imperfection seems like a big deal to them." When asked more specifically about the changes, he says that he used to get straight As and recently he has gotten some Cs and low Bs, which he says is "pretty typical of most kids in high school." He also states that he believes it is "normal" for kids his age to want to spend more time with his friends at 16 rather than with their families. He adds that his parents "don't get that and think that we should want to spend all of our free time with family."

When asked about his drinking, he admits to those "two times" his parents found him drunk, and says that the other times are not "that big of a deal." When asked to clarify what that means, he says that he drinks, but those two were the times when it "got out of control." He stated that the other times are more "normal," and he defined this as "drinking 'til you feel the buzz, but not to the point of passing out." He reported that he is drinking almost every weekend, but that it is "not a big deal" because he is "always around my friends and we drink at someone's house rather than at a bar somewhere." He was unable to report on average how many drinks per night he is consuming, as he is not "paying attention

J. W. Drisko and M. D. Grady, *Evidence-Based Practice in Clinical Social Work*,   209
Essential Clinical Social Work Series, DOI: 10.1007/978-1-4614-3470-2_15,
© Springer Science+Business Media New York 2012

to that stuff." However, upon further questioning, he did state that he loses track of the number of drinks he has each night but says that he "definitely has more than three or four" and that the number of drinks he has in an evening has increased. He denies the use of any other substances other than alcohol.

In discussing his parents' concerns, Jin states that he thinks his parents are "making a big deal out of normal American teenage behavior." He says that they do not understand him and his life because they did not grow up here. He says that he feels more American than Korean and "they cannot understand that reality." He reports that he does not feel that his drinking "is a big deal or a problem" and that "it is under control." He does not believe that his drinking is a "problem" since he does not drink alone, he only drinks with friends on the weekends, and he does not drink enough to "pass out each time." When questioned about his drop in grades, he replied that his GPA is "still fine" and that his parents' expectations "unreasonable" even though he has met them consistently in the past.

Jin, his siblings and his parents were born in North Korea. His parents held professional level jobs there until they fled with their family approximately 10 years ago. They are legal immigrants in America, on their way to citizenship, and feel very thankful to be here. The parents speak English pretty well with heavy accents, although Jin has none. Since arriving in America, his parents have had to work more working class jobs, but have placed a high value on education in the way that they have raised their children. Jin is the middle child. He has an older sister who is a sophomore at an Ivy League college. He also has a younger brother who is 14 and has just started high school. So far the younger brother is doing well academically, but is a little shy socially.

Jin's family's immigration to the U.S. was supported by a Korean Presbyterian church. Their local church has an active and large congregation. Although Jin's parents feel the loss of their country and family and friends who remain in Korea, they state that the Korean community they have found in the U.S. has become their family. Most of their social and family functions revolve around individuals from the church community. They do have a few extended family in the area who were also supported by the church in their immigration, but feel supported by all of the community, "blood relatives or not."

While their financial or social status is not as high as it was in Korea, they are relatively stable financially, live in a safe community where there are good schools and they have no health concerns. They state that there is no history of mental illness in their families to their knowledge, nor significant health problems. They are very concerned about Jin's alcohol use, as "drinking in our community is a sign of a serious problem." They believe that the drinking is increasing and feel that Jin is pulling farther and farther away from the family and their community. They are also concerned that when colleges see the drop in grades over the last year—his junior year in high school—that they will not accept him as this is such an important year in the college admissions process.

Jin currently meets the DSM-IV-TR criteria for Alcohol Abuse (305.00). He has demonstrated a maladaptive pattern of substance use leading to clinically significant impairment or distress, where he has recurrent substance use that is affecting his school work. He is continuing this alcohol use despite the interpersonal problems it is causing within his family. It is unclear at this point if he meets the criteria for dependence since Jin is not very forthcoming or clear about the increased amount of alcohol he uses and how much that has changed over time. More information from Jin would need to be reported to clarify whether he meets criteria for Alcohol Dependence rather than Abuse.

In addition, he does not appear to have traits of any Axis II disorders, and he is too young to be formally diagnosed with any personality disorders. In addition, he does not meet criteria for mental retardation nor does he have any Axis III medical health concerns. While his family is not wealthy, they are relatively stable financially and have stable housing and access to healthcare services through their employment. In addition, they have a strong support network around them.

Applying Steps of EBP to Jin's Needs

Step 1: Drawing on client needs and circumstances learned in a thorough assessment, identify answerable practice questions and related research information needs

This case is complicated by the fact that although Jin is technically the identified client, he does not believe that he has a problem of any kind. As such, he does not feel that he needs any sort of intervention. Jin's parents, however, believe strongly that he is drinking in excess and his drinking is causing a number of problems for him, including academic and family conflict. However, Jin's episodes of passing out clearly pose risk. As such, his drinking is a very real concern.

In addition, there are acculturation issues to consider. Jin is growing up in a very different culture from his parents. Although he was born in Korea, he identifies more with the American culture while his family remains strongly connected to the Korean community in their area. Jin is choosing to spend time with non-Koreans and made references several times to what he believes is typical for American teenagers. Given these differences between Jin and his parents, any intervention must be sensitive to the complexities of working with different levels of acculturation and cultural perspectives that are present in the one family.

Due to these complications discussed above, it is difficult to begin the EBP process and even identify what the practice question is. In speaking with Jin, he is willing to agree to work with his parents "only to get them off my back and so that maybe they will ease up and start to understand that I am not them and want to have a different life from what they had growing up." Therefore, he agrees to work with the therapist in a family format only, since he sees "this whole thing as their problem, not mine." Family conflict is clearly evident.

Given Jin's views, the clinician decides to "start where the client is" and is thankful that Jin is willing to engage at all in any form of therapeutic intervention. With this discussion, the clinician now has a searchable practice question: what are effective family interventions for families with an adolescent that abuses alcohol? Ideally, within this search, the clinician would also be able to explore cultural differences among the interventions and begin to determine which treatments might be most appropriate for Jin's family given their biculturalism.

In the **P.I.C.O.** model, the **P**opulation is adolescent male with substance abuse and family conflict. The **I**nterventions under consideration are psychotherapies or similar psychosocial interventions, including individual and family therapies. **C**omparisons would be between different therapies or psychosocial interventions as well as among medications and combinations of mediations and psychosocial therapies. The **O**utcomes would be decreasing Jin's alcohol use and increasing communication and family functioning within the family unit.

Step 2: Efficiently locate relevant research knowledge

In exploring the Cochrane Collaborative Library (http://www.cochrane.org/cochrane-reviews) using the search terms "family therapy" and "adolescent alcohol abuse," a long list of reviews appear. However, most of them are related to pharmacological issues, with a few psychosocial interventions. Foxcroft and Tsertsvadze (2011) completed a systematic review of universal school-based prevention programs for alcohol misuse in young people and found them promising but based on research of limited quality. Another review is "registered" but no results are yet available; nor are the authors named. This review is entitled "Universal family-based prevention programs for alcohol misuse in young people." (http://www2.cochrane.org/reviews/en/title_05845921347718672014101125 102357.html). A treatment focused program was also located for "cognitive behavioral therapy for substance abuse in young offenders." This too is under protocol and no results are provided as yet.

A search of the Campbell Collaboration library also led to no systematic reviews using the broad search terms "adolescent "and "alcohol." Several reviews of treatments for non-opioid substance use were located though all were in progress. No specific reviews of treatments for alcohol use or misuse were found.

Since the Cochrane and Campbell Collaboration Web sites did not yielded a great deal of relevant research information, another option is Substance Abuse and Mental Health Services Administration (SAMHSA; http://www.samhsa.gov/). This organization specializes in substance abuse issues and mental health services. It is run by the United States government. By typing into the search box "empirically supported family therapy alcohol abuse," a Treatment Improvement Protocol (TIP) was located, entitled *Substance Abuse Treatment and Family Therapy*, Series 39 (2004) (http://www.kap.samhsa.gov/products/tools/ad-guides/pdfs/QGA_39.pdf). TIPs are free treatment protocols provided by SAMHSA and provide best practice guidelines for practitioners. In this TIP, there are chapters exploring substance abuse and its impact on families. The TIP reports that different models of family therapy have been shown to be effective in working with families where there is substance abuse. This discussion includes a specific section on adolescents and a glossary chapter that discusses cultural differences. One of the sections is dedicated to working with individuals who are from an Asian culture.

Stated in the Executive Summary (http://www.ncbi.nlm.nih.gov/books/ NBK14505/) regarding cultural issues, the TIP reports:

> Although a great deal of research has been conducted related to both family therapy and culture and ethnicity, little research has concentrated on how culture and ethnicity influence core family and clinical processes. One important requirement is to move beyond ethnic labels and consider a host of factors—values, beliefs, and behaviors—associated with ethnic identity. Among major life experiences that must be factored into treating families touched by substance abuse is the complex challenge of determining how acculturation and ethnic identity influence the treatment process. (para. 17).

A further search located another report from the *Drug and Alcohol Services Information System* (DAIS; 2002) (http://www.oas.samhsa.gov/2k2/AsianTX/ AsianTX.htm) addressing the increase in substance use among Asian and Pacific Islanders that began in the 1990s. Although this report does not provide information on treatment, it may provide some information around trends and patterns among other individuals who identify as part of these cultural groups.

In addition, there is a second TIP, dated 2008, called *TIP 32: Treatment of Adolescents With Substance Use Disorders* (http://store.samhsa.gov/product/ SMA08-4080), that contains a chapter on family therapy as well as other issues related to adolescent substance abuse. Within the family therapy chapter, as with the first TIP, there are a number of guidelines offered for what to include within the treatment.

While these treatment protocols offer a great deal of information about the issues related to substance abuse among adolescents and its impact on the family, with some attention to cultural issues, the searches did not identify a particular model or intervention that appears to be more effective than any other. Citations to specific studies and their results were very rare.

A quick Google search did identify some specific models of intervention, such as Multidimensional Family Therapy, that have undergone randomized controlled clinical trials (RCTs) and have shown promising results for working with families with individuals who have abused substances. Six percent of the adolescents included in one of the studies identified as Asian, but the report did not state from what country they originated or their acculturation status (Liddle et al. 2001). In addition, the Liddle study included both marijuana abusers and alcohol abusers, and did not break down results by type of substance use. Liddle is also the originator of the multidimensional family theory model found to be the most effective in this single RCT. (In the meta-analysis examined next, Liddle is the only researcher to study the effectiveness of MDFT across 64 included publications.)

Still another search located a meta-analysis of adolescent substance abuse treatments that indicates that individual treatments are more effective than family treatments for adolescents who abuse alcohol, with behavioral interventions having the highest long-term effects (Tripodi et al. 2010). Based on 16 studies, the authors found that interventions significantly reduce adolescent alcohol use (Hedges $g = -0.61$; 95% confidence interval [CI], -0.83 to -0.40). Stratified analyses revealed larger effects for individual treatment ($g = -0.75$; CI, -1.05 to -0.40) compared with family- based treatments ($g = -0.46$; CI, -0.66 to -0.26) (Abstract).

They conclude that "individual-only interventions had larger effect sizes than family-based interventions and effect sizes decreased as length of follow-up increased. Furthermore, behavior-oriented treatments demonstrated promise in attaining long-term effects" (Abstract).

Step 3: Critically appraise the quality and applicability of this knowledge to the client's needs and situation

In this case, the clinician thinks that while the research supports taking an individual behavioral approach to Jin's alcohol abuse, the client factors in this case reduces the potential positive outcomes that such an intervention might have. Jin's refusal to participate in individual therapy reduces the likelihood that such an approach will be effective under the current circumstances. Also, as the parents are very concerned about Jin's recent withdrawal from the family as a unit, the clinician believes that by focusing on the family, he will be addressing several important issues related to this case. The first is that while individual family has been shown to be more effective, family therapy does have some empirical support and by using the TIPs from SAMHSA, he will be able to include research and best practice guidelines into his treatment approach. Second, Jin has stated that he will not participate in individual therapy, but has agreed to family therapy. In keeping with the adage of starting where the client is, having Jin participate in treatment at all is a first step in the engagement process and may eventually lead to his will-ingness to participate in an individually focused treatment later. In this case, client factors partially trumps the research, as the client refuses to participate in the potentially superior form of treatment. Third, Jin's family is very concerned about the family conflict that has arisen and Jin's withdrawal from the family. By focusing on the family as a unit, there will be time each week when Jin and his parents will be together, increasing their time together and the clinician can focus on the family conflict while working to address the alcohol abuse.

A family oriented plan will also allow for issues of acculturation to be examined, if they arise. Jin appears to feel under some pressure to follow the family's Korean practices and may feel stressed to also have to be part of American culture in school and with many peers. This may be an influence that exacerbates his drinking.

Step 4: Discuss the research results with the client to ensure they fit with the client's values and goals

The clinician now has the task of taking this information back to the clients: Jin's family. In the discussion with the clients, Jin confirms that he has only agreed to do family therapy. While it appears from the recent 2010 meta-analysis that individual therapy is more effective than family therapy, Jin's refusal to participate in individual family limits the choices that are options for Jin and his family.

However, the research information must be shared with the family and together the clinician and the clients make a decision. As Jin does not believe that his drinking is an issue, he does not feel that the individual therapy targets the primary issues concerning him or his family. While this viewpoint is in conflict with his parents who would like him to reduce his alcohol use, they all agree that they would like to improve their family functioning and communication among all members of the family. Given this focus, the family and the clinician agree to focus on family therapy at this time.

Additionally, the therapist discusses with the family whether they would be more comfortable to work with a therapist who is from Korea or from an Asian culture, should they be able to find one in their community. Jin strongly states that he does not want a therapist from Korea, as he wants someone who "will help my parents understand me as an American! We already are surrounded by Koreans and we need a different perspective." While his parents state that they would prefer to have someone from their own culture, they also state that they would prefer not to share the details of their life with someone who they might interact with socially in community events. They believe that the spiritual leaders at the church are different, but would worry that it would be awkward to work with someone from their community in such a capacity.

Step 5: Synthesizing the clinical needs and circumstances with the views of the client and the relevant research, develop a plan of intervention considering available options

Based on the previous conversation, the family, including Jin, agree to contract for 3 months of weekly family sessions. The clinical social worker has provided family therapy in the past, although not with individuals from Korea. Therefore, he has obtained permission from the parents to contact one of the leaders of the church they attend to ask additional questions about their culture. This will include both the Korean culture and their spiritual culture as well. The parents state that since they have already sought help with these leaders they are comfortable with these conversations and willingly give permission for the therapist to speak with these individuals. In addition, the therapist is part of a peer supervision group and is planning on seeking consultation from the group members, many of whom have worked cross-culturally throughout their careers.

The clinician located and read the full reports of the two TIPs from SAMHSA. He also read the abstracts of two articles on family therapy interventions by Liddle found on Google. This helps ensure that he is incorporating the essential components of effective family therapy into the intervention with Jin and his family. He hopes that Jin will eventually agree to participate in additional or adjunctive behavioral therapy to address his alcohol abuse as described by Tripodi and colleagues (2010). He is working with a friend who has university library privileges to obtain a copy of the full Tripodi meta-analysis. For now, he is incorporating the client's views into the current treatment plan.

Step 6: Implement the intervention

Before the treatment began, the clinical social worker asked to have releases signed authorizing him to speak with some of the leaders of the church. He was able to have a meeting with two of the church leaders and learned a bit more about the community in which Jin's family is a member. He also learned about the church and some of the teachings, as well as about some of the struggles that other families in their congregation have reported with their children of a similar age. The conversations helped the clinical social worker have a clearer contextual view of the family's world and begin to understand some of the conflicts reported by the family. The conversations were particularly useful in helping the social worker understand how differences in level of acculturation manifest in this community.

For Jin's family, the main challenge was to have Jin be an active participant and begin to address some of the concerns raised by his parents. Simultaneously, the clinical social worker also needed to help his parents understand the cultural influences Jin is exposed to that are different from their own adolescent experiences. It was difficult for the clinical social worker to accomplish both of the tasks described above. The initial goals agreed on by the family were to: 1) Identify structured time for the family to have time together; 2) Increase an understanding of the different cultural norms between America and Korea; and 3) Create a plan for addressing the school concerns. While the goals originally set on the initial treatment plan appeared to be modest at first, after a month of treatment, the clinical social worker realized that he needed to scale back on the goals, and revisit them. After the first month, the focus of treatment shifted to simply increasing effective communication between the family members. There was so much conflict that the other goals could not be addressed. Therefore, the clinical social worker moved to very basic communication skills, such as reflective listening, active listening, and "I statements."

By the third month of treatment, the family was able to begin to target the second of the original goals, which was to help members understand the cultural differences in which they experience(d) their adolescent years. Through their increased capacity for listening to each other, the family was able to have moments where they laughed about differences between their adolescent experiences. Both the parents and Jin were able to ask questions to each other in a non-defensive manner about these experiences. This shift allowed the family members begin to appreciate more what was important for each of them during adolescence. This new understanding allowed them to work on a plan with the clinical social worker to help the family identify some activities and events that would meet both what the parents wanted, but allow Jin some independence.

During the third month of treatment, the family began to address some of the school concerns, which led into concerns about Jin's friendships and other activities. It was during this time that the clinical social worker brought up the end of their three-month contract. All members of the family agreed that they were willing to work a bit longer and contracted again for another three months, which also "maxed out" the psychotherapy benefits offered by the parents' insurance companies.

While there was definitely progress on the goals, especially around the conflict within the family, the clinical social worker remained somewhat frustrated about his inability to address the substance abuse. Jin continued to deny that there was a problem, and it remained difficult to determine how much he was actually drinking. However, the parents reported that they now felt more confident in knowing where Jin was and who he was with when he was out with his friends. Jin said he did not feel he needed to be as secretive since his parents seemed to be more accepting of his need to be with his friends. So, while there was progress, the clinical social worker still remained concerned that he was not addressing this issue and hoped to offer Jin some individual sessions in the next month.

Chapter 16
Jennifer: A Young Homeless Woman Who has Borderline Personality Disorder

Jennifer is a 23-year-old white female. She was referred for mental health services by a staff member at a community homeless shelter. They arrived together, with the staffer doing most of the talking initially. Jennifer had been involved in several verbal and physical altercations with other residents at the shelter, and was finally asked not to return. Jennifer has no job or income, and no family or friends to ask for help. A recent boyfriend "kicked her out" a few weeks ago, and then left the area. He did not return texts or calls friends made on Jennifer's behalf. She has resided at the local shelter since his departure, and has now lost her chance to stay at the shelter.

Jennifer is tall, large framed, and muscular. She can be physically intimidating. Her clothes could use some washing, but she is clean and her hair neat. She says she "never got along well with anybody" and has been on her own for several years. She says her only living relative is her father, who is in jail on a 15-year sentence for sexually assaulting her as a young teenager. She has been in touch with him on and off, wanting to have "somebody" but always becoming upset as "he makes more promises he can't keep." "It's just filling the time for him." She does not mention his sentence has only 2 years left.

Jennifer was asked not to return to the shelter after pulling an old pay telephone from the wall and throwing it at another resident. She says it reminded her of the last call she got from her boyfriend, where everything "was sweet and wonderful" the day before he kicked her out and disappeared. The other person had a disagreement with Jennifer about a book that "got all out of proportion." This man had "tried to hit on me before," and got angry and insulting when she did not give him "what he wanted." Staff said she flew into a rage and a number of people had to break them up and separate them. Jennifer threw punches at the man who, they said "mainly covered up and tried to get away." Several less intense episodes had preceded this one, with different people involved.

Jennifer was born in the Midwest to parents who both worked in retail. "They were always busy and out." She is an only child and very quickly learned to take

J. W. Drisko and M. D. Grady, *Evidence-Based Practice in Clinical Social Work*, Essential Clinical Social Work Series, DOI: 10.1007/978-1-4614-3470-2_16, © Springer Science+Business Media New York 2012

care of herself. She says that at age four she was making breakfast for everybody. Her parents had loud arguments and some fights followed by "making up and making love." Jennifer saw this as a pattern. She says she was pretty much ignored until she reached puberty and then her father began to sexual abuse her. She says she enjoyed feeling important to him and the physical contact they had. When her mother literally walked in on them together, she turned around, walked to the phone, called the police about the abuse and left. "I guess she was so mad she dropped a dime on him. He deserved it. But I think she forced him out... the one good thing in my life." Still, her mother seems quite idealized at times despite her role in breaking up the family and abandoning Jennifer. Jennifer saw her father only a few more times as she went to foster care and her father went to jail. It is unclear what led him to move so quickly through the legal system, especially since the mother's 'whereabouts' were unknown almost immediately after the "call." She also recalls her mother saying, "You even had him taken away." Sometimes she thinks what happened is her fault. There seemed to be no extended family involvement, and only a neighbor baby sitter was recalled as a source of pleasure. "Mrs. Jones would play with me and do my hair."

Jennifer next lived in four different foster homes, each of which was "pretty good," but none of them "wanted me." A good home meant food, shelter, and clothing. Jennifer could not describe the characteristics of her foster parents beyond that they "took good care of me." She was moved several times and no plans for adoption proved viable. Still she said once, in a whisper, "each new place was like a wound." She dropped out of high school at 16, left foster care, and "ran away." Jennifer thought about going to the area where her father was in jail, but learned that it was small and isolated. Instead, she went to a moderate sized urban area where she lived on the streets prostituting and "living on others people's generosity." It was not clear if this generosity was a gloss over for the coercion she actually experienced. She was able to do food service work, but ended up quitting or being fired for disputes with other workers or her bosses. She seems both intelligent and quite verbal. She knows she is "moody" and has a "quick temper— like my father." She enjoys other people's humor, but almost never jokes.

Jennifer said she had "tried about every drug you can imagine" but found most of them made her feel "worse." She said pot and most pills made her "feel crazy" and that she avoided them. She said she liked "downers" and drinking that "made her forget." She acknowledged some binges, but said she did not drink much. However, she was not very specific about when and how much she drank. A long-time shelter staffer had said "it was a point in her favor that she wasn't 'big' into alcohol or drugs."

Jennifer has been briefly hospitalized on several occasions for suicidal threats and gestures. Most of these involve cutting her legs and wrists. She denied during assessment that she had been using drugs or alcohol. She denied any current suicidal ideation or plans. She says her cutting was always brought on "by being left" despite her very independent presentation. Even hints of sadness and loss are rare, and took several sessions to emerge. Her nonverbal presentation makes one feel like there is a veritable pool of sadness inside her. She has been connected with therapists several times by hospital staff, and says "I mainly blew them off." She truly seemed to doubt that other people are trustworthy.

When she was reminded she had "been left" just a short while before (the apparent precipitant of the phone incident), she became angry and loud, but insisted she did not want to hurt herself. "Him... well, that might be different. But he's gone." This little emotional "storm" was over quickly. When asked if the time in the hospital helped, Jennifer said it was good to be cared for, but mentioned nothing specific. "Those doctors and social workers kept asking me who I am. I don't really know... It gets worse when I am alone." Her wish: "to have a home where I am loved and taken care of." Her range of affect was very constricted and heavily weighted to the negative. People who were against her were "bad," only two shelter staffers were rated as "good." "It's hard enough bein' on the streets... it takes so much effort."

When asked where she might stay, she mentioned "the streets" or a shelter in a nearby town. "It's just starting to get really cold now; it ain't so bad," she said. Both Jennifer and the shelter worker said she was on a subsidized housing waiting list—with a 5-year wait. When asked if she would consider being part of a residential program, she said "Sure... you think they'd even take me?" the worker told her she would search for "what works" for people with her kind of needs, including worries about loss and a quick temper who were homeless. The worker was not sure that there were programs locally, and they would probably take some work to make sure they could be funded.

Step 1: Drawing on client needs and circumstances learned in a thorough assessment, identify answerable practice questions and related research information needs

Jennifer meets criteria for a Borderline Personality Disorder (BPD) diagnosis. Her history of sexual abuse, loss, and multiple foster placements also suggest a significant trauma history. She does not, however, meet criteria for Post Traumatic Stress Disorder. Her lack of attachment, impulsivity, self-harm, and coercive interpersonal relationships appear to replicate her family of origin's style of interaction at great social cost. She has very limited social support and few marketable skills for employment. It is unclear she could make, and sustain, a commitment to enter a treatment program. Her homelessness and lack of current insurance make finding services still more difficult. In her state, she would qualify to re-apply for public insurance. Another dimension to her situation is that she has "aged out" of services for teens under age 21 and yet has many of the issues they confront. In the service world she is just another adult.

In the P.I.C.O. model, the Population is people who have BPD along with people who are homeless. Given Jennifer's circumstances, it was not immediately clear where she would stay, and no additional resources to serve her need were immediately apparent. She could be long-term homeless. The Interventions under consideration are psychosocial interventions and possibly medication with the goals of reducing aggressive outbursts and more broadly to help Jennifer regulate her emotions, reduce suicidal ideation, gestures, and self-harm. In addition, the issues of her prior trauma and her relationship with her father are clearly of interest to Jennifer, though they are not immediate treatment priorities. Finding ongoing shelter or an apartment, and gainful employment to support it are also clear needs. Comparisons would be across different therapies and psychotherapy versus medication. Outcomes would include reducing aggressive outbursts, improved emotional regulation, reduced suicidal ideation and self-harm, and finding ongoing shelter. Interventions to help with her personality disorder may not necessarily coincide with her needs for shelter.

Step 2: Efficiently locate relevant research knowledge

PubMed revealed only three incidence studies for "BPD" + "homelessness," including one German field study indicating high levels of comorbid disorders and a common motive of flight from violent situations among these women (Torchalla et al. 2004). Using the same search terms in Google yielded quite a bit of information, mainly from the United Kingdom (i.e., http://handbooks.homeless.org.uk/ hostels/individuals/pd/rjapd). These sources ranged from efforts to create "low key" structured housing programs, to personal narratives, to a description of a program in Colorado to engage homeless persons who have BPD with mental health services by building an ongoing presence at soup kitchens. The connection between BPD and homelessness is common given how it can interfere with employment and, in turn, obtaining and maintaining housing. A major focus was on gaining housing and government support to get a "starting point" for other kinds of efforts. Though there was no large-scale research cited to support his point of view, the literature repeatedly pointed to having a place to live as the first order of business in helping people who have BPD. Organizations focused on homelessness are also looking for the connection between homelessness and treatment once they are in shelters or in some form of residential care. For example, the United Kingdom's Homeless Link Web site (http://handbooks.homeless.org.uk/hostels/ individuals/pd) specifically cited Bateman and Fonagy's partial hospitalization program as a potentially effective treatment program for persons who have BPD.

As discussed in Chapter 8, the Cochrane Collaboration states that two programs have preliminary empirical support as effective psychological treatments for BPD. There is also some suggestive support for "the use of second-generation antipsychotics, mood stabilizers, and omega-3 fatty acids, but require replication, since most effect estimates were based on single studies. The long-term use of these drugs has not been assessed" (Stoffers et al. 2010, authors' conclusion from the Abstract). This did not suggest medication as an initial approach to intervention for Jennifer.

Binks et al. (2009) summarize the research on psychotherapeutic interventions for BPD:

> In this review of the talking/behavioral therapies for people with BPD, we identified seven studies involving 262 people, over five separate comparisons. Dialectical behavior therapy (DBT) included treatment components such as prioritising a hierarchy of target behaviors, telephone coaching, groups skills training, behavioral skill training, contingency management, cognitive modification, exposure to emotional cues, reflection, empathy, and acceptance. DBT seemed to be helpful on a wide range of outcomes, such as admission to

hospital or incarceration in prison, but the small size of included studies limit confidence in their results. A second therapy, psychoanalytic orientated day hospital therapy, also seemed to decrease admission and use of prescribed medication and to increase social improvement and social adjustment. Again, this is an experimental treatment with too few data to really allow anyone to feel too confident of the findings. Even if these are trials undertaken by enthusiasts and difficult to apply to everyday care, they do suggest that the problems of people with BPD may be amenable to treatment (from the Plain language summary).

Both Linehan's DBT and Bateman and Fonagy's psychodynamically oriented partial hospitalization program have preliminary research support as effective for treating BPD. However, no mention is made of the effectiveness of these programs for the treatment of homeless people. McNeill (2005) refers to "adaptations" of DBT to better serve the needs of homeless people, but just what these adaptations are is not specified. (No follow-up article was located.) A partial hospital program *might* provide temporary shelter as part of the program.

The best research evidence suggests either entry into a psychodynamically oriented partial hospitalization program or a DBT program fully using Linehan's model. "Self harm or parasuicide may decrease after 6–12 months [of DBT] ($n = 63$, 1 RCT; RR 0.81 CI 0.66–0.98; NNT 12, CI 7–108)" (Binks et al. 2009, pp. 2 and 47). Another study documented that DBT significantly reduces anger scores for person who have BPD after 6 months of treatment compared to treatment as usual (p. 49). Results for improved self regulation were not reported. The psychoanalytically oriented partial hospital program significantly reduced inpatient admission ($n = 44$, 1 RCT; RR 0.04, CI 0.00–0.59; NNT 2, CI 3–6) (Binks et al. 2009, p. 2). It also improved social adjustment after 6–12 months (MD − 0.70, CI −1.08 to −0.32). Results for reduction of aggressive episodes and suicidal ideation and self-harm were not reported.

A search of the Campbell Collaboration library located several resources for the search term "homelessness." Most related to reviews registered but still not completed or reported. A powerpoint style report of a presentation by Antilla (2009) indicates that across several studies, a number of programs reduced mean days of homelessness. The target population was persons with mental illness (not further specified) and substance abuse. Assertive community treatment (ACT) proved very effective by visual inspection over a year to a year and a half after start of services. Case management services appear helpful. The search also revealed an abstract on a pilot study by Cavanaugh et al. (2009), provided descriptive information about a pilot program adapting DBT to a psychoeducational workshop to prevent interpersonal violence. Results of the study were not reported in the abstract.

Step 3: Critically appraise the quality and applicability of this knowledge to the client's needs and situation

Neither treatment program provided outcome data on all of Jennifer's concerns, but both DBT and a psychoanalytically informed day hospital program appeared to fit her concerns well in general. However, neither program's research data included any information about people who were homeless. Both programs appeared to presume clients had relatively stable and ongoing living situations.

The lack of such living situations might be viewed as making Jennifer quite different from the people included in these study results.

No program similar to Bateman and Fonagy's was available regionally. One DBT program was found, but had an eight-month or longer waiting list. This left no available therapeutic resources based on the best evidence possibilities for further discussion with Jennifer. Similarly, it was clear that she had "burned her bridges" with the available local shelters. She would likely be accepted at another shelter in a nearby town, but this left unresolved how she would be helped to avoid future aggressive incidents, as well as to find more permanent housing. It would also require yet another move and change, excluding her from the few local supports she trusted in.

Jennifer did not qualify for case management or assertive community treatment. Both programs are available in her community for persons with severe and persistent mental illness. Despite her hospitalizations, Jennifer does not meet criteria for such services. Severe and persistent mental illness does not lead to any priority in publicly subsidized housing. It might lead to access to housing programs for persons who have mental illness, but again, Jennifer does not qualify for such services.

Step 4: Discuss the research results with the client to ensure they fit with the client's values and goals

When these options, and their practical limitations, were discussed with Jennifer, she was very interested in the partial hospitalization program. Her interest had little to do with the program philosophy or its preliminary support as an effective program. Instead, she viewed the structure and support of a partial hospital program as useful to help "organize" her. Her response is consistent with a research summary on effective relationships for persons with personality disorders (Castonguay et al. 2006). A working group of clinicians and researchers, including Marsha Linehan, found considerable empirical support for intensive initial intervention for persons with personality disorders. They noted that regular mental health care, with weekly sessions and low intensity support for people who have personality disorders, was often ineffective. Nonetheless, access to such a program was not immediately available through a partial hospital or an intensively structured program. Neither access to empirically supported treatments nor access to long term of immediate shelter was available.

Step 5: Synthesizing the client's clinical needs and circumstances with the relevant research, finalize a shared plan of intervention collaboratively with the client

With no access to interventions supported by the best available evidence, Jennifer agreed to a plan of weekly session and some telephone contact if a crisis occurred. She endorsed a focus on planning to locate shelter and to, over time, look at how her "touchiness" (her word) kept her from housing, employment, and more fulfilling relationships. The clinical social worker noted in her record that she had a substantial and unexamined sexual trauma history, and that her father was nearing likely release from prison. Having a regular place to live would be a vital foundation for doing the psychological and interpersonal work facing Jennifer.

Step 6: Implement the Intervention

Jennifer left the office and headed for the streets. The lack of resources and her "burnt bridges" with several shelters left few immediate shelter or housing options. She did not seem overwhelmed by this result. She agreed to keep in touch and to drop in three days. At the three day check in, Jennifer had decided to move to a larger nearby city and stay at their shelter. She was unwilling to sign releases to allow staff to speak with staff at the new shelter about her needs. A week later she returned, unexpectedly, and said things were going well, "so far." She had changed her mind and agreed to sign releases, allowing sharing of information with the new shelter and its mental health consultant. Many of her needs remain unmet.

Part III
Evidence-Based Practice in Clinical Social Work Education and Ongoing Issues

Chapter 17
Evidence-Based Practice: Teaching and Supervision

A key goal of this book is to examine evidence-based practice (EBP) in a balanced and thorough manner. We have detailed the EBP decision-making process in several chapters. We have also pointed to a number of implementation challenges or controversies related to EBP in clinical practice. We see EBP as having both important strengths and unresolved limitations. Working backwards, one could argue that part of the reason these controversies exist in practice is because those who educate social workers also struggle with EBP. These differences and struggles are, in effect, transmitted to social work trainees. This chapter will give readers an overview of some of the challenges to training social workers in EBP. It will also examine different views on EBP among social work educators.

Teaching EBP

Recent national surveys indicate that social work educators support EBP (Bledsoe et al. 2007; Bledsoe et al. (in press); Rubin and Parrish 2007). Yet there still remains a great deal of controversy regarding how EBP should be integrated into social work education programs (Grady et al. 2010; Howard et al. 2007; Jenson 2007; Mullen et al. 2007; Shlonsky and Gibbs 2004; Springer 2007). Differences remain regarding the very definition of EBP (Powell et al. 2010; Rubin and Parrish 2007). In an effort to address and process these debates, a group of social work educators organized a conference in 2006 called the Symposium for Improving the Teaching of Evidence-Based Practice at the University of Texas at Austin (Springer 2007). Although the Symposium was an attempt to bring together social work educators to find a place of consensus among these issues, it appears that more questions than answers resulted from the conference. This may be typical of new and complex social movements.

Out of this Symposium, five major areas of debate regarding the training of social work students in EBP emerged that continue to be evident among social

J. W. Drisko and M. D. Grady, *Evidence-Based Practice in Clinical Social Work*, 229
Essential Clinical Social Work Series, DOI: 10.1007/978-1-4614-3470-2_17,
© Springer Science+Business Media New York 2012

work educators today (Springer 2007). These themes are: (1) defining EBP; (2) modeling the complexity of EBP in teaching; (3) examining social work curriculum; (4) coordinating social work professional organizations; and (5) shifting the culture of social work (Springer 2007, p. 619). Clinical social workers might raise additional questions about supports for EBP in agencies and in private practice. Further, some critical perspectives on EBM and EBP might be appropriate. Some social work researchers have questioned the EBP evidence hierarchy, noting it can be unduly restrictive and may devalue many useful forms of research (Black 1994; Popay and Williams 1998; Trinder 2000). Other social work researchers have called for the inclusion of more diverse voices and perspectives in EBP research (Petr 2009; Zayas et al. 2010). Like any social movement, EBP will have merits and limitations. The following section will address some salient issues within Springer's five themes.

Defining EBP

As we have stated throughout this book, EBP is a term that authors have used in many different ways, leading to a great deal of confusion among social work educators and practitioners. Part of the reason that this confusion exists may be because social work educators—and authors of EBP textbooks and articles—still do not use a common definition of EBP. This results in social work graduates having different definitions and meanings associated with the term (Springer 2007). Indeed, as we have discussed in Chapter 1 of this book, definitions of EBP vary with the author's purposes, emphases, and perspective. Results from a national survey of faculty members in MSW programs indicate that there remains a significant disparity among the faculty members regarding how EBP is defined (Rubin and Parrish 2007). We support the use of the Haynes, Devereaux, and Guyatt (2002a) four part model of the EBP practice decision-making process. Use of this definition is social work is endorsed by Gibbs and Gambrill (2002); Mullen and Shlonsky (2004); and Rubin (2008). Consensus on a definition of EBP would be very useful for orienting social work education.

In another survey, faculty members reported that although they view EBP as important, they do not necessarily use its core concepts to determine what they teach in the classroom (Grady et al. 2010). This adds further confusion about what is essential to teach about EBP and what is not. These varying views mean that what is taught about EBP, and how it is taught, will vary significantly among social work programs. Using research evidence to guide practice is the common thread throughout EBP definitions, but what kinds of research are valued may differ. Standards for research appraisal many also differ. Client preferences may be affirmed or omitted as a vital part of the EBP practice decision-making process. Clinical expertise may also be affirmed and emphasized. Such differences will result in varying levels of knowledge and skill regarding EBP with which social work practitioners enter the field. The risk is that EBP will be used as a "catchphrase for anything that is done with clients that can somehow be linked to an empirical study, regardless of the study's quality, competing evidence, or consideration of clients' needs" (Shlonsky and Gibbs 2004, p. 137).

Regardless of the formal education a clinical social worker receives, it is critical that active clinicians become educated about the EBP process and begin to apply it in all practice settings. It is especially important to understand the definition of EBP and the steps of the EBP practice decision-making process. Quality education requires clear thinking about EBP and its components.

As we have stated throughout this book, the clinician's professional expertise is the lynchpin in bringing the EBP process together. Regardless of the type of training a clinician has had regarding EBP during formal social work education, clinical social workers have a responsibility to use the EBP process to provide the most effective possible treatment that best fits the client's unique needs and circumstances. This includes careful assessment and the application of critical thinking during each phase of practice.

Modeling the Complexity of Evidence-Based Practice in Teaching

This theme covers several aspects of social work education and the teaching of EBP. EBP is a complex and multifaceted social process. We have attempted to portray EBM and EBP as multifaceted social movements. Academic, economic, and political forces are all evident within the larger EBP movement and its social context. This raises issues of *what* to teach about EBP. To describe it simply as a practice decision-making process without attention to larger economic and political forces omits attention to growing pressures practicing clinicians feel acutely. Such narrow descriptions strip EBP from its social context.

Similarly, while the EBM/EBP hierarchies of evidence have merit, they may also serve to limit attention to ways of knowing that are important to practice and to our clients. To emphasize experimental research may erode education on exploratory and descriptive approaches to research that allow for discovery and innovation. It may also limit the kinds of voices and perspectives valued in social work research and practice. Other important ways of knowing and research methods that can inform practice may receive reduced attention in social work education. We believe education about EBP should not come at the expense of attention to multiple ways of knowing and critical thinking. Each topic is valuable and important to social work education.

Teaching EBP in-depth would require considerable additional content in practice and in research classes as well as in the field practicum. Students would also need to be educated in literature search skills. Programs would need to expand EBP-related search content directed to sources such as PubMed and both the Cochrane Collaboration and Campbell Collaboration systematic review libraries. Appraising research knowledge on a clinical topic would link research and practice courses. In practice courses, the EBP practice decision-making process would need to be added to existing course content. To help students understand the methods on which EBP choices are made would require much more extensive teaching about large-scale statistical methods, of specific epidemiological statistical methods (such as odds ratios, numbers needed to treat, etc.). How to interpret meta-analysis statistics would also be important. How to read a systemic review and to appraise its overall quality would be necessary content. Learning to summarize complex research findings in order to state them clearly to clients of many different backgrounds would also be a new practice skill. Documenting use of the EBP model may also require specific content in client records. Finally, in the spirit of a holistic understanding of EBP, its impact on social policy, on the administration of practice, on supervision, and on the research debate over the merits and worth of different ways of knowing would all be important content for social work education at all levels. Critical thinking skills would be applicable to each of these content areas.

Another issue is *how* to teach EBP. According to Springer (2007), one controversy surrounds whether to teach the process of EBP versus teaching specific treatments (empirically supported treatments or ESTs). Springer asks the question, should social work educators teach students to be critical thinkers or feed them with "pearls of wisdom" (p. 620)? To teach EBP in-depth would require a major expansion of social work's curriculum content. This is in addition to an already crowded set of curriculum requirements. Addressing specific ESTs provides one option to limit the curricular burden. We argue, however, that teaching only about specific ESTs would not help students understand the EBP process adequately. Such an approach would ultimately limit student's preparation for practicing EBP in a changing social environment.

EBP has clear implications for teaching practice, for teaching research, for teaching human behavior theories, and for teaching social policy. While the Council on Social Work Education's (CSWE) 2008 accreditation standards do not currently specifically require EBP content, social work programs must teach about "research informed practice" and "practice informed research." Teaching EBP would be just one way to address how research informs practice. Practice evaluation would surely be another. It is less clear that EBP is an appropriate way to address how practice informs research.

Unfortunately, the broad phrases "research informed practice" and "practice informed research" are not well defined. The full text of the CSWE (2008) Educational Policy standard 2.1.6 reads:

> Social workers use practice experience to inform research, employ evidence-based interventions, evaluate their own practice, and use research findings to improve practice, policy, and social service delivery. Social workers comprehend quantitative and qualitative research and understand scientific and ethical approaches to building knowledge.

The standard requires content on both qualitative and quantitative research methods, scientific knowledge building, ethical issues, and practice evaluation. It also addresses the use of these methods "to improve practice, policy and social service delivery," implying critical analysis and application at micro-, meso-, and macro-levels of scale. Only wide ranging engagement with EBP content would fully address these standards. Focus on specific ESTs only would not.

Still another aspect issue is the *quality* of instruction in social work programs. In other words, how well do faculty members model EBP in the classroom by incorporating evidence regarding what makes an effective instructor? Springer (2007) states that there is both great emphasis on, and more rewards for, those faculty members who succeed in research and publication. On the other hand, there is not as much emphasis on, nor rewards for, those faculty members who are successful teachers. As a result of the reward structure in the academy, faculty members may not spend as much time learning about effective teaching strategies. This leads to varying levels of investment and quality among classroom instructors (Grady et al. (in press)). Educators can teach about EBP as a simple process or as a complex social phenomenon. It can be taught in ways that engage students and make its merits apparent, or in ways that make EBP just another form of research experience to be endured.

We believe it is essential to teach—in-depth—the clinical assessment and critical thinking skills that are required in the EBP decision-making process. This process requires clinicians to think carefully and holistically about the needs and goals of the client, the environmental context, and the research on potentially effective interventions that are appropriate for that client's unique needs and characteristics. As such, we believe that the focus in social work programs, both in the classroom and in field internships, needs to be on helping students examine critically the multitude of factors used in making a clinical decision *and* how to deliver the selected services using effective clinical skills. Determining what intervention might be the most appropriate is only the beginning of the clinical intervention process.

While the focus of this book is not to discuss effective clinical skills, we do want to emphasize that if educators only teach the process of EBP and exclude the importance of teaching assessment and other clinical skills, then clinical social workers will not be effective in delivering any service, even if it has strong research support. EBP does not replace good assessment and clinical practice skills. EBP seeks to guide clinicians in identifying several alternative options that are likely to be effective for a given client. Therefore, social work programs must focus on both the critical thinking skills needed to conduct the EBP process *and* simultaneously teach students how to be effective clinicians. Ideally, clinical social workers are capable of delivering several different kinds of treatments or services.

Examining the Social Work Curriculum

The literature on EBP and social work education focuses primarily on the content within social work curricula. Scholars have debated numerous issues regarding EBP in MSW programs. The broad issues include where in the curriculum EBP should be located (Howard et al. 2007; Jenson 2007; Mullen et al. 2007; Pollio and MacGowan 2010) and whether to emphasize lifelong learning and critical thinking (Gambrill 2006a; Mullen et al. 2007; Springer 2007). More specific issues include whether to focus only on discrete empirically supported treatments (Howard et al. 2007), and about teaching the specific skills needed for each step of the EBP process, such as the literature reviews (Howard et al. 2007; Shlonsky and Gibbs 2004). No clear consensus has emerged on these issues. All have relevance to understanding and doing EBP.

In addition to these valuable points, we believe that there are a few more issues regarding EBP in social work education programs. One of these is the critical importance of an assessment. As we emphasized in Chapter 4, a comprehensive and accurate assessment of the client's needs is critical to the EBP process, but is not an explicit part of it. We are concerned that in the rush to emphasize the need to use evidence in treatment decisions, educators may not emphasize the importance of a solid clinical assessment. Such an assessment informs the entire EBP and treatment process for each client. We believe that in order for the EBP process to work effectively, a clinician must be well trained in how to conduct a thorough assessment. Strong assessment skills allow clinical social workers to understand fully the complex needs of their client; whether it is the diagnosis or the environmental conditions in which treatment will take place, or both in combination.

We also think that the social work curriculum should include multiple practice theories. Further, students should be well supervised in the practice application of multiple theories. The EBP practice-decision making process encourages the identification of several alternatives that may help the client. Strong theoretical knowledge allows students to select from a greater range of intervention options. From these alternatives, client and clinician finalize a treatment plan based on research knowledge as well as the values and preferences of the client. Since treatments and services draw on many different theories, clinical social workers should learn and apply several different models in-depth and in detail.

An additional area that deserves more attention in the curriculum debate is field education. The Council for Social Work Education has identified field education as social work's "signature pedagogy" (CSWE 2008, EP 2.3). Much of the clinical training that social workers receive occurs in the field practicum. As a result, social work educators should spend more time on helping field educators and field advisors learn about and feel comfortable with EBP. In an effort to help bridge this gap, Grady (2010) outlined specific steps schools of social work can take to integrate EBP into the field. Some of these recommendations include trainings for field instructors on the EBP process, allowing field instructors greater access to electronic databases, offering trainings on conducting literature searches, offering trainings on research methods, and offering trainings on interpreting EBP reports and reviews. Field instructors must be well trained and familiar with the EBP practice decision-making process to apply it as educators.

It is well documented in the literature that clinicians in the field struggle with EBP (Bellamy et al. 2008; Nelson et al. 2006; Pollio 2006; Proctor et al. 2007). These same clinicians are often the field instructors or supervisors of students and new clinicians. It is therefore essential that social work educators make a strong effort to engage and partner with field clinicians so that they are well versed in EBP and can reinforce the learning that should be taking place in the classroom regarding EBP. Joining classroom and field to enhance EBP education requires additional efforts.

Coordinating Social Work Professional Organizations

Springer (2007, p. 623) states:

> It is not enough to discuss EBP within the confines of our ivory towers. It seems critical that we partner with key stakeholders representing and working in our communities to address some of the muddier issues (e.g., preparing social workers for practice in rural communities) facing the social work profession and the development of its workforce.

Springer identifies ways in which different social work organizations, such as Society for Social Work and Research, the National Association of Social Workers, and others have helped to contribute to the profession's movement toward the adoption of EBP. He also provides some examples of how smaller local organizations can play significant roles in educating about EBP. However, Springer also states that professional social work organizations can and should do more to help promote EBP within the profession. We further argue that they have a role to play in educating non-social workers about social work and EBP.

As social workers, we think about problems and practice on multiple levels of scale. We should apply our skills to improving practice effectiveness at several levels. How can our macro organizations partner with both individual clinicians and with the profession as a whole? How can the local or state clinical society help clinicians in EBP? Are there trainings they can sponsor? Are there resources they can make available, such as computer databases or the expertise of some members? How can practitioners who are more comfortable with EBP partner with local, state, and national organizations to help clinicians better understand EBP and offer effective services to their clients? These are all questions social work's professional organizations can address.

In comparison to other mental health professionals, MSW level clinical social workers have stronger professional organizations than do masters level psychologists or masters in marital and family therapy. In many states, social workers have more flexibility with insurance panels and higher reimbursement rates due to the efforts of social workers on the macro level. However, payers and policy makers perceive other professionals as being more open to and more trained in EBP that are social workers. Those same privileges may be questioned if our profession is not seen as current or evidence-based. Already, some other professionals view social workers as generally less knowledgeable about EBP. Other professions may argue that social workers do not base their practice decisions on research evidence (Murphy and McDonald 2004). Our professional organizations have the opportunity and responsibility to help educate within the profession, as well as beyond the profession, about social work and its relationship with EBP.

Shifting the Culture of Social Work

Almost a full decade ago, Gambrill and Gibbs (2002) argued that:

> Social workers want their physicians to rely on scientific criteria when they make recommendations for treatment, but [social workers] rely on weak evidentiary ground such as tradition when working with clients...what's good for the goose is not viewed as good for the gander (p. 39).

Changing the attitudes of social workers who are already in the field toward adopting a more evidence-based stance may be beyond the scope of what educational programs can do. However, educational programs can, and should, make the shift toward EBP with the early career social workers they are training. We encourage incorporating evidence-based attitudes and perspectives into every training they conduct in community-based settings. We also encourage critical thinking and critical perspectives on EBP, and excellence in assessment and practice skills.

To further assist in this aim, Springer (2007) asserts that social work educators need to discard the dichotomous view of EBP as *either* 'all good' *or* 'all bad.' Stated another way, that EBP is *either* focused on the clinical relationship *or* using a manual. EBP is more complex than the image many authors have commonly promoted. As we have attempted to show throughout this book and illustrated in the case examples, EBP is a multifaceted process. When professionals apply any process to unique individuals, complexity is magnified. However, EBP is a process that can help to orient and guide clinicians as they navigate the complexity of bringing together multiple sources of information to identify the most appropriate and informed treatment options for any given client(s). It seems that many social workers have yet to embrace this shift. Yet, it is vital for our profession to be viewed as one that uses evidence to make decisions, just as we expect other professionals to do. We should hold ourselves to the same level of standards and accountability to which we hold our own physicians. We expect our own providers to offer us options that work. Should not we do the same for our clients?

At the same time, clinical social workers should advocate for appropriate reimbursement policies and appropriate agency supports. Reimbursement rates for clinical social work services should reflect the additional time, knowledge, and effort the EBP process requires. The tension between limiting healthcare costs and providing appropriate compensation to providers can be framed as a difficult endeavor or as a hostile argument. Support for EBP in social work is likely to grow if it is implemented in ways that do not shift costs to providers nor limit client options. Shifting the culture of social work to support EBP may also require attention and advocacy in support of clinical social worker's compensation and working conditions. The administrative and policy dimensions of EBP can strongly impact its acceptance and use in clinical practice.

Supervision and EBP

The courses taken in any MSW program are only a portion of the training a clinical social worker receives. Yet any clinical social worker knows that the field experiences and supervision received during internships is a critical component in gaining competence. Supervision is also seen as essential to social workers post-graduation, not only because all states require it before a clinical social worker can be independently licensed, but because it is seen as a core component of a clinician's professional development (Osborn and Davis 2009; Rothstein 2001; Willer 2009). Supervision and consultation are life-long parts of good clinical practice.

One of the most commonly used definitions of supervision comes from Bernard and Goodyear (2009) who define supervision as:

> an intervention provided by a more senior member of a profession to a more junior member or members of that same profession. This relationship is evaluative, extends over time, and has the simultaneous purposes of (1) enhancing the professional functioning of the more junior person(s) (2) monitoring the quality of the professional functional services offered to the client(s) she, he or they see(s), and (3) serving as a gatekeeper of those who are to enter the particular profession. (p. 7)

However, as Osborn and Davis (2009) note when the supervision is using an EBP framework, there are additional issues that should be considered beyond the definition provided above.

First, if an early career clinician using the EBP process identifies a particular model of intervention to use with a client, there may be an assumption that the supervisor is competent in that model as well and can adequately supervise that individual. This assumption may not always be accurate. In other words, how do we assure that the supervisor is knowledgeable and skilled in the selected type of practice? Or does that supervisor need to be trained in this, and other, models in order to provide adequate supervision? Can the supervisor still be an appropriate guiding resource if not trained in the specific treatment model? Supervisors will face a number of new challenges in overseeing EBP practice learning.

Second, Osborn and Davis (2009, p. 66) raise the issue of the "splintering of clinical practice." Here they refer to the tension between helping a supervisee with a set of prescribed skills needed for a particular model and the broader professional development issues that may not be specific to any single model. Such issues include, among others, ethical challenges, social diversity and the differential use of self. By focusing too much on a particular practice model and the skills related to that model, supervisors may miss the larger professional development needs of the supervisee. This is a concern parallel to one that is often raised in the field by social workers: if a clinician focuses too much on a model, then the larger issues facing a client may be missed or not adequately addressed (Bellamy et al. 2008; Pollio 2006).

Finally, Osborn and Davis (2009) raise an issue similar to one identified by Springer (2007) around competence. Supervisors "increasingly need to supply evidence that their work with clinicians yields beneficial results for clients" and that this evidence needs to "demonstrate effectiveness beyond supervisee satisfaction or even supervisee competence" (p. 66). In effect, they apply the logic of EBP to evaluating the effectiveness of supervision. This is an area for further conceptual development and research. We note that it is very much like the use of practice outcomes to evaluate teachers discussed in Chapter 3. The EBP logic may be increasingly used to appraise the effectiveness of professionals, supervisors, and teachers in social work.

The topic of clinician competence is the primary focus of much of the literature concerning EBP and supervision (see Henggeler et al. 2002). Many articles focus mainly on how to increase the competence of clinicians in a particular model of intervention, such as multisystemic therapy (Henggeler et al. 2002). Yet, we agree with Osborn and Davis' (2009) concern about the potential for splintering in supervision and losing sight of the larger professional development aspects that clinicians cite as being an essential part of their supervisory experiences (Altoma-Mathews 2001; Rothstein 2001). Supervisors should encourage their supervisees to embrace the EBP process, which may lead to the need to increase their competence and skill level in a particular empirically supported model. At the same time, supervisors must simultaneously attend to the professional needs of the supervisee, such as focusing on ethical dilemmas, use of self, boundaries, self-disclosure, countertransference, theoretical knowledge, environmental and systemic factors. An effective supervisory relationship is one that simultaneously helps clinicians learn and improve skills, while keeping attention on the larger clinical and professional issues facing the practitioner.

Summary

It is possible that social workers and educators hold the key to changing the way EBP is viewed within the social work profession and outside of it as well. These individuals have the privilege and responsibility of training future practitioners who will eventually become the educators and supervisors of future generations. Through the educational process, these individuals will disseminate their views as to the definition and importance of EBP. Their actions will shape whether or not EBP is viewed as an approach with "potential as a way to guide social workers in delivering effective services" to clients (Springer 2007, p. 623). Yet, as is clear in the literature, there remains disagreement among those who teach and supervise social workers about what should be taught about EBP and how to go about teaching it effectively.

Through its consideration of the multiple factors that must be evaluated before making a treatment decision, we view the EBP decision making process as part of a holistic approach to working with clients. Therefore, we encourage educators and supervisors to bring that same approach to their work with social work trainees. We encourage a holistic approach to teaching EBP. Social workers must gain a range of knowledge, value, and skills. These must include how to conduct a thorough assessment, how to engage clients in the treatment planning process, and how to identify the best available evidence. Social workers must also learn how to be open and flexible, and to consider the complexities of clinical work beyond the skills that are associated with any one intervention. Effective clinical work is more than technique (Norcross 2011; Wampold 2010). Educators and supervisors need to communicate that EBP involves a multitude of skills and find effective strategies to help their students and supervisees gain competence and confidence in their ability to translate those skills to their clinical work with clients.

Chapter 18
Continuing Issues Regarding Evidence-Based Practice in Practice

In the preceding chapters, we have attempted to show how social workers can use evidence-based practice (EBP) to enhance practice with their clients, and how to incorporate the principles of EBP into clinical decision-making processes. We think that the EBP process is a "public idea" that is actively shaping public opinion about healthcare practices (Tanenbaum, 2003). It is also shaping funding and administrative practices, research funding priorities, and even research education for mental health professionals. Evidence-based medicine (EBM) and EBP have many supporters. For example, the Open Clinical (undated) organization states that:

For supporters, EBM has three main advantages:

1) It offers the surest and most objective way to determine and maintain consistently high quality and safety standards in medical practice.
2) It can help speed up the process of transferring clinical research findings into practice.
3) It has the potential to reduce healthcare costs significantly.

The approach, however, is not without its opponents. These consider that EBM risks downplaying the importance of clinical experience and expert opinion, and that the conditions under which clinical trials used to define best practice take place are hard to replicate in routine practice. (Benefits section)

Despite many potential advantages, there are also continuing issues reading the use of EBP in clinical social work practice.

In this chapter, we summarize and review several of the unresolved issues and challenges raised about EBM and EBP. We hope that this review prompts the reader to think critically about EBP and social work. We also hope that this review will prompt discussions with others in the profession and promote solutions that make EBP more optimally useful in practice.

J. W. Drisko and M. D. Grady, *Evidence-Based Practice in Clinical Social Work*,
Essential Clinical Social Work Series, DOI: 10.1007/978-1-4614-3470-2_18,
© Springer Science+Business Media New York 2012

Challenges to Evidence-Based Practice in Practice

There are a number of challenges to the EBP movement. There are also challenges within the social work profession regarding the adoption and acceptance of EBP. In fact, EBP has been met with resistance by many social workers working in various settings (Bellamy et al. 2008; Murphy and McDonald 2004; Nelson et al. 2006; Pollio, 2006; Proctor et al. 2007; Rosen, 2003; Trinder, 2000a, b). Below is a discussion of some of the everyday challenges that some social workers and other mental health professionals have documented that they face in using EBP.

Social Justice and Evidence-Based Practice

As discussed previously in Chapter 2, and Chapter 4 for many social workers EBP appears to be at odds with some of the core values of social work. These include inadequately addressing structural issues that may contribute to social justice concerns and further pushing social work toward a limited medical model orientation rather than promoting biopsychosocial and interdisciplinary models (Baines, 2006; Murphy and McDonald, 2004; Rosen, 2003; Trinder, 2000a). With a heavy reliance on the medical model to orient practice questions and literature searches, systemic, cultural, and other social diversity issues are not given priority equal to individual pathology. This seems inconsistent with core social work value on social justice. It also devalues social work's unique person-in-environment worldview. Since most EBM/EBP research projects are aimed at individual interventions rather than the systemic causes of mental health problems, the focus of most research remains on the resolution of an individual's deficits rather than on the broader social structures that also contribute to human suffering, such as poverty or racism. Similarly, EBP research rarely examines sources of strength and resilience in clients.

We also note that most EBM/EBP research discussed in social work is directed to determining treatment outcomes. We have also adopted this focus in this book. Readers should keep in mind that EBP research can also address prevention programs and even the effects of policies (Rubin, 2008). Another focus of EBP research is the cost benefit analysis of specific procedures. Yet social justice efforts have not yet been included in the EBP framework, nor prioritized for funding.

Limitations to Available Research

While we note that EBP has begun to alter priorities for research funding, most treatments and service programs have not been studied using high quality methods. The large number of specific DSM diagnoses, including their subtypes, means that more than 1,000 specific diagnoses would need to be studied to have even a beginning database of 'what works' in mental health. In reality most high quality studies focus, appropriately, on high incidence and high cost disorders such as depression, anxiety, and schizophrenia. This means that the concerns of many clients, including children and elders, are not reflected in some Cochrane or Campbell systematic reviews for practice use. Clinical social workers will have to search for individual studies, which takes considerable time and expert research evaluation skills. There is also no guarantee that at the end of a search the results will offer clear and relevant guidance for practice decision making.

With the arrival of both new and revised psychiatric diagnoses in DSM-V, it is unclear if the results of research based on older criteria remain fully applicable in practice. Clinical social workers will need to critically examine older research to insure it is truly relevant and applicable to all new DSM-V diagnostic categories. Any revised diagnosis will require careful review for its fit with older research.

As social workers, we also think that DSM diagnoses are only starting points for evaluating real-world client needs. We have noted throughout this book that clients with comorbid disorders, with significant social stressors, and who may suffer from socially structured oppression are not yet well addressed by EBM and EBP outcome research. Galea et al. (2011) used a meta-analysis of the Medline research reports to estimate that 176,000 deaths in the United States in 2000 were caused by racial segregation, 162,000 to low social support, and 133,000 to individual level poverty. They conclude that "the estimated number of deaths attributable to social factors in the United States is comparable to the number attributed to pathophysiological and behavioral causes" (Abstract). The evidence base on which EBM and EBP rests needs enormous expansion to be optimally useful for practice decision making. Social work's person-in-environment world-view can add significantly to the conceptualization of EBM and EBP research.

Ironically, clinical social workers and others who undertake the EBP literature searches often suffer from information overload (Tanjong-Ghogomu et al. 2009). Lots of information is available in print and online, but finding truly useful and relevant research results may be all the more difficult due to the sheer volume of available material. Even with sources for high quality systematic reviews and excellent search tools, finding useful research can be like finding a needle in a haystack. Both the lack of specific research and the volume of available research information combine to make 'doing' EBP difficult and time consuming.

Realities of Real-World Practice

Other critiques of EBP are that empirically supported interventions (ESIs) do not take into account the "messiness" of real life practice (Bellamy et al. 2008; Murphy and McDonald, 2004; Nelson et al. 2006; Pollio, 2006; Proctor et al. 2007; Rosen, 2003). One social worker states that highly controlled studies are "irrelevant" and "absurd" (Nelson et al. 2006, p. 404) regarding their utility for practitioners.

As discussed throughout this book, EBM/EBP researchers generally seek to study narrowly defined and tightly controlled samples to insure homogeneity. Most often, the selection criteria highlight only a single diagnosis or a diagnosis in combination with specific client demographic criteria (most often age and/or gender).

These limitations translate into a very narrow group of individuals who are actually studied in EBP research. The samples may, or may not, be representative of the larger and more diverse, often multiproblem, populations who apply for clinical services. Results of high quality studies may be based on samples that are quite different from the typical clients with whom a social worker is working. For example, a clinician is working with a 10-year-old Asian-American girl who has experienced a trauma and now has a diagnosis of Post-Traumatic Stress Disorder as well as a severe learning disability. It will be difficult to locate research reports that capture both her complex diagnostic picture as well as her cultural back-ground. For social workers who work in diverse settings with diverse clients, applying the findings from a research study can feel unrealistic or impossible. One social worker in a study regarding the applicability of research findings to her practice stated, "Our kids don't come in nice neat packages. Most have multiple diagnoses, and I don't know what's out there for kids with multiple diagnoses" (Nelson et al. 2006, p. 409). Another stated "The research has to be with out-of-control kids, not control kids" (Nelson, et al. 2006, p. 404). These quotes reflect the wariness that many social workers have about how to transfer what is done in a "lab" with what they see in the "real world."

Accessibility of Research

For other social workers, the accessibility of research further limits use of currently available knowledge. This has two parts. First, social workers find it difficult to locate research findings. Second, they also question their ability to understand and evaluate the research they can locate (Bellamy et al. 2008; Proctor et al. 2007). For example, a study aimed at translating empirically supported interventions (ESIs) into a community-based practice setting. One participating social worker said "To me, the evaluations of the research, it's like really complicated, and the statistical stuff, to me, I start to zone out." Another said "I can't see myself going through 15 articles and calculating the effect size" (Bellamy et al. 2008, pp. 63–64). EBP research summaries can be very complex and detailed. Most MSW level social work education does not adequately prepare clinical practitioners to critically evaluate research reports including statistical results. The plain language abstracts of Cochrane Collaboration and Campbell Collaboration systematic reviews may be easier to understand, but most still contain many unfamiliar statistics.

Further complicating the interpretation of research is that the majority of empirical research articles reporting findings regarding a particular intervention are not written for clinicians but for other researchers (Yunong and Fengzhi, 2009). This makes it a challenge for lay clinicians to understand the findings of different research projects and apply those findings to their own practices. We hope that through this book, we have made the evaluation of the research a bit more accessible and less daunting by sharing various ideas and resources. We also provide readers with research review materials in Chapters 6–8 and in the Glossary. However, the reality is that for many social workers, the prospect of evaluating research evidence remains a difficult and intimidating task.

We also note that each of the literature searches completed for the cases in this book took no less than three hours. Where there was no systematic review, literatures searches for individual articles often took much longer. Funding and other supports for the time to locate and evaluate relevant research literature must be made available to make doing EBP realistic.

Ignores the Expertise of the Clinician

We have emphasized throughout this book that the clinician is the 'glue' that integrates the components of the EBP process. Still, many clinical social workers think that EBP ignores the expertise of the clinician. Some clinicians say that "Therapy is still an art" (Proctor et al. 2007, p. 483). Clinicians often believe that researchers do not understand the interpersonal processes that make up clinical practice. Some clinicians say that researchers need to be more informed about the nuances of actual practice and that many research interventions are unrealistic given practice realities (Brekke, Ell, and Palinkas, 2007). In addition, social work has been built as a profession, "very much around the clinical experience of people" (Murphy and McDonald, 2004, p. 131). The ability to form relationships among clients is seen as central to the work that social workers do in the field. Yet the role of the therapeutic relationship is not often included in EBM and EBP outcome research. The therapeutic relationship and the working alliance are also viewed as key active ingredients in clinical change by many clinical researchers in allied mental health professions. Studies that directly address clinical expertise should be part of EBP research.

Going even further, some social workers believe that EBP and lists of empirically supported treatments (ESTs) have been created by governmental or other monitoring bodies without regard for the actual needs of the clients or the challenges in implementing the interventions (Baines, 2006; Bellamy et al. 2008). As discussed in Chapter 2, the push by governmental agencies or managed care companies for the use of prescribed ESIs or ESTs has created the feeling that clinicians cannot be trusted to design and implement their own interventions; rather they need an administrator or a manual to tell them what to do with their clients (Pollio, 2006). As such, many clinicians have resisted the movement, which they believe dismisses an essential part of their professional identity and expertise (Baines, 2006; Bellamy et al. 2008; Pollio, 2006).

We argue that healthcare economics largely drives many efforts to limit professional autonomy. Healthcare companies and public regulatory agencies use inconsistent standards to certify lists of ESIs and ESTs. We have noted that insurance payers may endorse specific treatments despite the fact that Cochrane Collaboration and Campbell Collaboration systematic reviews show little or no support for these treatments. Healthcare organization and public funding agencies should follow the lead of organizations that seek transparent and high quality research results. The standards and decision-making processes of funders should also be open and transparent. That said, funders face the same limitations to finding high quality outcome studies that clinicians face: there is simply no strong outcome research on many mental health care issues.

Logistics and Realities of Evidence-Based Practice Implementation

Finally, there are concerns among social workers that EBP sounds like a wonderful concept in theory, but the logistics of implementing EBP and ESIs found in the search process into clinical settings render them unrealistic. This is due to time, training, and money restraints that make it too difficult for many agencies to sustain such practices. Specifically, budget restrictions make it difficult for agencies to both fund the actual intervention found to be effective in a search, as well as allow supervision and training time, all of which takes away from the productivity of the workers (Proctor et al. 2007).

Statements that express these sentiments come from two separate studies that interviewed practitioners and agency directors regarding the challenges of implementing and sustaining ESIs within their agencies. One agency director stated "A treatment may be the best thing in the world, but if we can't fund it, we can't do it" (Nelson et al. 2006, p. 402). Another stated that "Supervision takes people off-line" (Proctor et al. 2007, p. 483). Other clinical social workers and agency directors have noted that high caseloads and the need to maximize billable time do not allow for the luxury of reading research articles and attending training on various ESIs (Murphy and McDonald, 2004; Proctor et al. 2007). Administrative practices may undermine the implementation of EBP.

To use an example to illustrate some of these challenges, imagine a clinician who meets with Chad, a 15-year Caucasian male who is involved in the juvenile justice system, has a diagnosis of conduct disorder, and is at risk of being placed out of his home. The clinician is interested in learning about the most effective interventions to help Chad with both the conduct disorder behaviors, and to attempt to keep him in his home. After completing an initial search, the clinician finds that Multisystemic Treatment (MST) (Henggeler and Lee, 2003; Schoenwald et al. 2000) appears to be an empirically supported treatment for the client's needs. The demographics of clients included in several outcome studies match with Chad's in terms of race, age, diagnosis, and presenting problem. On all accounts, MST seems like a very appropriate and potentially efficacious treatment for Chad. (We must note that a

Campbell Collaboration systematic review of MST by Littell et al. (2005) questions its effectiveness regarding out of home placement, arrests, and convictions.)

The clinician's excitement about finding a likely effective intervention is quickly damped once she learns that MST can be conducted only through agencies that have acquired the training and licensing to provide this intervention (Schoenwald et al. 2000). In other words, unless her agency opted to get the training, receives the license and follows the protocols of the licensing body for MST, she is unable to offer this service to her client. The agency where the social worker works is based in a small rural community, with a very limited budget and staff. It would be economically unrealistic for the agency to pursue the supervision and training needed to become a provider of MST. In the meantime Chad's challenges remain. In searching for other options in her community, she learns that no local agency is a licensed MST provider. While the clinical social worker has found a good match for Chad and his needs, she is not able to offer him such a service, nor is she able to offer him other evidence-based alternatives within his own community.

The example of Chad highlights that EBP is a starting point in practice decision making. The clinical social worker must use the best available evidence to inform her or his clinical decision, in conjunction with the client's needs, values and goals, and the clinical context. When the research points to only a few likely effective options, there is even more need for clinical expertise in interpreting and synthesizing all of the factors in the client's presentation. While the EBP search process located likely effective treatments for Chad, the practice realities obligated the clinician to revise the search and incorporate the additional information into the clinical decision-making process.

Questions Related to Modifying the Intervention

Another challenge faced by social workers is whether modifying an intervention is appropriate and allowed in EBP. That is, must an ESI be used only in full, exactly as the authors describe it? Many ESIs and ESTs, like Multisystemic Therapy or Linehan's Dialectical Behavior Therapy (DBT), have strict treatment protocols that have been followed in efficacy studies to make for internally valid research. In the field, however, the realities of practice come into play. In practice it is up to the clinician to determine whether such interventions can be modified for the client's benefit. Questions include how, when, where, and in what situations should the intervention be modified.

One clinician said:

> If we decide that there were some approaches or interventions that were useful, there is still a whole piece missing, and that is how we would actually implement—with whom, why, when—and that is not in the literature, that is where the creative part is. (Bellamy et al. 2008, p. 66)

Clinicians often make modifications to a treatment in order to combine the art and science of clinical practice (Graybeal, 2007; Messer, 2004; Pollio, 2006; Weinberger and Rasco, 2007). After doing so, however, can the clinician be confident that the modified intervention maintains the essential ingredients needed for it to be effective?

The clinician-researchers who have developed intervention models often work hard to ensure that only those individuals who have been trained and supervised in the model can legitimately state that they are actually using the model in practice. They do this to protect the treatment fidelity of the model. Such treatment models include MST (Schoenwald et al. 2000) and Eye-Movement Desensitization and Reprocessing (EMDR; Shapiro and Maxfield, 2002). Yet, by copyrighting these interventions, and certifying trained providers, they have become less accessible to many clinicians due to financial, training, and supervision challenges.

If a clinical social worker uses a copyrighted treatment that he or she has learned about, and modifies it based on the needs of the client, can it still be labeled as the original model? If it does *not* prove to be effective with that client, did the model fail or was it the *way in which* the model was implemented that was ineffective?

Practice anecdotes indicate that clinicians and agencies do frequently modify copyrighted and detailed treatment protocols. These vary from minor alterations in content or timing of delivery to using only the group components of models that originally included both group and individual components. While modifying treatments may be common in practice, it is unclear how such modification fits with the EBP model. Delivering a modified treatment without research support may be a way of avoiding or evading EBP. It is also unclear if a modified treatment might open clinicians to legal suit for malpractice or for violation of professional ethics. This would appear to be a greater risk if the original treatment plan identified a specific model, which was not fully delivered. Funders might also challenge payment for modified treatments. The issue of if, and if, how much, modification to ESIs is allowable in EBP remains minimally explored and unresolved.

Social Workers Compared to Other Professionals in the Evidence-Based Practice Movement

Whether due to the concerns discussed above or to other issues, social workers have lagged behind other mental health and medical professionals regarding their training and knowledge of the EBP principles and empirically supported practice models (Bellamy et al. 2006; Brekke et al. 2007; Murphy and McDonald, 2004; Weismann et al. 2006). In a national study of accredited training programs in psychiatry, psychology, and social work Weismann et al. (2006) found that social work programs required the least amount of training and supervision in ESTs in comparison to the other disciplines. This is despite claims by many social work programs that they provide strong clinical training. The authors concluded that

"There is a considerable gap between research evidence for psychotherapy and clinical training. Until the training programs in the major disciplines providing psychotherapy increase training in EBT [evidence based therapy], the gap between research evidence and clinical practice will remain" (p. 925).

This lack of training in social work programs surrounding EBP and the use of ESIs and ESTs may have negative consequences for social workers who work in multidiscipline settings. In one study at a community hospital that delivers services through interdisciplinary teams, researchers surveyed the different disciplines about their perceptions of the knowledge base of the other professionals (Murphy and McDonald, 2004). Of all of the professions included, social work was the only one for which respondents raised concerns regarding a lack of knowledge and skills in using EBP. This puts social workers at a disadvantage when compared to other professionals on the same team. One nurse in the study stated that social workers "come from a non-medical background and they fit into teams, but often operate differently...it's pretty airy fairy" (p. 134). A physiotherapist stated in reference to social workers "some of them just don't have any real evidence base...they seem not to" (p. 134). The social workers themselves identified that their lack of knowledge of EBP "problematic" for them in their work settings and they felt that concerns were raised about the "validity of social work practice" on their teams (Murphy and McDonald, 2004, p. 132). One social worker stated that "Professionally we are being devalued because we're unable to compete in that context" (p. 134).

Chapter Summary

The continuing issues raised above by clinical social workers and the profession's relationship with EBP are indeed challenging. We believe that in order for social work to remain a respected profession, it must find a way to balance the criticisms and concerns of EBP with the strengths presented in this book. As discussed previously, social workers are viewed by other professionals as having less knowledge of EBP when compared to other health and mental health professionals (Murphy and McDonald, 2004). In order for our profession to be seen as relevant and knowledgeable in today's current practice climate, social workers must embrace the tools needed to practice within an EBP context. We also need to take leadership in exploring these unresolved issues related to applying EBP in everyday clinical practice.

Our goal in this chapter is to clearly present the challenges of doing EBP. We have already pointed out its many strengths through this book. We also provide in Appendix B a summary listing of both the strengths and the limitations of EBP. Learning, and critically examining, EBP will help clinical social workers understand its complexity from several different perspectives. We hope that readers will be motivated to think about how to help individual practitioners and the profession as a whole address these concerns.

Chapter 19
Conclusion

Throughout this book, we have attempted to show how to implement the evidence-based practice (EBP) decision-making process in a way that feels manageable and realistic in everyday practice. We hope that the previous chapters have provided clinical practitioners with the tools and the knowledge necessary to have confidence in their ability to use EBP to inform practice decisions in many settings and with a wide range of clients. While EBP is a process with both strengths and limitations, we believe that social workers must engage with EBP as a way of providing the best possible care to the clients they serve. Evidence-based medicine (EBM) and EBP are valuable steps toward realizing Dr. Archie Cochrane's goals of increasing effective treatments, reducing benign treatments, and eliminating harmful and ineffective treatments. EBP is an important step in improving professional accountability. EBP moves social work from the "empirically based practice" world of single case outcome evaluation into the realm of large-scale outcome research.

We have examined EBM and EBP from three different perspectives. First, EBP is widely promoted as a practice decision-making process. Second, EBP is also actively used to promote certain administrative and economic interests. Third, we argue that it is also used to promote certain research priorities and academic positions. We think all three perspectives help professionals understand the complexity of EBM and EBP as "public ideas" and as social movements. Looking at EBP only as a practice decision-making process omits the context in which it is promoted, critiqued, funded, and researched.

Still, EBM and EBP are most often discussed as practice decision-making processes. This is indeed the perspective of the McMaster Group of physicians who have so clearly and effectively promoted the inclusion of population-based scale outcome research into routine clinical practice (Guyatt et al. 2008; Sackett et al. 1996). The EBP practice decision-making process is also widely promoted within social work (Gambrill, 2001; Gibbs, 2002; Thyer, 2011). We agree this is a key, and valuable, part of EBM and EBP.

J. W. Drisko and M. D. Grady, *Evidence-Based Practice in Clinical Social Work*, 251
Essential Clinical Social Work Series, DOI: 10.1007/978-1-4614-3470-2_19,
© Springer Science+Business Media New York 2012

The six-step EBM/EBP practice decision-making process provides a clear method for social workers to identify, locate, evaluate, and utilize research knowledge for practice. While we find the steps of the EBP process very useful, we also note that they are silent on assessment. To start the EBP practice decision-making process, a high quality, thorough assessment is assumed. We think assessment can be a challenging process and is often incomplete. We are concerned that contemporary clinical practice policies and administrative practices do not always allow for the thorough assessment that is the hidden foundation of the EBP practice decision-making process (Drisko and Grady, 2011). We offer an outline of a social work assessment in Appendix A.

The EBP process begins by requiring a clear formulation of the practice issues presented by your client. The EBP process then promotes location and evaluation of relevant population-based research. Recent innovations in online materials and search tools aid in the location of research results. New international professional organizations have developed and promoted preliminary standards for evaluating clinical research. They have also developed libraries of high quality research results, most notably the Cochrane Library for medical and psychiatry topics and the Campbell Library for social welfare, education, and criminal justice topics. While these libraries may lack results on specific practice topics of interest to clinical social workers, their knowledge bases are growing rapidly. Social workers are increasingly authors of systematic reviews.

The contemporary EBM and EBP practice decision-making process obligates shared discussion with the client about the alternative treatments and services located in the research review. While some medical texts on EBM appear to make this step a simple 'reporting out' of research results, clinical social workers may use it as an opportunity to actively involve clients in decision making. We believe this is consistent with core social work values and useful for engaging clients in the therapeutic process. Active engagement in informed, shared practice decision making can be an empowering aspect of practice. EBP also allows client values and preferences to override research results in practice decision making. The EBP practice decision-making process highlights the critical importance of professional expertise in combining clinical circumstances, client values, and preferences with research knowledge to guide practice. The EBM/EBP movement has actively promoted the use of quantitative research results in practice decision making, but it neither omits professional expertise and judgment, nor client views and autonomy.

It is our position that practice evaluation is an integral part of doing good practice. We find merit in many forms of practice evaluation. However, we think the population scale research logic highlighted in EBM and EBP research is very different from the single case evaluation methods used to evaluate everyday practice efforts. Single case evaluation does not allow the determination of cause and effect relationships fundamental to the EBP research hierarchy. It may reflect the perspective of researchers unfamiliar with practice that evaluation is 'tacked on' to EBP while assessment is omitted from it. We support the importance of practice evaluation but do not view it as part of the EBP practice decision-making process. We understand that professionals may have different views on this issue.

Other Perspectives on Evidence-Based Practice

To understand EBM and EBP more fully, it is also important to examine these social movements from multiple perspectives. The practice decision-making process is one key part of EBM and EBP, but it does not capture the movement in full. How EBM and EBP are promoted for economic purposes at policy and administrative levels, and how they are used to promote certain types of research also matter. How EBP shapes research will have important consequences for education in social work and allied professions, and for clinical supervision.

Evidence-Based Practice as a Shaping Influence on Research and Education

From a second perspective, EBP and population scale research are vital sources of knowledge for practice. Dr. Archie Cochrane's effort to increase effective treatments, reduce ineffective treatments, and eliminate harmful treatments is a very worthy endeavor. That this viewpoint has been adopted worldwide shows its value. Yet large-scale, population-based research cannot be the only source of knowledge used to inform and expand social work's knowledge of what helps clients achieve their goals. Other kinds of knowledge and other types of research must also inform clinical social work practice and the policies that shape it (Lietz and Zayas, 2010). We find merit and worth in both EBP and in "many ways of knowing" (Hartman, 1994). Non-experimental research allows for innovation and discovery in ways that are necessary to learn about changing practice needs and changing social circumstances. Such methods also allow for discovery and inclusion about social diversity in ways that are too often omitted or underrepresented in EBM and EBP research. Maximizing the internal validity of research on practice is a worthy goal for many important purposes. Still, the results of experimental research must address the questions and needs of clinical social work practitioners more fully to encourage them to make the best use of EBP. Questions of *what* generates changes in clinical practice and *how* individual clinicians and their agencies impact practice outcomes needs further study. Questions about modifying empirically supported treatments to meet specific client needs and service limitations also need further conceptualization and study. Such research should not be at odds with high quality quantitative studies of the outcomes of clinical social work practice.

EBM and EBP are actively shaping research training, priorities, and funding. They promote large-scale experimental research methods and medical model views of problems and outcomes. In academics, they also shape the content of research courses. We argue that EBP has many merits but does not always value and encourage diverse ways of knowing. From one perspective, it is a battleground for defining 'the best research' when different research methods are appropriate to varied research questions, varied research purposes and varied audiences who need research information. There is no single 'best' approach to research. Social work students should be educated in many different research approaches and methods for different uses.

Social work educators have a long way to go to help practitioners understand the research methods used in EBP and to critically appraise EBP results. This book provides detailed information on how to implement EBP in clinical social work practice. Littell et al. (2008) provide an excellent introduction to the details of interpreting systematic reviews. Gilgun's (2005a) "Four Cornerstones of Evidence Based Practice" provides a valuable introduction to EBP research assumptions and methods. Many social work texts on research methods offer useful starting points for understanding EBP research. Still standards for accreditation only broadly promote "research informed practice" and "practice informed research" (CSWE, 2008, EP 2.1.6). How to more actively include the knowledge and expertise of clinical social work practitioners, and of clients, must be explored and resolved. EBP shaped and guided only by researchers will not be fully embraced by real-world practitioners, nor will it fully meet the needs of real-world clients.

Evidence-Based Practice as a Public Idea that Shapes Policy and Practice Funding

From a third perspective, EBM and EBP are public ideas that are being actively used in the process of managing health care costs. This is an important public issue affecting rich and poor, and old and young. To make health care accessible to the greatest number of people, efficiency is important. *How* such decisions are made matters to both professionals and to our clients.

Dr. Archie Cochrane believed improving patient outcomes and reducing ineffective treatments would simultaneously reduce overall healthcare costs. This may be more likely in countries with single payer, national healthcare systems than in countries with a patchwork of paid insurance plans and many for-profit healthcare corporations. Health care costs in the United States have increased far beyond the average level of overall inflation for many years. Annual increases in health care costs far outpace increases in inflation and personal income (KaiserEDU.org 2010). Health care costs and cost increases have reached a crisis point.

In this context, the public ideas of EBM and EBP actively shape public opinion (Tanenbaum 2003). As quoted in Chapter 2, the conflict between professional autonomy and administrative oversight of EBP is often portrayed as competent, research informed, administrators pitted against ineffective, and incompetent practitioners. Using the EBP practice decision-making process makes clear that clinical social workers are research informed. Yet if a goal of the tighter administrative oversight of practitioners is to limit the types and number of treatments and services solely to generate cost savings, practitioners must be much more active voices in the healthcare debate. We find it odd that the lists of "empirically supported" treatments and services created by states and insurance companies often do not match with the treatments found to be effective by Cochrane Collaboration and Campbell Collaboration systematic reviews. It is often quite unclear *who* created these lists of funded treatment, and *what standards* they applied in making these determinations. A basic premise of EBM and EBP systematic reviews is transparency: that readers can review exactly how decisions were made in great detail. Such transparency is often lacking in the lists of approved treatments and services created by states and insurance companies. We argue that it should be fully transparent for professionals and for the people who pay for coverage. Administrators, policy makers, and funders might more fully embrace and enact the methods of the EBP movement.

Making the Most of Professional Expertise

The professional expertise and knowledge of clinical social work practitioners is one vital part of the contemporary EBP process. EBM and EBP embrace and include professional expertise in the application of the EBP practice decision-making process. We argue that professional expertise should be much more widely incorporated into the definition of EBP questions and its research methods. We also argue, along with Petr (2009), that client views and multiple voices should be much more part of the EBP research. EBP should expand from a narrow view of symptom reduction to a larger view that also includes enhancement of capacities and empowerment. Such a larger view of the outcomes of effective treatments is more fully consistent with social work's core professional values.

We note that EBP provides a forum in which social workers can disseminate their research and practice wisdom in an intentional manner. When clinical social work practitioners contribute to research and knowledge about what works in treatment, the field, the profession, and most importantly, clients benefit. Social workers have an opportunity to help shape how EBP is understood and implemented. We must use this influence to support high quality practice processes and outcomes, and to ensure our efforts best meet the needs of out clients at macro-, messo-, and micro levels.

Staying Close to Cases and to the Realities
of Clinical Social Work Practice

As we have attempted to show through the case examples examined in this book, there are still significant gaps in the research knowledge of what works in treatment for certain clinical presentations and for certain populations. EBP is based on the assumption that evidence should inform treatment, yet there are many times when little or no high quality evidence is available to inform the practitioner about what forms of intervention have been shown to be effective with similar clients. Intervention outcome research is a growing yet limited body of knowledge. The professional knowledge and expertise of clinical social work practitioners will be a critical component in increasing this body of knowledge around what actually works in practice.

Professional expertise and practice knowledge is the integrating factor in EBP. We argue that the EBP decision-making process pays much too little attention to assessment. The EBM and EBP models appear to assume a thorough and adequate assessment has been completed, though many contemporary mental health policies and administrative practices fail to support thorough assessment. Single session assessment is often insufficient to learn about a client's needs and circumstances. Clinical social work uses many different models of assessment which address different aspects of client's needs and situations. These models also formulate clinical needs and problems in ways that go far beyond symptom reduction. Most require multiple measures of outcome to demonstrate effectiveness. How EBP fits with the models of assessment clinical social workers use needs more examination. More research on the kinds of complex problems social workers confront in practice also needs to be completed.

Even with an accurate assessment, clients may still be offered services that are inappropriate for them. There is a growing emphasis within many mental health and human service organizations to offer clients a selection of empirically supported treatments (ESTs) or empirically supported interventions (ESIs). Some funders and policy makers restrict money and other benefits, such as certification or licensing, to organizations that do not deliver a preselected set of ESTs or ESIs that have been identified by these third parties as "effective" (Proctor et al. 2007). One administrator who was interviewed in Proctor et al.'s (2007) study stated, "There's not going to be a new dollar on the street that's not going to be associated with EBPs. Period…. There's not going to be a new dollar that comes out to do non-EBPs" (p. 488). As noted, such lists of ESTs and "EBPs" may be inconsistent with the results found by independent searches of the Cochrane or Campbell databases for the same disorders. With such policies, there is a risk of clients only being offered a limited type of services that do not align with their needs and personal goals. Practitioners may be put in a position of having to offer services that they know are not appropriate for the client. Neither client values and autonomy nor professional expertise are honored; the EBP practice decision-making process is overridden by administration. In those instances, it is essential to refer clients to other agencies that may provide a better fit for the needs of the clients. Yet due to financial realities, there may be pressure to encourage clients to remain at the original agency so the agency will not lose that potential revenue. Agencies, policy makers, and providers all want to offer clients treatments that work. How restrictive or limited is the vision of 'what works,' and from whose point of view effectiveness is assessed, will be important to watch as EBP is embraced in various practice settings.

Is Evidence-Based Practice Effective?

EBP is based on the premise that clinicians should be using evidence to inform their practice decisions, yet there is no evidence on whether using such an approach actually improves outcomes with mental health clients (Trinder, 2000a; Westen, 2006). In using the model of population scale research, there have been no trials in which randomly selected clinicians are divided into groups that use EBP and do not use EBP, then comparing which clients had better outcomes. (Note that such a study would have likely have many confounds, low internal validity, and some ethical challenges.) While everyone appears to agree to that using evidence is a good thing, it is still not clear whether adopting this process will measurably improve the outcomes for the clients social workers serve in their practice settings. Nor is it clear that EBP will reduce service costs.

We raise this issue not to dismiss or negate any parts of what we have described throughout this book. EBP is a valuable process for determining the best possible treatment options for clients and should be a part of the clinical decision-making process. Well-conceptualized, high quality research can improve practice outcomes. However, it is important to note that just as in many areas of social work, there is much still unknown about what happens during the change process. The mechanisms behind clinical changes in mental health need further study and identification. In the meantime, clinical social workers must use all forms of knowledge that are available to them, as they work tirelessly with their clients to find solutions to the complex internal and external experiences with which our clients struggle.

We encourage clinical social workers to engage with, and critically examine, both the strengths and limitations of EBP. It is an important social movement and a practice decision-making process that will better inform clinical practice. The voices and views of both clinical social workers and our clients must be active parts of the future of EBP.

Appendix A
An Outline for a Biopsychosocial Assessment and Intervention Plan

I. Referral
How and why did the client(s) get to the agency? Is the client self-referred? Is the client voluntary or involuntary?

II. Description of Client
Who is the client? Briefly document relevant identifying information including: Age, gender identity, marital/partner status, race, ethnicity, sexual orientation, religion, social class, income source(s), disabilities, level of education, prominent health issues, medications, substance use, and legal issues.

III. Presenting Issues and Concerns
What are the client's complaints? What are the larger presenting issues? How does the client view these concerns/issues? How do other people (family, friends, agency, work, school, courts, physicians, religious community, you, etc.) view the concerns/issues?

When did these concerns/issues begin? Is there an identifiable precipitant? Why is the client coming in now?

How has the client dealt with these or similar concern/issues in the past? What would the client most want help with?

IV. Assessment of Relevant Contextual, Historical, and Intrapersonal Factors

    a. **Current context** What are the family, social community, work, and other issues relevant to an understanding of the client and the problem? (An eco-map and/or a family genogram, identifying family, and environmental resources may help clarify these intertwining issues.)

        • Are the client's basic needs met? (Housing, food, clothing, utilities, emergency, or situational needs such as diaper services or money for medicine or care of pets while inpatient?) What are the clients' strengths in meeting basic needs? Are these needs met in a culturally appropriate/sensitive manner?

J. W. Drisko and M. D. Grady, *Evidence-Based Practice in Clinical Social Work*,
Essential Clinical Social Work Series, DOI: 10.1007/978-1-4614-3470-2,
© Springer Science+Business Media New York 2012

- What are the clients' income sources? Are they stable? Can they be improved? What are the clients' strengths in meeting basic needs? Is this income obtained in a culturally appropriate/sensitive manner?
- Are there language issues for the client in the services and communities to which they relate? In meeting basic needs? In the school or workplace? Are interpreters available? Is language training accessible if sought? What strengths and challenges does language pose for the clients?
- If the client has disability issues, how adapted/accessible are home, neighborhood, workplace, schools, stores, and professionals? How are communication needs met? How are transportation needs met? Does the client have access to needed equipment for safety and for daily living skills? Does the client have training to use such equipment/devices? How is this disability understood in the clients' cultural context? What strengths are evident related to this disability?
- Are the client's medical and dental needs met? (This includes routine checkups, assessment of illnesses, emergency care, immunizations, dental care, rehabilitation services, access to medications or rehabilitation equipment, access to nursing help, and access to long-term care, etc,) Are the services culturally appropriate? Accessible?
- Are the client's safety needs met? (Domestic violence, abuse or neglect of children or elders, violence in housing, neighborhood, and specific threats?) Is the client's physical environment safe? (Free of fire hazards, with accessible fire escapes, no lead paint, etc.?)
- Does the client pose a hazard to the safety of self or others; specifically is there suicide risk or lethality risk? Fire setting risk? (If any of these apply, a specific detailed evaluation and documentation is also required.)
- Is domestic, partner, or marital violence an issue? If so, is a safety plan in place?
- Are there child protective, disability, or elder protective issues for the clients? If so, is there a service plan? What services are involved? What services/needs are ignored?
- Are there legal issues for the clients? Any court involvement, restraints, obligations? Are there obligatory services, costs, or settlements unpaid?
- What is the client's immigration status? Could this be a source of being unsafe or exploited?
- What is the client's religion or spiritual beliefs? What level of involvement do they have with their religion or spiritual organization, its practices, and its community? Does the client have other connections to spirituality? How do these (religion and/or spirituality) shape the meaning of the client's life?
- What are the client's recreational interests? How and where are these met? Are there barriers to recreational activities?
- What are the client's key social supports? Are they accessible?

- Are there important social policy or social structural aspects to the client's situation and problem? Has (or could) the client joined with others to address these issues? How?

b. **Historical influences** Summarize, as relevant, past material about

- Client's childhood, including developmental history.
- Relationships with family of origin.
- School and work history.
- Previous experiences with social, medical or psychological services.
- Intimate relationships.

c. **Coping strengths and weaknesses**

- What are the client's key self-reported strengths? Are there other strengths you observe or can infer?
- How does the client process information? Protect themselves from anxiety and stress? Who do they turn to for support and nurturance?
- How does the client characteristically interact with others? Are these strategies successful in meeting the client's needs? Are they routinely problematic? Can the client show flexibility in style of interaction?
- How do these strengths, challenges, and abilities fit with the client's social and institutional resources? What resources or obstacles facilitate or inhibit the client's mastering current issues/concerns?
- What role do current life cycle tasks play in relation to the concerns and issues that have been identified?

V. Formulation

Develop a brief, clear, biopsychosocial summary of the above material that integrates relevant developmental, theoretical (i.e., psychodynamic, cognitive-behavioral, P–I–E, family systems, or risk and resiliency), family, and sociocultural issues. How would you state the client's dilemma in easily understood words that capture the key concerns and strengths?

VI. Plan for Intervention

Drawing upon the formulation, describe your plan for intervention. Identify your goals, separating immediate from long term. What would be the core elements of a treatment contract with this client? Are there elements that might be uncomfortable or unacceptable to the client?

VII. The Best Research Evidence

Given the proposed plan for intervention, what does the research evidence indicate are the best likely effective treatments or services to discuss with the client? Are the treatments realistically available and can they be funded? Are these treatments likely to be accepted by the client?

VIII. Values and Ethics: The Worker's own Values and Experience

What are the value, ethical, diversity, personal reactions, and other challenging issues that surface in this case? Will these alter what you can offer and provide?

IX. Organizational Issues
How will your agency mission and practices shape further service delivery? What organizational factors aid successful services for this case? What factors are barriers or impede services for this case?

X. Social Change Goals
What social change goals can be part of, or related to, your work with the client? What resources might you mention to the client as ways to promote the changes they wish to help make? What resources might you help connect the client with to promote these changes? How might you work to promote social changes related to this client and case?

© 1997, 2005 by James Drisko and Carolyn DuBois—used with permission from the authors

Appendix B
A Bullet Point Summary of the Merits and the Limitations of Evidence-Based Practice

In this appendix we offer a very brief overall summary of the merits EBM/EBP and the concerns and issues scholars and practitioners have raised about it. Each of these issues has been examined in greater detail in this book.

The Merits of EBP

The General and Practice Merits of EBP

(1) EBP offers a method for clinical social workers to include the use of research evidence in treatment planning, in diagnostic determination, and in the understanding of etiology and prognosis. It helps clinicians select among treatments in manner that includes knowledge of comparative outcomes for large samples. EBP provides policy planners with important data for determining the cost-benefit of specific treatments and procedures.

(2) The current EBP practice decision-making model makes research evidence one key part of practice decision making while also emphasizing the client's clinical needs, patient values and preferences, and the clinical social worker's expertise. Specific aspects of the clinical picture, the client's values, and preferences may override research evidence in clinical decision making. Clinical expertise is used to deterring the relative emphasis to be placed on each component of the practice decision-making process.

(3) EBP should help keep practice up-to-date. The obligation to search current research will bring new knowledge to bear on practice. It should speed up the application of new knowledge in day-to-day clinical practice. It provides a method for clinicians to manage 'information overload.'

J. W. Drisko and M. D. Grady, *Evidence-Based Practice in Clinical Social Work*,
Essential Clinical Social Work Series, DOI: 10.1007/978-1-4614-3470-2,
© Springer Science+Business Media New York 2012

(4) The EBP can help ensure that nothing is overlooked when the EBP practice decision-making process is fully applied after a thorough clinical assessment.

(5) EBP should help make practice more effective, ideally for individual clients as well as for clients overall.

(6) Evidence-based practice can empower clinicians to develop independent views and positions regarding practice claims and controversies. It supports their ability to make alternative treatment choices with a clear rationale.

Methodological Merits

(7) Well-conceptualized and carefully implemented experimental studies (RCTs) of large samples provide a strong basis for documenting that a specific treatment leads to specific outcomes. Carefully applied, these research designs have strong internal validity. This allows researchers to say that a specific treatment *causes* a specific change (or does not cause such a change).

(8) The use of probabilistic, statistical methods proves a clear and well-developed method for making decisions about differences among treatments. EBP applies a well-developed technology for making claims that a specific treatment leads to a specific change (or does not lead to such a change).

(9) EBP promotes the aggregation of multiple studies on a topic. This emphasis has the practical effect of increasing the combined sample size on which calculations and decisions are made. It benefits clinicians by emphasizing large-scale calculations of outcomes; allowing for better representation of large populations than do individual studies (that often use small samples).

(10) EBM/EBP, and particularly the efforts of Cochrane Collaboration methods groups, have led to the creation of quality standards for systematic reviews of research that are transparent and very demanding. Other groups have created standards for reporting systematic reviews that both promote quality and help readers understand the research processes being reported.

(11) The aggregation of multiple RCTs through carefully conceptualized and implemented systematic reviews provides a clear methodology (statistical meta-analysis) for determining the magnitude of treatment effects (i.e., effect sizes, odds ratios, number needed to treat).

(12) The aggregation of multiple RCTs also provides a clear methodology for identification of treatment risks and harms that might not be identified in small-scale outcome studies (so long as the measured outcomes are wide ranging).

Administrative and Policy Merits

(13) Both for individual clients and in the aggregate, EBP should make practice more efficient, by increasing the use of effective treatments and reducing the number of ineffective, benign, and harmful treatments delivered. This should reduce overall costs.

(14) EBM/EBP provides a methodology to help policy makers and funders make choices about which treatments are effective and which are benign, ineffective, or harmful.

(15) EBM/EBP provides a clear rationale for making funding choices.

(16) EBP may provide a rationale for the determination of comparative provider effectiveness.

Research Merits

As noted in the Methodological Merits section above, EBM and EBP have led to many refinements and elaborations of research methods. EBP represents the application of very large-scale (population scale) epidemiological research methods and results to clinical practice decision making. It is an expanded application of an existing, and well-developed, research methodology, rather than a new form of research endeavor.

(17) EBM and EBP have identified, and actively promoted, the need for many more studies of treatment outcome and effectiveness (as well as the effectiveness of diagnostic procedures, the etiology of illnesses and disorders, and the prognosis of disorders). EBM and EBP provide a strong rationale for increasing research funding.

(18) EBM and EBP have shifted research funding priorities heavily toward studies of the effectiveness of treatments, and of diagnostic procedures.

Ethical Merits

(19) EBP is ethical in that clients are offered treatments that are demonstrated to be effective (though they may decline them based on their own values and beliefs).

(20) EBP may provide a public good by reducing or eliminating ineffective and harmful healthcare services. This may also reduce unnecessary healthcare spending and may reduce healthcare costs.

Questions and Continuing Issues About EBP

General Concerns About EBP

(1) There is no evidence that adapting the EBM/EBP model will make health and mental healthcare services more effective or less costly. Medications with demonstrated effectiveness sometimes prove to have harmful side effects after they have been widely used. EBP could end up increasing mental healthcare costs, especially if empirically supported but labor intensive models of treatment such as DBT begin to be widely used for the treatment of personality disorders.

(2) EBP adopts a particular definition of evidence drawing upon large-scale, quantitative research. This definition has been promoted by many physicians, policy makers and funders, psychologists, social workers, nurses, and educators. On the other hand, many professionals from the same groups question the narrow nature of this definition of 'evidence.' They note that some useful forms of research are devalued by the EBP research hierarchy. They also note that it is an act of economic, political, academic, and social power to set a definition of evidence, setting up relative winners and losers. Clinical practitioners question the completeness of EBP's definition of evidence and its relevance to direct practice. Some academic researchers have started to reframe EBP as "Science-based Research" (SBR) to reclaim the word 'evidence' as much broader and varied than is defined in the EBP evidence hierarchy and methods.

(3) EBP offers what is often called an 'objective' approach to scientific knowledge building, but it fails to address theory in many instances. Science is typically defined as a circular process starting with inductive knowledge building based on observation, leading to the creation of theories, which are then tested based on deductive hypotheses or predictions. Based on the result of these tests, theory is revised and modified. New hypotheses and predictions are generated. EBP applies an empiricist approach, comparing treatments outcomes and effects of large groups of people, but does not attend to theories that explain how treatments works or why groups differ that is fundamental to good science.

(4) While EBM and EBP research methods are well developed and increasingly transparent, they value internal validity over external validity and ecological validity. That is, those characteristics of research that allow claims that a treatment caused a change are valued over considerations of to whom research results are applicable, and in what settings and situations. Some researchers call EBM/EBP research 'lab science' that may not be relevant or applicable to the complexity of real-world clinical practice.

(5) EBP results may be so complex that clinical practitioners from many professions can not interpret them correctly, and may be unable to critically

evaluate their strengths and limitations. This has led to the development of a new area of 'translational research' in which researchers help develop ways to make research results more applicable and more useful to practitioners. Practitioners are not widely involved in the conceptualization or implementation of such translational models.

(6) The medical model orientation of EBP addresses mainly personal characteristics and disorders with little attention to social factors and social context. For social workers this narrow focus omits balanced attention to persons in environments. It also omits attention to factors that point to risks and sources of resiliency and factors that may render even the best treatment ineffective (i.e., lack of trust or motivation, of full participation, of full adherence with a treatment plan).

(7) Social workers and others note EBP research often fails to identify and address the needs of socially diverse communities. The bulk of medical and social science research uses middle class whites as its samples. Many large-scale research reports simply do not address or identify the specific subpopulations they include or omit. As population demographics in many countries show growing racial, ethnic, and other forms of diversity, EBP does not include sufficient attention to their often different needs and values to guide knowledge development and practice. This is evident both in the questions EBP research addresses, and in the failure to identify and study the specific needs of social groups. Systematic review standards do not emphasize social diversity as an important variable in health care.

(8) EBP research values the researcher-defined evaluations of clients and clinical professionals. Yet a multidimensional model of EBP has been offered by Petr (2008) which actively seeks out the perspectives of clients and of other community members in their own words and voices, not just through standardized measures of disorders. Why not actively include the views of clients and other community members in outcome research and in searches for the best available evidence?

(9) Some social workers argue that the restrictive medical model emphasis of EBM and EBP fails to address social work's core value on social justice.

Practice Concerns

(10) Client populations in real-world practice settings are often very different from the samples used in outcome research. The complex social circumstances and multiple problems and multiple diagnoses of social work clients make it difficult to apply results of studies that exclude comorbid diagnoses and ignore social circumstances.

(11) Access to research results is a mix of free and paid print and online resources. Both individual clinical social workers and many agencies do not have access to the most current paid research results.

(12) Training in EBP, and in empirical supported treatments, is not adequately funded. Supervision on such therapies is also inadequately funded. Agencies do not provide time and support to fully implement the EBP practice decision-making process. This appears to be, in large part, due to reimbursement policies which do not fund the time such efforts require. Learning and doing EBP is a cost shifted onto individual providers rather than supported as a valuable part of the healthcare system.

(13) Even when the EBP practice decision-making process points to empirically supported treatments that are acceptable to the client, such services may not be available in all areas. (The Jennifer case examined in Chapter 16 is an example of this dilemma.) Ironically, some such services may not be reimbursed by state or insurance companies as they do not appear on their lists of empirically supported treatments (ESTs).

(14) It is unclear if treatments and services that are based upon empirically supported treatments (ESTs) can claim demonstrated effectiveness when they are modified to meet local circumstances and needs. It is unclear if ESTs that are not delivered fully according to treatment programs or manuals, and by appropriately trained and certified providers, can claim any empirical support for their altered treatments.

Methodological Concerns

(15) It is often unclear how relevant and applicable large-scale research results are to any individual client. EBP uses medical model definitions of individual disorders. These often include many components in a 'menu' of options. Clients may fit a diagnosis based on presenting with 5 of 7 to 12 characteristics. This may create subtypes of people within a diagnostic category that are not differentiated in EBP conceptualization or in EBP research. This may make EBP findings more or less relevant to individual clients within the same large diagnostic category.

(16) EBP uses measures of disorders that vary widely in content, comprehensiveness, and psychometric properties. Many standardized measures used in research have highly variable scores on concurrent validity. The measures on which EBP outcomes are based may themselves be suspect. The psychometric properties of measures are often omitted from, or minimally reported, in research reports. These measures may also not have been tested for validity and reliability for diverse social groups.

(17) Research on clinical processes are not a major part of EBP research but are of great interest to clinical practitioners. What factors within a treatment model make the treatment effective? How are individual differences and preferences best accommodated in clinical practice? There is research that demonstrates that even "demonstrated effective" therapies may not lead to good outcomes unless a good working alliance between client and clinician is in place (see, for example, Castonguay, Goldfried, Wiser, Raue and

Hayes 1996). How does the relationship and the alliance differentially impact outcomes?

(18) The active roles of both client and clinical are not widely addressed in EBP research. Common factor research suggests that the client is the largest source of variation in clinical outcome. Why are not client differences more studied? Clinical practitioners also vary in strengths, styles and skills. Why are not differences among clinicians studied in detail?

(19) Investigator bias and/or allegiance bias is underexamined in EBP research. Studies may be conceptualized and designed in ways which overtly or covertly favor one theory over another. This bias may also extend to favoring one type of outcome, or type of treatment, over others. In turn, researchers fail to question adequately whether their own biases may influence the design, implementation, results, and interpretations of their studies.

Administrative and Policy Issues

(20) While rising healthcare costs are a concern to everyone, who does it benefit to portray clinical practitioners as lacking in knowledge or skill, or even as incompetent? Is not there a way to address financial concerns that is less accusatory and inflammatory? Why are the financial concerns of professionals suspect while the motives of for-profit healthcare corporations are assumed to be righteous and are not examined as equally suspect?

(21) Managed care policies and practices may actively discourage acceptance of EBP by practitioners. It is even possible that managed care administrative practices may directly conflict with the emphasis on clinical expertise as the integrating factor in the EBP practice decision-making model. That is, if treatments with empirically demonstrated effectiveness are not authorized by managed care companies, or if their lists of reimbursable treatment differ from those of major research organizations, managed care practices may directly conflict with the use of the best available evidence in clinical practice.

Glossary

Absolute Risk Reduction (ARR) also known as Absolute Risk Difference: In epidemiology a measure of the effectiveness of a treatment. ARR is the risk of an outcome for the control group minus risk of the same outcome for the treated group. An ARR of 0 means there is no difference due to a treatment. Negative values indicate that treatment reduces the risk of unwanted outcomes, i.e., an ARR of −12% means the treatment leads to 12% fewer rehospitalizations. This is a positive treatment effect.

AMSTAR: Stands for the Assessment of Multiple Systematic Reviews is an 11 item measurement tool for the assessment of quality in systematic reviews.

Analysis of Variance or ANOVA or *F* test: In statistics a test used to determine differences across two or more groups on an interval level dependent outcome variable. ANOVA only determines difference across all the groups, so it is often used in combination with *post hoc* or *a posteriori* tests that identify if specific groups differ one from another. Common *post hoc* tests include the Tukey-B, Bonferroni, and LSD [Least Significant Difference].

Attribution Bias: Refers to the possibility that creators of a treatment might consciously or unconsciously favor their own theories treatments or methods leading to a falsely positive implementation of services or falsely positive interpretation of research results.

Bias: In general bias is any unknown or unidentified influence that alters the results of a study or its interpretation. Biases may be systematic or random, intentional, or unintentional. In experiments or RCTs, bias is any influence that affects the results of a trial or its interpretation other than the specified intervention under study.

Blinding: A research technique involving the concealment of an intervention or any other influence that might consciously or unconsciously influence study

J. W. Drisko and M. D. Grady, *Evidence-Based Practice in Clinical Social Work*,
Essential Clinical Social Work Series, DOI: 10.1007/978-1-4614-3470-2,
© Springer Science+Business Media New York 2012

results from patients clinicians, and/or researchers. Single blinding involves concealment from participants but not from the researchers doing the study. Double blinding involves concealment from both researchers and participants. Blinding in psychosocial interventions can be very difficult.

Boolean Operators: Commands used to specify the logical connections among search terms. The most common Boolean operators are "Or" (which yields all content on both terms), "And" (which yields only content including both terms), and "Not" (which excludes all content with the specified term). They are widely used in electronic database searches.

Campbell Collaboration: An international volunteer, organization promoting high quality outcome research in education, social welfare, and crime and justice. Works in close cooperatively with the Cochrane Collaboration. Named in honor of psychologist Dr. Donald T. Campbell who was a pioneering research methodologist.

Case Control Study: In research design a naturalistic design in which participants with an outcome of interest (known as "cases") and control patients with different outcomes are compared for exposure to specific risk or resiliency factors.

Case-Series: In research design a naturalistic design in which participants who show a specific target outcome are studied without using controls.

Case Study: In research design a naturalistic design which focuses on just one, or very few, cases. Cases may be individuals, groups, families, organizations, or communities. Case studies often provide in-depth information about the focal case and the intervention process.

Chi-square Statistic: In statistics a test used to show if a relationship exists among nominal or categorical variables, such as gender or ethnicity.

Cochrane Collaboration: An international volunteer, organization begun in 1993 to promote standards for medical and psychiatric outcome research and to increase the use of high quality research results in practice and policy. Established and publishes the *Cochrane Handbook for Systematic Reviews of Interventions*, widely acknowledge as the most clear and rigorous set of procedures for summarizing quantitative outcome research. Named in honor of physician Dr. Archibald Cochrane who argued for including large scale research results in treatment planning.

Cohen's d: A statistical measure of effect size summarizing the magnitude of change. Small effects are in the 0.00–0.20 range moderate effects are in the 0.21–0.79 range, and large effects are 0.80 or higher. Effects sizes of 0.20 may also be interpreted as a 55% success rate, 0.50 as a 62% success rate, and 0.80 as a 69% success rate.

Cohort Study: In research design a naturalistic design comparing two distinct groups (or cohorts) of clients, one which has a received a specific exposure or intervention and another which has not, to determine how the groups differ over time on a specific outcome.

Conceptual Definition also called a Theoretical Definition: Are definitions stated in terms of concepts or theories not specific measures. To define theoretically is to create a hypothetical construct acknowledged as useful within a profession. For example, that depression is generated by dysfunctional cognitions in cognitive theory, or that repetitive patterns of early childhood cognition and interaction may be unconsciously continued as transference in psychodynamic theory. Contrasts with operational definition.

Confidence Interval (CI): In statistics the range around a study's main statistical result within which the unknown true or population value is determined to be located. Defined as a range of values between specific lower and higher limits, if a statistical result falls within the CI, it is statistically significant. If it does not, the result is not statistically significant. In research reports, study outcomes that fall within the CI are statically significant, while those that fall outside the CI are not. In Forest plots used in meta-analyses, if the null result falls within the CI, the result is not statistically significant. CIs allows for sampling error in estimating how well a study's sample reflects the larger but unknown, population the study seeks to represent. Smaller CIs are preferable to large CIs as the point estimate is likely more representative of the larger population.

Confounding Variable also Known as Confounds: An extraneous variable that is not under explicit study but which may impact both the independent and dependent variables. Confounding variables undermine the internal validity of studies most often by increasing false positives or Type I errors.

Continuous Variable: In measurement a variable that may take on any value, including fractions or decimal values between whole numbers. Opposite of a discrete variable.

CONSORT: Stands for Consolidated Standards of Reporting Trials begun in 1993, is an international medical working group seeking to improve standards for the reporting of randomized controlled trials (RCTs). The CONSORT statement offers a standard, detailed, format for reporting the results of RCTs.

Criterion Level: In statistics the probability that, in comparison to a defined null hypothesis, a statistical test will generate a false-positive error. In research, the criterion level is used by researchers to make a determination that an observed result is unlikely to have occurred by chance alone. The common criterion levels are $p < .05$ (or less than 1 chance in 20) or the more conservative $p < 0.01$ (or less than 1 chance in 100).

Degrees of Freedom: In statistics the number of values in a distribution that are free to vary. Degrees of freedom are used to help determine if the value of a statistic is statistically significant compared to a previously selected criterion level or probability.

Discrete Variable: In measurement a variable that may only take on whole number values, such as number of children in a family. Opposite of a continuous variable.

Effect Size: In statistics a measure of the magnitude of experimental effects. Effect sizes go beyond simple statistical significance to measure the size of the observed effect. Effect sizes are typically reported using the Cohen's d statistic for large samples and the Hedge's g statistic for small samples. d and g values are interpreted as 0.00–0.19 indicates no effect, from 0.20 to 0.49 as a small effect, from 0.50 to 0.79 as a moderate effect and over 0.80 as a large effect. Odds ratios and relative risk are also measures of effect size used with binary data.

Effectiveness Studies: Research studies done on real-world clinical populations rather than as fully controlled experiments. Effectiveness studies reflect everyday practice conditions well but often allow for threats to the interval validity of study results.

Efficacy Studies: Research studies done as very carefully controlled experiments. In clinical trials efficacy studies often involve diagnostic procedures and other efforts to insure treatment fidelity that are not typical of everyday practice. They seek to demonstrate treatment effects under ideal controlled conditions with very few threats to internal validity.

Epidemiology: The study of the relationships of the various factors determining the frequency and distribution of diseases.

Event Rate: In epidemiology the proportion of clients in a group or population for whom a specific result or event is observed.

False Negative: In everyday usage deciding there is no problem based on a test or procedure where a problem actually exists. In statistics, a false negative, or Type II error, occurs when statistical test results lead to acceptance of a null hypothesis that is actually incorrect.

False Positive: In everyday usage deciding a problem based on a test or procedure where no problem exists. In statistics, a false positive, or Type I error, occurs when statistical test results lead to rejection of a null hypothesis that is actually correct.

Fidelity: The degree to which an intervention treatment, or service adheres to the manual, principles, or rules that define the original intervention, treatment, or service. An intervention that omits aspects of the defined treatment, or is not fully implemented, or is delivered by poorly trained personnel may be said to lack fidelity to the defined model.

Forrest Plot: A chart or diagram representing the results of individual studies included in a meta-analysis. Forrest plots clearly portray how individual study results compare to the mean outcome of the meta-analysis as a whole. This makes individual study results that were better or worse than the mean for all studies quickly apparent.

Funnel Plot: A flow chart documenting how the results of trials in a meta-analysis are affected by publication bias.

Generalization: The ability to apply the results of any single study based on a specific sample to the larger population from which the sample was drawn.

GRADE: Begun in 2000 the GRADE working group is a collaboration of health professionals working to develop a common approach to grading the quality of quantitative research results.

Heterogeneity: In statistics a property of a dataset, indicating how similar or varied are the cases that constitute it. In meta-analysis and in systematic reviews, a measure of variation or difference among trials included in the review. Forest plots graphically display heterogeneity of results. The χ^2 (Chi-square) statistic is often used as a test of significant differences among combined study results. The I^2 statistic is also used to measure the parentage of variation not due to chance alone. I^2 values of less than 25% are considered low by convention.

Incidence: In epidemiology the number of new cases of illness arising during a specified time period for a defined population.

Intention-to-Treat: In research design a design in which client data are analyzed in the groups to which they were originally assigned, despite the possibility that they may have switched treatment types (or arms) during the study. Such changes often occur for clinical reasons to maximize positive outcomes for the client. For example, a client with serious side effects to a medication might be switched to a group not receiving medications but would still be analyzed at the end of the study in the original group that received medication. In sampling, specifying how non-compliant cases and drop outs are handled in the study analysis.

Interval Level Variable: In measures and statistics a measure with mutually exclusive categories, a clear hierarchy of values, and equal intervals between each value. An example is I.Q. scores which are normed on a value of 100 with a standard deviation of 15 points (and a value of zero has no clear meaning).

Likelihood Ratio: In epidemiology the likelihood that a given result is expected in a person with the disorder of interest compared to the likelihood of the same result in persons without the disorder.

MeSH: An abbreviation for the Medical Subject Headings created by the United States National Library of Medicine. MeSH provides a thesaurus of medical terms (including psychiatry and psychology) used by many databases and libraries. Very useful to target precise literature searches.

Mean: In statistics the numerical average of observed scores. Only appropriate to use with interval or ratio level measures.

Median: In statistics the category that divides a distribution of scores into two equal parts. Only appropriate to use with ordinal, interval or ratio level measures.

Meta-analysis: In statistics are methods for combining the results of several quantitative studies exploring related content using weighted effect sizes. Statistically, meta-analytic results overcome the limited statistical power inherent in studies using small sample sizes by combining studies and increasing overall sample size. Results of meta-analysis are often reported as effect sizes, in Forrest plots, or in Funnel plots. Meta-analysis originally refereed to combined literature search efforts and statistical methods, but the design of systematic reviews have largely replaced meta-analytic search methods. Meta-analysis statistics are a key part of systematic reviews.

Mode: In statistics the most frequent score. Appropriate to use with all levels of measure.

Nominal Level Variable: In measures and statistics a categorical measure with mutually exclusive values but without a clear hierarchy of values or equal intervals between values. For example, gender defined by the categories female, male, and other.

Number Needed to Harm (NNH): In the epidemiological literature a measure summarizing the number of clients who must to be treated in order for one negative outcome to occur compared to untreated controls. Lower values (i.e., two or three) represent greater risk of harmful effects due to the treatment compared to controls.

Number Needed to Treat (NNT): In the epidemiological literature a measure summarizing the number of clients who must be treated in order to prevent one negative outcome over the course of the treatment. Lower values (i.e., two or three) represent greater positive effects over the course of treatment.

Odds: In probability theory a summary measure calculated as the ratio of an event occurring to not occurring. If hospitalization occurs for 25% of clients with a disorder, its odds are calculated as the probability of occurrence/1–probability of occurrence, or 25/75%, or one in three.

Operational Definition: An operational definition defines a concept in terms of a specific measurement process. Contrasts with theoretical or conceptual definitions.

Ordinal Level Variable: In measures and statistics a measure with mutually exclusive categories and a clear hierarchy of values, but lacking equal intervals between values. An example is highest level of school completed, scored in the hierarchy, 'none,' 'some elementary,' 'completed elementary,' 'some middle school,' 'completed middle school', etc. The categories include unequal numbers of years but do represent a hierarchy of schooling.

Outlier: In statistics a term for a case or element of a distribution that is much higher or much lower than are the great majority of values.

p **value:** In statistics the probability that a particular result would have happened by chance alone. Compared to a defined criterion level, or alpha level, the *p* value is used to decide if observed results are unlikely to have occurred by chance alone.

P.I.C.O. (or P.I.C.O.T.): An acronym used to guide the formulation of practice questions. *P* stands for patient *I* for intervention, *C* for comparison (to contrast with the intervention), and *O* for outcome of interest. *T* stands for type of question which may address treatment, diagnosis, etiology, prognosis or cost effectiveness.

Point Estimate: In statistics an estimate based on a sample of treated clients used to represent the unknown population value. Since the population value for all possible persons whom might receive a treatment is often unknown, point estimates based on large probability samples are used as the best estimates of these unknown values. Point estimates are best reported with confidence intervals for the estimate.

Prevalence: In epidemiology the baseline risk of a specific disorder occurring in a population, usually reported as a proportion or a percentage.

Prevalence Rate: The proportion or percentage of a population that has a target characteristic such as a major depressive episode, often over a specific period of time.

PRISMA: An abbreviation for Preferred Reporting Items for Systematic Reviews and Meta-Analyses. PRISMA is a working group of researchers who seek to improve the reporting of systematic reviews. PRISMA offers a 27 item checklist for reviewing the quality of systematic reviews and meta-analyses updating QUORUM reporting standards.

Probability Sample: A sample in which every case has equal chance of selection.

PubMed: A database of the United States National Library of Medicine that compiles over 20 million citations from the electronic biomedical literature including online books (but not print books). Also a valuable gateway to many free full text articles.

Publication Bias: In systematic reviews and meta-analysis a bias due to omission of important but unavailable research reports. Publication bias can be due to an inadequate search strategy, exclusion of reports in different languages, but is most often due to omission of unpublished reports, including those with negative findings (that are less likely to be published in journals).

QUORUM: An abbreviation for Quality of Reporting of Meta-analyses. QUO-RUM was a working group of researchers who sought to improve the reporting of meta-analyses and systematic reviews. QUORUM produced a checklist for reviewing the quality of systematic reviews and meta-analyses and a chart format for summarizing literature searches.

QUORUM Chart: A flow-chart style diagram used to display visually the literature search and review process in a meta-analysis or systematic review. Makes plain why research reports were included or excluded from a given analysis and the numbers of reports included at each stage of the analysis.

r **or Pearson's** *r***:** A statistic used to assess association or correlation between two interval or ratio level variables.

r_s **or Spearman's rho:** A statistic used to assess association or correlation between two ordinal level variables or one interval level and one ordinal level variable.

Random: In statistics refers to an equal chance of selection for all members of a population of sampling frame. Randomization limits biased assignment of cases to treated and control conditions in experiments or RCTs.

Randomized Controlled Trial (RCT) also Known as a Randomized Controlled Clinical Trial: In research design, an experimental research design used in clinical research. Clients are randomly assigned into treatment and control groups, assessed at baseline and again after treatment concludes. Both groups are compared on the same outcome variable(s). RCTs allows determination of changes caused by the treatment, and for attribution of cause and effect relationships: that the treatment caused any changes observed. May also be referred to as a *parallel-group design*, since randomization is used to generate equivalent—or parallel—treated and control groups.

Ratio Level Variable: In measures and statistics a measure with mutually exclusive categories, a clear hierarchy of values, equal intervals between each value, and a non-arbitrary zero point such as age in years.

Relative Risk (RR) also Known as the Risk Ratio: RR is the ratio of the probability of an event occurring in a treated group divided by the probability of its occurring in an untreated group (or a known prevalence rate). It is a measure of improvement due to treatment. An RR of 1 shows no difference in outcomes between the groups. Values greater than 1 means that the treatment increases the risk of the outcome which is good for positive outcomes but bad for unwanted outcomes. (The treated group fared better) Values less than 1 mean that the treatment reduces risk of the outcome, which is good for unwanted outcomes but bad for positive outcomes. (The untreated group fared better).

Relative Risk Reduction (RRR): A widely used measure of medical treatment effect calculated as 1 − RR. RRR summaries the reduction in an unwanted outcome in the treated group compared to the control group. An RRR of 50%

would indicate that 50% fewer treated clients were rehospitalized after treatment compared to controls.

Reliability: In tests and measures refers to how consistently a measure produces similar scores over time, setting and administrator, not based on any changes in the content under study.

Sensitivity: In standardized tests a measure of how well a test can capture very small changes.

Specificity: In epidemiology refers to the proportion of people without a disorder who have (correctly) a negative test.

Sampling Error: In statistics the uncertainty generated by collecting data from a sample rather than from every member of a population.

Systematic Review: A peer-reviewed research summary on a specified topic involving systematic and transparent searching, evaluation, selection, and meta-analytic summarizing of all high quality relevant results found in the literature. The standards for a systematic review are set by the *Cochrane Handbook for Systematic Reviews of Interventions*, but many published reports use different, and often much lower, quality standards. Cochrane reviews heavily emphasize quantitative, experimental research.

t **test:** In statistics a test used to determine differences between two groups of a nominal level independent variable on an interval level outcome variable. t Tests are useful for determining if differences exist with small sample sizes.

Treatment as Usual: Used as a comparison intervention in some experiments or RCTs refers to the treatment or services routinely available in a community. A limitation of treatment as usual as a comparison group is that it may be composed of many different treatments, with varying fidelity of delivery. The choice of such services may also be subject to several forms of bias. In favor of this approach is that, done well, it represents routine care and can be a reasonable, naturalistic, basis for comparison of treatment effects.

Validity: The extent to which a variable measures what it is intended to measure. There are several types of validity. In research design *internal validity* refers to the ability of an experiment research design to make cause and effect attributions when fully and carefully implemented. The *external validity* of a study refers to how well results based on the study sample can be generalized to other people and settings. *Statistical conclusion validity* refers to how fully and carefully the statistical analysis was completed. In tests and measures, validity refers to how well the measure represents the concepts and content they are intended to capture.

z **Scores:** In statistics and in meta-analysis individual scores may be converted mathematically from their original scales into z scores which have a mean value of 0 and a standard deviation of 1. The relative distribution among scores in a distribution is not altered in this process, but the label for each value is changed to a new, common, metric. This allows different interval or ratio level measures, with different ranges, to be meaningfully compared in meta-analysis.

References

Aberson, C. (2010). *Applied power analysis for the behavioral sciences.* New York: Routledge Academic.

Abu-Bader, S. (2006). *Using statistical methods in social work practice.* New York: Lyceum Books.

Achenbach, T. (1991). *Manual for the child behavior checklist/4–18 and 1991 profile.* Burlington, VT: University of Vermont Department of Psychiatry.

Achenbach, T. (1992). *Manual for the child behavior checklist/2–3 and 1992 profile.* Burlington, VT: University of Vermont Department of Psychiatry.

Achenbach, T., & Rescorla, L. (2000). *Manual for the ASEBA preschool forms and profiles.* Burlington, VT: University of Vermont Department of Psychiatry.

Achenbach, T., & Rescorla, L. (2001). *Manual for the ASEBA school-age forms and profiles.* Burlington, VT: University of Vermont Research Center for Children, Youth, and Families.

Addis, M., & Krasnow, A. (2000). A national survey of practicing psychologists' attitudes toward psychotherapy treatment manuals. *Journal of Consulting and Clinical Psychology, 68*(2), 331–339.

Agency for Healthcare Research and Quality. (2002). Expanding patient-centered care to empower patients and assist providers. *Research in Action.* Issue #5. Retrieved from www.ahrq.gov/qual/ptcareria.pdf

Ainsworth, M. (1978). *Patterns of attachment: A psychological study of the strange situation.* New York: Lawrence Erlbaum Associates.

Alexander, K., Peterson, E., Granger, C., Casas, A. C., Van der Werf, F., Armstrong, P., et al. (1998). Potential impact of evidence-based medicine in acute coronary syndromes: Insights from GUSTO-IIb. *Journal of the American College of Cardiology, 32,* 2023–2030.

Alliance of Psychoanalytic Organizations. (2006). *Psychodynamic diagnostic manual (PDM).* Silver Spring, MD: Psychodynamic Diagnostic Manual.

Altoma-Mathews, C. (2001). On my own: My experiences finding supervision. *Reflections, 7,* 73–79.

Amedeo, G. (1997). The theory, practice, and evaluation of the phenomenological method as a qualitative research procedure. *Journal of Phenomenological Psychology, 28*(2), 235–260.

American Academy of Child and Adolescent Psychiatry. (2005). Practice parameter for the assessment and treatment of children and adolescents with reactive attachment disorder of infancy and early childhood. *Journal of the American Academy of Child and Adolescent Psychiatry, 44*(11), 1206–1219.

American Psychiatric Association. (2000a). *Diagnostic and statistical manual of mental disorders* (4th ed., text revision). Washington, DC: American Psychiatric Publishing, Inc.

American Psychiatric Association. (2000b). *Desk reference to the diagnostic criteria from DSM-IV-TR*. Washington, DC: Author.

American Psychiatric Association. (2006). Psychiatric evaluation guidelines. *Psychiatric evaluation of adults* (2nd ed.). Retrieved from www.psychiatryonline.com/pracGuide/pracGuideChapToc_1.aspx

American Psychiatric Association. (2011a). DSM-5 overview: The future manual. Retrieved from www.dsm5.org/about/Pages/DSMVOverview.aspx

American Psychiatric Association. (2011b). Proposed DSM-5 organizational structure and disorder names. Retrieved from www.dsm5.org/proposedrevision/Pages/proposed-dsm5-organizational-structure-and-disorder-names.aspx

American Psychiatric Association. (2011c). Proposed revisions: Personality disorders. www.dsm5.org/proposedrevision/Pages/PersonalityDisorders.aspx

American Psychological Association. (2009). *Publication manual of the American Psychological Association* (6th ed.). Washington, DC: American Psychological Association.

American Psychological Association. (2006). Evidence-based practice in psychology (A report of the APA task force on evidence-based practice). *American Psychologist, 61*, 271–285.

Anastas, J. (1999). *Research design for social work and the human services* (2nd ed.). New York: Columbia University Press.

Andreason, N., & Black, D. (2006). *Introductory textbook of psychiatry* (4th ed.). Washington, DC: American Psychiatric Association.

Andrews, G., Creamer, M., Crino, R., Hunt, C., Lampe, L., & Page, A. (2002). *The treatment of anxiety disorders: Clinician guides and patient manuals*. New York: Cambridge University Press.

Antilla, S. (2009). Housing programs and case management for reducing homelessness. Paper presented at the Campbell Collaboration Colloquium, Oslo, May 18, 2009. Retrieved from www.campbellcollaboration.org/artman2/uploads/1/Anttila_housing_programs.pdf

Arnd-Caddigan, M. & Pozzuto, R. (2010). Evidence-based practice and the purpose of clinical social work. *Smith College Studies in Social Work, 80*, 35–53.

Associated Press (2010, December 13). Some Alaskan parents fined if kids skip school. Retrieved from www.foxnews.com/us/2010/12/13/alaska-parents-fined-kids-skip-school/#ixzz1NTeOsepm

Baik, S., Gonzales, J., Bowers, B., Anthony, J., Tidjani, B., & Susman, J. (2010). Reinvention of depression instruments by primary care clinicians. *Annals of Family Medicine, 8*(3), 224–230.

Bains, D. (2006). 'If you could change one thing': Social service workers and restructuring. *Australian Social Work, 59*(1), 20–34.

Ballenger, J. (2003). Selective serotonin reuptake inhibitors in the treatment of anxiety disorders. In D. Nutt & J. Ballenger (Eds.), *Anxiety disorders* (pp. 339–361). Malden, MA: Blackwell.

Barlow, D., Craske, M., Cerny, J., & Klosko, J. (1989). Behavioral treatment of panic disorders. *Behavior Therapy, 20*(2), 261–282.

Barlow, D., Nock, M., & Hersen, M. (2008). *Single case experimental designs: Strategies for studying behavior change* (3rd ed.). New York: Allyn and Bacon.

Barrett, A. (2008). Evidence based medicine and shared decision making: The challenge of getting both evidence and preferences into health care. *Patient Education and Counseling, 73*(3), 407–412.

Bateman, A., & Fonagy, P. (1999). The effectiveness of partial hospitalization in the treatment of borderline personality disorder: A randomized controlled trial. *American Journal of Psychiatry, 156*, 1563–1569.

Bateman, A., & Fonagy, P. (2001). Treatment of borderline personality disorder with psycho-analytically oriented partial hospitalization: An 18-month follow-up. *American Journal of Psychiatry, 158*, 36–42.

Beck, A., Steer, R., Ball, R., & Ranieri, W. (1996). Comparison of Beck Depression Inventories-IA and -II in psychiatric outpatients. *Journal of Personality Assessment, 67*(3), 588–597. doi: 10.1207/s15327752jpa6703_13.

Becker-Weidman, A. (2006a). Treatment for children with trauma-attachment disorders: Dyadic developmental therapy. *Child and Adolescent Social Work Journal, 23*(2), 147–171.

Becker-Weidman, A. (2006b). Dyadic developmental psychotherapy: A multi-year follow-up. In S. Sturt (Ed.), *New developments in child abuse research*. Hauppauge, NY: Nova Science Publishers.

Belenky, M., Clinchy, B., Goldberger, N., & Tarule, J. (1986). *Women's ways of knowing*. New York: Basic Books.

Bellamy, J., Bledsoe, S., Mullen, E., Fang, L., & Manuel, J. (2008). Agency-university partnerships for evidence-based practice in social work. *Journal of Social Work Education, 44*, 55–75.

Bellamy, J., Bledsoe, S.E., & Traube, D. (2006). The current state of evidence based practice in social work: A review of the literature and qualitative analysis of expert interviews. *Journal of Evidence-Based Social Work, 3*, 23–48.

Benedek, D., & Wynn, G. (Eds.). (2011). *Clinical manual for management of PTSD*, Arlington, VA: American Psychiatric Publishing.

Berger, P., Sachs, G., Amering, M., Holzinger, A., Bankier, B., & Katschnig, H. (2004). Personality disorder and social anxiety predict delayed response in drug and behavioral treatment of panic disorder. *Journal of Affective Disorders, 80*, 75–78.

Bergin, A., & Garfield, S. (Eds.). (1971). *Handbook of psychotherapy and behavior change: An empirical analysis*. New York: Wiley.

Bergin, A., & Garfield, S. (Eds.). (1978). *Handbook of psychotherapy and behavior change* (2nd ed.). New York: Wiley.

Bergin, A., & Garfield, S. (Eds.). (1986). *Handbook of psychotherapy and behavior change* (3rd ed.). New York: Wiley.

Bergin, A., & Garfield, S. (Eds.). (1994). *Handbook of psychotherapy and behavior change* (4th ed.). New York: Wiley.

Bernard, J., & Goodyear, R. (2009). *Fundamentals of clinical supervision* (4th ed.). Upper Saddle River, NJ: Pearson Education.

Bernstein, C. (2011). Meta-structure in DSM-5 process. *Psychiatric News, 46*(5), 7.

Berzoff, J., Flanagan, L., & Hertz, P. (2007). *Inside out and outside in: Psychodynamic clinical theory and psychopathology in contemporary multicultural contexts*. Northvale, NJ: Jason Aronson.

Beutler, L. (2000). David and Goliath: When empirical and clinical standards of practice meet. *American Psychologist, 55*(9), 997–1007.

Binks, C., Fenton, M., McCarthy, L., Lee, T., Adams, C., & Duggan, C. (2009). Psychological therapies for people with borderline personality disorder. Cochrane Database of Systematic Reviews, Issue 1. Art. No.: CD005652. doi: 10.1002/14651858.CD005652

Black, N. (1994). Why we need qualitative research. *Journal of Epidemiological Community Health, 48*, 425–426.

Blanck, G., & Blanck, R. (1979). *Ego psychology II*. New York: Columbia University Press.

Blanck, G., & Blanck, R. (1994). *Ego psychology* (2nd ed.). New York: Columbia University Press.

Bledsoe, S.E., Bellamy, J., Wike, T., Grady, M., Dinata, E., Killian, C. & Rosenberg, K. (in press). Agency university partnerships for evidence-based practice: A national survey of schools of social work. *Social Work Research*.

Bledsoe, S., Weissman, M., Mullen, E., Ponniah, K., Gameroff, M., Verdeli, H., et al. (2007). Empirically supported psychotherapy in social work training programs: Does the definition of evidence matter? *Research on Social Work Practice, 17*, 449–455.

Bloom, M., & Fischer, J. (1982). *Evaluating practice: Guidelines for the accountable professional*. Englewood Cliffs, NJ: Prentice-Hall.

Bloom, M., Fischer, J., & Orme, J. (2003). *Evaluating practice: Guidelines for the accountable professional* (4th ed.). Boston: Allyn & Bacon.

Bogan, C., & English, M. (1994). *Benchmarking for best practices: Winning through innovative adaptation*. New York: McGraw-Hill.

Bowen, M. (1978). *Family therapy in clinical practice*. Northvale, NJ: Jason Aronson.

Brandell, J. (2010a). *Theory and practice in clinical social work*. Thousand Oaks, CA: Sage.

Brandell, J. (2010b). Contemporary psychoanalytic perspectives on attachment. *Psychoanalytic Social Work, 17*(2), 132–157.

Brandell, J., & Ringel, S. (2004). Psychodynamic perspectives on relationship: Implications of new findings from human attachment and the neurosciences for social work education. *Families in Society, 85*(4), 549–556.

Bratton, S., Landreth, G., Kellam, T., & Blackard, S. (2006). *CPRT package: Child-parent relationship therapy (CPRT) treatment manual*. New York: Routledge.

Brekke, J., Ell, K., & Palinkas, L. (2007). Translational science at the National Institute of Mental Health: Can social work take it rightful place? *Research on Social Work Practice, 17*, 123–133. doi:10.1177/1049731506293693.

Bringhurst, D., Watson, C., Miller, S., & Duncan, B. (2006). The reliability and validity of the outcome rating scale: A replication study of a brief clinical measure. *Journal of Brief Therapy, 5*(1), 23–30.

Brown, L. (2005). The neglect of lesbian, gay, bisexual and transgendered clients. In J. Norcross, L. Beutler, & R. Levant (Eds.), *Evidence-based practices in mental health* (pp. 346–352). Washington, DC: American Psychological Association.

Brush, J. (2010, January 11). Letters: Looking at ways to treat depression. *The New York Times Online*. Retrieved Janaury 12, 2010 from www.nytimes.com/2010/01/12/opinion/l12warner.html

Buetow, S., & Kenealy, T. (2000). Evidence-based medicine: The need for a new definition. *Journal of Evaluation of Clinical Practice, 6*(2), 85–92.

Buetow, S., & Mintoft, B. (2011). When should patient intuition be taken seriously? *Journal of General Internal Medicine, 26*(4), 433–436.

Cameron, M., & Keenan, E. K. (2010). The common factors model: Implications for transtheoretical clinical social work practice. *Social Work, 55*(1), 63–73.

Campbell, A., & Hemsley, S. (2009). Outcome rating scale and session rating scale in psychological practice: Clinical utility of ultra-brief measures. *Clinical Psychologist, 13*(1), 1–9.

Campbell, D., & Stanley, J. (1963). *Experimental and quasi-experimental designs for research*. New York: Wadsworth.

Campbell, M., Fitzpatrick, R., Haines, A., Kinmouth, A., Sandercock, P., Spiegelhalter, D., et al. (2000). Framework for design and evaluation of complex interventions to improve health. *British Medical Journal, 321*, 694. doi:10.1136/bmj.321.7262.694.

Carey, B. (2008, January 17). Antidepressant studies unpublished. *The New York Times*. Retrieved from www.nytimes.com/2008/01/17/health/17depress.html?scp=3&sq=The%20New%20York%20Times%20-%20January%2017,%202008&st=cse.

Carr, A. (2002). *Prevention: What works with children and adolescents?: A critical review of psychological prevention programmes for children, adolescents and their families*. New York: Routledge.

Carr, A. (2009). *What works with children, adolescents and adults?* New York: Routledge.

Carter, B., & McGoldrick, M. (Eds.). (2004). *The expanded family life cycle: Individual, family, and social perspectives* (3rd ed.). Boston, MA: Allyn & Bacon.

Castonguay, L., & Beutler, L. (Eds.). (2006a). *Principles of therapeutic change that work*. New York: Oxford: University Press.

Castonguay, L., & Beutler, L. (2006b). Common and unique principles of therapeutic change: What do we know and what do we need to know? In L. Castonguay and L. Beutler (Eds.). *Principles of therapeutic change that work* (pp. 353–369). New York: Oxford: University Press.

Castonguay, L., Goldfried, M., Wiser, S., Raue, P., & Hayes, A. (1996). Predicting the effect of cognitive therapy for depression: A study of unique and common factors. *Journal of Consulting and Clinical Psychology, 64*, 497–504.

Cavanaugh, M., Gelles, R., & Solomon, P. (2009). A pilot RCT exploring the effectiveness of the DPEW in decreasing potential risk of violence of IPV. Paper presented at the Campbell Collaboration Colloquium, Oslo, May 18–20, 2009. Retrieved from www.campbellcollaboration.org/artman2/uploads/1/Conference_Abstracts_v2.pdf

Centre for Evidence Based Medicine. (2009). Rating the evidence. Retrieved from www.cebm.net/index.aspx?o=1025

Center for Substance Abuse Treatment. (2007). *Counselor's treatment manual: Matrix intensive outpatient treatment for people with stimulant use disorders.* DHHS Publication No. (SMA) 07-4152. Rockville, MD: Substance Abuse and Mental Health Services Administration. Retrieved from http://kap.samhsa.gov/products/manuals/matrix/index.htm

Chaffin, M., Hanson, R., Saunders, B., Nichols, T., Barnett, D., Zeanah, C., et al. (2006). Report of the APSAC task force on attachment therapy, reactive attachment disorder, and attachment problems. *Child Maltreatment, 11*(1), 76–89.

Chambless, D., & Hollon, S. (1998). Defining empirically supported therapies. *Journal of Clinical and Consulting Psychology, 66*, 7–18.

Chambon, A. (1994). The dialogical analysis of case materials. In W. Reid & E. Sherman (Eds.), *Qualitative research in social work* (pp. 205–215). New York: Columbia University Press.

Chen, Y. (2002). Chinese classification of mental disorders (CCMD-3): Towards integration in international classification. *Psychopathology, 35*(2/3), 171–175.

Children Unlimited, Inc. (2004). Attachment Center of South Carolina. www.children-onlimited.org/attachment_center_of_south_carol.htm (Wimmer, Vonk & Bordnick report this URL was active in June, 2005, but it is no longer as of 2009; Google and Bing searches for the organization led to no active online results.)

Chinese Society of Psychiatry. (2001). *Chinese classification of mental disorders.* Ginan: Chinese Society of Psychiatry, Committee on the Chinese Classification of Mental Disease.

Christensen, P., & Kristiansen, I. (2006). Number-needed-to-treat (NNT)—Needs treatment with care. *Basic and Clinical Pharmacology and Toxicology, 99*(1), 12–16.

Chorpita, B., Becker, K., & Daleiden, E. (2007). Understanding the common elements of evidence-based practice: Misconceptions and clinical examples. *Journal of the American Academy of Child and Adolescent Psychiatry, 46*, 647–652.

Chorpita, B., Bernstein, A., & Daleiden, E. (2008). Driving with roadmaps and dashboards: Using information resources to structure the decision models in service organizations. *Administration Policy Mental Health, 35*, 114–123.

Clarkin, J., Yeomans, F., & Kernberg, O. (2006). *Psychotherapy for borderline personality: Focusing on object relations.* Arlington: VA: American Psychiatric Publishing.

Clinical evidence handbook. (2009/2010). BMJ Publishing group. (British Medical Journal; www.clincialevidence.com).

Cochrane, A. (1972). Effectiveness and efficiency: Random reflections on health services. London: Nuffield Provincial Hospitals Trust. Excerpts are also available online at www.cochrane.org/about-us/history/archie-cochrane

Cochrane, A., & Blythe, M. (1989). *One man's medicine.* London: BMJ (Memoir Club).

Cohen, J. (1988). *Statistical power analysis for the behavioral sciences* (2nd ed.). New York: Routledge Academic.

Colditz, G., Manson, J., & Hankinson, S. (1997). The nurses' health study: 20-year contribution to the understanding of health among women. *Journal of Women's Health, 6*(1), 49–62.

Columbia University Biometrics Research Division. (undated). What is the reliability of the SCID-II? Retrieved from www.scid4.org/psychometric/scidII_reliability.html

Congress, E. P. (1994). The use of culturegrams to assess and empower culturally diverse families. *Families in Society, 75*, 531–540.

CONSORT Group. (2010). The CONSORT statement. Retrieved from www.consort-statement.org/home/

Cook, T., & Campbell, D. (1979). *Quasi-experimentation: Design & analysis issues for field settings.* New York: Houghton Mifflin.

Corcoran, J., & Walsh, J. (2006). *Clinical assessment and diagnosis in social work practice.* New York, NY: Oxford University Press.

Corcoran, K., & Fischer, J. (2007). Measures for clinical practice: A sourcebook (4th ed.). [Two volume set]. NY: Oxford University Press

Cortes, D., Mulvaney-Day, N., Fortuna, L., Reinfeld, S., & Alegría, M. (2008). Patient-provider communication: Understanding the role of patients activation for Latinos in metal health treatment. *Health Education Behavior, 36*(1), 1–17.

Council on Social Work Education (CSWE). (2001). *Educational policy and accreditation standards.* Alexandria, VA: Author.

Council on Social Work Education (CSWE). (2008). *Educational policy and accreditation standards.* Alexandria, VA: Author.

Cowger, C. (1984). Statistical significance tests: Scientific ritualism or scientific method? *Social Service Review, 8*(3), 358–372.

Dana, J., & Loewenstein, G. (2003). A social science perspective on gifts to physicians from industry. *Journal of the American Medical Association, 290*(2), 252–255. doi: 10.1001/jama.290.2.252.

Dar, R., Serlin, R., & Omer, H. (1994). Misuse of statistical tests in three decades of psychotherapy research. *Journal of Consulting and Clinical Psychology, 62*(1), 75–82.

Dattalo, P. (2008). *Determining sample size: Balancing power, precision, and practicality.* New York: Oxford University Press.

Davenloo, H. (Ed.). (1978). *Basic principles and techniques of short-term dynamic psychotherapy.* New York: Jason Aaronson.

Davis, I. (1994). Integrating qualitative and quantitative methods in practice evaluation in clinical research. In W. Reid & E. Sherman (Eds.), *Qualitative research in social work* (pp. 423–434). New York: Columbia University Press.

Dean, R., & Reinherz, H. (1986). Psychodynamic practice and single system designs: The odd couple. *Journal of Social Work Education, 22,* 71–81.

DeVellis, R. F. (2003). *Scale development: Theory and applications* (2nd ed.). Thousand Oaks, CA: Sage Publications.

Dickersin, K. (1990). The existence of publication bias and risk factors for its occurrence. *Journal of the American Medical Association, 263,* 1385–1389.

Dillon, S. (August 31, 2010). Formula to grade teachers' skill gains acceptance, and critics. *The New York Times.* Retrieved from www.nytimes.com/2010/09/01/education/01teacher. html?ref=magazine&pagewanted=all (print version September, 1, 2010, p. A1).

Dixon, L., Lucksted, A., Stewart, B., Burland, J., Brown, C.H., Postrado, L., McGuire, & C., Hoffman, M. (2004). Outcomes of a peer-taught 12-week family-to-family education program for severe mental illness. *Acta Psychiatr Scandanvia, 109,* 207–215.

Dixon, L., Stewart, B., Burland, J., Delahanty, J., Lucksted, A., & Hoffman, M. (2001). Pilot study of the effectiveness of the family-to-family education program. *Psychiatric Services, 52,* 965–967. doi:10.1176/appi.ps.52.7.965.

Dixon-Woods, M., Bonas, S., Booth, A., Jones, D., Miller, T., Sutton, J., et al. (2006a). How can systematic reviews incorporate qualitative research? *A Critical Perspective. Qualitative Research, 6*(1), 27–44.

Dixon-Woods, M., Cavers, D., Agarwal, S., et al. (2006b). Conducting a critical interpretive synthesis of the literature on access to healthcare by vulnerable groups. *BMC Medical Research Methodology, 6.* (electronic journal). Retrieved January 2, 2007 from www.biomedcentral.com/1471-2288/6/3

Drisko, J. (2001). How do clinical social workers evaluate practice? *Smith College Studies in Social Work, 71*(3), 419–439.

Drisko, J. (2004). Common factors in psychotherapy effectiveness: Meta-analytic findings and their implications for practice and research. *Families in Society, 85*(1), 81–90.

Drisko, J. (2009). *Effective therapeutic interventions for reactive attachment disorder: A mixed-method systematic research synthesis*. New Orleans, LA: Juried paper presented at the Society for Social Work and Research.

Drisko, J. (2010). Technology in teaching. In J. Anastas (Ed.), *Teaching in social work: An educator's guide to theory and practice* (pp. 115–150). New York: Columbia University Press.

Drisko, J. (2011). Researching clinical practice. In J. Brandell (Ed.), *Theory and practice in clinical social work* (2nd ed., pp. 717–738). Thousand Oaks, CA: Sage.

Drisko, J., & DuBois, C. (2000). *Social work assessment format*. Northampton, MA: Unpublished manuscript used in classes at the Smith College School for Social Work.

Drisko, J., & Grady, M. (2011, October). Thorough clinical assessment: The hidden foundation of evidence-based practice. Paper presented at the Annual Program Meeting of the Council on Social Work Education, Atlanta, GA

Drisko, J., & Zilberstein, K. (2008). What works in treating reactive attachment disorder: Parent's perspectives. *Families in Society, 89*(3), 476–486.

Duggal, R., & Menkes, D. (2011). Evidence-based medicine in practice. *International Journal of Clinical Practice, 65*(6), 639–644. doi:10.1111/j.1742-1241.2011.02681.x.

Duncan, B., Miller, S., Sparks, J., Claud, D., Reynolds, L., Brown, J., et al. (2003). The session rating scale: Preliminary psychometric properties of a "working" alliance measure. *Journal of Brief Therapy, 3*(1), 3–12.

Ebell, M. (2001). *Evidence-based diagnosis: A handbook of clinical prediction rules*. New York: Springer.

Edmond, T., Megivern, D., Williams, C., Rochman, E., & Howard, M. (2006). Integrating evidence-based practice and social work field education. *Journal of Social Work Education, 42*, 377–396.

Elks, M., & Kirkhart, K. (1993). Evaluating effectiveness from the practitioner perspective. *Social Work, 38*(5), 554–563.

Elkin, I., Shea, T., Watkins, J., et al. (1989). National Institute of Mental Health treatment of depression collaborative research program: General effectiveness of treatments. *Archives of General Psychiatry, 46*, 971–982

Ellis, P. (2010). *The essential guide to effect sizes: An introduction to statistical power, meta-analysis and the interpretation of research results*. New York: Cambridge University Press.

Endicott, J., Spitzer, R., Fleiss, J., & Cohen, J. (1976). The Global Assessment Scale: A procedure for measuring overall severity of psychiatric disturbance. *Archives of General Psychiatry, 33*, 766–771

Evans, C., & Fisher, M. (1999). Collaborative evaluation with service users. In I. Shaw & J. Lishman, (Eds.), *Evaluation and social work practice* (pp. 101–117). Thousand Oaks, CA: Sage.

Fals-Borda, O., & Rahman, M. (Eds.). (1991). *Action and knowledge: Breaking the monopoly with participatory action research*. Lanham, MD: Apex Press.

First, M., Gibbon, M., Spitzer, R., Williams, J., & Benjamin, L. (1997). *Structured clinical interview for DSM-IV Axis II personality disorders (SCID-II)*. Washington, DC: American Psychiatric Press.

Flyvbjerg, B. (2001). *Making social science matter: Why social inquiry fails and how it can succeed again*. New York: Cambridge University Press.

Foucault, M. (1964). *Madness and civilization: A history of insanity in the age of reason*. New York: Random House.

Foxcroft, D.R., & Tsertsvadze, A. (2011). Universal school-based prevention programs for alcohol misuse in young people. Cochrane Database of Systematic Reviews 2011, Issue 5. Art. No.: CD009113. doi: 10.1002/14651858.CD009113

Frank, J. D., & Frank, J. B. (1991). *Persuasion and healing: A comparative study of psychotherapy* (3rd ed.). Baltimore: Johns Hopkins University Press.

Fraser, M., Richman, J., & Galinsky, M. (1999). Risk, protection, and resilience: Toward a conceptual framework for social work practice. *Social Work Research, 23*(3), 131–143.

Freedman, (2010, January 11). Letters: Looking at ways to treat depression. *The New York Times Online*. Retrieved Jan. 12, 21010 from www.nytimes.com/2010/01/12/opinion/112warner.html

Freud, S (1923). *Das Ich und das Es*. [The Ego and the Id]. Vienna, Austria: Internationaler Psycho-analytischer Verlag.

Friedman, R. (2010, January 11). Before you quit antidepressants. *The New York Times Online*. Retrieved 1 12 10 from www.nytimes.com/2010/01/12/health/12mind.html

Fonagy, P., Target, M., Cottrell, D., Phillips, J., & Kurtz, Z. (2005). *What works for whom? A critical review of treatments for children and adolescents*. New York: Guilford.

Fournier, J., DeRubeis, R., Hollon, S., Dimidjian, S., Amsterdam, J., Shelton, R., et al. (2010). Antidepressant drug effects and depression severity: A patient-level meta-analysis. *Journal of the American Medical Association, 303*(1), 47–53.

Furr, R.M., & Bacharach, V. (2007). Psychometrics: An introduction. Thousand Oaks, CA: Sage

Furukawa, T., Watanabe, N., & Churchill, R. (2007). Combined psychotherapy plus antidepressants for panic disorder with or without agoraphobia. *Cochrane Database of Systematic Reviews* 2007, Issue 1. Art. No.: CD004364. DOI: 10.1002/14651858.CD004364.pub2.

Gabbard, G. (2010). *Long-term psychodynamic psychotherapy: A basic text*. Arlington, VA: American Psychiatric Publishing.

Galea, S., Tracy, M., Hoggatt, K., DiMaggio, C., & Karpati, A. (2011, June 16). Estimated deaths attributable to social factors in the United States. *American Journal of Public Health*. Published online ahead of print June 16, 2011:e1–e10. doi:10.2105/AJPH.2010.300086

Gambrill, E. (2001). Social work: An authority-based profession. *Research on Social Work Practice, 11*, 166–175.

Gambrill, E. (2003). Evidence-based practice: Implications for knowledge development and use in social work. In A. Rosen & E. Proctor (Eds.), *Developing practice guidelines for social work intervention* (pp. 37–58). New York: Columbia University Press.

Gambrill, E. (2006a). *Critical thinking in clinical practice: Improving the quality of judgments and decisions* (2nd ed.). New York: Wiley.

Gambrill, E. (2006b). *Social work practice: A critical thinker's guide* (2nd ed.). New York: Oxford University Press.

Gambrill, E., & Gibbs, L. (2002). Making practice decisions: Is what's good for the goose good for the gander? *Ethical Human Sciences and Services, 4*, 31–46.

Gibbs, L. (2002). *Evidence-based practice for the helping professions: A practical guide*. Belmont, CA: Brooks-Cole.

Gibbs, L., & Gambrill, E. (2002). Evidence-based practice: Counterarguments to objections. *Research on Social Work Practice, 12*(3), 452–476.

Gilgun, J. (2005a). The four cornerstones of evidence-based practice. *Research on Social Work Practice, 15*(1), 52–61.

Gilgun, J. (2005b). Evidence-based practice, descriptive research and the resilience-schema-gender-brain functioning (RSGB) assessment. *British Journal of Social Work, 35*(6), 843–862.

Gilgun, J., Daly, K., & Handel, G. (1992). *Qualitative methods in family research*. Thousand Oaks, CA: Sage.

Golden, R., Gaynes, B., Ekstrom, R., Hamer, R., Jacobsen, F., Suppes, T., et al. (2005). The efficacy of light therapy in the treatment of mood disorders: A review and meta-analysis of the evidence. *American Journal of Psychiatry, 162*, 656–662.

Goldenberg, M. (2006). On evidence and evidence-based medicine: Lessons from the philosophy of science. *Social Science & Medicine, 62*(11), 2621–2632. doi: 10.1016/j.socscimed.2005.11.031.

Goldenberg, M. (2009). Iconoclast or creed? Objectivism, pragmatism and the hierarchy of evidence. *Perspectives in Biology and Medicine, 52*(2), 168–187.

Goldman, J., & Shih, T. (2011). The limitations of evidence-based medicine: Applying population-based recommendations to individual patients. *Virtual Mentor, 13*(1), 26–30.

Goldstein, E. (1995). *Ego psychology and social work practice* (2nd ed.). New York: Free Press.

Goldstein, E. (2001). *Object relations theory and self psychology in social work practice*. New York: Free Press.

Goldstein, E., Miehls, D., & Ringel, S. (2009). *Advanced clinical social work practice: Relational principles and techniques*. New York: Columbia University Press.

Goodheart, C., Kazdin, A., & Sternberg, R. (Eds.). (2006). *Evidence-based psychotherapy: Where research and practice meet*. Washington, DC: American Psychological Association.

Gould, N. (2010). Integrating qualitative evidence in practice guideline development: Meeting the challenge of evidence-based practice for social work. *Qualitative Social Work, 9*(1), 93–109.

Glickman, S., McHutchison, J., Peterson, E., Cairns, C., Harrington, R., Califf, R., et al. (2009). Ethical and scientific implications of the globalization of clinical research. *New England Journal of Medicine, 360*, 816–823.

Grading of Recommendations Assessment, Development and Evaluation (GRADE) Working Group. (undated). Grading the quality of evidence and the strength of recommendations. Retrieved from http://www.gradeworkinggroup.org/intro.htm

Grady, M. (2010). The missing link: The role of social work schools and evidence-based practice. *The Journal of Evidence-Based Social Work, 7*, 400–411.

Grady, M., Powers, J., Naylor, S. & Despard, M. (2011). Measuring the implicit program: Initial development and results of a MSW survey. *Journal of Social Work Education, 47*, 463–487. doi: 10.5175/JSWE.2011.200900119

Grady, M., Werkmeister-Rozas, L., & Bledsoe, S. (2010). Are curriculum decisions based on the evidence? How social work faculty members make choices in curriculum decisions. *Journal of Evidence-Based Social Work, 7*, 466–480.

Gray, G. (2004). *Concise guide to evidence-based psychiatry*. Arlington, VA: American Psychiatric Publishing.

Graybeal, C. (2007). Evidence for the art of social work. *Families in Society, 88*, 513–523.

Greene, J., Doughty, J., Marquart, J., Ray, M., & Roberts, L. (1988). Qualitative evaluation audits in practice. *Evaluation Review, 12*(4), 352–375.

Green, M., & Ruff, T. (2005). Why do residents fail to answer their clinical questions? A qualitative study of barriers to practicing evidence-based medicine. *Academic Medicine, 80*(2), 176–182.

Greenhalgh, T. (2010). *How to read a paper: The basics of evidence based medicine* (4th ed.). Hoboken, NJ: BMJ Books; Blackwell-Riley.

Grey, S., & Zide, M. (2008). *Psychopathology: A competency-based assessment model for social workers* (2nd ed.). Belmont, CA: Thompson/Brooks Cole.

Grinnell, R., & Unrau, Y. (2010). *Social work research and evaluation* (9th ed.). New York: Oxford.

Groopman, J. (2010, February 11). Health care: Who knows 'best.' *The New York Review of Books.*

Groopman, J., & Hartzman, P. (2011a). *Your medical mind: How to decide what is right for you.* New York: Penguin.

Groopman, J. & Hartzman, P. (2011b, September 21). Becoming mindful of medical decision making. *Fresh Air with Terry Gross.* Transcript retrieved from www.npr.org/templates/transcript/transcript.php?storyId=140438982

Guyatt, G. (1991). Evidence-based medicine. *American College of Physician's Journal Club (Annals of Internal Medicine), 114*(suppl 2), A-16.

Guyatt, G., Cairns, J., Churchill, D., Cook, D., Haynes, B, Hirsh, J., et al. [The Evidence-Based Medicine Working Group]. (1992). Evidence-based medicine: A new approach to teaching the practice of medicine. *Journal of the American Medical Association, 268*(17), 2420–2425. doi: 10.1001/jama.1992.03490170092032

Guyatt, G., Cook, D., & Haynes, B. (2004). Evidence based medicine has come a long way (Editorial). *British Medical Journal [BMJ], 329*(7473), 990–991.

Guyatt, G., Rennie, D., Meade, M., & Cook, D. (2008). Preface to users' guides to the medical literature: *Essentials of evidence-based clinical practice* (2nd ed). New York: McGraw-Hill. Also available online at http://jamaevidence.com/resource/preface/520

Habermas, J. (1990). *The philosophical discourse of modernity*. Cambridge, MA: MIT Press.

Haley, J. (1971). *Changing families: A family therapy reader*. New York: Grune & Stratton.

Hammersley, M. (2005). Is the evidence based practice movement doing more harm than good? *Evidence and Policy, 1*(1), 85–100.

Hansen, H. F., & Rieper, O. (2009). The evidence movement: The development and consequences of methodologies in review practices. *Evaluation, 15*(2), 141–163. doi: 10.1177/1356389008101968.

Harding, S. (1986). *The science question in feminism*. Ithaca, NY: Cornell University Press.

Hartman, A. (1990). Many ways of knowing. *Social Work, 35*(1), 3–4.

Hartman, A. (1994). Many ways of knowing. In W. Reid & E. Sherman (Eds.), *Qualitative research in social work* (pp. 459–463). Washington, DC: NASW Press.

Hartman, A., & Laird, J. (1983). *Family centered social work practice*. New York, NY: The Free Press.

Haynes, R., Devereaux, P., & Guyatt, G. (2002a). Clinical expertise in the era of evidence based medicine and patient choice. *Evidence-based Medicine, 7*, 36–38.

Haynes, R., Devereaux, P., & Guyatt, G. (2002b). Physicians' and patients' choices in evidence based practice. *British Medical Journal (BMJ), 324*, 1350.

Henggeler, S., Schoenwald, S., Liao, J., Letourneau, E., & Edwards, D. (2002). Transporting efficacious treatments to field settings: The link between supervisory practices and therapist fidelity in MST programs. *Journal of Clinical Child Psychology, 31*, 155–167.

Henggeler, S., & Lee, T. (2003). Multisystemic treatment of serious clinical problems. In A. Kazdin & J. Weisz (Eds.), *Evidence-based psychotherapies for children and adolescents* (pp. 301–322). New York, NY: Guilford Press.

Hepworth, D., Rooney, R., Rooney, G., Strom-Gottfried, K., & Larsen, J. (2010). *Direct social work practice: Theory and skills* (8th ed.). Belmont, CA: Brooks-Cole.

Herdt, G., & de Vries, B. (2004). *Gay and lesbian aging: Research and future directions*. New York: Springer.

Hersen, M., & Van Hasselt, V. (1996). *Sourcebook of psychological treatment manuals for adult disorders*. New York: Plenum Press.

Higgins J., & Green, S. (Eds.). (2011). *Cochrane handbook for systematic reviews of interventions, version 5.1.0*. Available from www.cochrane-handbook.org

Hodges, K., Xue, Y., & Wotring, J. (2004). The use of CAFAS to evaluate outcomes for youth with severe emotional disturbance served by public mental health. *Journal of Child and Family Studies, 13*(3), 325–339.

Hollis, F. (1964). *Casework: A psychosocial therapy*. New York: Random House.

Hopewell, S., Loudon, K., Clarke, M.J., Oxman, A., Dickersin, K. (2009). Publication bias in clinical trials due to statistical significance or direction of trial results. *Cochrane Database of Systematic Reviews, 2009*, Issue 1. Art. No.: MR000006. doi: 10.1002/14651858. MR000006.pub3

Horowitz, L., Alden, L., Wiggins, J., & Pincus, A. (2000). *Inventory of interpersonal problems manual*. Odessa, FL: The Psychological Corporation.

Horvath, A., & Bedi, R. (2002). The alliance. In J. Norcross (Ed.), *Psychotherapy relationships that work: Therapist contributions and responsiveness to patients* (pp. 37–69). New York, NY: Oxford University Press.

Horvath, A., & Symonds, B. (1991). Relation between working alliance and outcome in psychotherapy: A meta-analysis. *Journal of Consulting Psychology, 38,* 139–149.

Howard, M., Allen-Meares, P., & Ruffolo, M. (2007). Teaching evidence-based practice: Strategic and pedagogical recommendations for schools of social work. *Research on Social Work Practice, 17,* 561–568.

Hubble, M., Duncan, B., Miller, S., & Wampold, B. (2010). Introduction. In B. Duncan, S. Miller, B. Wampold, & M. Hubble (Eds.), *The heart & soul of change* (2nd ed., pp. 23–46). Washington, DC: American Psychological Association.

Hudson, W. (1982) *The clinical measurement package: A field manual.* Homewood, IL: Dorsey Press

Hughes, D. (2004). An attachment-based treatment of maltreated children and young people. *Attachment and Human Development, 6*(3), 263–278.

Hughes, D. (2006). *Building the bonds of attachment: Awakening love in deeply troubled children* (2nd ed.). Northvale, NJ: Jason Aronson.

Hughes, D. (undated). The P.LA.C.E. model. Retrieved from http://www.danielhughes.org/html/PLACE.html

Huxley, P. (1986). Statistical errors in papers in the *British Journal of Social Work* (Volumes 1–14). *British Journal of Social Work, 16*(6), 645–658.

Institute for the Advancement of Social Work Research. (2008). *Evidence-based practice.* Washington, DC: NASW Press.

Jagaroo, V., Maxwell, D., & Satake, E. (2008). *Handbook of statistical methods: Single subject design.* San Diego, CA: Plural Publishing.

Jayaratne, S. (1978). Analytic procedures for single subject designs. *Social Work Research and Abstracts, 14*(3), 30–40.

Johnson, L., Miller, S., & Duncan, B. (2000). The Session rating scale 3.0. Chicago: Author. Online at http://scottdmiller.com/node/13

Jones, R. (1996). *Handbook of test and measurements for black populations* (2 vols.). Hampton, VA: Cobb & Henry.

Jorm, A., Morgan, A., & Hetrick, S. (2008). Relaxation for depression. *Cochrane Database of Systematic Reviews, 4,* Art. No.: CD007142. Retrieved from: http://www2.cochrane.org/reviews/en/ab007142.html DOI: 10.1002/14651858.CD007142.pub2

KaiserEDU.org. (2010). U.S. health care costs. Retrieved from www.kaiseredu.org/Issue-Modules/US-Health-Care-Costs/Background-Brief.aspx

Karls, J., & Wandrei, K. (1994). *Person-in-environments system: The PIE classification system for social functioning problems.* Washington, DC: NASW Press.

Kazdin, A. (2002). *Research design in clinical psychology* (4th ed.). New York: Allyn & Bacon.

Kazi, M. (1998). *Single-case evaluation by social workers.* Hants, UK: Avebury Publishing.

Kazi, M., & Wilson, J. (1996). Applying single-case evaluation in social work. *British Journal of Social Work, 26*(5), 699–717.

Kelsey, J., Whittemore, A., Evans, A., & Thompson, W. (1996). *Methods in observational epidemiology* (2nd ed.). New York: Oxford University Press.

Kirk, S. (2005). Critical perspectives. In S. Kirk (Ed.), *Mental disorders in the social environment: Critical perspectives* (pp. 1–22). New York: Columbia University Press.

Kirk, S., & Kutchins, H. (1988). Deliberate misdiagnosis in mental health practice. *Social Service Review, 62*(2), 225–237.

Kohut, H. (1977). *The analysis of the self.* Madison, CT: International Universities Press.

Kraemer, H., & Thiemann, S. (1987). *How many subjects? Statistical power analysis in research.* Thousand Oaks, CA: Sage.

Kratochwill, T. R. (Ed.). (1978). *Single subject research: Strategies for evaluating change.* New York: Academic Press.

Kreuger, L., & Stretch, J. (2000). How hypermodern technology in social work bites back. *Journal of Social Work Education, 36*(1), 103–114.

Krupnick, J., Sotsky, S., Elkin, I., Simmens, S., Moyer, J., Watkins, J., et al. (1996). The role of the therapeutic alliance in psychotherapy and pharmacotherapy outcome: Findings in the National Institute of Mental Health treatment of depression collaborative research program. *Journal of Consulting and Clinical Psychology, 64*, 532–539.

Kuhn, T. (1996). *The structure of scientific revolutions* (3rd ed.). Chicago, IL: University Chicago Press.

Kutchins, H., & Kirk, S. (1988). The business of diagnosis: DSM-III and clinical social work. *Social Work, 33*(3), 215–220.

Kuzel, A. (1999). Sampling in qualitative research. In B. Crabtree & Miller (Eds.), *Doing qualitative research* (pp. 33–46). Thousand Oaks, CA: Sage.

Kvernbekk, T. (2011). The concept of evidence in evidence-based practice. *Educational Theory, 61*(5), 515–532.

Lai, N.M., Teng, C.L., & Lee, M.L. (2011). Interpreting systematic reviews: are we ready to make our own conclusions? A cross-sectional study. *BMC Medicine, 9*, 30. Retrieved from www.ncbi.nlm.nih.gov/pmc/articles/PMC3100234/pdf/1741-7015-9-30.pdf

Lam, R., Levitt, A., Levitan, R., Enns, M., Morehouse, R., Michalak, E., et al. (2006). The Can-SAD study: A randomized controlled trial of the effectiveness of light therapy and fluoxetine in patients with winter seasonal affective disorder. *American Journal of Psychiatry, 163*(5), 805–812.

Lambert, M. (1992). Implications of outcome research for psychotherapy integration. In J. Norcross & J. Goldstein (Eds.), *Handbook of psychotherapy integration* (pp. 94–129). New York: Basic Books.

Lambert, M. (Ed.). (2004). *Bergin and Garfield's handbook of psychotherapy and behavior change* (5th ed.). New York: Wiley.

Lambert, M. (2010). *Prevention of treatment failure: The use of measuring, monitoring, and feedback in clinical practice*. Washington, DC: American Psychological Association.

Lambert, M., & Barley, D. (2001). Research summary on the therapeutic relationship and psychotherapy outcome. *Psychotherapy: Theory, Research, Practice, Training, 38*(4), 357–361.

Lambert, M., Hansen, N., & Harmon, S. C. (2010). Outcome questionnaire system (The OQ System): Development and practical applications in healthcare settings. In M. Barkham, G. Hardy, & J. Mellor-Clark (Eds.), *Developing and delivering practice-based evidence: A guide for the psychological therapies* (pp. 141–154). New York: Wiley-Blackwell.

Lambert, M., Hansen, N., Umphress, V., Lunnen, L., Okiishi, J., Burlingame, G., et al. (1996). *Administration and scoring manual for the OQ-45-2*. Stevenson, MD: American Professional Credentialing Services.

Lambert, M., & Ogles, B. (2004). The efficacy and effectiveness of psychotherapy. In M. Lambert (Ed.), *Bergin and Garfield's handbook of psychotherapy and behavior change* (5th ed., pp. 139–193). New York: Wiley.

Lambert, M., Smart, D., Campbell, M., Hawkins, E., Harmon, C., & Slade, K. (2006). Psychotherapy outcome, as measured by the OQ-45, in African American, Asian/Pacific Islander, Latino/a, and Native American clients compared with matched Caucasian clients. *Journal of College Student Psychotherapy, 20*(4), 17–29.

Lambert, M., & Vermeersch, D. (2008). Measuring and improving psychotherapy outcome in routine practice. In S. Brown & R. Lent (Eds.), *Handbook of counseling psychology* (4th ed., pp. 233–248). Hoboken, NJ: Wiley.

Lang, N. (1994). Integrating the data processing of qualitative research and social work practice to advance the practitioner as knowledge builder: Tools for knowing and doing. In W. Reid & E. Sherman (Eds.), *Qualitative Research in Social Work* (pp. 265–278). New York: Columbia University Press.

LeCroy, C. (2008). *Handbook of evidence-based treatment manuals for children and adolescents*. New York: Oxford University Press.

Leeper, J. (undated). Choosing the correct statistical test. Retrieved from http://bama.ua.edu/~jleeper/627/choosestat.html

Légaré, F., Elwyn, G., Fishbein, M., Frémont, P., Frosch, D., Gagnon, M., et al. (2008). Translating shared decision-making into health care clinical practices: Proof of concepts. *Implementation Science, 3*, 2. doi:10.1186/1748-5908-3-2.

Légaré, F., Bekker, H., Desroches, S., Drolet, R., Politi, M., Stacey, D., et al. (2011). How can continuing professional development better promote shared decision-making? *Perspectives from an international collaboration. Implementation Science, 6*, 68. doi: 10.1186/1748-5908-6-68

Lehman, A. (2010). Adopting evidence based practices: Our hesitation waltz. *Schizophrenia Bulletin, 36*(1), 1–2.

Lenth, R. (2008). Java applets for power and sample size. Retrieved March 2, 2011 from www.stat.uiowa.edu/~rlenth/Power/

Lester, V. (1997). Behavior change as reported by caregivers of children receiving holding therapy. Retrieved from www.attach.org/lester.htm

Levant, R., & Silverstein, L. (2005). Gender is neglected by both evidence-based practices and treatment as usual. In J. Norcross, L. Beutler, & R. Levant (Eds.), *Evidence-based practices in mental health* (pp. 338–345). Washington, DC: American Psychological Association.

Levy, M. (2011, January 20). Lebanon school district sued over excessive truancy fines.*The Huffington Post*. Retrieved from www.huffingtonpost.com/2011/01/20/pennsylvania-truancy-fines_n_811833.html

Levy, T., & Orlans, M. (undated). Clinical research shows corrective attachment therapy™ works. Online paper Retrieved March 4, 2007, from www.attachmentexperts.com/treatment_outcome.html

Liddle, H., Dakof, G., Parker, K., Diamond, G., Barrett, K., & Tejeda, M. (2001). Multidimensional family therapy for adolescent drug abuse: Results from a randomized controlled trial. *American Journal of Drug and Alcohol Abuse, 27*, 651–688.

Lieberman, A. (2003). The treatment of attachment disorder in infancy and early childhood: Reflections from clinical intervention with late-adopted foster care children. *Attachment & Human Development, 5*(3), 279–282.

Lietz, C., & Zayas, L. E. (2010). Evaluating qualitative research for social work practitioners. *Advances in Social Work, 11*(2), 188–202.

Linehan, M. (1993). *Skills training manual for treating borderline personality disorder*. New York: Guilford Press.

Litschge, C., Vaughn, M., & McCrea, C. (2010). The empirical status of treatments for children and youth with conduct problems: An overview of meta-analytic studies. *Research on Social Work Practice, 20*(1), 21–35.

Littell, J. (2011). Evidence-based practice versus practice-based research. Paper presented at the Society for Social Work and Research, Tampa, FL, January 15, 2011.

Littell, J., Corcoran, J., & Pillai, V. (2008). *Systematic reviews and meta-analysis*. New York: Oxford University Press.

Littell, J., Popa, M., & Forsythe, B. (2005). Multisystem therapy for social, emotional and behavioral problems in youth aged 10–17. Campbell Systematic Reviews, 2005:1. Retrieved from www.campbellcollaboration.org/library.php (with search term multisystemic therapy).

Lock, J., Le Grange, D., Agras, W. S., & Dare, C. (2002). *Treatment manual for anorexia nervosa: A family-based approach*. New York: Guilford Press.

Loewy, E. (2007). Ethics and evidence-based medicine: Is there a conflict? *Medscape General Medicine, 9*(3), 30. Retrieved from www.medscape.com/viewarticle/559977_8

Los Angeles Times. (undated). Grading the teachers: Value-added analysis. (A series of articles published over the summer of 2010). Retrieved from www.latimes.com/news/local/teachers-investigation/

Lyotard, J.-F. (1984). *The postmodern condition*. Minneapolis, MN: University of Minnesota Press.

Mace, C., Moorey, S., & Roberts, B. (Eds.). (2001). *Evidence in the psychological therapies: A critical guide for practitioners.* Philadelphia, PA: Taylor & Francis.

Machin, D., & Campbell, M. (2005). *The design of studies for medical research.* New York: Wiley.

Mahler, M., Pine, F., & Bergman, A. (2000). *The psychological birth of the human infant: Symbiosis and individuation.* New York: Basic Books.

Marshall, M., Lockwood, A., Bradley, C., Adams, C., Joy, C., & Fenton, M. (2000). Unpublished rating scales: A major source of bias in randomised controlled trails of treatment for schizophrenia. *British Journal of Psychiatry, 176,* 249–252.

Martin, D., Garske, J., & Davis, M. K. (2000). Relation of the therapeutic alliance with outcome and other variables: A meta-analytic review. *Journal of Consulting and Clinical Psychology, 68*(3), 43–50.

Mayo Clinic. (2011). *Stress basics.* Retrieved from www.mayoclinic.com/health/stress-management/MY00435

McDowell, T. (2000). Practice evaluation as a collaborative process: A client's and a clinician's perceptions of helpful and unhelpful moments in a clinical interview. *Smith College Studies in Social Work, 70*(2), 375–387.

McGauran, N., Wiesler, B., Kreis, J., Schüler, Y.-B., Kölsch, H., & Kaiser, T. (2010). Reporting bias in medical research: A narrative review. *Trials, 11,* 37.

McMaster Group—The Department of Epidemiology and Biostatistics, McMaster University Health Sciences Center. (1991). How to read clinical journals, [part] I: Why to read them and how to start reading them critically. *Canadian Medical Association Journal, 124*(5), 555–558.

McQuay, H., & Moore, A. (1997). Using numerical results from systematic reviews in clinical practice. *Annals of Internal Medicine, 126,* 712–720. Retrieved from www.medicine.ox.ac.uk/bandolier/booth/painpag/NNTstuff/numeric.htm

McNeill, C. (2005, December 13). Dialectical behavioral therapy for homeless patients with borderline personality disorder. Paper presented that the American Public Health Association 133rd annual meeting, Philadelphia, PA. Abstract retrieved from http://apha.confex.com/apha/133am/techprogram/paper_103492.htm

Messer, S. (2004). Evidence-based practice: Beyond empirically supported treatments. *Professional Psychology: Research and Practice, 35*(6), 580–588.

Michigan Quality Improvement Consortium. (2010, January). Primary care diagnosis and management of adults with depression. Southfield (MI): Michigan Quality Improvement Consortium. Retrieved from http://guidelines.gov/content.aspx?id=15647&search=major+depression

Miller, S., & Duncan, B. (2000). *The outcome rating scale.* Chicago: Author.

Miller, S., Duncan, B., Brown, J., Sorrell, R., & Chalk, M. (2006). Using formal client feedback to improve retention and outcome: Making ongoing, real-time assessment feasible. *Journal of Brief Therapy, 5*(1), 5–22.

Miller, S., Duncan, B., Brown, J., Sparks, J., & Claud, D. (2003). The outcome rating scale: A preliminary study of the reliability, validity, and feasibility of a brief visual analog measure. *Journal of Brief Therapy, 2,* 91–100.

Milrod, B., Leon, A., Busch, F., Rudden, M., Schwalberg, M. Clarkin, J., Aronson, A., Singer, M., Turchin, W., Klass, E.T., Graf, E., Teres, J., & Shear, M.K. (2007). A randomized controlled clinical trial of psychoanalytic psychotherapy for panic disorder. *American Journal of Psychiatry, 164,* 265–272.

Minneapolis VA Health Care System. (2010). Mental health: Evidence based treatments. Retrieved September 22, 2011 from www.minneapolis.va.gov/services/Mental Health/MHebt.asp

Minuchin, S. (1974). *Families and family therapy.* Cambridge, MA: Harvard University Press.

Moher, D., Cook, D., Eastwood, S., Olkin, I., Rennie, D., & Stroup, F. (1999). Improving the quality of reports of meta-analyses of randomized controlled trails: The Quorom group statement. *Lancet, 354*(9193), 1896–1900.

Moher, D., Liberati, A., Tetzlaff, J., & Altman, D. (2009). Preferred reporting items for systematic reviews and meta-analyses: the PRISMA statement. *British Medical Journal (BMJ), 339*, b2535. doi:10.1136/bmj.b2535.

Moore, M. (1988). What sort of ideas become public ideas? In R. Reich (Ed.), *The power of public ideas* (pp. 55–84). Cambridge, MA: Ballinger Publishing.

Mullen, E., & Shlonsky, A. (2004, September 24). From concept to implementation: The challenges facing evidence-based social work. Powerpoint from the Faculty Research & Insights: A Series Featuring CUSSW Faculty Research. Retrieved from www.columbia.edu/.../Mullen & Shlonsky no notes 09-26-04.ppt

Mullen, E., Shlonsky, A., Bledoe, S., & Bellamy, J. (2005). From concept to implementation: Challenges facing evidence-based social work. *Evidence & Policy: A Journal of Research, Debate and Practice, 1*(1), 61–84.

Murphy, A., & McDonald, D. (2004). Power, status, and marginalisation: Rural social workers and evidence-based practice in interdisciplinary teams. *Australian Social Work, 57*, 127–136.

Murray, E., Pollack, L., White, M., & Lo, B. (2007). Clinical decision-making: Physicians' preferences and experiences. *BMC (Bio Med Central) Family Practice, 8*, 10.

Myeroff, R. (1997). Comparative effectiveness of attachment therapy with the special needs adoptive population. Dissertation Abstracts International: Section B: The Sciences and Engineering, Vol 58(6-B), Dec 1997. pp. 3323. ISSN:0419-4217 (Print) Order Number:AAM9736716

Myeroff, R. L., Mertlich, G., & Gross, G. (1999). Comparative effectiveness of holding therapy with aggressive children. *Child Psychiatry and Human Development, 29*(4), 303–313.

Myers, L., & Thyer, B. (1997). Should social work clients have the right to effective treatment? *Social Work, 42*, 288–298.

National Alliance of the Mentally Ill. (2011). *New study: Support groups help parents of adult children living with mental illness, create advocates and leaders; 2010 NAMI National Convention will address family education.* Retrieved from: www.nami.org/Content/Content Groups/Press_Room1/20102/June17/New_Study_Support_Groups_Help_Parents_of_Adult_ Children_Living_with_Mental_Illness,_Create_Advocates.htm

National Association of Social Workers. (2005a). *NASW standards for clinical social work in social work practice.* Washington, DC: NASW Press.

National Association of Social Workers. (2005b). *NASW standards social work practice in health care settings.* Washington, DC: NASW Press.

National Association of Social Workers (NASW). (2008). *Code of ethics.* Washington, DC: NASW Press.

Nelkin, D. (1996). The science wars: Responses to a marriage failed. *Social Text, 46/47*(14), 93–100.

Nelson, A. (2008). Addressing the threat of evidence-based practice to qualitative inquiry through increasing attention to quality: A discussion paper. *International Journal of Nursing Studies, 45*(2), 316–322.

Nelson, L. (1993). Epistemological communities. In L. Alcoff & E. Potter (Eds.), *Feminist epistemologies* (pp. 121–160). New York: Routledge.

Nelson, T., Steele, R., & Mize, J. (2006). Practitioner attitudes toward evidence-based practice: themes and challenges. *Administration and Policy in Mental Health, 33*, 398–409. doi: 10.1007/s10488-006-0044-4.

Nespor, J. (2006). Methodological inquiry: The uses and spaces of paradigm proliferation. *International Journal of Qualitative Studies in Education, 19*, 115–128.

Noblit, G., & Hare, R. (1988). *Meta-ethnography: Synthesizing qualitative studies.* Newbury Park, CA: Sage.

Nolen-Hoeksema, S. (2001). Gender differences in depression. *Current Directions in Psychological Science, 10*(5), 173–176.

Norcross, J. (2010). The therapeutic relationship. In B. Duncan, S. Miller, B. Wampold, & M. Hubble (Eds.), *The heart & soul of change* (2nd ed., pp. 113–141). Washington, DC: American Psychological Association.

Norcross, J. (Ed.). (2011). *Psychotherapy relationships that work: Evidence-based responsiveness* (2nd ed.). New York: Oxford.

Norcross, J., Hogan, T., & Koocher, G. (2008). *Clinicians' guide to evidence-based practices.* New York: Oxford University Press.

Norman, G., & Streiner, D. (Eds.). (2003). *PDQ Statistics* (3rd ed.). Shelton, CT: People's Medical Publishing House (PMPH).

Nugent, W. (1992). Psychometric characteristics of self-anchored scales in clinical application. *Journal of Social Service Research, 15*(3/4), 137–152.

Nye, C. (1994). Discourse analysis methods and clinical research: A single case study. In E. Sherman & W. Reid. (Eds.), Qualitative research in social work (pp. 216–227). New York: Columbia University Press.

O'Connor, T., & Zeanah, C. (2003). Attachment disorders: Assessment strategies and treatment implications. *Attachment and Human Development, 5*(3), 223–244.

Ogles, B., Lambert, M., & Masters, K. (1996). *Assessing outcome in clinical practice.* Boston: Allyn and Bacon.

Olkin, R., & Taliferro, G. (2005). Evidence-based practices have ignored people with disabilities. In J. Norcross, L. Beutler, & R. Levant (Eds.), *Evidence-based practices in mental health* (pp. 3352–3358). Washington, DC: American Psychological Association.

Ollendick, T., King, N., & Chorpita, B. (2006). Empirically supported treatments for children and adolescents. In P. Kendall (Ed.), *Child and adolescent therapy: Cognitive-behavioral procedures.* New York: Guilford Press.

Open Clinical. (undated). Evidence based medicine (Benefits section). Retrieved from www.openclinical.org/ebm.html

Orlinsky, D., Rønnestad, M., & Willutzki, U. (2004). Fifty years of process-outcome research: Continuity and change. In M. Lambert (Ed.), *Bergin and Garfield's handbook of psychotherapy and behavior change* (5th ed., pp. 307–390). New York, NY: Wiley Press.

Osborn, C. J., & Davis, T. E. (2009). Ethical issues in the clinical supervision of evidence-based practices. In N. Pelling, J. Barletta, P. Armstrong, N. Pelling, J. Barletta, & P. Armstrong (Eds.), *The practice of clinical supervision* (pp. 56–80). Bowen Hills, QLD Australia: Australian Academic Press.

Otterman, S. (2011, May 25). Tests for pupils, but the grades go to teachers. *The New York Times Online.* Retrieved fromwww.nytimes.com/2011/05/24/education/24tests.html?_r=1&ref=education

Overall, J., & Gorham, D. (1962). The brief psychiatric rating scale. *Psychological Reports, 10*, 799–812.

Oxford University Centre for Evidence-based Medicine. (2009, January). Study designs. Retrieved from www.cebm.net/index.aspx?o=1039

Oxford University Centre for Evidence-based Medicine. (2009, March). Levels of evidence. Retrieved from www.cebm.net/index.aspx?o=1025.

Oxford University Centre for Evidence-based Medicine. (2009, April). Asking focused questions. Retrieved from /www.cebm.net/index.aspx?o=1036

Oxford University Centre for Evidence-based Medicine. (2011). The Oxford levels of evidence 2011. Retrieved from www.cebm.net/mod_product/design/files/CEBM-Levels-of-Evidence-2.1.pdf

Palombo, J. (1985). The treatment of borderline neurocognitively impaired children: A perspective from self psychology. *Clinical Social Work Journal, 13*, 117–128.

Panzarino, P., & Kellar, J. (1994). Integrating outcomes, quality and utilization data for profiling behavioral health providers. *Behavioral Healthcare Tomorrow, 3*(6), 27–30.

Park, K. (1990). Book review of Avicenna in renaissance Italy: The canon and medical teaching in Italian universities after 1500 by Nancy G. Siraisi. *The Journal of Modern History, 62*(1), 169–170.

Patel, S., & Bakken, S. (2010). Preferences for participation in decision making among ethnically diverse patients with anxiety and depression. *Community Mental Health Journal, 46*(5), 466–473. doi:10.1007/s10597-010-9323-3.

Patel, S., Bakken, S., & Ruland, C. (2009). Recent advances in shared decision making for mental health. *Current Opinion in Psychiatry, 21*(6), 606–612.

Patton, M. Q. (1990). *Qualitative evaluation and research methods* (2nd ed.). Newbury Park, CA: Sage.

Pautasso, M. (2010). Worsening file-draw problem in the abstracts of natural, medical and social science databases. *Scientometrics,*. doi:10.1007/s11192-010-0233-5.

Perlman, F., & Brandell, J. (2010). Psychoanalytic theory. In J. Brandell (Ed.), *Theory and practice in clinical social work* (pp. 41–80). Thousand Oaks, CA: Sage.

Percevic, R., Lambert, M., & Kordy, H. (2006). What is the predictive value of responses to psychotherapy for its future course? Empirical explorations and consequences for outcome monitoring. *Psychotherapy Research, 16*(3), 364–373.

Petr, C. (Ed.). (2009). *Multidimensional evidence based practice: Synthesizing knowledge, research, and values.* New York: Routledge.

Pollio, D. (2006). The art of evidence-based practice. *Research on Social Work Practice, 16,* 224–232. doi:10.1177/1049731505282981.

Popay, J., & Williams, G. (1998). Qualitative research and evidence-based healthcare. *Journal of the Royal Society of Medicine, 91*(Supp 35), 32–37.

Postal, L., & Balona, D.-M. (2011, January, 18). It's time to grade parents, new bill proposes. *The Orlando [FL] Sentinel.*http://articles.orlandosentinel.com/2011-01-18/news/os-teachers-grade-parents-20110118_1_parental-involvement-parent-appeals-grade-parents

PracticeWise. (2008). *Practicewise clinical dashboard.* Retrieved August 1, 2008 from www.practicewise.com. Retrieved from: www.practicewise.com/web/

Pratt, J., Rhine, J., Smith, B., Stuart, C., & Greenwood, J. (1940). *Extra-sensory perception after sixty years.* New York: Henry Holt.

Price, L. (2010, January 11). Letters: Looking at ways to treat depression. *The New York Times Online.* Retrieved January 12, 2010 from www.nytimes.com/2010/01/12/opinion/l12 warner.html

Probst, B. (2011). Walking the tightrope: Using diagnostic and environmental perspectives in clinical practice. Unpublished doctoral dissertation, Fordham University School of Social Work

Proctor, E., Knudsen, K., Fedoravicius, N., Hovmand, P., Rosen, A., & Perron, B. (2007). Implementation of evidence-based practice in community behavioral health: Agency director perspectives. *Administration and Policy in Mental Health, 34,* 479–488. doi:10.1007/s10488-007-0129-8.

Proctor, E., & Rosen, A. (2006). Concise standards for developing evidence-based practice guidelines. In A. Roberts & K. Yeager (Eds.), *Foundations of evidence-based social work practice* (pp. 93–102). New York, NY: Oxford University Press.

Powell, K., Abrefa-Gyan, T., Williams, C., & Rice, K. (2010, October 15). Perceptions and realities in evidence-based practice: Implications for social work education. Paper presented at the Annual Program Meeting of the Council on Social Work Education, Portland, Oregon

Quine, W.V.O. (1953). Two dogmas of empiricism. In W.V.O. Quine (Ed.), *From a logical point of view* (pp. 20–46). Cambridge, MA: Harvard University Press.

Randolph, E. (2000). *Manual for the Randolph attachment disorder questionnaire.* Evergreen, CO: Attachment Center Press.

Raphael, D. (2000). The question of evidence in health promotion. *Health Promotion International, 15*(4), 355–367. doi: 10.1093/heapro/15.4.355

Ravetz, J. (1979). *Scientific knowledge and its social problems.* Oxford: Oxford University Press.

Reed, G., & Eisman, E. (2006). Uses and misused of evidence: Managed care, treatment guidelines, and outcomes measurement in professional practice. In C. Goodheart, A. Kazdin, & R. Sternberg (Eds.), *Evidence-based psychotherapy: Where practice and research meet* (pp. 13–35). Washington, DC: American Psychological Association.

Reese, R., Toland, M., Slone, N., & Norsworthy, L. (2010). Effect of client feedback on couple psychotherapy outcomes. *Psychotherapy, 47,* 616–630.

Reich, R. (1988). *The power of public ideas.* Cambridge, MA: Ballinger Publishing.

Reid, W. (1994). The empirical practice movement. *Social Service Review, 68*(2), 165–184.

Reilly, P., & Shopshire, M. (2002). *Anger management for substance abuse and mental health clients: A cognitive behavioral therapy manual.* Washington, DC: SAMHSA.

Review: Light therapy is an effective treatment for seasonal affective disorder. Retrieved from http://ebmh.bmj.com/content/9/1/21.full.pdf

Riessman, C. (Ed.). (1994). *Qualitative studies in social work research.* Thousand Oaks, CA: Sage.

Richardson, W., Wilson, M., Nishikawa, J., & Hayward, R. (1995). The well-built clinical question: A key to evidence-based decisions [Editorial]. *American College of Physicians Journal Club, 123,* A12–A13.

Roberts, A., & Yeager, K. (2004). *Evidence-based practice manual.* New York: Oxford University Press.

Rodwell [O'Connor], M.C. (1998). *Social work constructivist research.* New York: Garland

Rodwell, M. C., & Woody, D. (1994). Constructivist evaluation: The policy/practice context. In W. Reid & E. Sherman (Eds.), *Qualitative Research in Social Work* (pp. 315–327). New York: Columbia University Press.

Rorty, R. (1979). *Philosophy and the mirror of nature.* Princeton, NJ: Princeton University Press.

Rosen, A. (2003). Evidence-based social work practice: Challenges and promise. *Social Work Research, 27,* 197–208.

Roth, A., & Fonagy, P. (2005). *What works for whom? A critical review of psychotherapy research* (2nd ed.). New York: Guilford.

Rothstein, J. (2001). Clinical supervision–then and now: The professional development of social workers. *Reflections, 7,* 61–71.

Rubin, A. (2008). *Practitioner's guide to using research for evidence-based practice.* Hoboken, NJ: Wiley.

Rubin, A., & Babbie, E. (2008). *Research methods for social work* (7th ed.). Belmont, CA: Brooks/Cole.

Rubin, A., & Parrish, D. (2007). Views of evidenced-based practice among faculty in master of social work programs: A national survey. *Research on Social Work Practice, 17,* 110–122.

Ruckdeschel, R. (1999). Qualitative clinical research and evaluation. In I. Shaw & J. Lishman (Eds.), *Evaluation and social work practice* (pp. 251–264). Thousand Oaks, CA: Sage.

Ruckdeschel, R., Earnshaw, P., & Firrik, A. (1994). The qualitative case study and evaluation: issues, methods and examples. In W. Reid & E. Sherman (Eds.), *Qualitative research in social work* (pp. 251–264). New York: Columbia University Press.

Rust, J., & Golombok, S. (2009). *Modern psychometrics: The science of psychological assessment* (3rd ed.). New York: Routledge.

Sackett, D., Richardson, W., Rosenberg, W., & Haynes, R. (1997). *Evidence-based medicine: How to practice and teach EBM.* New York: Churchill Livingston.

Sackett, D., Rosenberg, W., Muir Gray, J., Haynes, R., & Richardson, W. (1996). Editorial: Evidence based medicine: What it is and what it isn't. *British Medical Journal, 312,* 71–72.

Sackett, D, Straus, S., Richardson, W., Rosenberg, W., & Haynes, R. (2000). *Evidence-based medicine: How to practice and teach EBM* (2nd ed.). Edinburgh: Churchill Livingstone.

Sanderson, W., & Woody, S. (1995, 1996). *Manuals for empirically validated treatments: A project of the Task Force on Psychological Interventions, Division of Clinical Psychology, American Psychological Association.* Washington, DC: American Psychological Association.

Sandler, J. (1962). Hampstead index as an instrument of psychoanalytic research. *International Journal of Psychoanalysis, 43,* 287–291.

Sandelowski, M., & Barroso, J. (2007). *Handbook for synthesizing qualitative research.* New York: Springer Publishing.

Scargle, J. (2000). Publication bias: The "file-drawer problem" in scientific inference. *Journal of Scientific Exploration, 14*(2), 94–106.

Schoenwald, S. K., Brown, T. L., & Henggeler, S. W. (2000). Inside multisystemic therapy: Therapists, supervisory, and program practices. *Journal of Emotional and Behavioral Disorders, 8*, 113–127.

Schwandt, T. (2005). The centrality of practice to evaluation. *American Journal of Evaluation, 26*, 95–105.

Shadish, W., Cook, T., & Campbell, D. (2001). *Experimental and quasi-experimental designs for generalized causal inference* (2nd ed.). New York: Wadsworth.

Sheafor, B., & Horejsi, C. (2011). *Techniques and guidelines for social work practice* (9th ed.). New York: Prentice Hall.

Shapiro, D., Harper, H., & Startup, M., et al. (1994). The high water mark of the drug metaphor: A meta-analytic critique of process-outcome research. In R. Russell (Ed.), *Reassessing psychotherapy research* (pp. 1–8; 26–31). New York: Guilford.

Shapiro, F., & Maxfield, L. (2002). Eye movement desensitization and reprocessing (EMDR): Information processing in the treatment of trauma. *Psychotherapy in Practice, 58*, 933–946.

Shaw, I. (1999). *Qualitative evaluation*. London: Sage.

Shaw, I., & Lishman, J. (Eds.). (1999). *Evaluation and social work practice*. Thousand Oaks, CA: Sage.

Sherman, E., & Reid, W. (Eds.). (1994). *Qualitative research in social work*. New York: Columbia.

Shlonsky, A., & Stern, S. (2007). Reflections on the teaching of evidence-based practice. *Research on Social Work Practice, 17*, 603–611.

Shojania, K., Sampson, M., Ansari, M., Ji, J., Doucette, S., & Moher, D. (2007). How quickly do systematic review of out of date? *Annals of Internal Medicine, 141*(4), 224–233.

Silverman, W. (1996). Cookbooks, manuals and paint by numbers: Psychotherapy in the 1990s. *Psychotherapy, 33*, 2017–2215.

Smith, E. (1995). A passionate, rationale response to the 'manualization' of psychotherapy. *Psychological Bulletin, 22*, 36–40.

Smyke, A., & Zeanah, C. (1999) Disturbances of attachment interview. Retrieved from http://download.lww.com/wolterskluwer_vitalstream_com/PermaLink/CHI/A/00004583-920020800-00014.doc

Snyder, J., & Gauthier, C. (2008). *Evidence-based medical ethics: Cases for practice-based learning*. New York: Springer.

Solomon, P., Cavanaugh, M., & Draine, J. (2009). *Randomized controlled trails*. New York: Oxford University Press.

Spence, D. (1982). *Narrative truth and historical truth: Meaning and interpretation in psychoanalysis*. New York: W.W. Norton.

Spitzer, R., Williams, J., Gibbon, M., & First, M. (1990). *Structured clinician interview for DSM-III-R Axis II Disorders, (SCID-II)*. Washington, DC.: American Psychiatric Press.

Springer, D. (2007). The teaching of evidence-based practice in social work higher education— Living by the Charlie Parker dictum: A response to papers by Shlonsky and Stern, and Soydan. *Research on Social Work Practice, 17*, 619–624.

Sridharan, L., & Greenland, P. (2009). Editorial policies and publication bias: The importance of negative studies (editorial commentary). *Archives of Internal Medicine, 169*, 1022–1023.

Staller, K. (2006). Railroads, runaways, and researchers: Returning evidence rhetoric to its practice base. *Qualitative Inquiry, 12*(3), 503–522.

Stark, K., Streusand, W., Krumholz, L., & Patel, P. (2010). Cognitive-behavioral therapy for depression: The ACTION treatment program for girls. In J. Weisz & A. Kazdin (Eds.), *Evidence-based psychotherapies for children and adolescents* (2nd ed., pp. 93–109). New York: Guilford.

Steele, R., Elkin, T., & Roberts, M. (Eds.). (2007). *Handbook of evidence-based therapies for children and adolescents: Bridging science and practice*. New York: Springer.

Stern, D. (2004). *The present moment in psychotherapy and everyday life.* New York: W.W. Norton.

Stoffers, J., Völlm, B., Rücker, G., Timmer, A., Huband, N., & Lieb, K. (2010). Pharmacological interventions for borderline personality disorder. *Cochrane Database of Systematic Reviews* 2010, Issue 6. Art. No.: CD005653. doi: 10.1002/14651858.CD005653.pub2.

Strupp, H. & Binder, J. (1984). *Psychotherapy in a new key: A guide to time-limited dynamic psychotherapy.* New York: Basic Books.

Strupp, H., & Binder, J. (1985). *Psychotherapy in a new key.* New York: Basic Books.

Sue, S., & Zane, N. (2005). Ethnic minority populations have been neglected by evidence-based practice. In J. Norcross, L. Beutler, & R. Levant (Eds.), *Evidence-based practices in mental health* (pp. 329–337). Washington, DC: American Psychological Association.

Summers, R., & Barber, J. (2010). *Psychodynamic therapy: A guide to evidence-based practice.* New York: Guilford.

Swenson, S., Buell, S., Zettler, P., White, M., Ruston, D., & Lo, B. (2004). Patient-centered communication: Do patients really prefer it? *Journal of General Internal Medicine, 19*(11), 1069–1079.

Swigonski, M. (1994). The logic of feminist standpoint theory for social work research. *Social Work, 39*(4), 387–393.

Tabachnick, B., & Fidell, L. (2007). *Using multivariate statistics* (5th ed.), New York: Pearson Educational Inc.

Tanenbaum, S. (2003). Evidence-based practice in mental health: Practical weakness meets political strengths. *Journal of Evidence in Clinical Practice, 9,* 287–301.

Tanjong-Ghogomu, E., Tugwell, P., & Welch, V. (2009). Evidence based practice and the Cochrane Collaboration. *Bulletin of the New York University Hospital for Joint Diseases, 67*(2), 198–205.

Thaler, K., Chapman, A., Gaynes, B. Kaminski, A., & Gartlehner, G. (2010). Second-generation antidepressants for seasonal affective disorder (SAD) (Protocol). *Cochrane Database of Systematic Reviews* 2010, Issue 7. Art. No.: CD008591. doi: 10.1002/14651858.CD008591.

Telch, C., Argas, W.S., & Linehan, M. (2001). Dialectic behavior therapy for binge eating disorder. *Journal of Consulting and Clinical Psychology, 69*(6), 1061–1065.

Terman, M. (2006). Therapeutics: Is light therapy an effective treatment for seasonal affective disorder? *Evidence Based Mental Health, 9,* 21. doi: 10.1136/ebmh.9.1.21.

Thombs, B., & Jewett, L. (2009). Letter: Analyzing effectiveness of long-term psychodynamic psychotherapy. *Journal of the American Medical Association, 301*(9), 930.

Thompson, B. (2001). 402 Citations questioning the indiscriminate use of null hypothesis significance tests in observational studies. Retrieved from http://warnercnr.colostate.edu/~anderson/thompson1.html

Thyer, B. (2011). *Evidence-based practice versus practice-based research. Paper presented at the Society for Social Work and Research.* Tampa, FL, January 15, 2011.

Thyer, B., & Myers, L. (2007). *A social worker's guide to evaluating practice outcomes.* Alexandria, VA: Council on Social Work Education.

Tonelli, M. (1998). The philosophical limits of evidence-based medicine. *Academic Medicine, 73*(12), 1234–1240.

Tonelli, M. (2001). The limits of evidence-based medicine. *Respiratory Care, 46*(2), 1435–1440.

Torchalla, I., Albrecht, F., Buchkremer, G., & Langue, G. (2004). Homeless women with psychiatric disorders: A field study. *Psychiatric Praxis, 31*(5), 228-235. [Article in German.]

Towle, A., & Godolphin, W. (1999). Framework for teaching and learning informed shared decision making. *British Medical Journal (BMJ), 319*(7212), 766–771.

Trepper, T., McCollum, E., DeJong, P., Korman, H., Gingerich, W., & Franklin, C. (undated). Solution focused therapy: Treatment manual for working with individuals (preliminary). *Research Committee of the Association for Solution Focused Therapy.* Retrieved from www.sfbta.org/Research.pdf

Trinder, L. (2000a). A critical appraisal of evidence based practice. In L. Trinder & S. Reynolds (Eds.), *Evidence-based practice: A critical appraisal* (pp. 212–241). Ames, IA: Blackwell Science.

Trinder, L. (2000b). Evidence based practice in social work and probation. In L. Trinder & S. Reynolds (Eds.), *Evidence-based practice: A critical appraisal* (pp. 138–162). Ames, IA: Blackwell Science.

Trinder, L. (2000c). Introduction: The context of evidence based practice. In L. Trinder & S. Reynolds (Eds.), *Evidence-based practice: A critical appraisal* (pp. 1–16). Ames, IA: Blackwell Science.

Trinder, L., & Reynolds, S. (Eds.). (2000). *Evidence-based practice: A critical appraisal*. Ames, IA: Blackwell Science.

Tripodi, S. J., Bender, K., Litschge, C., & Vaughn, M. G. (2010). Interventions for reducing adolescent alcohol abuse: A meta-analytic review. *Archives of Pediatric Adolescent Medicine, 164*, 85–91.

Tripodi, T. (1994). *A primer on single subject design for clinical social workers.* Washington, DC: National Association of Social Workers.

Turner, F. (2002). *Diagnosis in social work: New imperatives*. Binghamton, NY: Haworth.

Tuhiwai Smith, L. (1999). *Decolonizing methodologies: Research and indigenous peoples*. Dunedin: NZ: University of Otego Press.

Tuunainen, A., Kripke, D. & Endo, T. (2004). Light therapy for non-seasonal depression. *Cochrane Database of Systematic Reviews,* Issue 2. Art. No.: CD004050. doi: 10.1002/14651858.CD004050.pub2

Shea, B., Grimshaw, J., Wells, G., Boers, M., Andersson, N., Hamel, C., et al. (2007). Development of AMSTAR: A measurement tool to assess the methodological quality of systematic reviews. *BMC Medical Research Methodology, 7*, 10. doi:10.1186/1471-2288-7-10.

Simon, S. (2008). Clinical research statistics web pages. Retrieved match 7, 2001 from http://www.childrensmercy.org/stats/overview.asp

Sistrom, C., & Garvan, C. (2004). Proportions, odds, and risk. *Radiology, 230*(1), 12–19. doi: 10.1148/radiol.2301031028.

Smith, M., Glass, G., & Miller, T. (1980). *The benefits of psychotherapy*. Baltimore, MD: Johns Hopkins University Press.

United States Department of Health and Human Services. (1999). *Mental health: A report of the Surgeon General*. Rockville, MD: U.S. Department of Health and Human Services, Substance Abuse and Mental Health Services Administration, Center for Mental Health Services, National Institutes of Health, and National Institute of Mental Health. Cited section is online at www.surgeongeneral.gov/library/mentalhealth/chapter5/sec3.html

Ventimiglia, J., Marschke, J., Carmichael, P., & Loew, R. (2000). How do clinicians evaluate their practice effectiveness? A survey of clinical social workers. *Smith College Studies in Social Work, 70*(2), 287–306.

Wakefield, J. (2005). Disorders versus problems of living in DSM: Rethinking social work's relationship to psychiatry. In S. Kirk (Ed.), *Mental disorders in the social environment: Critical perspectives*. New York: Columbia University Press.

Walsh, J. (2010). *Theories for direct social work practice* (2nd ed.). Belmont, CA: Thompson Brooks/Cole.

Wampold, B. (2001). *The great psychotherapy debate: Models, methods and findings*. Mahwah, NJ: Erlbaum.

Wampold, B. (2010). *The basics of psychotherapy: An introduction to theory and practice*. Washington, DC: American Psychological Association.

Watanabe, N., Churchill, R., & Furukawa, T. (2009). Combined psychotherapy plus benzodiazepines for panic disorder. *Cochrane Database of Systematic Reviews* 2009, Issue 1. Art. No.: CD005335. DOI: 10.1002/14651858.CD005335.pub2.

Weinbach, R., & Grinnell, R. (2009). *Statistics for social workers* (8th ed.). New York: Prentice-Hall.

Weinberger, J., & Rasco, C. (2007). Empirically supported common factors. In S. Hofmann & J. Weinberger (Eds.), *The art and science of psychotherapy* (pp. 103–129). New York, NY: Taylor & Francis Group.

Weissman, M. M., Verdeli, H., Gameroff, M. J., Bledsoe, S. E., Betts, K., Mufson, L., & … Wickramaratne, P. (2006). National survey of psychotherapy training in psychiatry, psychology, and social work. *Archives of General Psychiatry, 63*, 925–934. doi: 10.1001/archpsyc.63.8.925.

Wennberg, J. (1984). Dealing with medical practice variations: A proposal for action. *Health Affairs, 3*, 6–12.

Westen, D. (2006). Transporting laboratory validated treatments to the community will not necessarily produce better outcomes. In J. Norcross, L. Beutler, & R. Levant (Eds.), *Evidence-based practices in mental health* (pp. 383–392). Washington, DC: American Psychological Association.

Wiborg, I., & Dahl, A. (1996). Does brief dynamic psychotherapy reduce the relapse rate of panic disorder? *Archives of General Psychiatry, 53*(8), 689–694.

Willer, J. (2009). The supervisor-supervisee relationship. In J. Willer (Ed.), *The beginning psychotherapist's companion* (pp. 13–24). Lanham, MD: Rowman & Littlefield Publishers, Inc.

Wilson, K., Mottram, P., Sivananthan, A., & Nightingale A. (2001). Antidepressants versus placebo for the depressed elderly. *Cochrane Database of Systematic Reviews* 2001, Issue 3. Art. No.: CD000561. doi: 10.1002/14651858.CD000561.

Wilson, K., Mottram, P., & Vassilas, C. (2008). Psychotherapeutic treatments for older depressed people *Cochrane Database of Systematic Reviews* 2008, Issue 1. Art. No.: CD004853. doi: 10.1002/14651858.CD004853.pub2.

Wilt, T., MacDonald, R., Rutks, I., Shamliyan, T., Taylor, B., & Kane, R. (2008). Systematic review: Comparative effectiveness and harms of treatments for clinically localized prostate cancer. *Annals of Internal Medicine, 148*(6), 435–448.

Wimmer, J., Vonk, M., & Bordnick, P. (2009). A preliminary investigation of the effectiveness of attachment therapy for adopted children with reactive attachment disorder. *Child & Adolescent Social Work Journal, 26*(4), 351–360.

Winnicott, D. (1992). *The child, the family and the outside world.* New York: Perseus Books.

World Health Organization. (2007). *International classification of diseases* (10th ed., version 2). Retrieved from http://apps.who.int/classifications/apps/icd/icd10online/.

Writing Group for the Women's Health Initiative Investigators. (2002). Risks and benefits of estrogen plus progestin in healthy postmenopausal women: Principal results from the Women's Health Initiative randomized controlled trial. *Journal of the American medical Association, 288*(3), 321–333.

Yunong, H., & Fengzhi, M. (2009). A reflection on reasons, preconditions, and effects of implementing evidence-based practice in social work. *Social Work, 54*, 177–181.

Zayas, L., Drake, B., & Jonson-Reid, M. (2010). Overrating or dismissing the value of evidence based practice: Consequences for clinical practice. *Clinical Social Work Journal, 39*(4), 400–405. doi:10.1007/s10615-010-0306-1.

Zilberstein, K. (2006). Clarifying core characteristics of attachment disorders: A review of current research and theory. *American Journal of Orthopsychiatry, 76*(1), 55–64.

Zulman, D., Sussman, J., Chen, X., Cigolle, C., Blaum, C., & R. Hayward. (2011, February 1). Examining the evidence: A systematic review of the inclusion and analysis of older adults in randomized controlled trials. *Journal of General Internal Medicine*, online. doi: 10.1007/s11606-010-1629-x.

Index

CPSIA information can be obtained at www.ICGtesting.com
Printed in the USA
LVOW10s0803040414

380339LV00002B/92/P